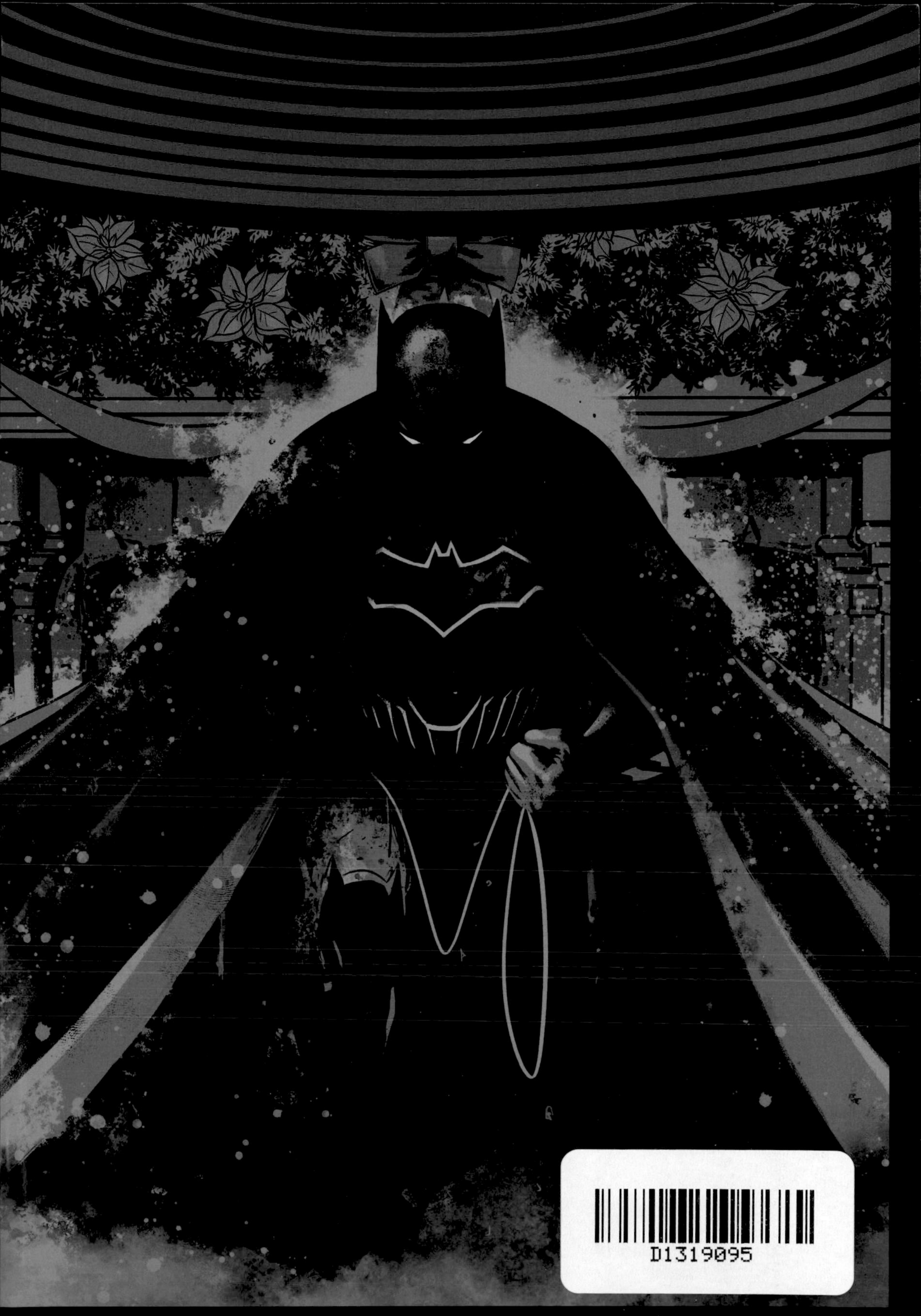

A Very DC Rebirth Holiday Sequel

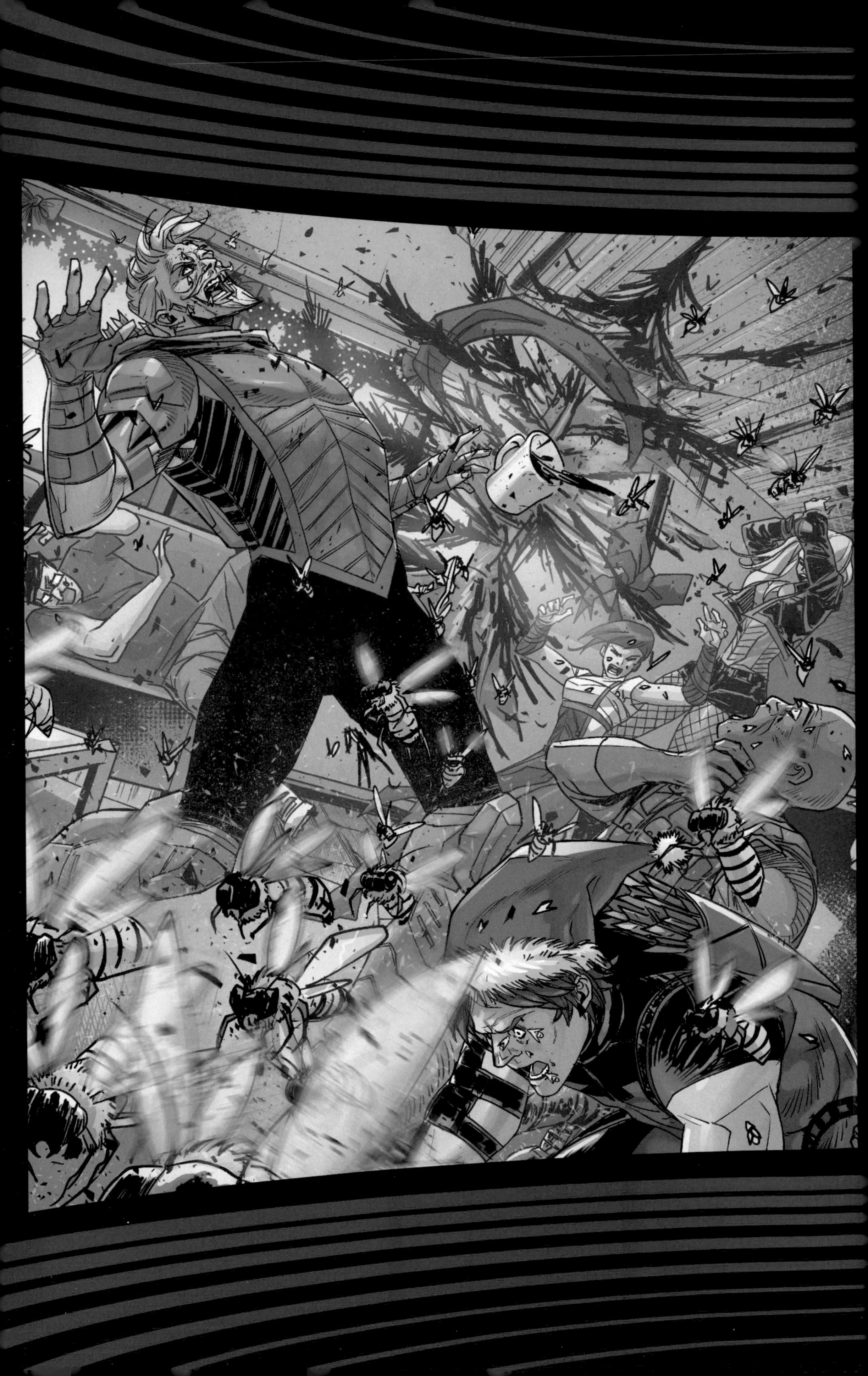

A Very DC Rebirth Holiday Sequel

JEFF LEMIRE * DENNY O'NEIL * MAIRGHREAD SCOTT * TOM KING * JOSHUA WILLIAMSON
CHRISTOPHER PRIEST * DAN DiDIO * SHEA FONTANA * SCOTT BRYAN WILSON
GREG RUCKA * MIKE FRIEDRICH * BENJAMIN PERCY * HOPE LARSON * ROB WILLIAMS
writers

GIUSEPPE CAMUNCOLI * CAM SMITH * STEVE EPTING * PHIL HESTER
ANDE PARKS * FRANCESCO FRANCAVILLA * NEIL GOOGE * TOM GRUMMETT
SCOTT HANNA * MATTHEW CLARK * SEAN PARSONS * OTTO SCHMIDT * NIC KLEIN
BILQUIS EVELY * NEAL ADAMS * DICK GIORDANO * ELEONORA CARLINI
SAMI BASRI * V KEN MARION * SANDU FLOREA
artists

TOMEU MOREY * DAVE McCAIG * TRISH MULVIHILL * FRANCESCO FRANCAVILLA
IVAN PLASCENCIA * JEROMY COX * ROB SCHWAGER * OTTO SCHMIDT * NIC KLEIN
ROMULO FAJARDO JR. * JERRY SERPE * HI-FI * JESSICA KHOLINNE * DINEI RIBEIRO
colorists

CLAYTON COWLES * DERON BENNETT * CLEM ROBINS * TOM NAPOLITANO
WILLIE SCHUBERT * TRAVIS LANHAM * CARLOS M. MANGUAL
DAVE SHARPE * STEVE WANDS
letterers

ANDY KUBERT and BRAD ANDERSON
collection cover artists

SUPERMAN created by JERRY SIEGEL and JOE SHUSTER
SUPERBOY created by JERRY SIEGEL
By special arrangement with the Jerry Siegel family
BATMAN created by BOB KANE with BILL FINGER
WONDER WOMAN created by WILLIAM MOULTON MARSTON

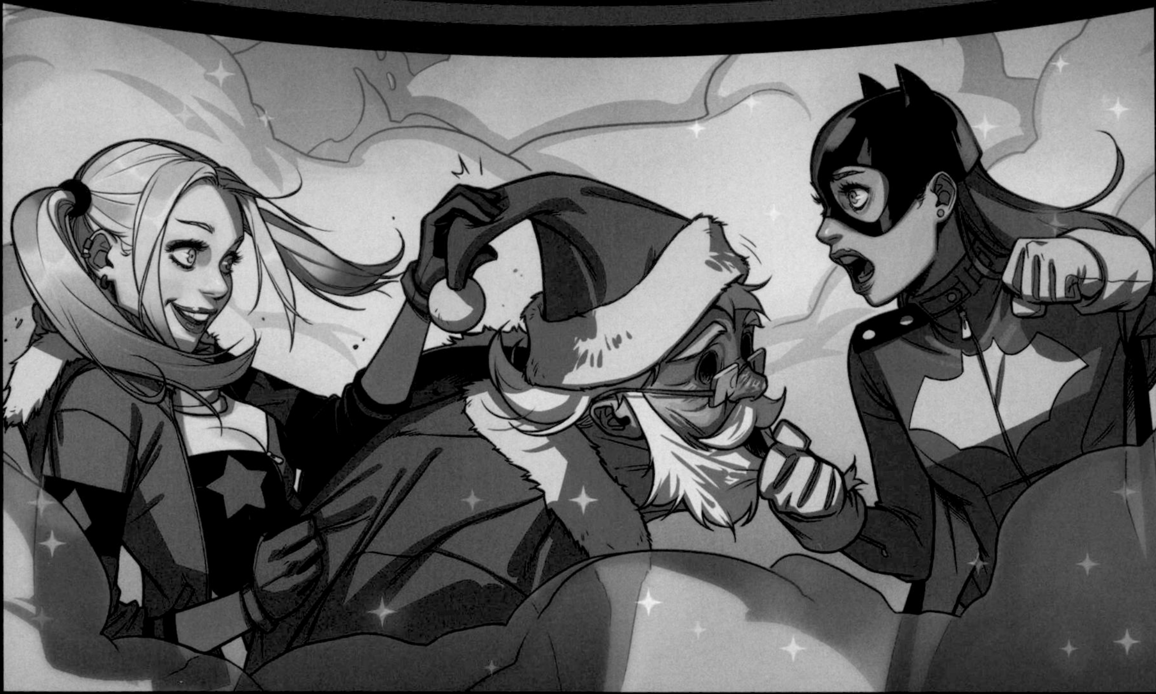

ALEX ANTONE DAVE WIELGOSZ JULIE SCHWARTZ ANDY KHOURI PAUL KAMINSKI Editors - Original Series
HARVEY RICHARDS BRITTANY HOLZHERR Associate Editors - Original Series * **ANDREA SHEA** Assistant Editor - Original Series
JEB WOODARD Group Editor - Collected Editions * **TYLER-MARIE EVANS** Editor - Collected Edition
STEVE COOK Design Director - Books * **MEGEN BELLERSEN** Publication Design

BOB HARRAS Senior VP - Editor-in-Chief, DC Comics
PAT McCALLUM Executive Editor, DC Comics

DAN DiDIO Publisher * **JIM LEE** Publisher & Chief Creative Officer
AMIT DESAI Executive VP - Business & Marketing Strategy, Direct to Consumer & Global Franchise Management
BOBBIE CHASE VP & Executive Editor, Young Reader & Talent Development * **MARK CHIARELLO** Senior VP - Art, Design & Collected Editions
JOHN CUNNINGHAM Senior VP - Sales & Trade Marketing * **BRIAR DARDEN** VP - Business Affairs
ANNE DePIES Senior VP - Business Strategy, Finance & Administration * **DON FALLETTI** VP - Manufacturing Operations
LAWRENCE GANEM VP - Editorial Administration & Talent Relations * **ALISON GILL** Senior VP - Manufacturing & Operations
JASON GREENBERG VP - Business Strategy & Finance * **HANK KANALZ** Senior VP - Editorial Strategy & Administration * **JAY KOGAN** Senior VP - Legal Affairs
NICK J. NAPOLITANO VP - Manufacturing Administration * **LISETTE OSTERLOH** VP - Digital Marketing & Events * **EDDIE SCANNELL** VP - Consumer Marketing
COURTNEY SIMMONS Senior VP - Publicity & Communications * **JIM (SKI) SOKOLOWSKI** VP - Comic Book Specialty Sales & Trade Marketing
NANCY SPEARS VP - Mass, Book, Digital Sales & Trade Marketing * **MICHELE R. WELLS** VP - Content Strategy

A VERY DC REBIRTH HOLIDAY SEQUEL

DC Comics, 2900 West Alameda Ave., Burbank, CA 91505
Printed by LSC Communications, Kendallville, IN, USA. 10/5/18. First Printing.
ISBN: 978-1-4012-8496-1

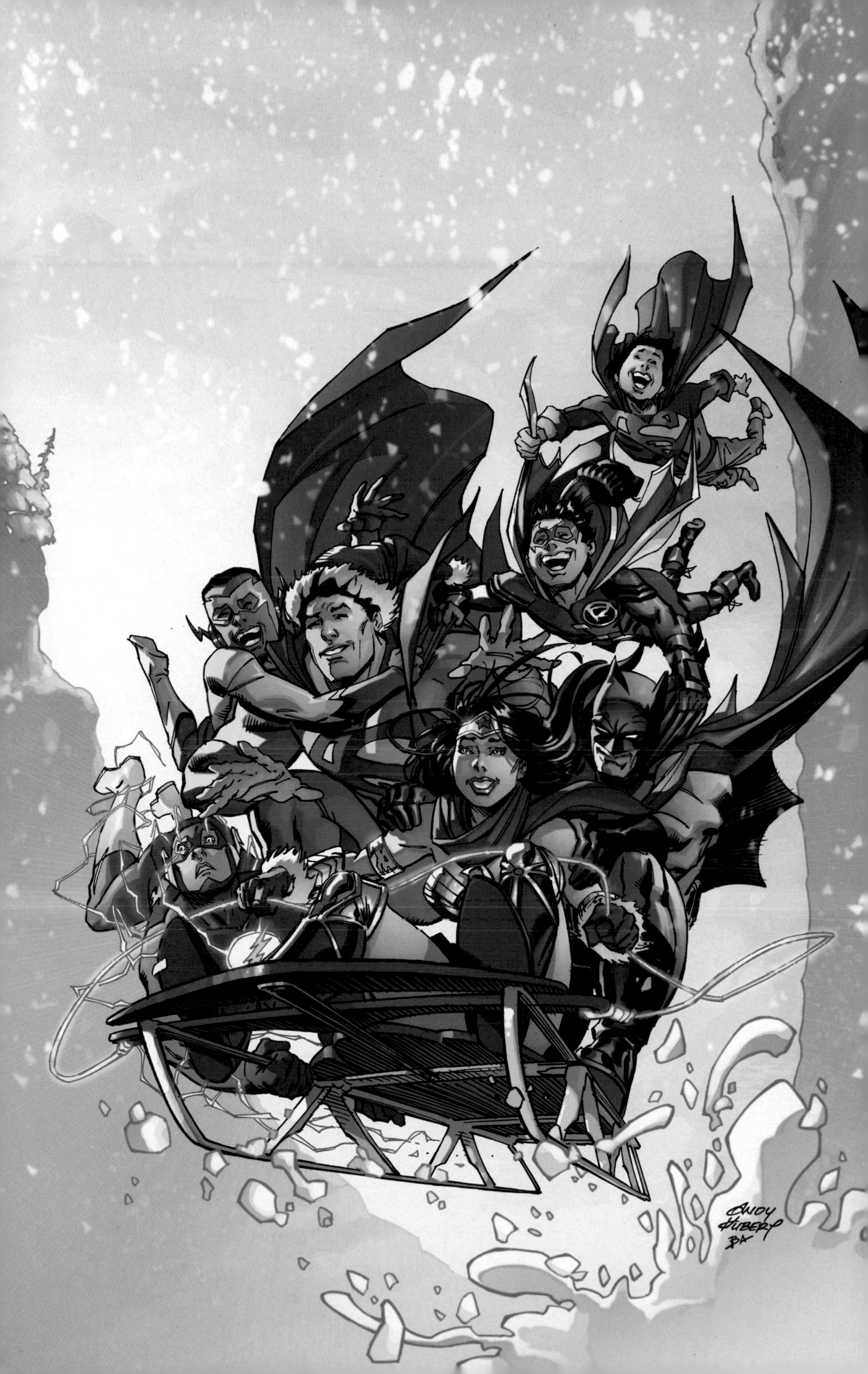
ANDY KUBERT BA

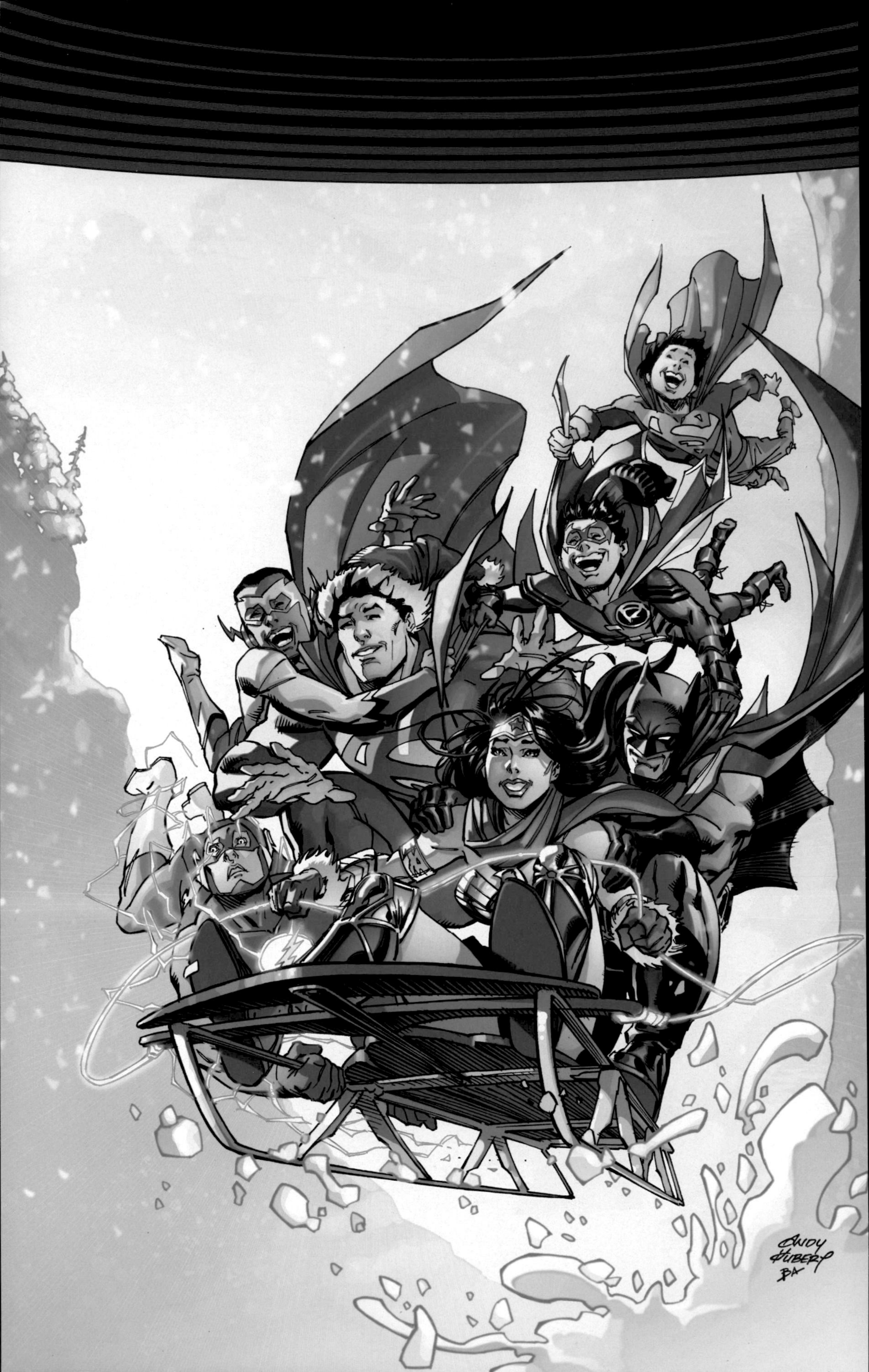

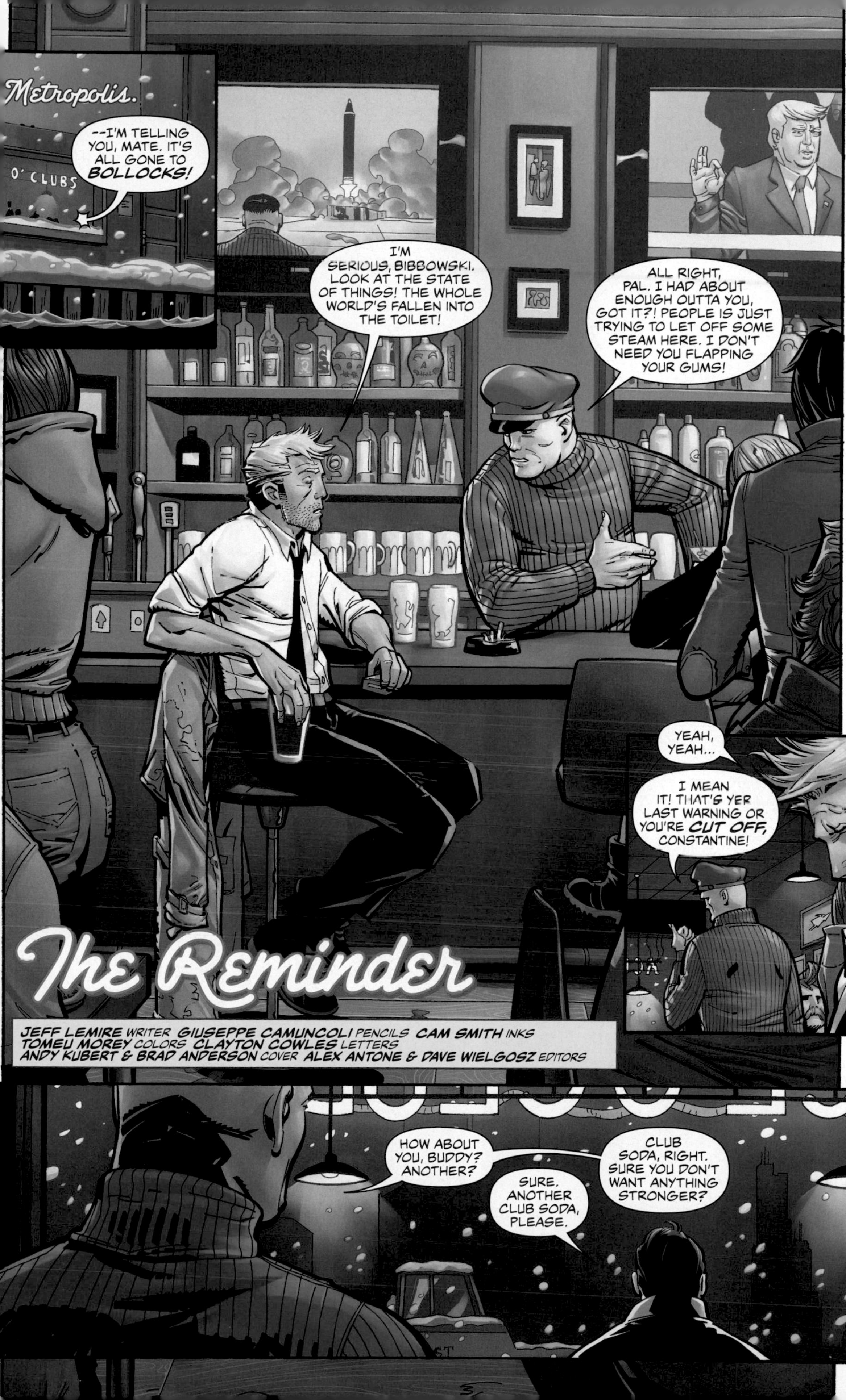
Metropolis.
--I'M TELLING YOU, MATE. IT'S ALL GONE TO BOLLOCKS!
O' CLUBS
I'M SERIOUS, BIBBOWSKI. LOOK AT THE STATE OF THINGS! THE WHOLE WORLD'S FALLEN INTO THE TOILET!
ALL RIGHT, PAL. I HAD ABOUT ENOUGH OUTTA YOU, GOT IT?! PEOPLE IS JUST TRYING TO LET OFF SOME STEAM HERE. I DON'T NEED YOU FLAPPING YOUR GUMS!
YEAH, YEAH...
I MEAN IT! THAT'S YER LAST WARNING OR YOU'RE CUT OFF, CONSTANTINE!
The Reminder
JEFF LEMIRE WRITER GIUSEPPE CAMUNCOLI PENCILS CAM SMITH INKS
TOMEU MOREY COLORS CLAYTON COWLES LETTERS
ANDY KUBERT & BRAD ANDERSON COVER ALEX ANTONE & DAVE WIELGOSZ EDITORS
HOW ABOUT YOU, BUDDY? ANOTHER?
SURE. ANOTHER CLUB SODA, PLEASE.
CLUB SODA, RIGHT. SURE YOU DON'T WANT ANYTHING STRONGER?

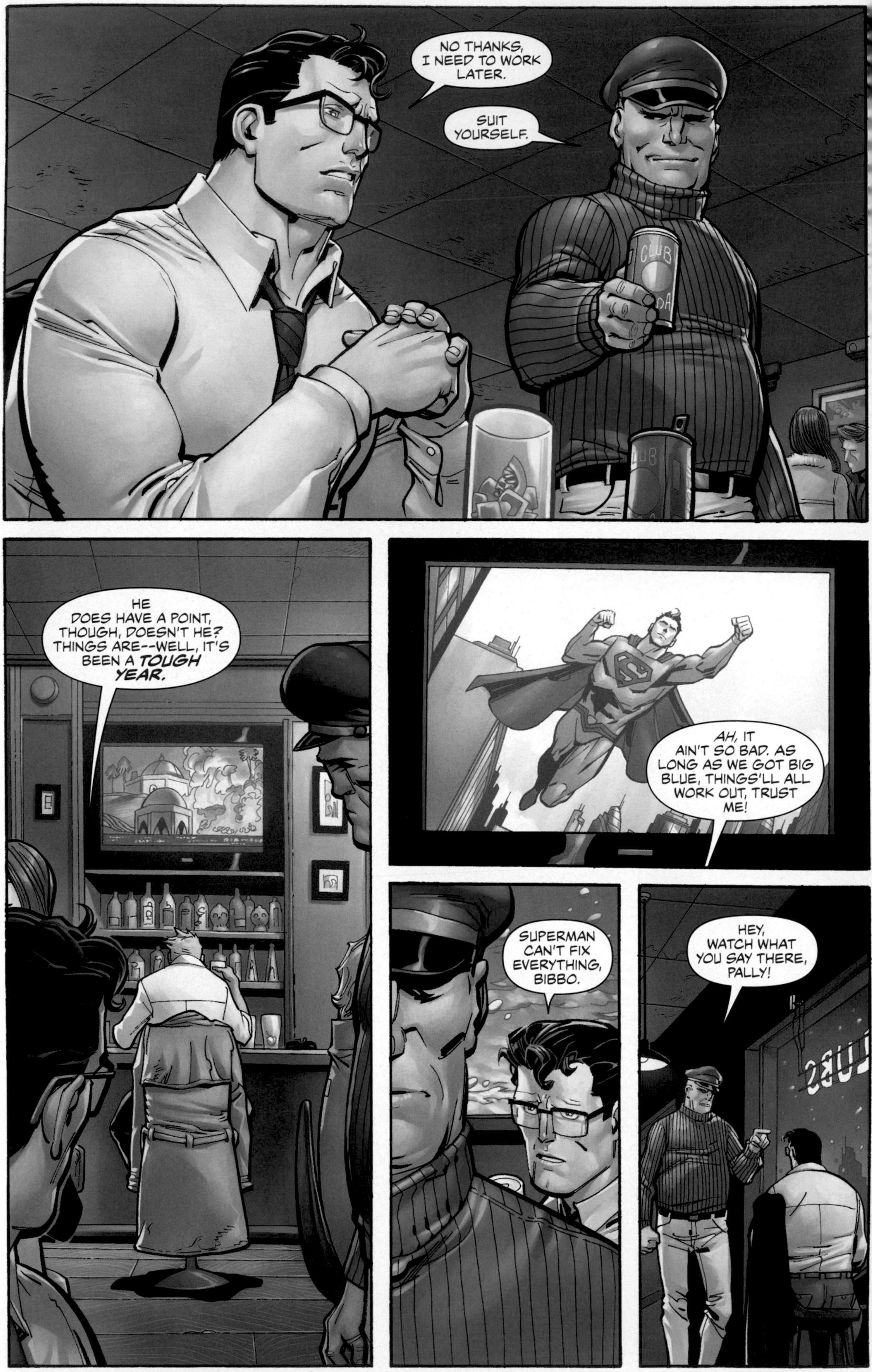
NO THANKS, I NEED TO WORK LATER.
SUIT YOURSELF.
HE DOES HAVE A POINT, THOUGH, DOESN'T HE? THINGS ARE--WELL, IT'S BEEN A TOUGH YEAR.
AH, IT AIN'T SO BAD. AS LONG AS WE GOT BIG BLUE, THINGS'LL ALL WORK OUT, TRUST ME!
SUPERMAN CAN'T FIX EVERYTHING, BIBBO.
HEY, WATCH WHAT YOU SAY THERE, PALLY!

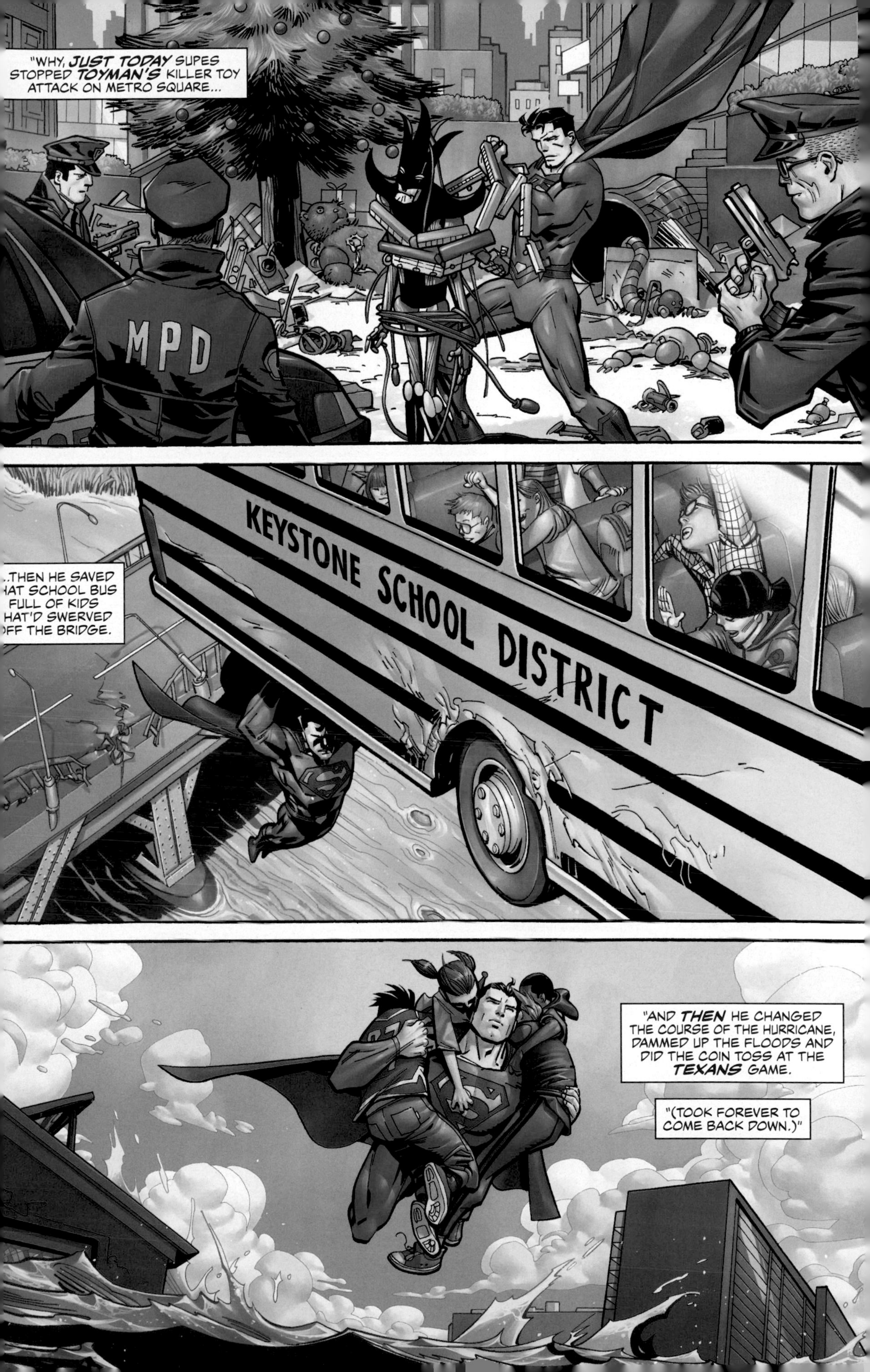
"WHY, JUST TODAY SUPES STOPPED TOYMAN'S KILLER TOY ATTACK ON METRO SQUARE...
MPD
..THEN HE SAVED HAT SCHOOL BUS FULL OF KIDS HAT'D SWERVED FF THE BRIDGE.
KEYSTONE SCHOOL DISTRICT
"AND THEN HE CHANGED THE COURSE OF THE HURRICANE, DAMMED UP THE FLOODS AND DID THE COIN TOSS AT THE TEXANS GAME.
"(TOOK FOREVER TO COME BACK DOWN.)"

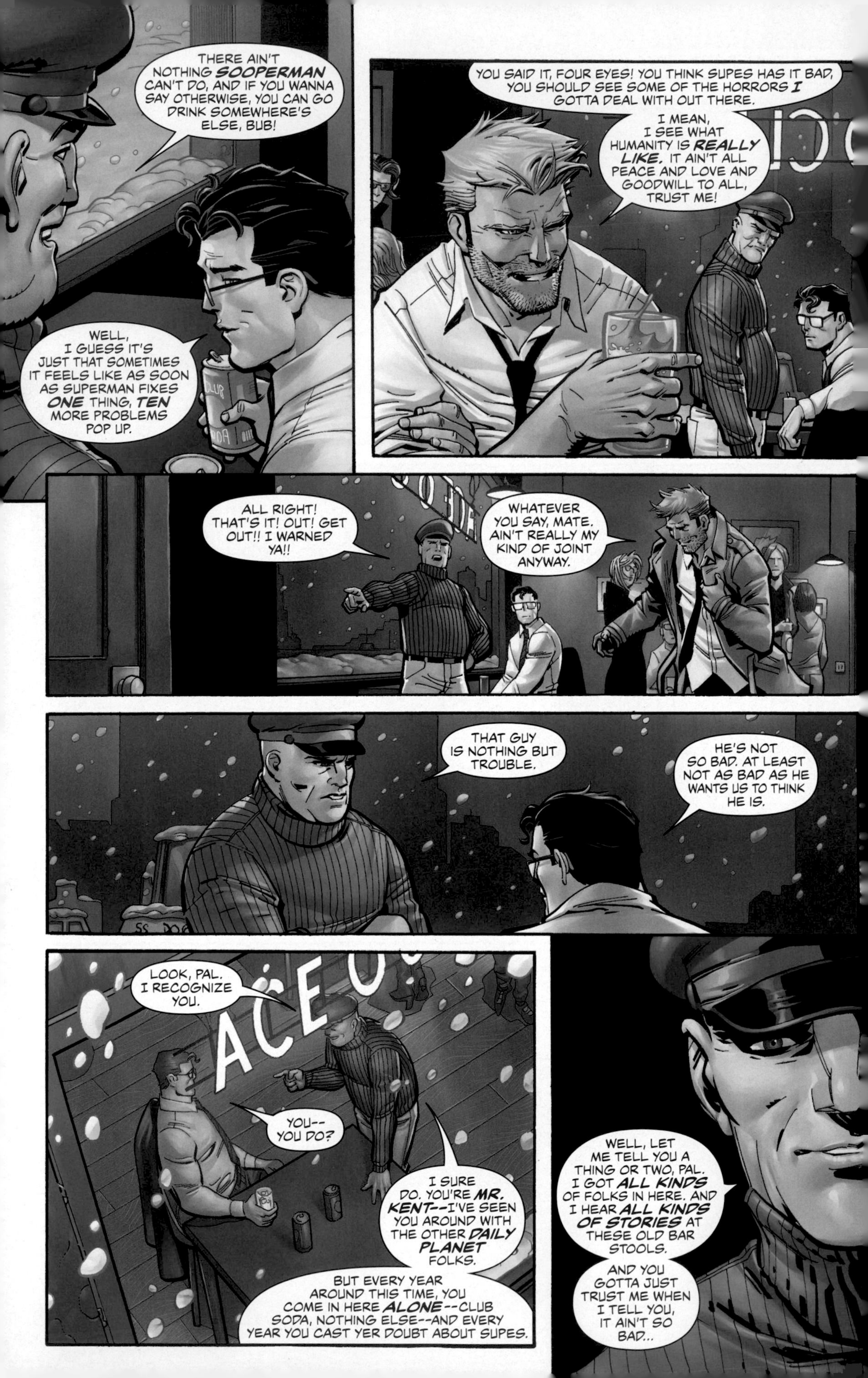

THERE AIN'T NOTHING SOOPERMAN CAN'T DO, AND IF YOU WANNA SAY OTHERWISE, YOU CAN GO DRINK SOMEWHERE'S ELSE, BUB!
WELL, I GUESS IT'S JUST THAT SOMETIMES IT FEELS LIKE AS SOON AS SUPERMAN FIXES ONE THING, TEN MORE PROBLEMS POP UP.
YOU SAID IT, FOUR EYES! YOU THINK SUPES HAS IT BAD, YOU SHOULD SEE SOME OF THE HORRORS I GOTTA DEAL WITH OUT THERE.
I MEAN, I SEE WHAT HUMANITY IS REALLY LIKE. IT AIN'T ALL PEACE AND LOVE AND GOODWILL TO ALL, TRUST ME!
ALL RIGHT! THAT'S IT! OUT! GET OUT!! I WARNED YA!!
WHATEVER YOU SAY, MATE. AIN'T REALLY MY KIND OF JOINT ANYWAY.
THAT GUY IS NOTHING BUT TROUBLE.
HE'S NOT SO BAD. AT LEAST NOT AS BAD AS HE WANTS US TO THINK HE IS.
LOOK, PAL. I RECOGNIZE YOU.
YOU-- YOU DO?
I SURE DO. YOU'RE MR. KENT--I'VE SEEN YOU AROUND WITH THE OTHER DAILY PLANET FOLKS.
BUT EVERY YEAR AROUND THIS TIME, YOU COME IN HERE ALONE--CLUB SODA, NOTHING ELSE--AND EVERY YEAR YOU CAST YER DOUBT ABOUT SUPES.
WELL, LET ME TELL YOU A THING OR TWO, PAL. I GOT ALL KINDS OF FOLKS IN HERE. AND I HEAR ALL KINDS OF STORIES AT THESE OLD BAR STOOLS.
AND YOU GOTTA JUST TRUST ME WHEN I TELL YOU, IT AIN'T SO BAD...

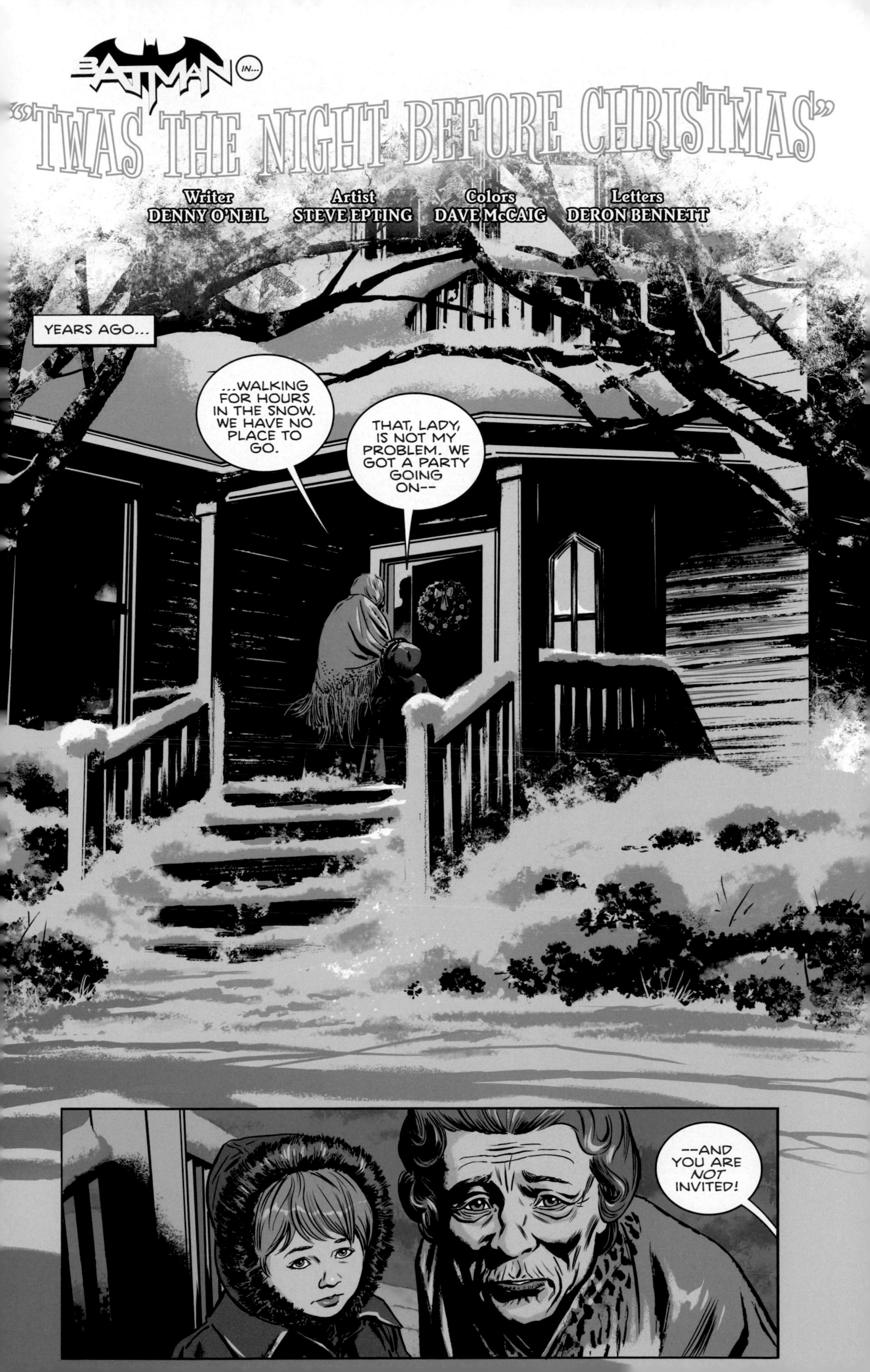
BATMAN IN...
"'TWAS THE NIGHT BEFORE CHRISTMAS"
Writer DENNY O'NEIL
Artist STEVE EPTING
Colors DAVE McCAIG
Letters DERON BENNETT
YEARS AGO...
...WALKING FOR HOURS IN THE SNOW. WE HAVE NO PLACE TO GO.
THAT, LADY, IS NOT MY PROBLEM. WE GOT A PARTY GOING ON--
--AND YOU ARE NOT INVITED!

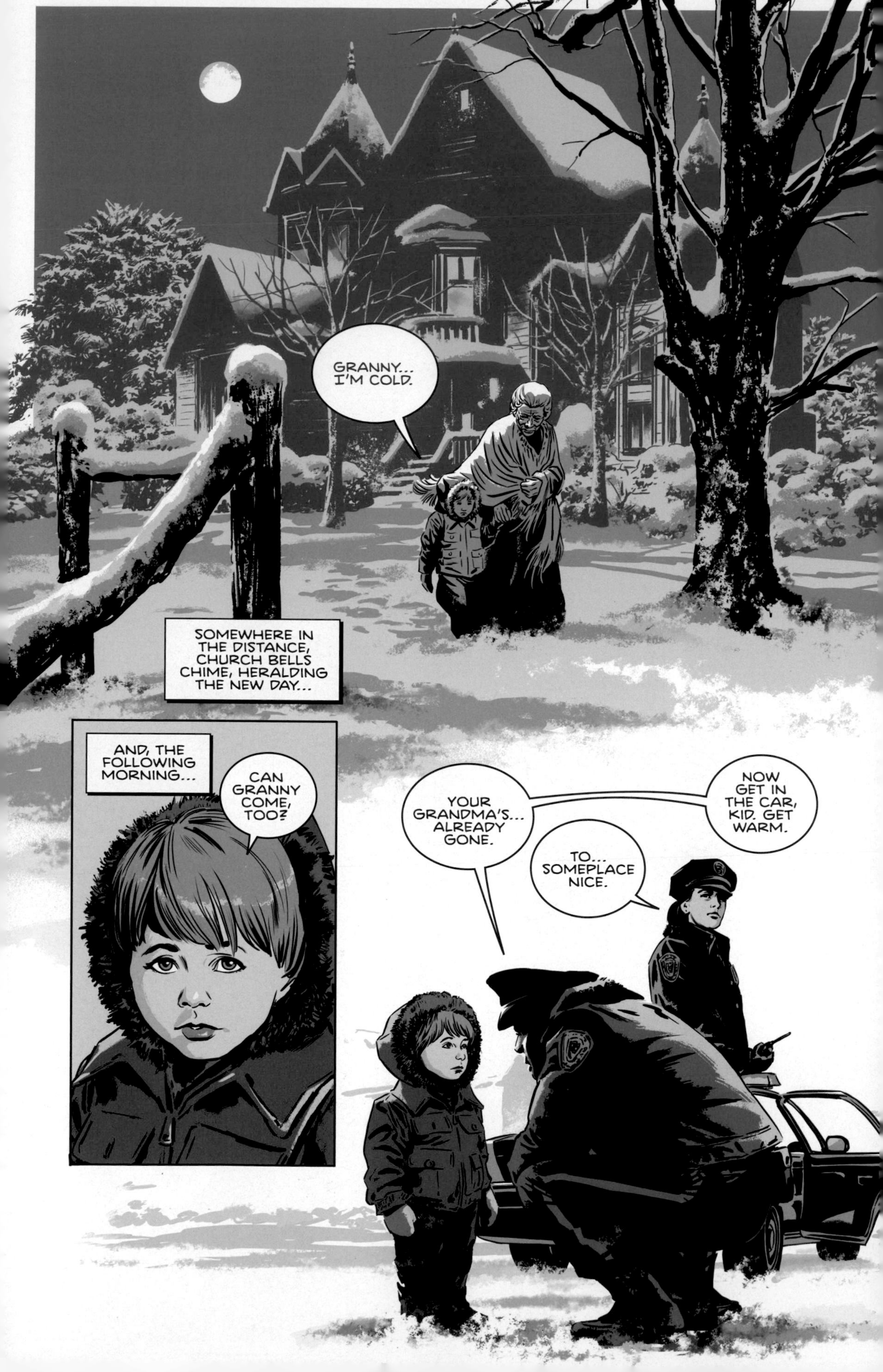
GRANNY... I'M COLD.
SOMEWHERE IN THE DISTANCE, CHURCH BELLS CHIME, HERALDING THE NEW DAY...
AND, THE FOLLOWING MORNING...
CAN GRANNY COME, TOO?
YOUR GRANDMA'S... ALREADY GONE.
TO... SOMEPLACE NICE.
NOW GET IN THE CAR, KID. GET WARM.

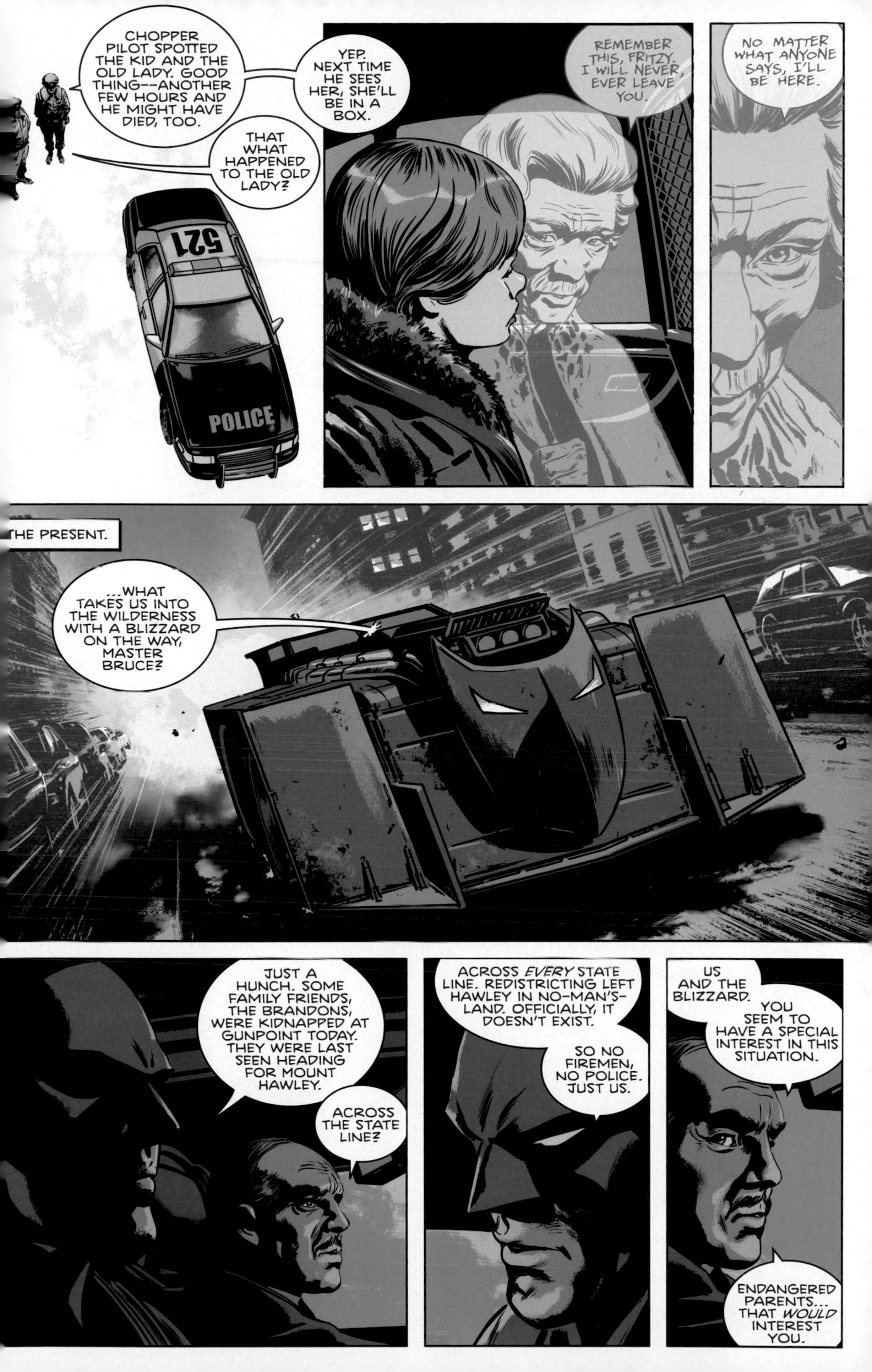
CHOPPER PILOT SPOTTED THE KID AND THE OLD LADY. GOOD THING--ANOTHER FEW HOURS AND HE MIGHT HAVE DIED, TOO.
THAT WHAT HAPPENED TO THE OLD LADY?
YEP. NEXT TIME HE SEES HER, SHE'LL BE IN A BOX.
521
POLICE
REMEMBER THIS, FRITZY. I WILL NEVER, EVER LEAVE YOU.
NO MATTER WHAT ANYONE SAYS, I'LL BE HERE.
THE PRESENT.
...WHAT TAKES US INTO THE WILDERNESS WITH A BLIZZARD ON THE WAY, MASTER BRUCE?
JUST A HUNCH. SOME FAMILY FRIENDS, THE BRANDONS, WERE KIDNAPPED AT GUNPOINT TODAY. THEY WERE LAST SEEN HEADING FOR MOUNT HAWLEY.
ACROSS THE STATE LINE?
ACROSS *EVERY* STATE LINE. REDISTRICTING LEFT HAWLEY IN NO-MAN'S-LAND. OFFICIALLY, IT DOESN'T EXIST.
SO NO FIREMEN, NO POLICE. JUST US.
US AND THE BLIZZARD.
YOU SEEM TO HAVE A SPECIAL INTEREST IN THIS SITUATION.
ENDANGERED PARENTS... THAT *WOULD* INTEREST YOU.

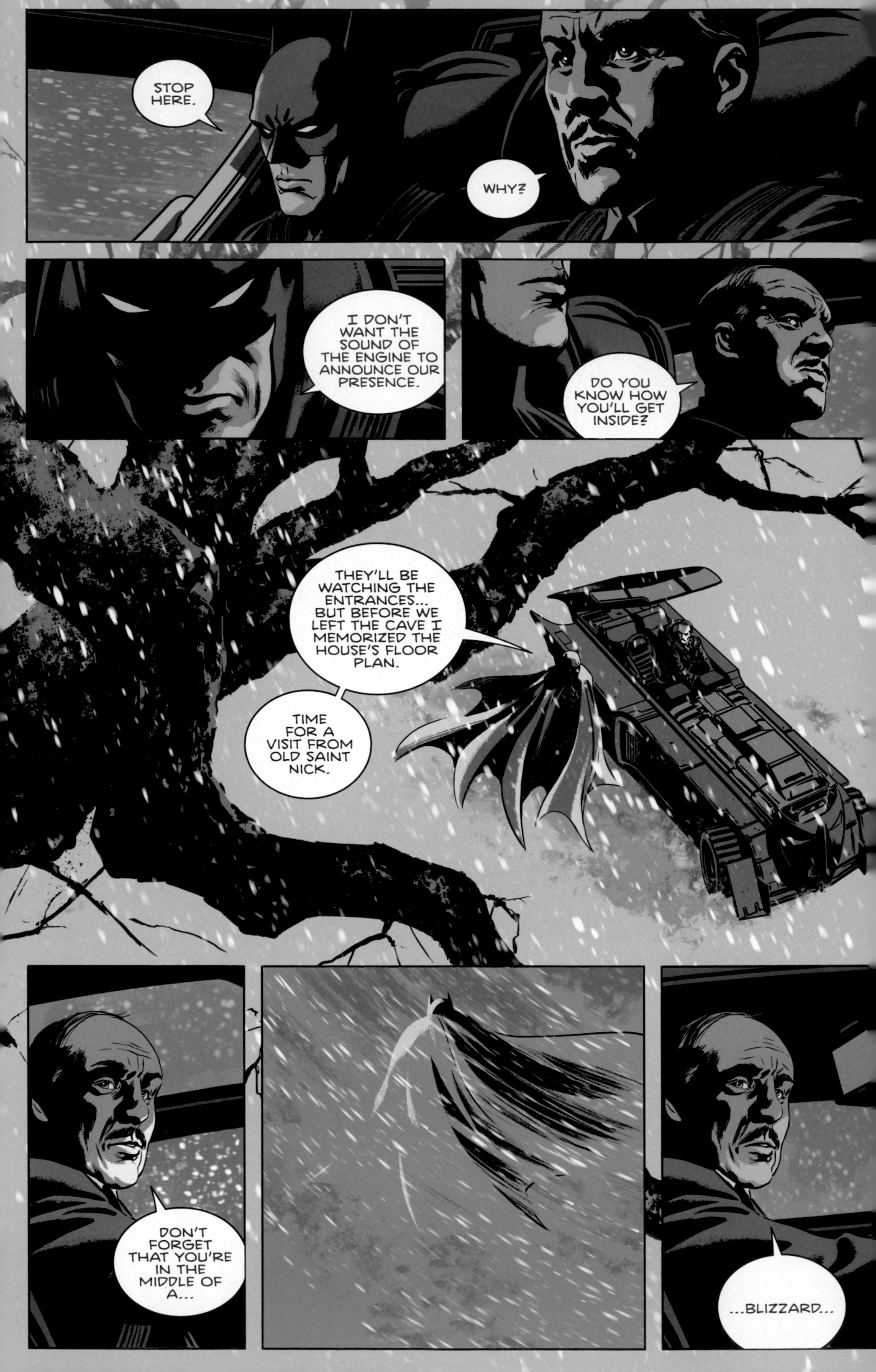
STOP HERE.
WHY?
I DON'T WANT THE SOUND OF THE ENGINE TO ANNOUNCE OUR PRESENCE.
DO YOU KNOW HOW YOU'LL GET INSIDE?
THEY'LL BE WATCHING THE ENTRANCES... BUT BEFORE WE LEFT THE CAVE I MEMORIZED THE HOUSE'S FLOOR PLAN.
TIME FOR A VISIT FROM OLD SAINT NICK.
DON'T FORGET THAT YOU'RE IN THE MIDDLE OF A...
...BLIZZARD...

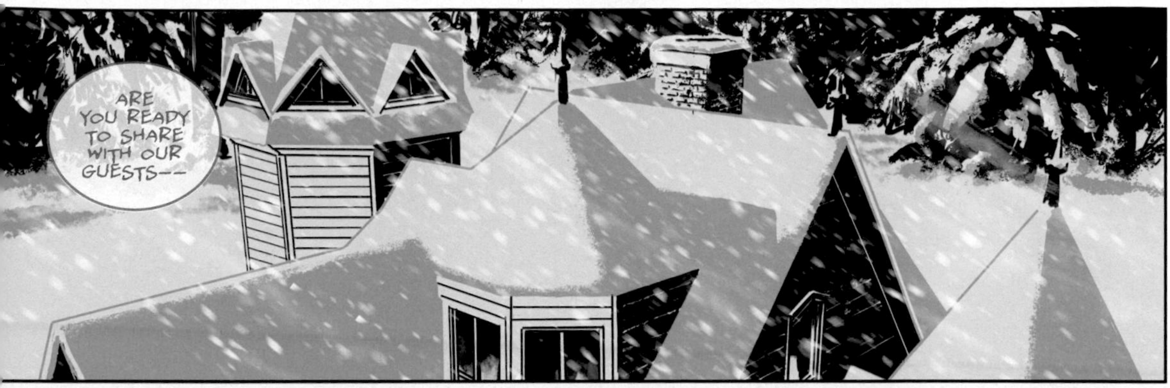
ARE YOU READY TO SHARE WITH OUR GUESTS--

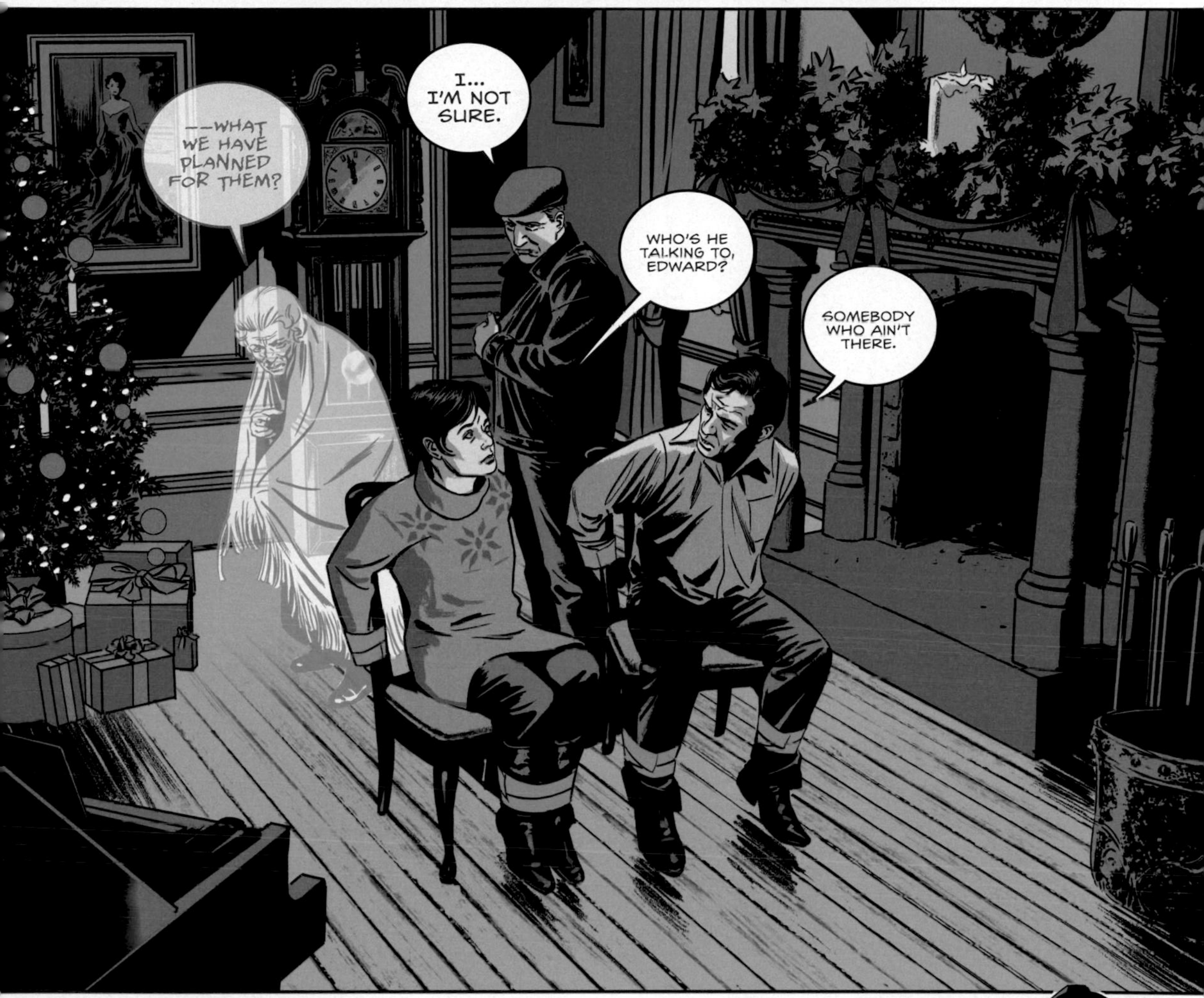
--WHAT WE HAVE PLANNED FOR THEM?
I... I'M NOT SURE.
WHO'S HE TALKING TO, EDWARD?
SOMEBODY WHO AIN'T THERE.

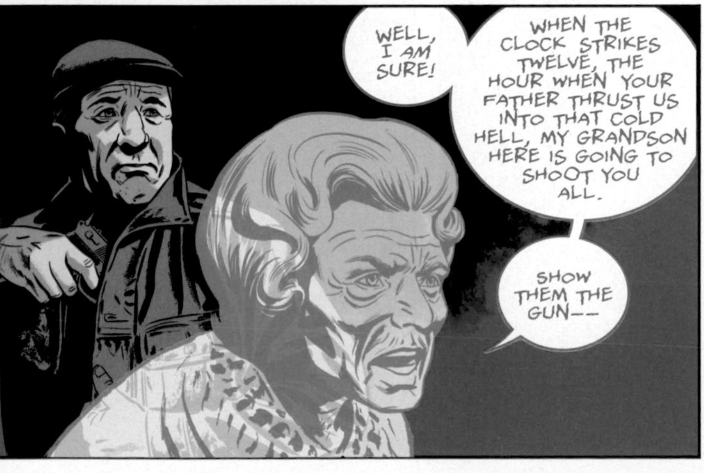
WELL, I *AM* SURE!
WHEN THE CLOCK STRIKES TWELVE, THE HOUR WHEN YOUR FATHER THRUST US INTO THAT COLD HELL, MY GRANDSON HERE IS GOING TO SHOOT YOU ALL.
SHOW THEM THE GUN--

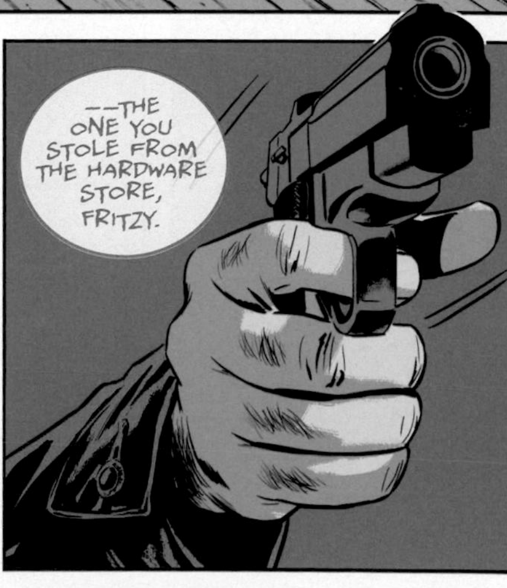
--THE ONE YOU STOLE FROM THE HARDWARE STORE, FRITZY.

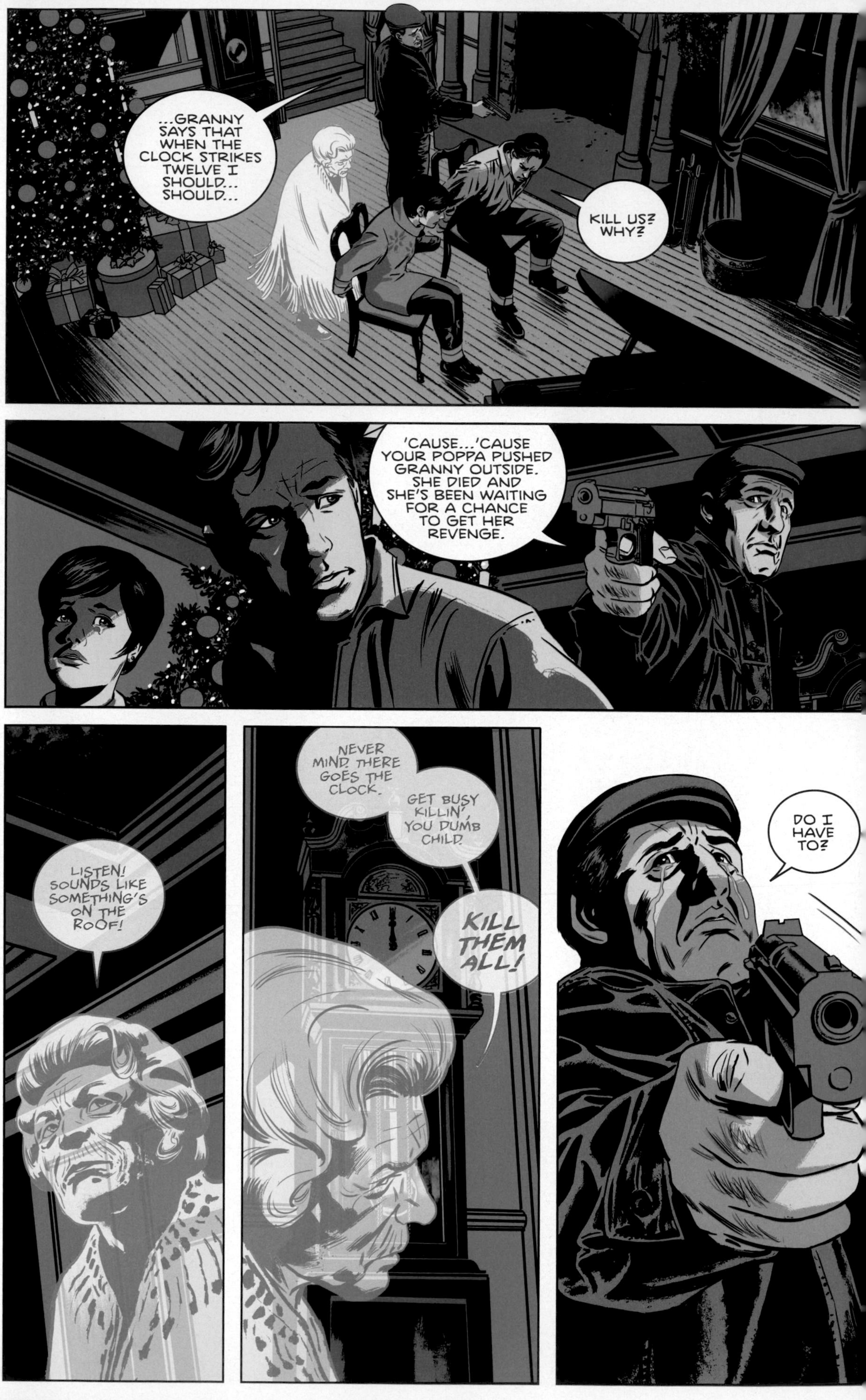
...GRANNY SAYS THAT WHEN THE CLOCK STRIKES TWELVE I SHOULD... SHOULD...
KILL US? WHY?
'CAUSE...'CAUSE YOUR POPPA PUSHED GRANNY OUTSIDE. SHE DIED AND SHE'S BEEN WAITING FOR A CHANCE TO GET HER REVENGE.
LISTEN! SOUNDS LIKE SOMETHING'S ON THE ROOF!
NEVER MIND. THERE GOES THE CLOCK.
GET BUSY KILLIN', YOU DUMB CHILD.
KILL THEM ALL!
DO I HAVE TO?

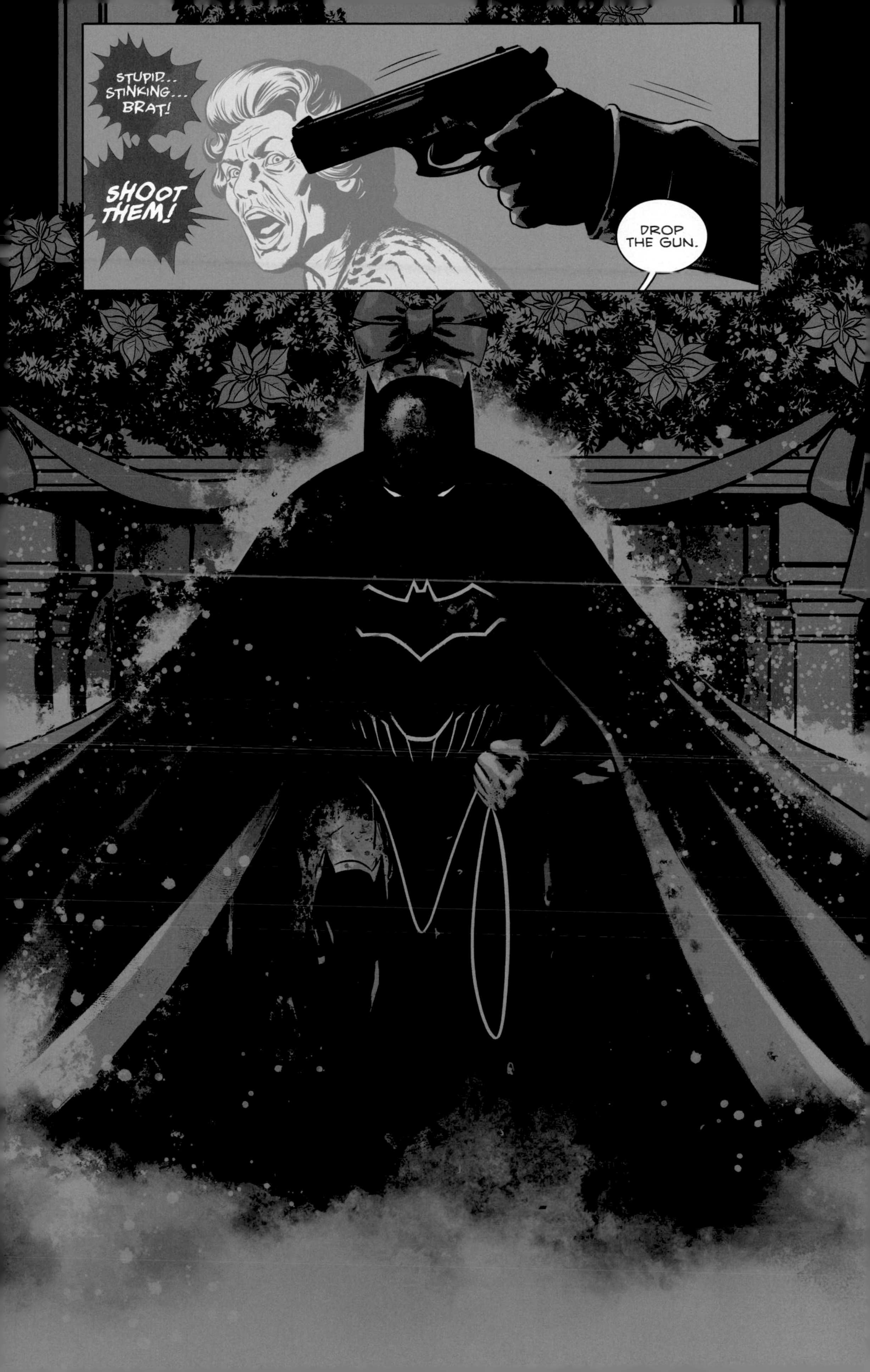
STUPID... STINKING... BRAT!
SHOOT THEM!
DROP THE GUN.

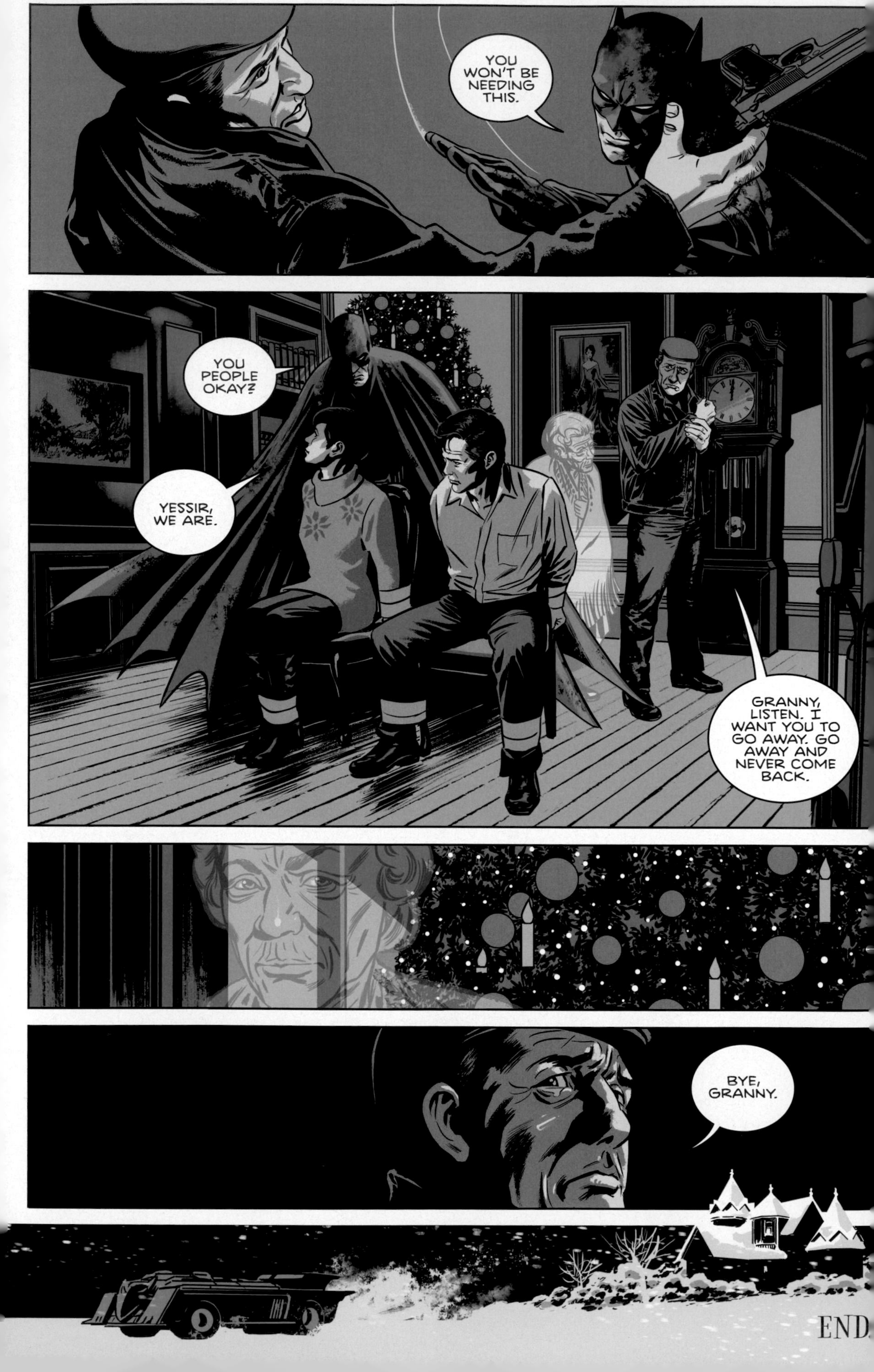
YOU WON'T BE NEEDING THIS.
YOU PEOPLE OKAY?
YESSIR, WE ARE.
GRANNY, LISTEN. I WANT YOU TO GO AWAY. GO AWAY AND NEVER COME BACK.
BYE, GRANNY.
END.

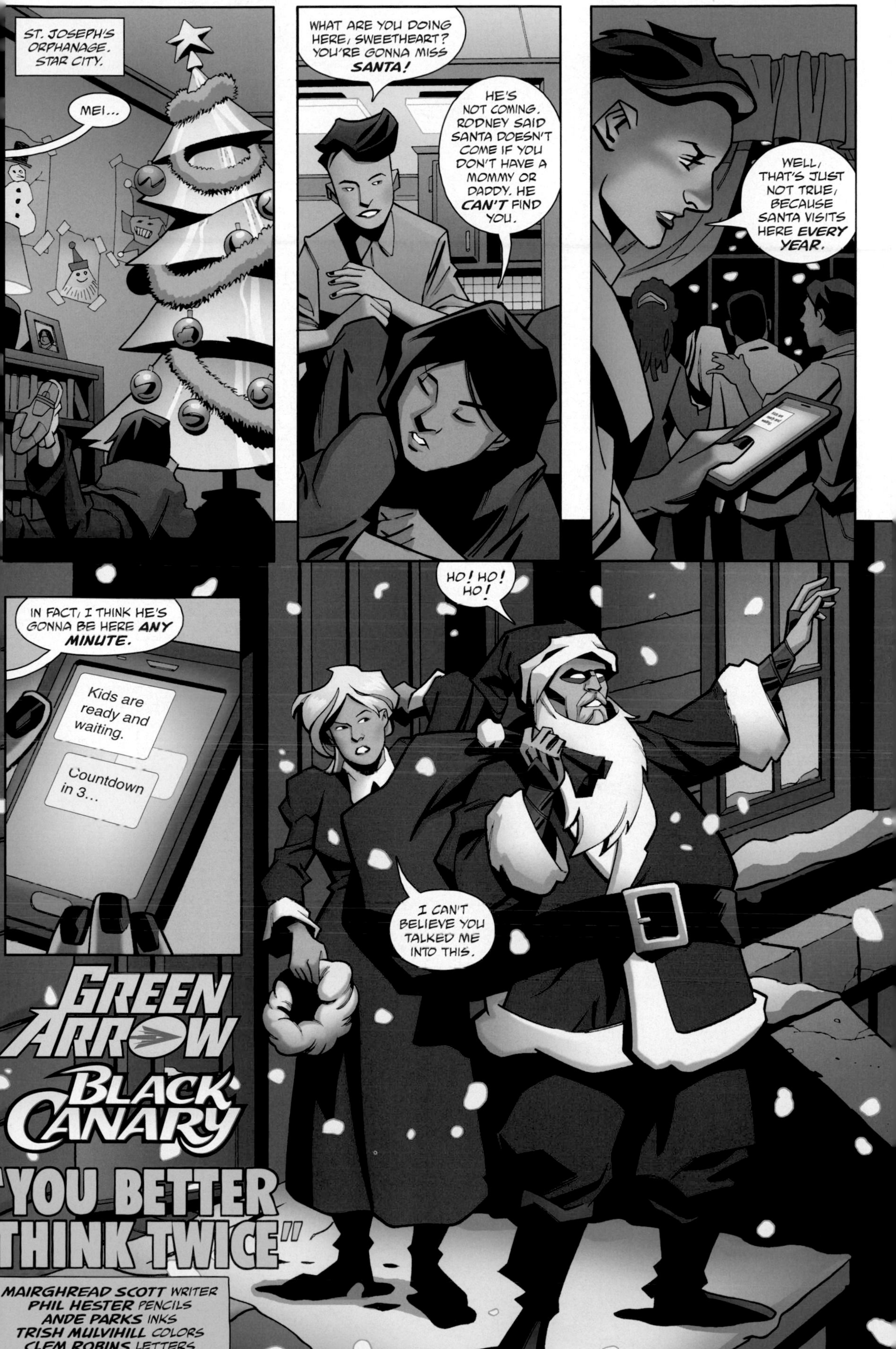
ST. JOSEPH'S ORPHANAGE. STAR CITY.
MEI...
WHAT ARE YOU DOING HERE, SWEETHEART? YOU'RE GONNA MISS SANTA!
HE'S NOT COMING. RODNEY SAID SANTA DOESN'T COME IF YOU DON'T HAVE A MOMMY OR DADDY. HE CAN'T FIND YOU.
WELL, THAT'S JUST NOT TRUE, BECAUSE SANTA VISITS HERE EVERY YEAR.
IN FACT, I THINK HE'S GONNA BE HERE ANY MINUTE.
Kids are ready and waiting.
Countdown in 3...
HO! HO! HO!
I CAN'T BELIEVE YOU TALKED ME INTO THIS.
GREEN ARROW
BLACK CANARY
"YOU BETTER THINK TWICE"
MAIRGHREAD SCOTT WRITER
PHIL HESTER PENCILS
ANDE PARKS INKS
TRISH MULVIHILL COLORS
CLEM ROBINS LETTERS

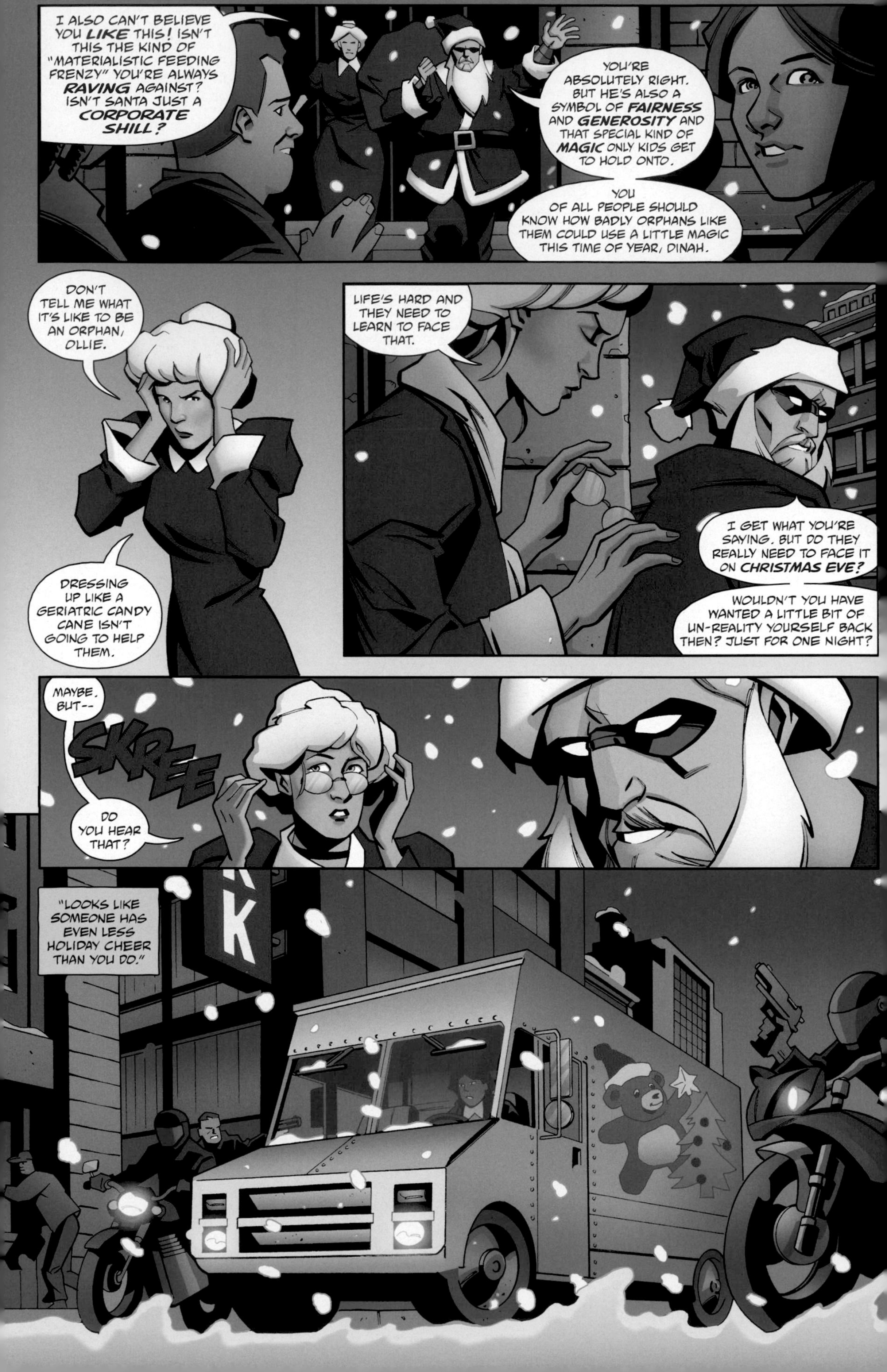
I ALSO CAN'T BELIEVE YOU LIKE THIS! ISN'T THIS THE KIND OF "MATERIALISTIC FEEDING FRENZY" YOU'RE ALWAYS RAVING AGAINST? ISN'T SANTA JUST A CORPORATE SHILL?
YOU'RE ABSOLUTELY RIGHT. BUT HE'S ALSO A SYMBOL OF FAIRNESS AND GENEROSITY AND THAT SPECIAL KIND OF MAGIC ONLY KIDS GET TO HOLD ONTO.
YOU OF ALL PEOPLE SHOULD KNOW HOW BADLY ORPHANS LIKE THEM COULD USE A LITTLE MAGIC THIS TIME OF YEAR, DINAH.
DON'T TELL ME WHAT IT'S LIKE TO BE AN ORPHAN, OLLIE.
DRESSING UP LIKE A GERIATRIC CANDY CANE ISN'T GOING TO HELP THEM.
LIFE'S HARD AND THEY NEED TO LEARN TO FACE THAT.
I GET WHAT YOU'RE SAYING. BUT DO THEY REALLY NEED TO FACE IT ON CHRISTMAS EVE?
WOULDN'T YOU HAVE WANTED A LITTLE BIT OF UN-REALITY YOURSELF BACK THEN? JUST FOR ONE NIGHT?
MAYBE. BUT--
SKREEE
DO YOU HEAR THAT?
"LOOKS LIKE SOMEONE HAS EVEN LESS HOLIDAY CHEER THAN YOU DO."

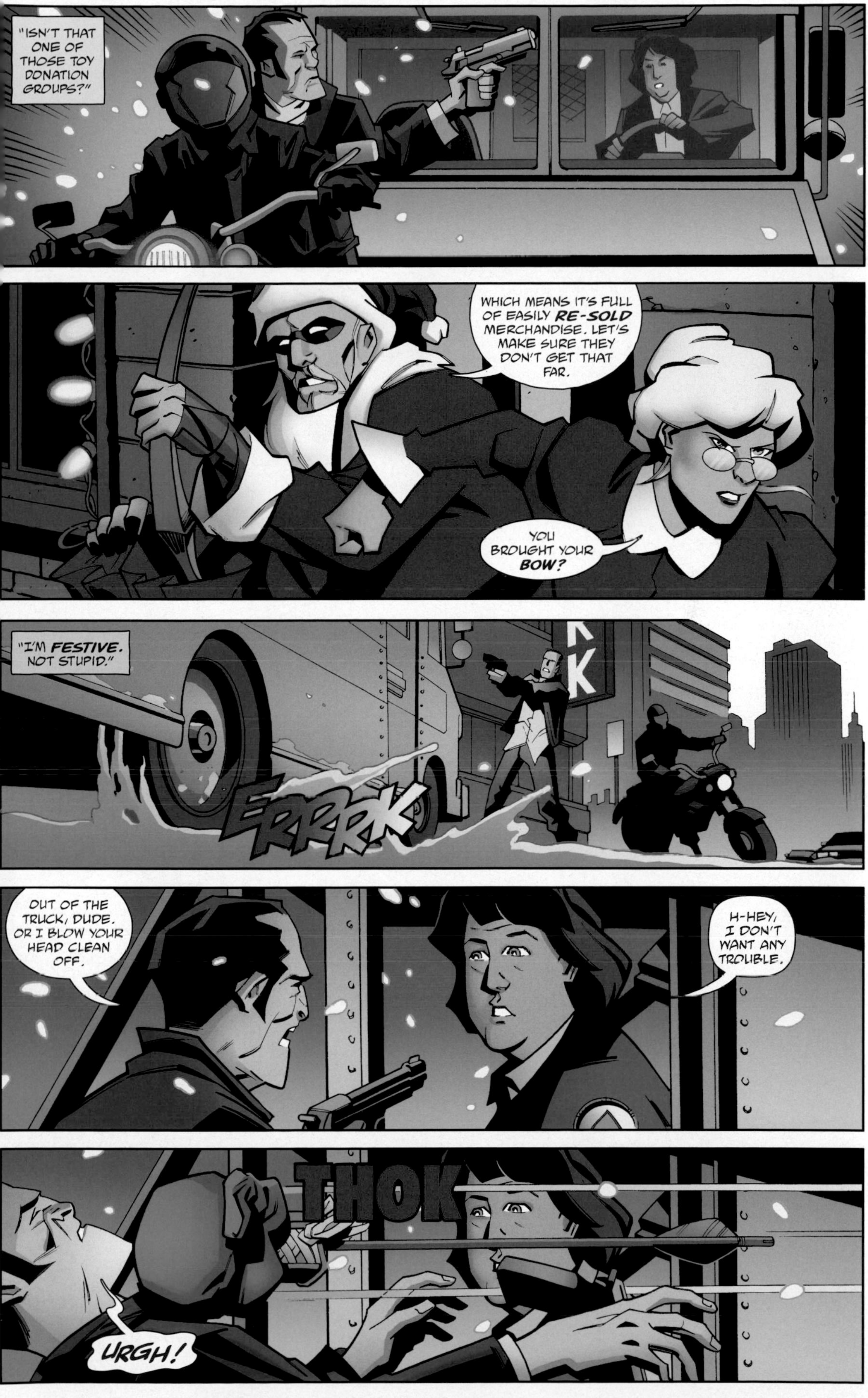
"ISN'T THAT ONE OF THOSE TOY DONATION GROUPS?"
WHICH MEANS IT'S FULL OF EASILY **RE-SOLD** MERCHANDISE. LET'S MAKE SURE THEY DON'T GET THAT FAR.
YOU BROUGHT YOUR **BOW?**
"I'M **FESTIVE.** NOT STUPID."
ERRRK
OUT OF THE TRUCK, DUDE, OR I BLOW YOUR HEAD CLEAN OFF.
H-HEY, I DON'T WANT ANY TROUBLE.
THOK
URGH!

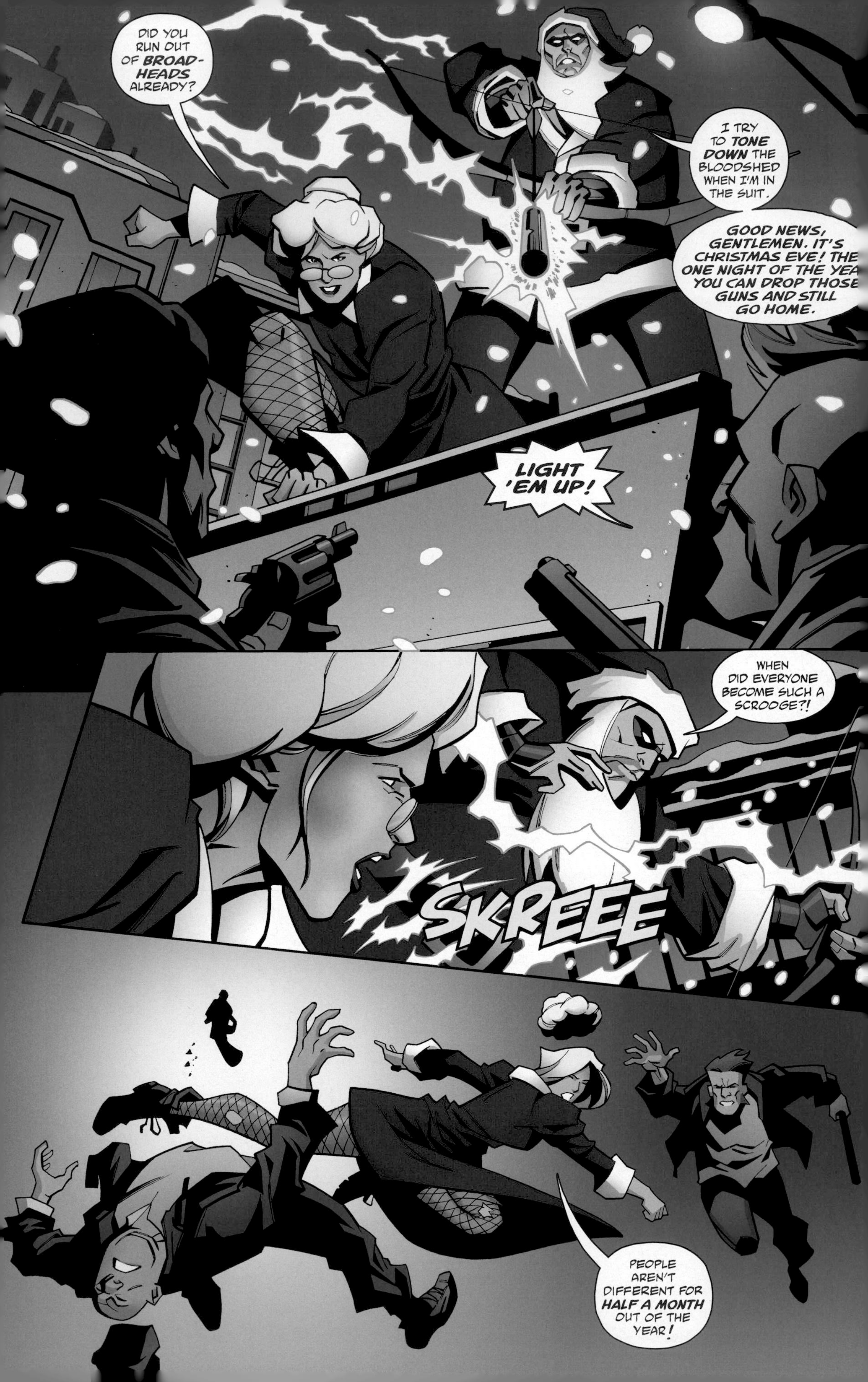
DID YOU RUN OUT OF BROAD-HEADS ALREADY?
I TRY TO TONE DOWN THE BLOODSHED WHEN I'M IN THE SUIT.
GOOD NEWS, GENTLEMEN. IT'S CHRISTMAS EVE! THE ONE NIGHT OF THE YEA YOU CAN DROP THOSE GUNS AND STILL GO HOME.
LIGHT 'EM UP!
WHEN DID EVERYONE BECOME SUCH A SCROOGE?!
SKREEE
PEOPLE AREN'T DIFFERENT FOR HALF A MONTH OUT OF THE YEAR!

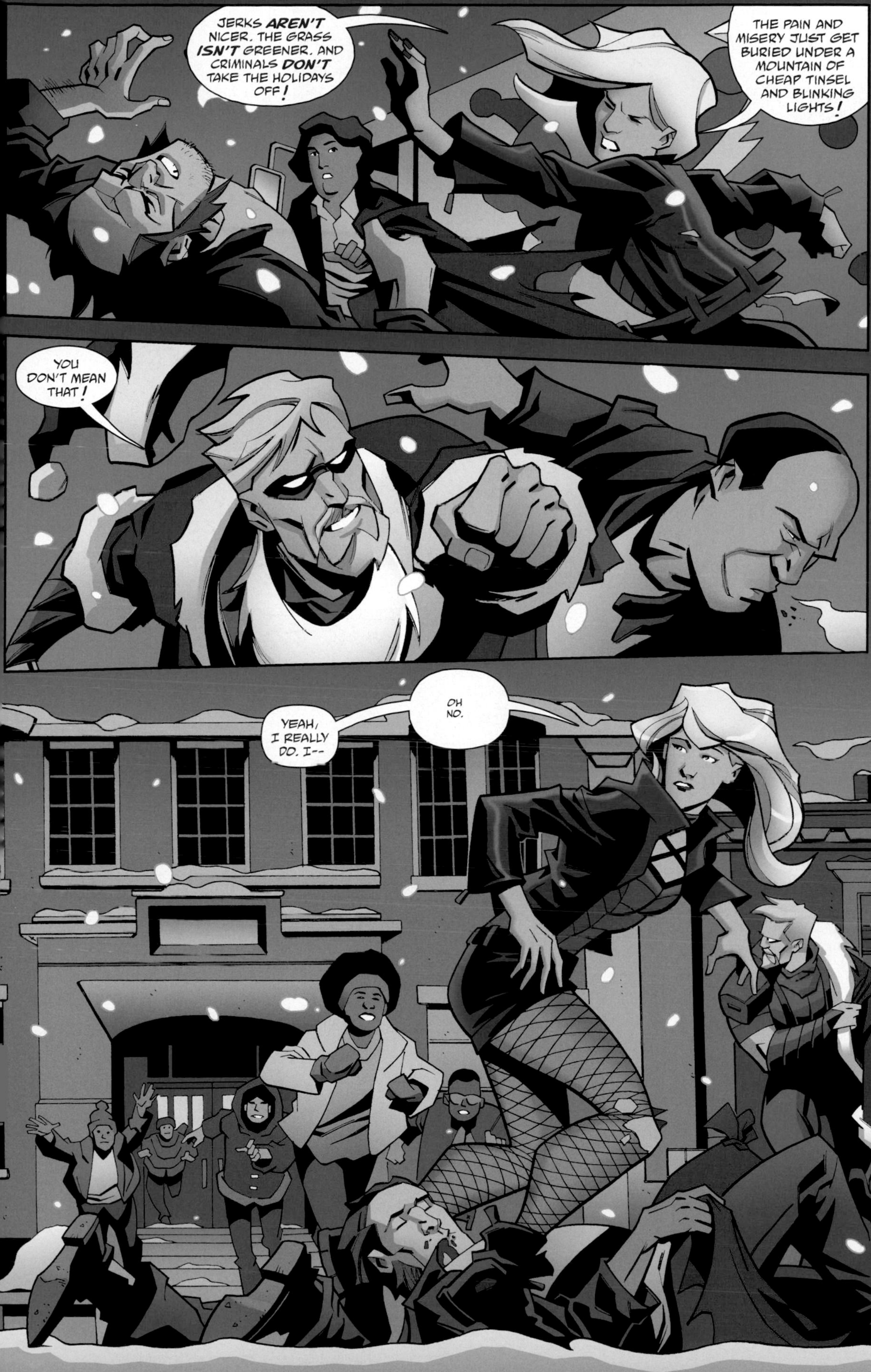

JERKS **AREN'T** NICER. THE GRASS **ISN'T** GREENER. AND CRIMINALS **DON'T** TAKE THE HOLIDAYS OFF!
THE PAIN AND MISERY JUST GET BURIED UNDER A MOUNTAIN OF CHEAP TINSEL AND BLINKING LIGHTS!
YOU DON'T MEAN THAT!
YEAH, I REALLY DO. I--
OH NO.

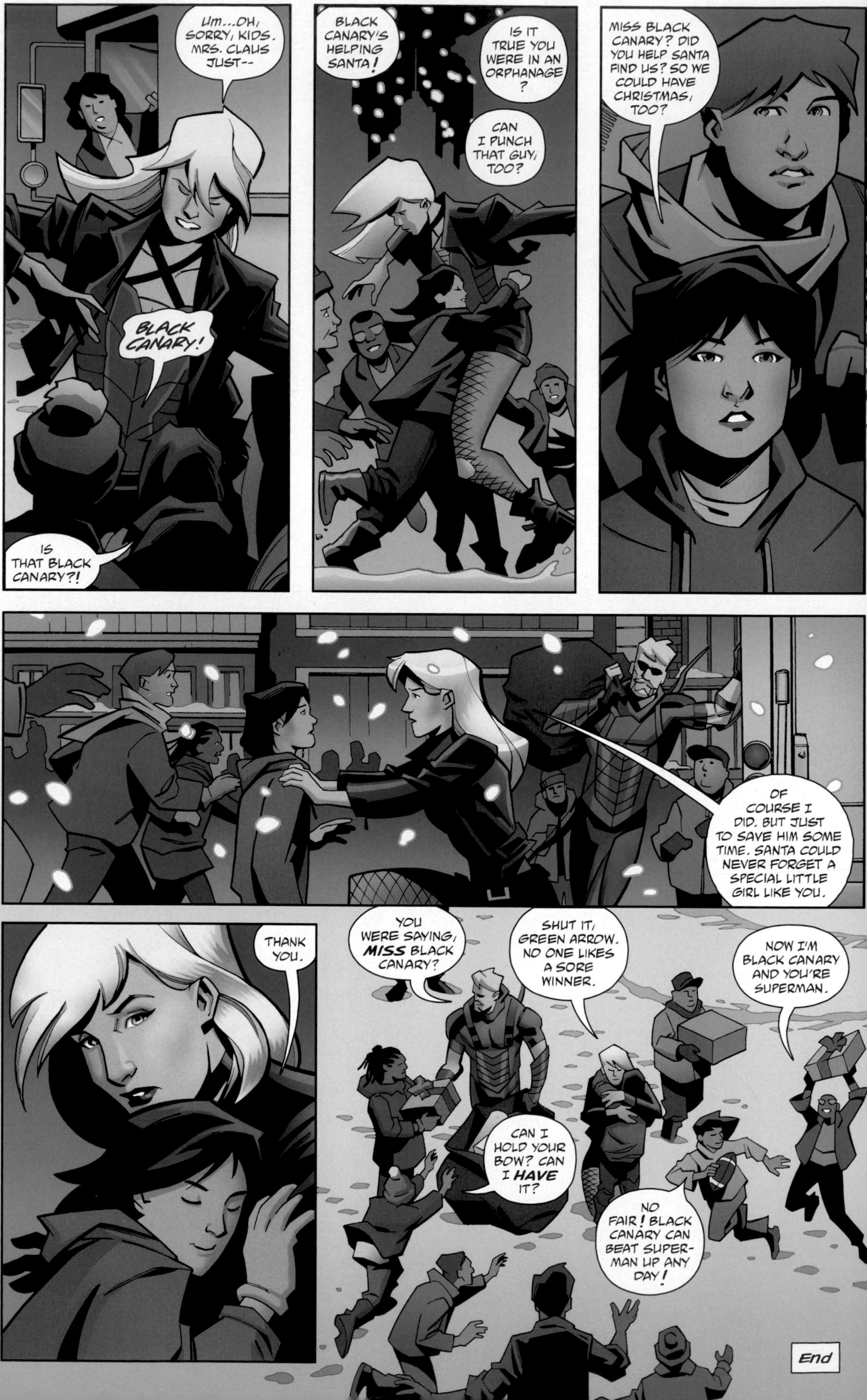
UM...OH, SORRY, KIDS. MRS. CLAUS JUST--
BLACK CANARY!
IS THAT BLACK CANARY?!
BLACK CANARY'S HELPING SANTA!
IS IT TRUE YOU WERE IN AN ORPHANAGE?
CAN I PUNCH THAT GUY, TOO?
MISS BLACK CANARY? DID YOU HELP SANTA FIND US? SO WE COULD HAVE CHRISTMAS, TOO?
OF COURSE I DID. BUT JUST TO SAVE HIM SOME TIME. SANTA COULD NEVER FORGET A SPECIAL LITTLE GIRL LIKE YOU.
THANK YOU.
YOU WERE SAYING, MISS BLACK CANARY?
SHUT IT, GREEN ARROW. NO ONE LIKES A SORE WINNER.
NOW I'M BLACK CANARY AND YOU'RE SUPERMAN.
CAN I HOLD YOUR BOW? CAN I HAVE IT?
NO FAIR! BLACK CANARY CAN BEAT SUPER-MAN UP ANY DAY!
End

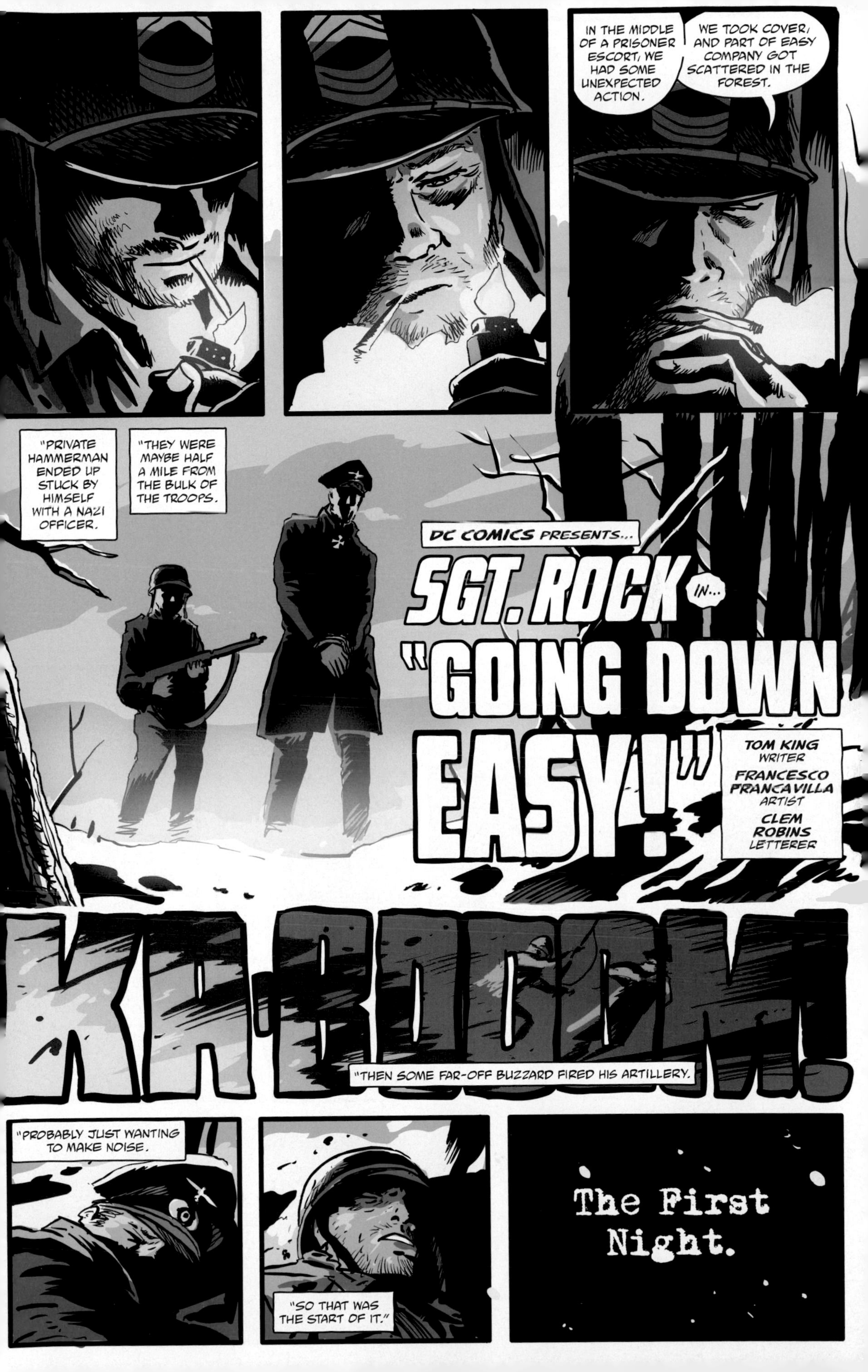
IN THE MIDDLE OF A PRISONER ESCORT, WE HAD SOME UNEXPECTED ACTION.
WE TOOK COVER, AND PART OF EASY COMPANY GOT SCATTERED IN THE FOREST.
"PRIVATE HAMMERMAN ENDED UP STUCK BY HIMSELF WITH A NAZI OFFICER.
"THEY WERE MAYBE HALF A MILE FROM THE BULK OF THE TROOPS.
DC COMICS PRESENTS...
SGT. ROCK IN...
"GOING DOWN EASY!"
TOM KING WRITER
FRANCESCO FRANCAVILLA ARTIST
CLEM ROBINS LETTERER
KA-BOOM!
"THEN SOME FAR-OFF BUZZARD FIRED HIS ARTILLERY.
"PROBABLY JUST WANTING TO MAKE NOISE.
"SO THAT WAS THE START OF IT."
The First Night.

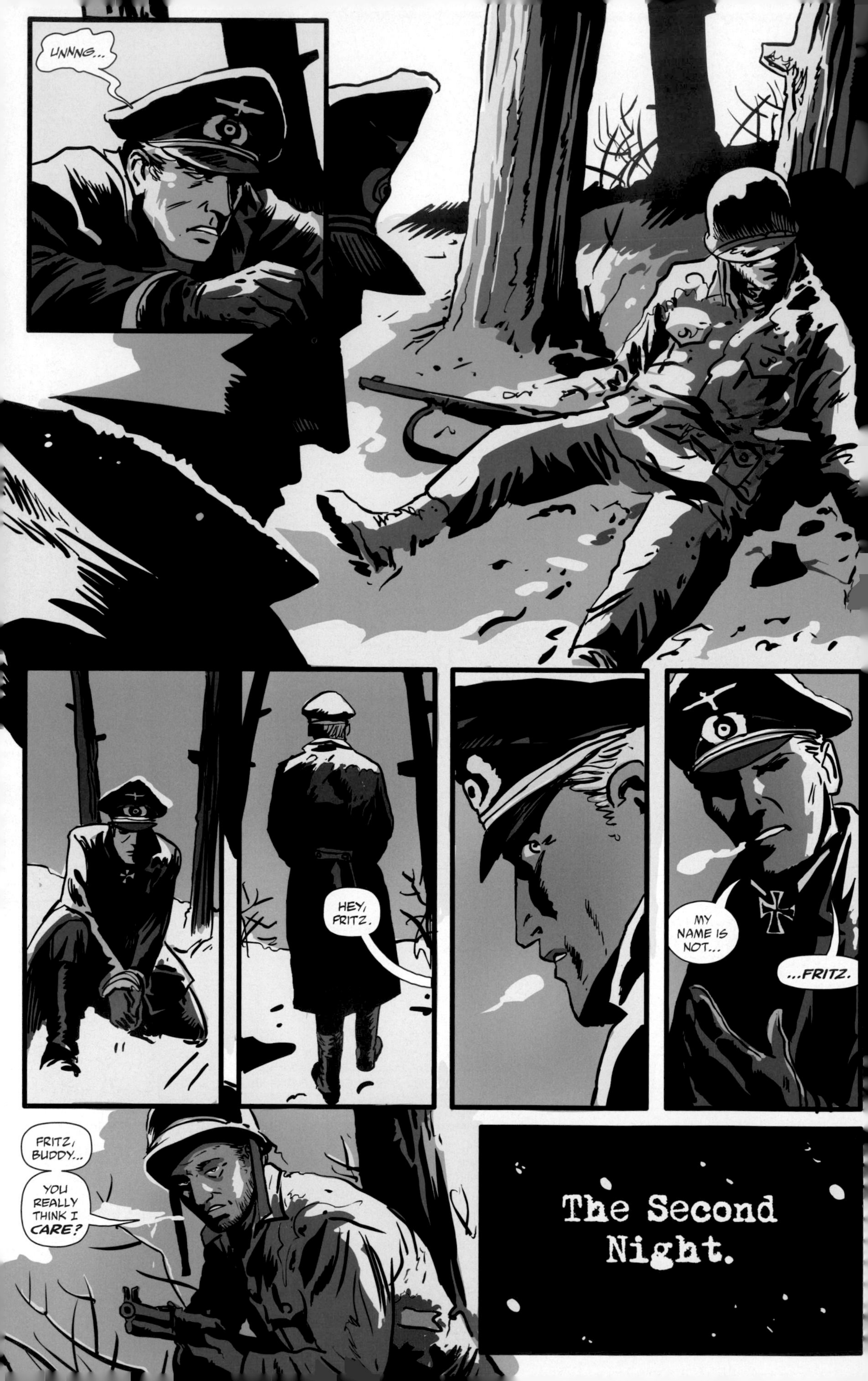
UNNNG...
HEY, FRITZ.
MY NAME IS NOT...
...FRITZ.
FRITZ, BUDDY...
YOU REALLY THINK I *CARE?*
The Second Night.

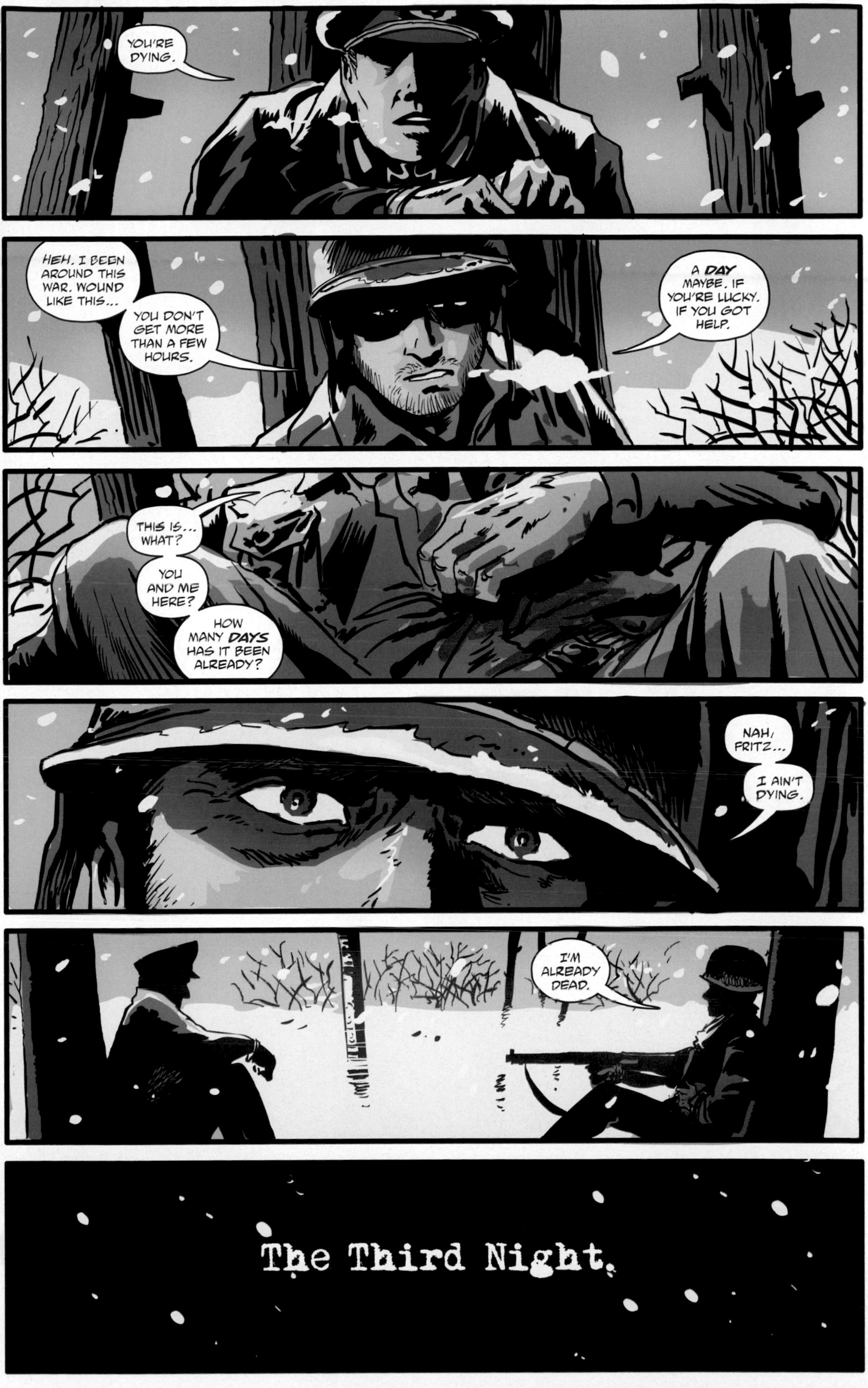
YOU'RE DYING.
HEH. I BEEN AROUND THIS WAR. WOUND LIKE THIS...
YOU DON'T GET MORE THAN A FEW HOURS.
A DAY MAYBE. IF YOU'RE LUCKY. IF YOU GOT HELP.
THIS IS... WHAT?
YOU AND ME HERE?
HOW MANY DAYS HAS IT BEEN ALREADY?
NAH, FRITZ...
I AIN'T DYING.
I'M ALREADY DEAD.
The Third Night.

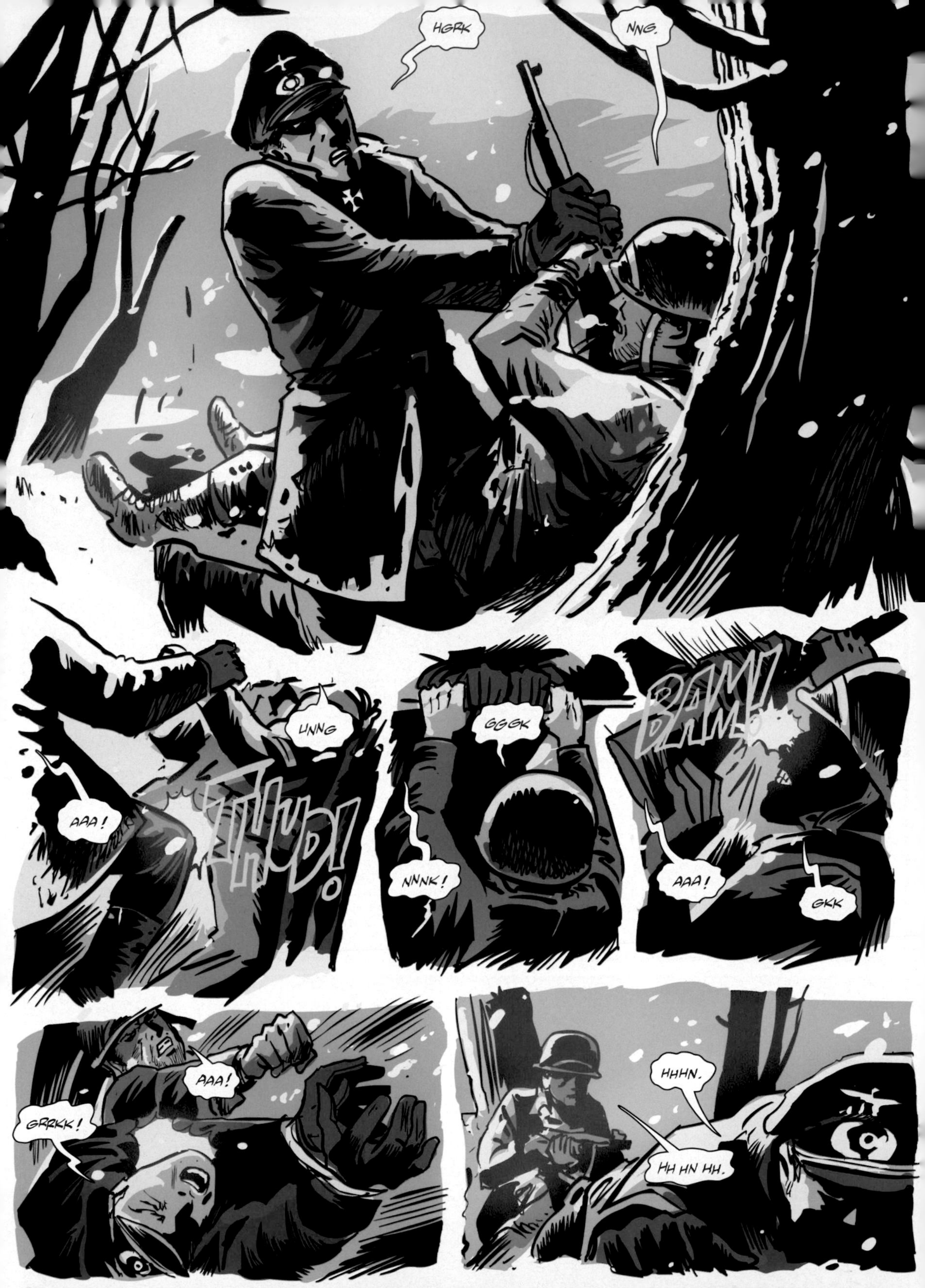
HGRK
NNG.
UNNG
AAA!
THUD!
GGGK
NNNK!
BAM!
AAA!
GKK
AAA!
GRRKK!
HHHN.
HH HN HH.

The Fourth Night.

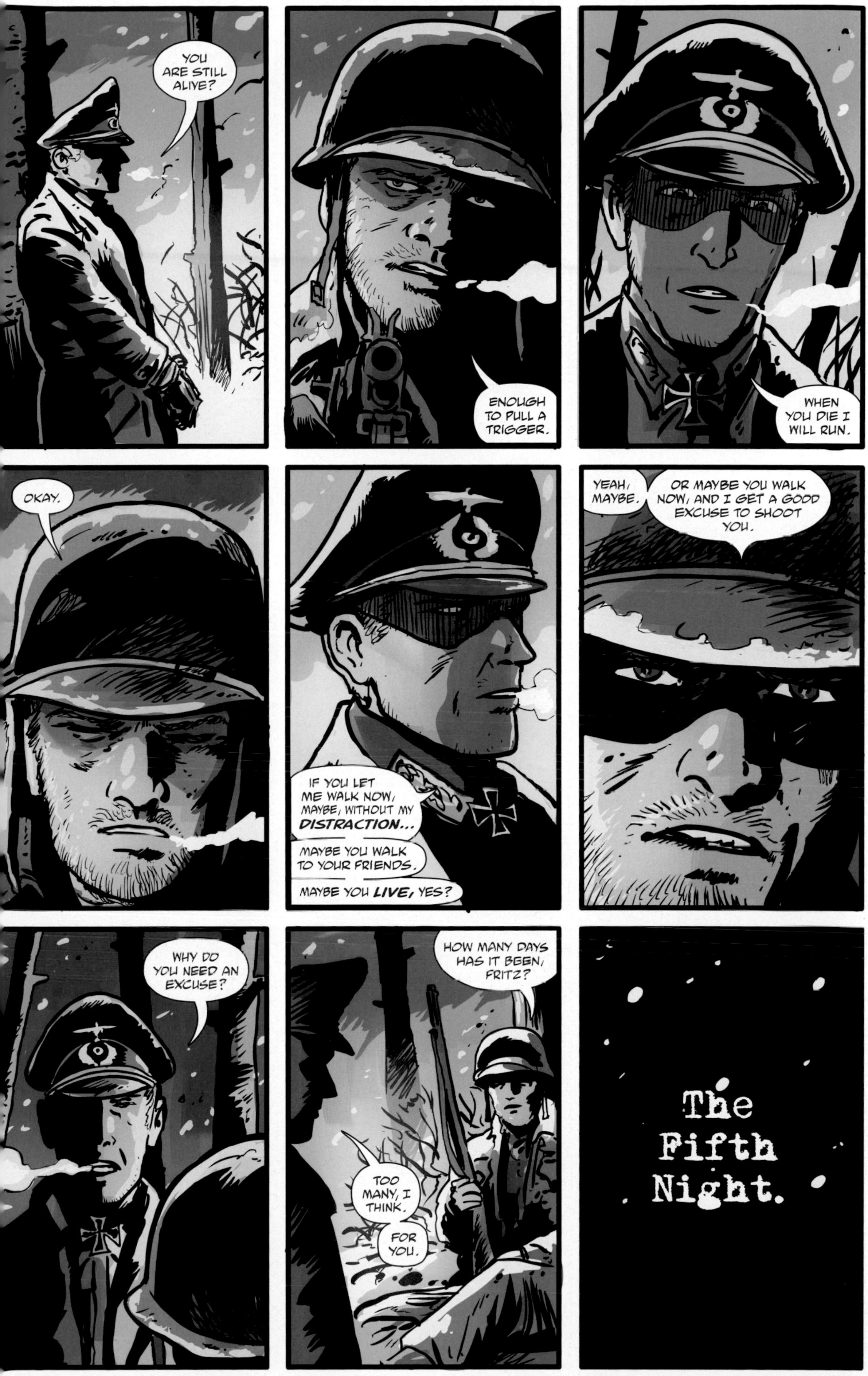
YOU ARE STILL ALIVE?
ENOUGH TO PULL A TRIGGER.
WHEN YOU DIE I WILL RUN.
OKAY.
IF YOU LET ME WALK NOW, MAYBE, WITHOUT MY DISTRACTION...
MAYBE YOU WALK TO YOUR FRIENDS.
MAYBE YOU LIVE, YES?
YEAH, MAYBE.
OR MAYBE YOU WALK NOW, AND I GET A GOOD EXCUSE TO SHOOT YOU.
WHY DO YOU NEED AN EXCUSE?
HOW MANY DAYS HAS IT BEEN, FRITZ?
TOO MANY, I THINK.
FOR YOU.
The Fifth Night.

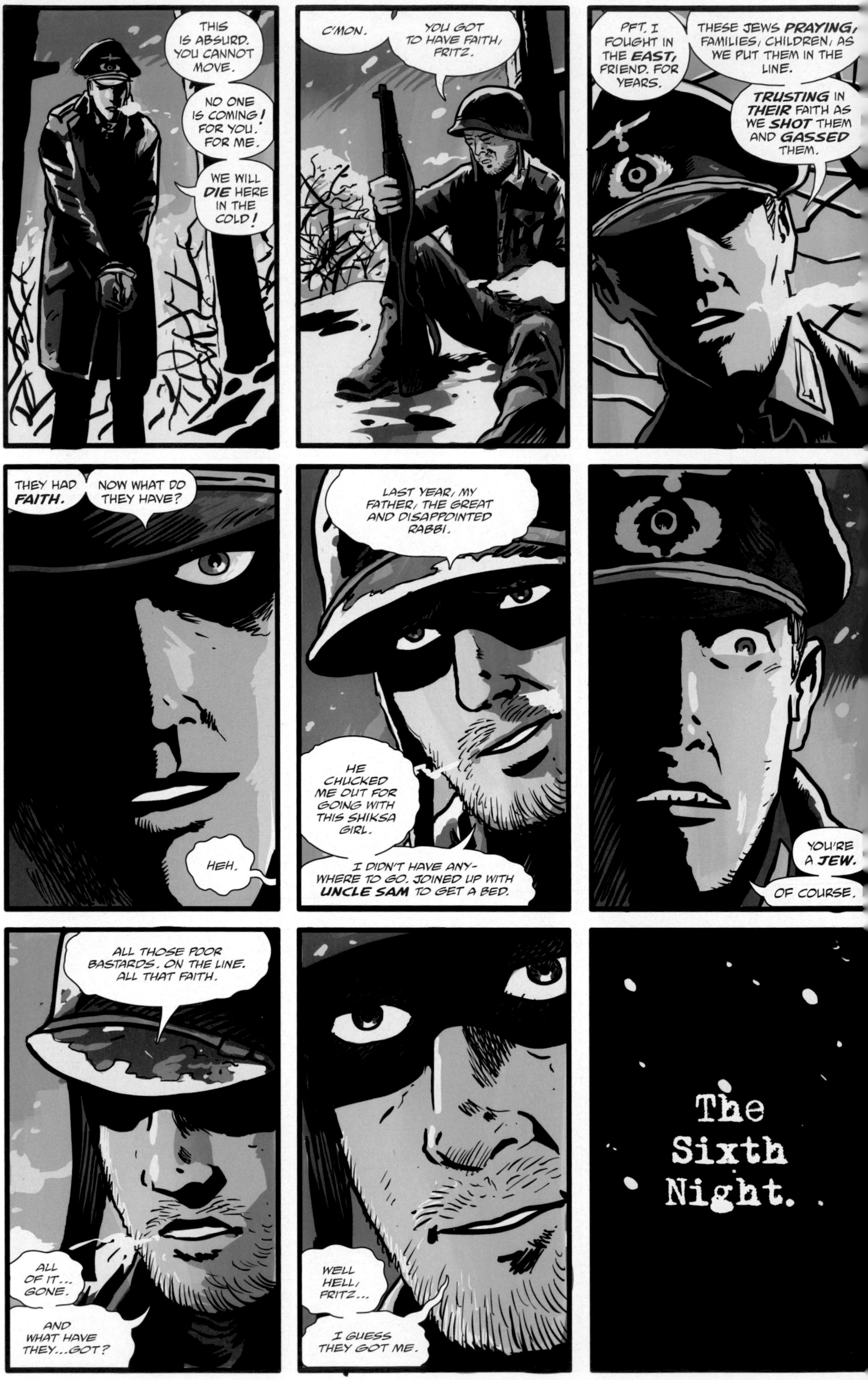
THIS IS ABSURD. YOU CANNOT MOVE.
NO ONE IS COMING! FOR YOU. FOR ME.
WE WILL DIE HERE IN THE COLD!
C'MON.
YOU GOT TO HAVE FAITH, FRITZ.
PFT. I FOUGHT IN THE EAST, FRIEND. FOR YEARS.
THESE JEWS PRAYING, FAMILIES, CHILDREN, AS WE PUT THEM IN THE LINE.
TRUSTING IN THEIR FAITH AS WE SHOT THEM AND GASSED THEM.
THEY HAD FAITH.
NOW WHAT DO THEY HAVE?
HEH.
LAST YEAR, MY FATHER, THE GREAT AND DISAPPOINTED RABBI.
HE CHUCKED ME OUT FOR GOING WITH THIS SHIKSA GIRL.
I DIDN'T HAVE ANY-WHERE TO GO. JOINED UP WITH UNCLE SAM TO GET A BED.
YOU'RE A JEW.
OF COURSE.
ALL THOSE POOR BASTARDS. ON THE LINE. ALL THAT FAITH.
ALL OF IT... GONE.
AND WHAT HAVE THEY...GOT?
WELL HELL, FRITZ...
I GUESS THEY GOT ME.
The Sixth Night.

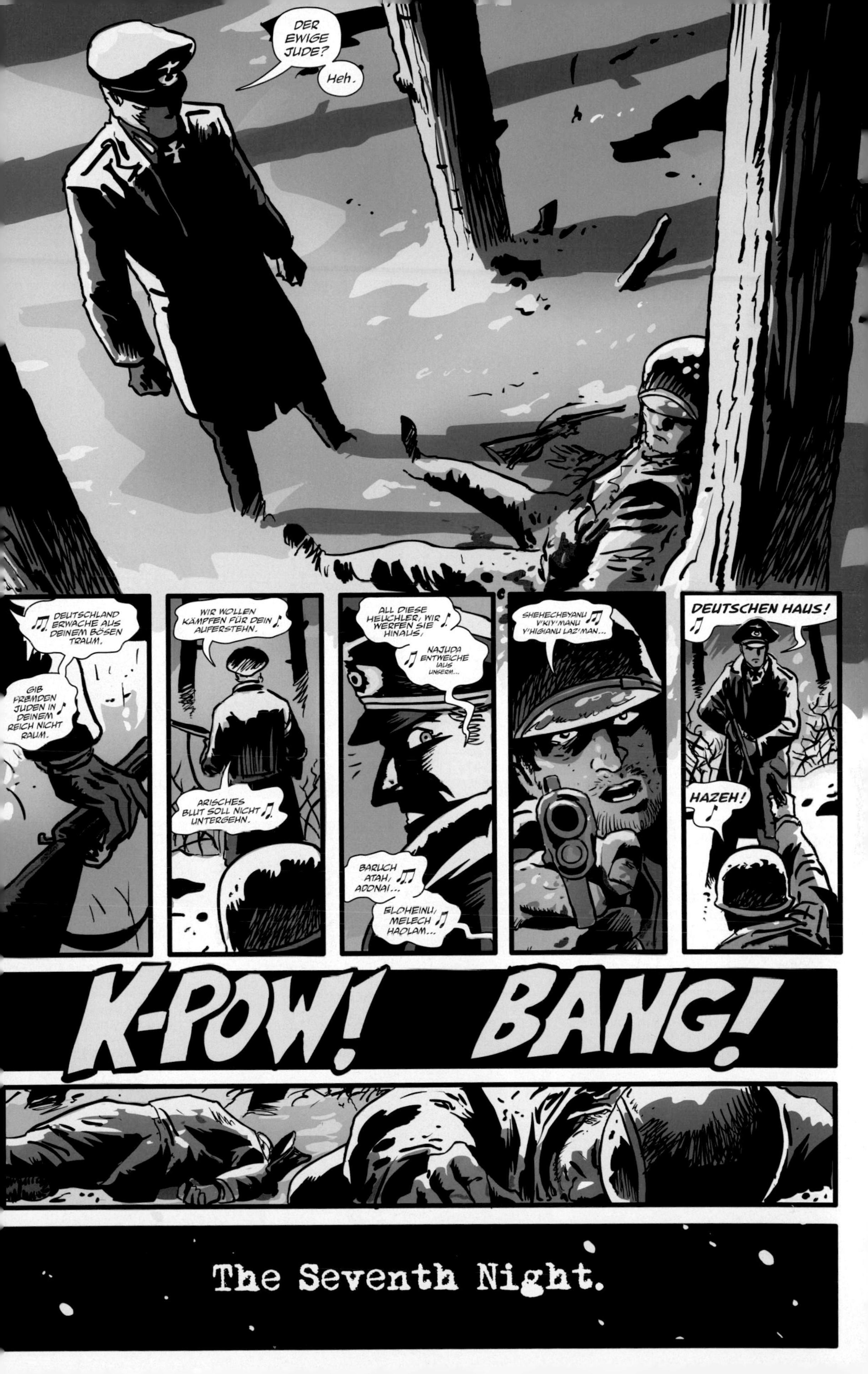
DER EWIGE JUDE?
Heh.
DEUTSCHLAND ERWACHE AUS DEINEM BÖSEN TRAUM.
GIB FREMDEN JUDEN IN DEINEM REICH NICHT RAUM.
WIR WOLLEN KÄMPFEN FÜR DEIN AUFERSTEHN.
ARISCHES BLUT SOLL NICHT UNTERGEHN.
ALL DIESE HEUCHLER, WIR WERFEN SIE HINAUS,
NAJUDA ENTWEICHE IAUS UNSERM...
BARUCH ATAH, ADONAI...
ELOHEINU, MELECH HAOLAM...
SHEHECHEYANU V'KIY'MANU V'HIGIANU LAZ'MAN...
DEUTSCHEN HAUS!
HAZEH!
K-POW!
BANG!
The Seventh Night.

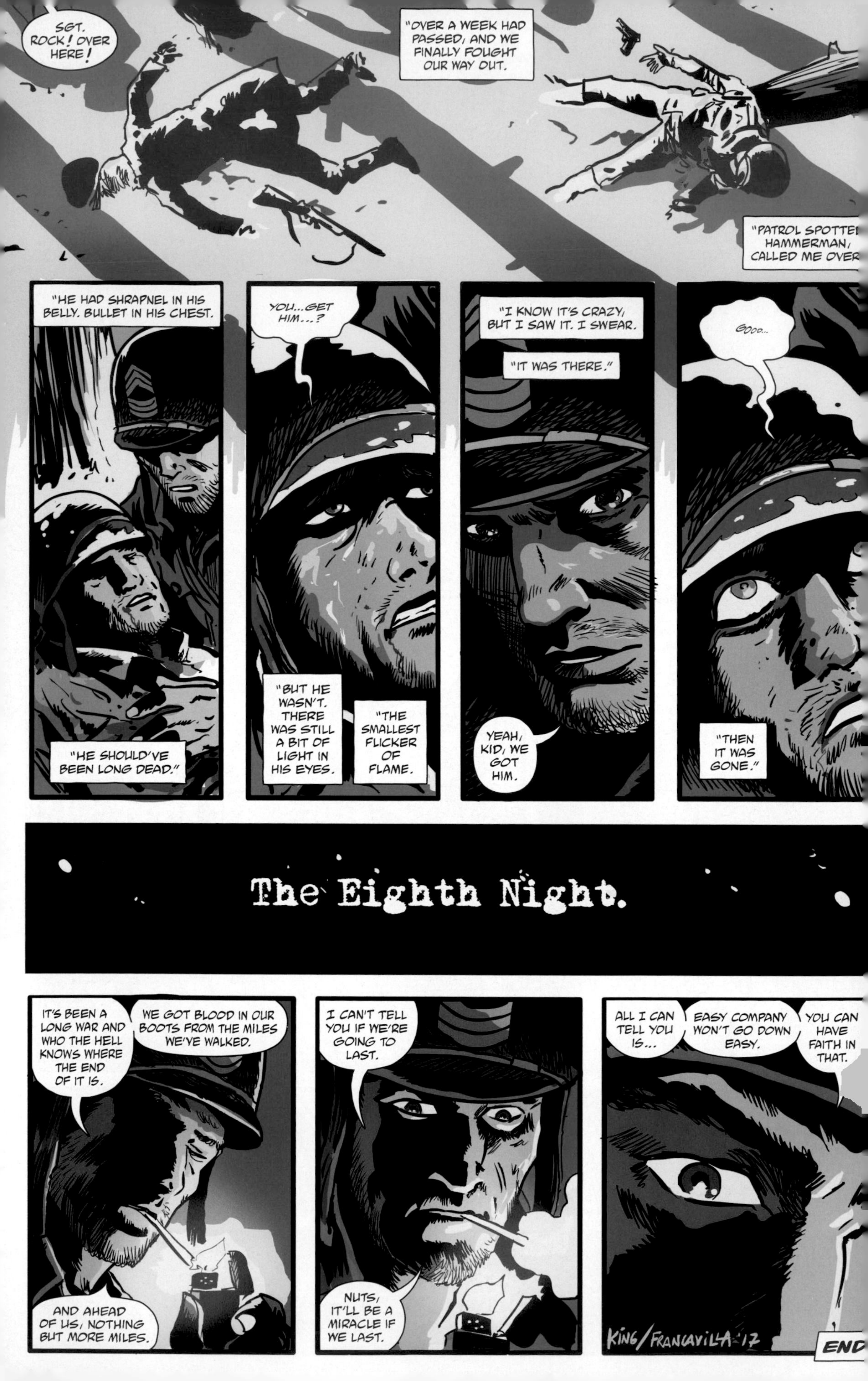
SGT. ROCK! OVER HERE!
"OVER A WEEK HAD PASSED, AND WE FINALLY FOUGHT OUR WAY OUT.
"PATROL SPOTTER HAMMERMAN, CALLED ME OVER
"HE HAD SHRAPNEL IN HIS BELLY. BULLET IN HIS CHEST.
"HE SHOULD'VE BEEN LONG DEAD."
YOU...GET HIM...?
"BUT HE WASN'T. THERE WAS STILL A BIT OF LIGHT IN HIS EYES.
"THE SMALLEST FLICKER OF FLAME.
"I KNOW IT'S CRAZY, BUT I SAW IT. I SWEAR.
"IT WAS THERE."
YEAH, KID, WE GOT HIM.
GOOD...
"THEN IT WAS GONE."
The Eighth Night.
IT'S BEEN A LONG WAR AND WHO THE HELL KNOWS WHERE THE END OF IT IS.
WE GOT BLOOD IN OUR BOOTS FROM THE MILES WE'VE WALKED.
AND AHEAD OF US, NOTHING BUT MORE MILES.
I CAN'T TELL YOU IF WE'RE GOING TO LAST.
NUTS, IT'LL BE A MIRACLE IF WE LAST.
ALL I CAN TELL YOU IS...
EASY COMPANY WON'T GO DOWN EASY.
YOU CAN HAVE FAITH IN THAT.
KING/FRANCAVILLA '17
END

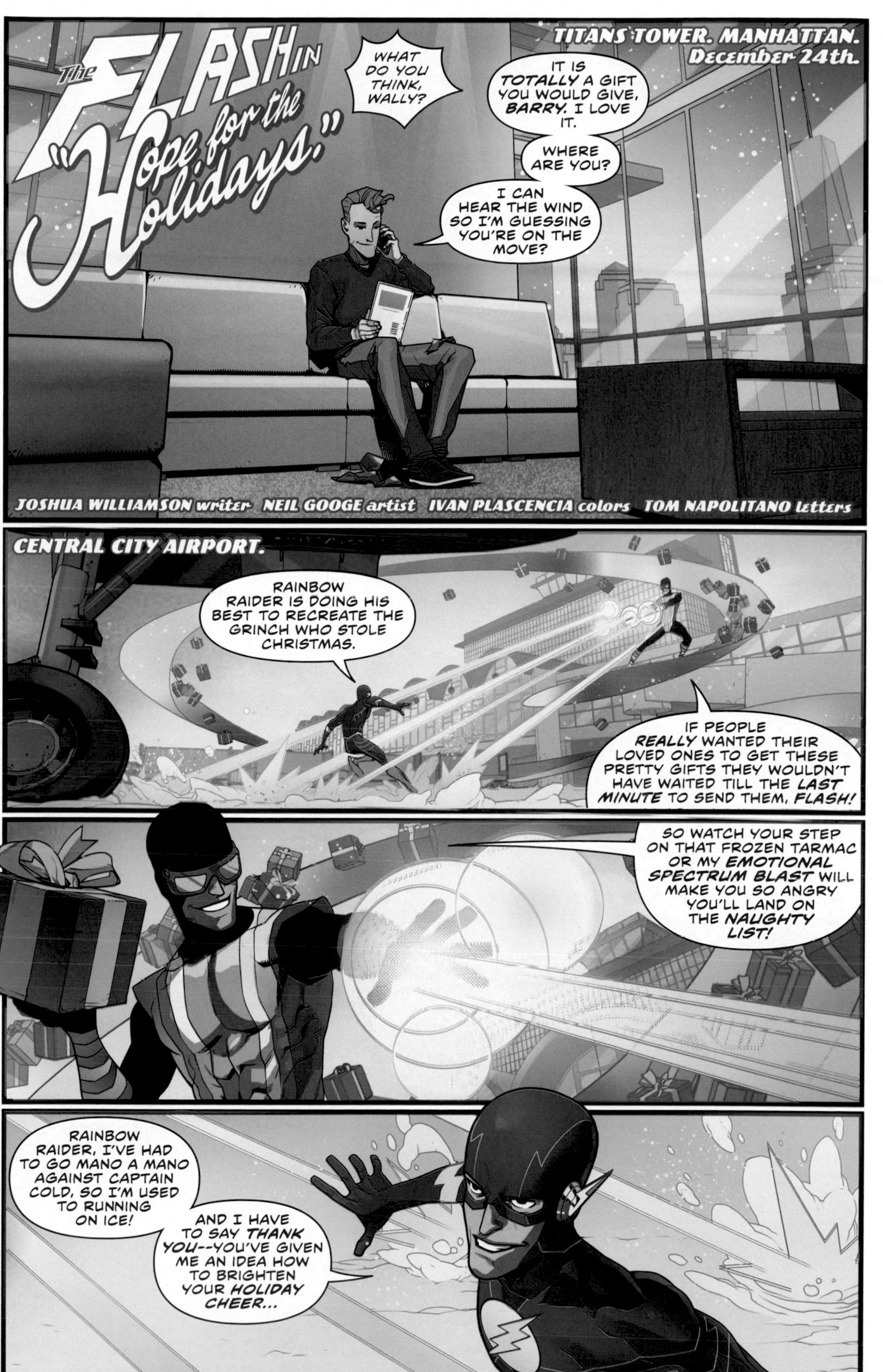
The FLASH in
"Hope for the Holidays."
TITANS TOWER. MANHATTAN. December 24th.
WHAT DO YOU THINK, WALLY?
IT IS TOTALLY A GIFT YOU WOULD GIVE, BARRY. I LOVE IT.
WHERE ARE YOU?
I CAN HEAR THE WIND SO I'M GUESSING YOU'RE ON THE MOVE?
JOSHUA WILLIAMSON writer NEIL GOOGE artist IVAN PLASCENCIA colors TOM NAPOLITANO letters
CENTRAL CITY AIRPORT.
RAINBOW RAIDER IS DOING HIS BEST TO RECREATE THE GRINCH WHO STOLE CHRISTMAS.
IF PEOPLE REALLY WANTED THEIR LOVED ONES TO GET THESE PRETTY GIFTS THEY WOULDN'T HAVE WAITED TILL THE LAST MINUTE TO SEND THEM, FLASH!
SO WATCH YOUR STEP ON THAT FROZEN TARMAC OR MY EMOTIONAL SPECTRUM BLAST WILL MAKE YOU SO ANGRY YOU'LL LAND ON THE NAUGHTY LIST!
RAINBOW RAIDER, I'VE HAD TO GO MANO A MANO AGAINST CAPTAIN COLD, SO I'M USED TO RUNNING ON ICE!
AND I HAVE TO SAY THANK YOU--YOU'VE GIVEN ME AN IDEA HOW TO BRIGHTEN YOUR HOLIDAY CHEER...

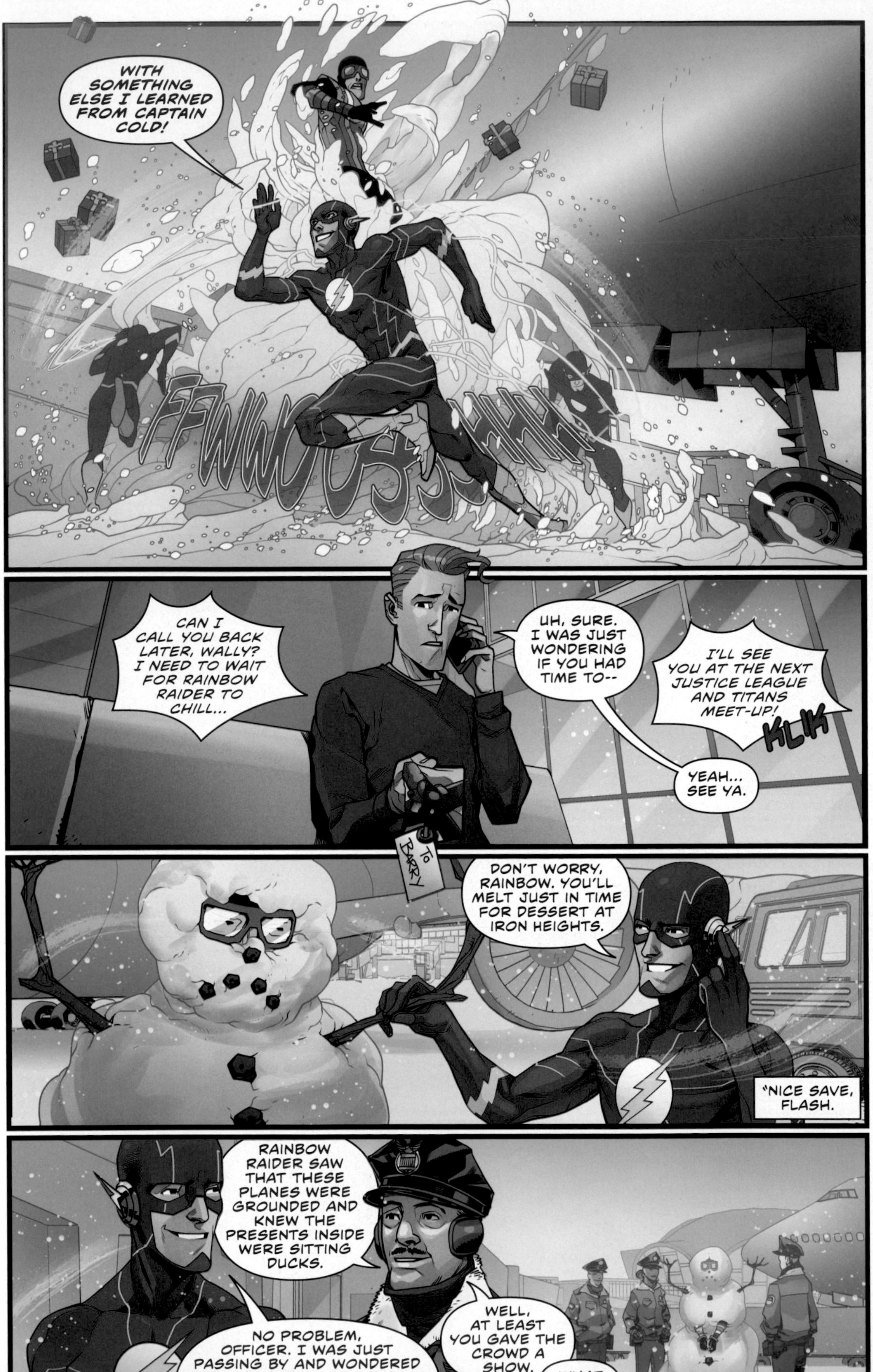

WITH SOMETHING ELSE I LEARNED FROM CAPTAIN COLD!
FFWWOOSSSHHH
CAN I CALL YOU BACK LATER, WALLY? I NEED TO WAIT FOR RAINBOW RAIDER TO CHILL...
UH, SURE. I WAS JUST WONDERING IF YOU HAD TIME TO--
I'LL SEE YOU AT THE NEXT JUSTICE LEAGUE AND TITANS MEET-UP!
KLIK
YEAH... SEE YA.
TO BARRY
DON'T WORRY, RAINBOW. YOU'LL MELT JUST IN TIME FOR DESSERT AT IRON HEIGHTS.
"NICE SAVE, FLASH.
RAINBOW RAIDER SAW THAT THESE PLANES WERE GROUNDED AND KNEW THE PRESENTS INSIDE WERE SITTING DUCKS.
NO PROBLEM, OFFICER. I WAS JUST PASSING BY AND WONDERED HOW A RAINBOW COULD BE IN THE SKY DURING A SNOWSTORM.
WELL, AT LEAST YOU GAVE THE CROWD A SHOW.
WHAT CROWD?

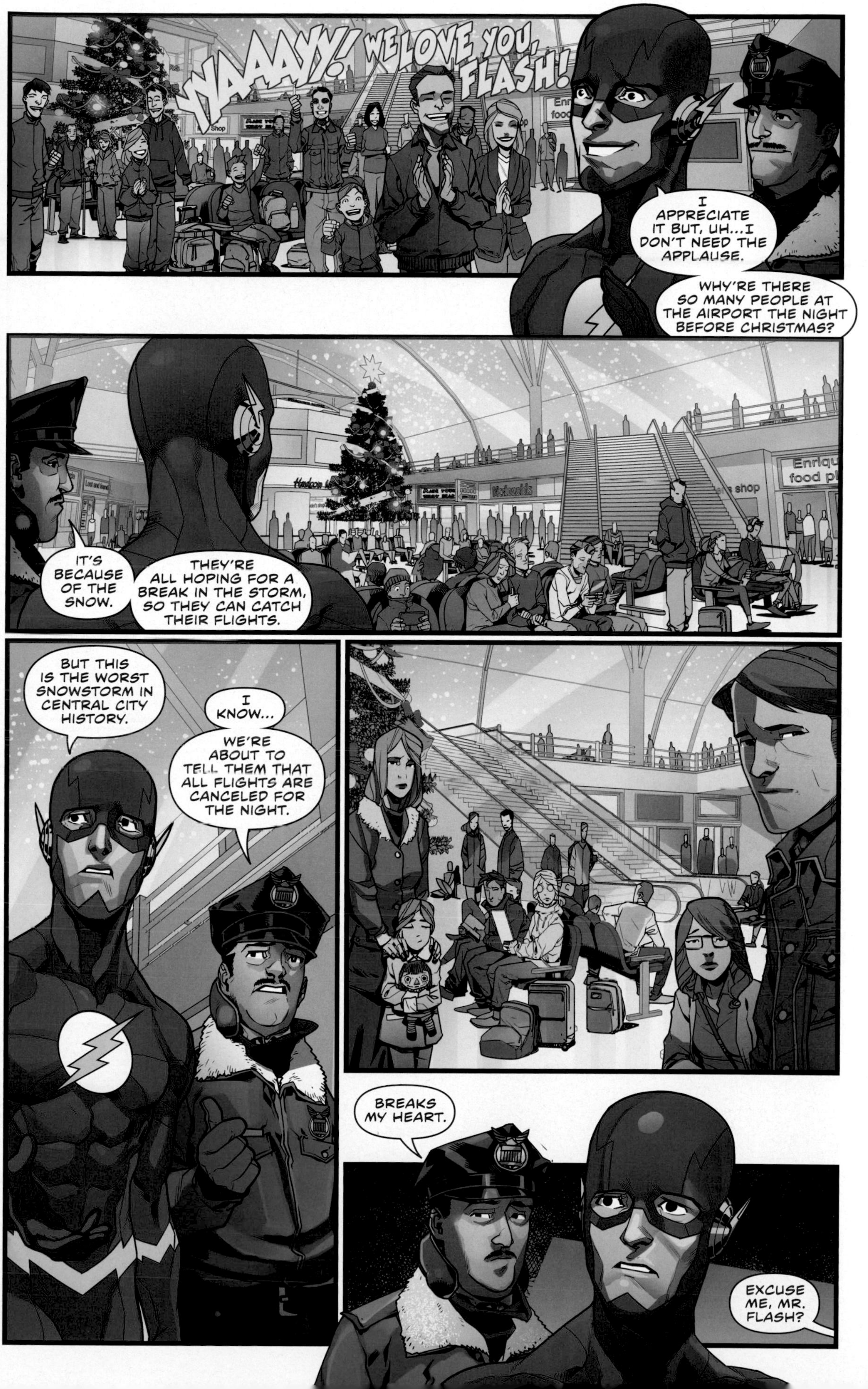
YAAAYY! WE LOVE YOU, FLASH!
I APPRECIATE IT BUT, UH...I DON'T NEED THE APPLAUSE.
WHY'RE THERE SO MANY PEOPLE AT THE AIRPORT THE NIGHT BEFORE CHRISTMAS?
IT'S BECAUSE OF THE SNOW.
THEY'RE ALL HOPING FOR A BREAK IN THE STORM, SO THEY CAN CATCH THEIR FLIGHTS.
BUT THIS IS THE WORST SNOWSTORM IN CENTRAL CITY HISTORY.
I KNOW...
WE'RE ABOUT TO TELL THEM THAT ALL FLIGHTS ARE CANCELED FOR THE NIGHT.
BREAKS MY HEART.
EXCUSE ME, MR. FLASH?

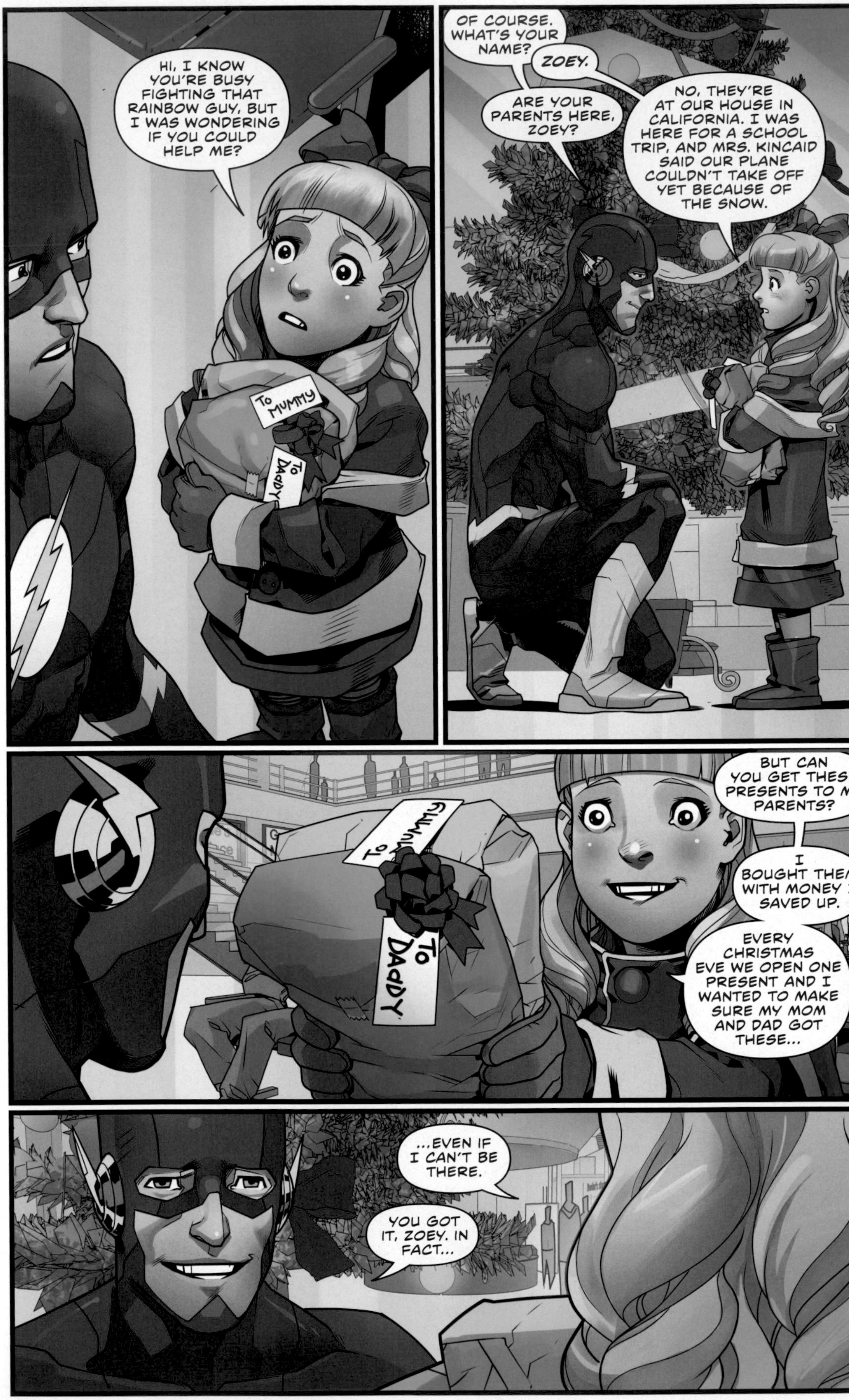
HI, I KNOW YOU'RE BUSY FIGHTING THAT RAINBOW GUY, BUT I WAS WONDERING IF YOU COULD HELP ME?
TO MUMMY
TO DADDY
OF COURSE. WHAT'S YOUR NAME?
ZOEY.
ARE YOUR PARENTS HERE, ZOEY?
NO, THEY'RE AT OUR HOUSE IN CALIFORNIA. I WAS HERE FOR A SCHOOL TRIP, AND MRS. KINCAID SAID OUR PLANE COULDN'T TAKE OFF YET BECAUSE OF THE SNOW.
TO MUMMY
TO DADDY
BUT CAN YOU GET THESE PRESENTS TO MY PARENTS?
I BOUGHT THEM WITH MONEY I SAVED UP.
EVERY CHRISTMAS EVE WE OPEN ONE PRESENT AND I WANTED TO MAKE SURE MY MOM AND DAD GOT THESE...
...EVEN IF I CAN'T BE THERE.
YOU GOT IT, ZOEY. IN FACT...

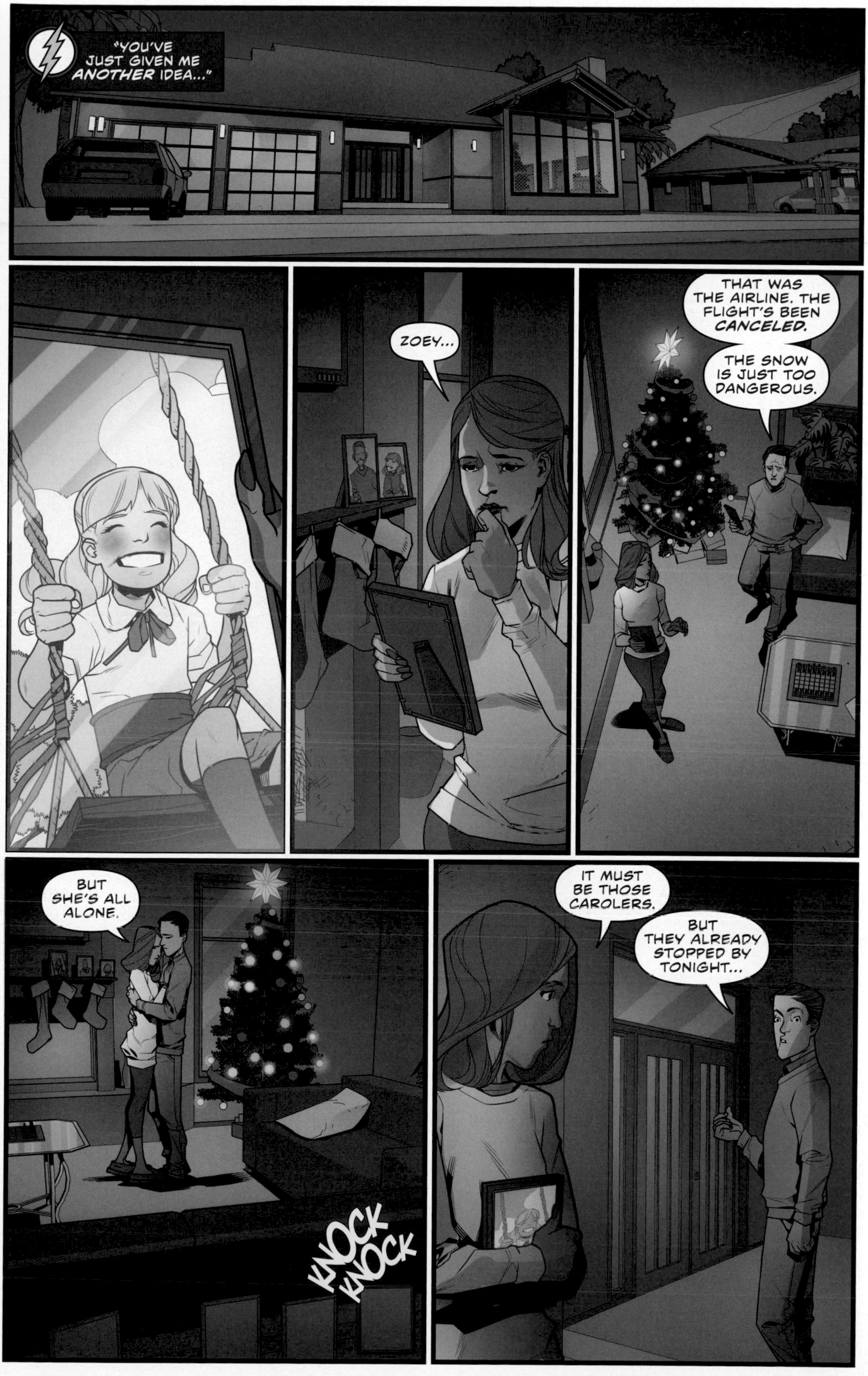
"YOU'VE JUST GIVEN ME ANOTHER IDEA..."
ZOEY...
THAT WAS THE AIRLINE. THE FLIGHT'S BEEN CANCELED.
THE SNOW IS JUST TOO DANGEROUS.
BUT SHE'S ALL ALONE.
KNOCK KNOCK
IT MUST BE THOSE CAROLERS.
BUT THEY ALREADY STOPPED BY TONIGHT...

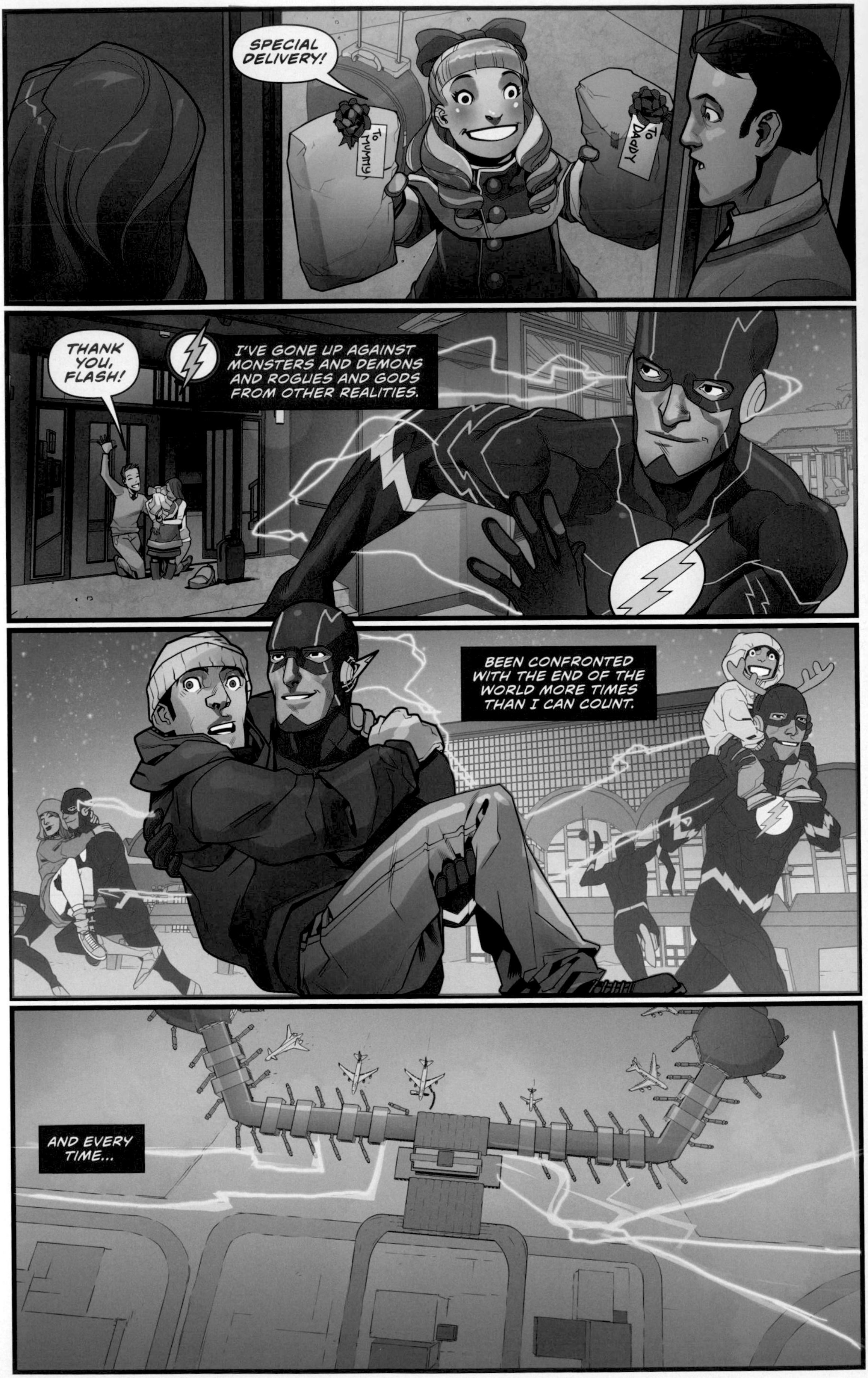
SPECIAL DELIVERY!
TO MUMMY
TO DADDY
THANK YOU, FLASH!
I'VE GONE UP AGAINST MONSTERS AND DEMONS AND ROGUES AND GODS FROM OTHER REALITIES.
BEEN CONFRONTED WITH THE END OF THE WORLD MORE TIMES THAN I CAN COUNT.
AND EVERY TIME...

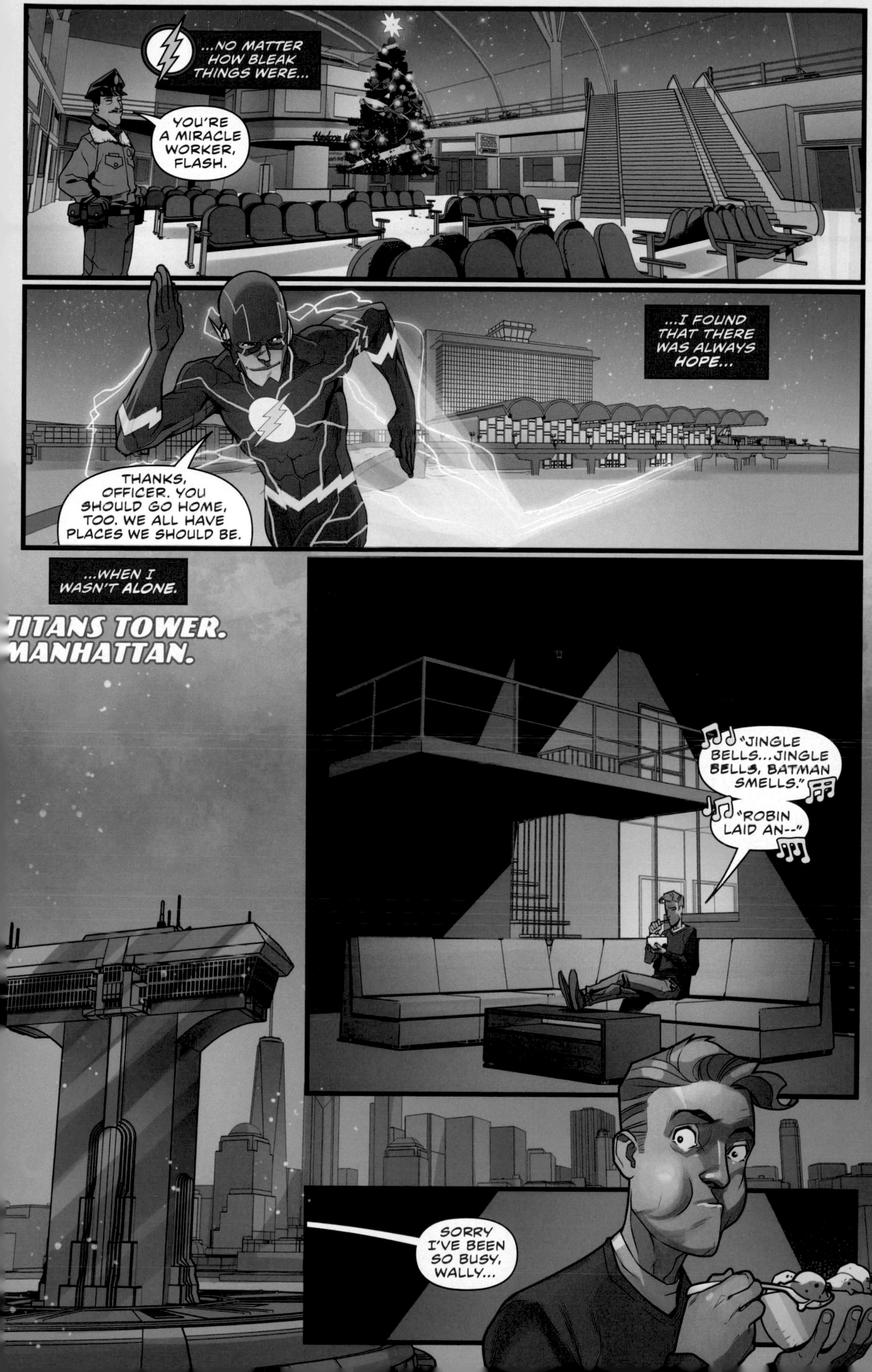
...NO MATTER HOW BLEAK THINGS WERE...
YOU'RE A MIRACLE WORKER, FLASH.
...I FOUND THAT THERE WAS ALWAYS HOPE...
THANKS, OFFICER. YOU SHOULD GO HOME, TOO. WE ALL HAVE PLACES WE SHOULD BE.
...WHEN I WASN'T ALONE.
TITANS TOWER. MANHATTAN.
"JINGLE BELLS...JINGLE BELLS, BATMAN SMELLS."
"ROBIN LAID AN--"
SORRY I'VE BEEN SO BUSY, WALLY...

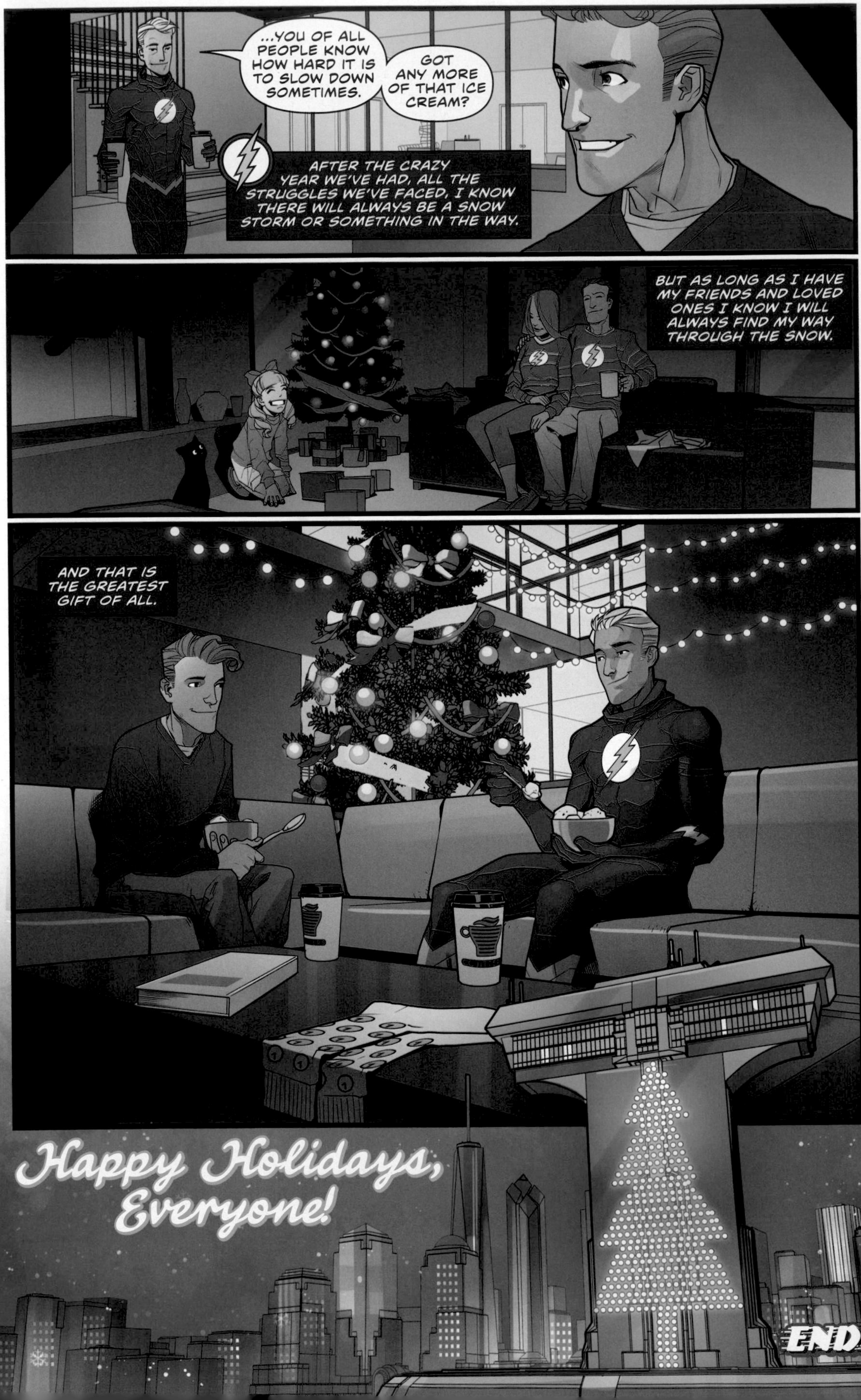
...YOU OF ALL PEOPLE KNOW HOW HARD IT IS TO SLOW DOWN SOMETIMES.
GOT ANY MORE OF THAT ICE CREAM?
AFTER THE CRAZY YEAR WE'VE HAD, ALL THE STRUGGLES WE'VE FACED, I KNOW THERE WILL ALWAYS BE A SNOW STORM OR SOMETHING IN THE WAY.
BUT AS LONG AS I HAVE MY FRIENDS AND LOVED ONES I KNOW I WILL ALWAYS FIND MY WAY THROUGH THE SNOW.
AND THAT IS THE GREATEST GIFT OF ALL.
Happy Holidays, Everyone!
END.

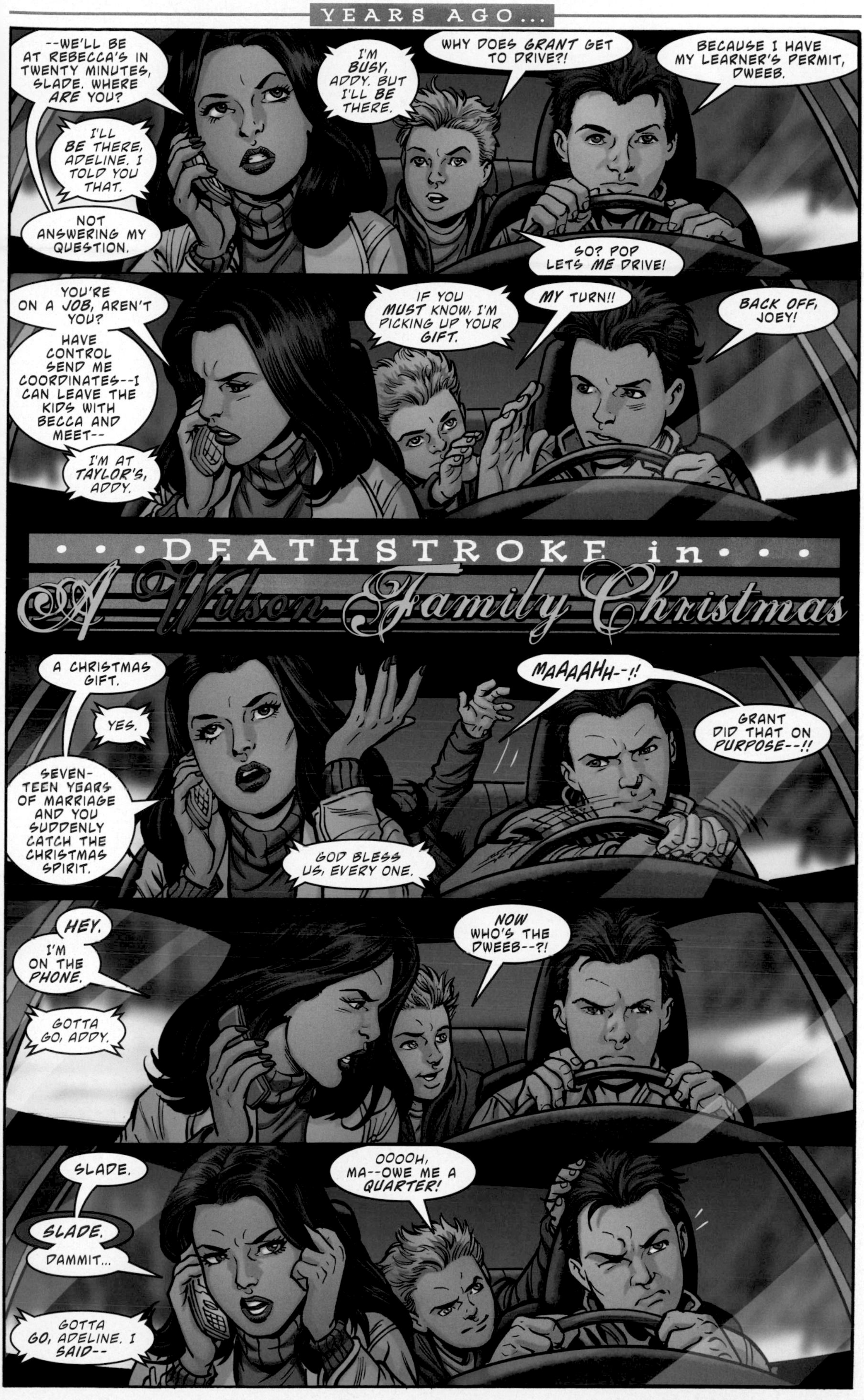
YEARS AGO...
--WE'LL BE AT REBECCA'S IN TWENTY MINUTES, SLADE. WHERE ARE YOU?
I'LL BE THERE, ADELINE. I TOLD YOU THAT.
NOT ANSWERING MY QUESTION.
I'M BUSY, ADDY. BUT I'LL BE THERE.
WHY DOES GRANT GET TO DRIVE?!
BECAUSE I HAVE MY LEARNER'S PERMIT, DWEEB.
SO? POP LETS ME DRIVE!
YOU'RE ON A JOB, AREN'T YOU?
HAVE CONTROL SEND ME COORDINATES--I CAN LEAVE THE KIDS WITH BECCA AND MEET--
I'M AT TAYLOR'S, ADDY.
IF YOU MUST KNOW, I'M PICKING UP YOUR GIFT.
MY TURN!!
BACK OFF, JOEY!
• • • DEATHSTROKE in • • •
A Wilson Family Christmas
A CHRISTMAS GIFT.
YES.
SEVENTEEN YEARS OF MARRIAGE AND YOU SUDDENLY CATCH THE CHRISTMAS SPIRIT.
GOD BLESS US, EVERY ONE.
MAAAAHH--!!
GRANT DID THAT ON PURPOSE--!!
HEY. I'M ON THE PHONE.
GOTTA GO, ADDY.
NOW WHO'S THE DWEEB--?!
SLADE.
SLADE.
DAMMIT...
GOTTA GO, ADELINE. I SAID--
OOOOH, MA--OWE ME A QUARTER!

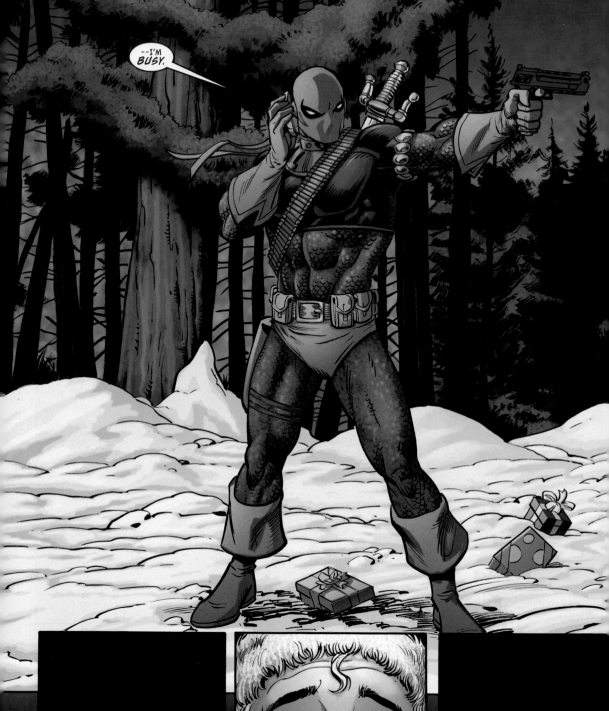

PRIEST
— story —

TOM GRUMMETT
— pencils —

SCOTT HANNA
— inks —

"Bearing Gifts, We Traverse Afar"

MARYLAND

CHRISTMAS EVE

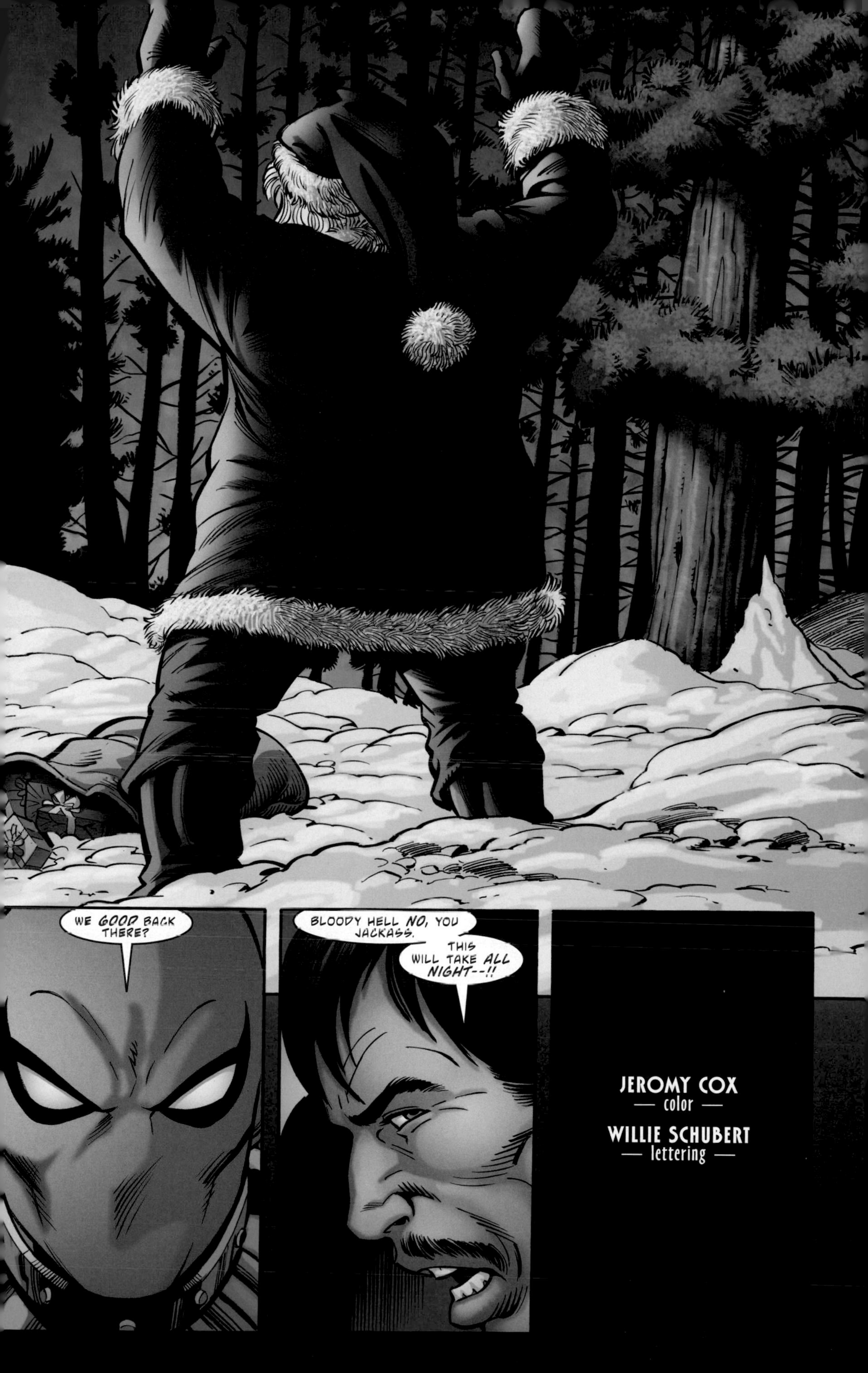
WE GOOD BACK THERE?
BLOODY HELL NO, YOU JACKASS.
THIS WILL TAKE ALL NIGHT--!!
JEROMY COX
— color —
WILLIE SCHUBERT
— lettering —

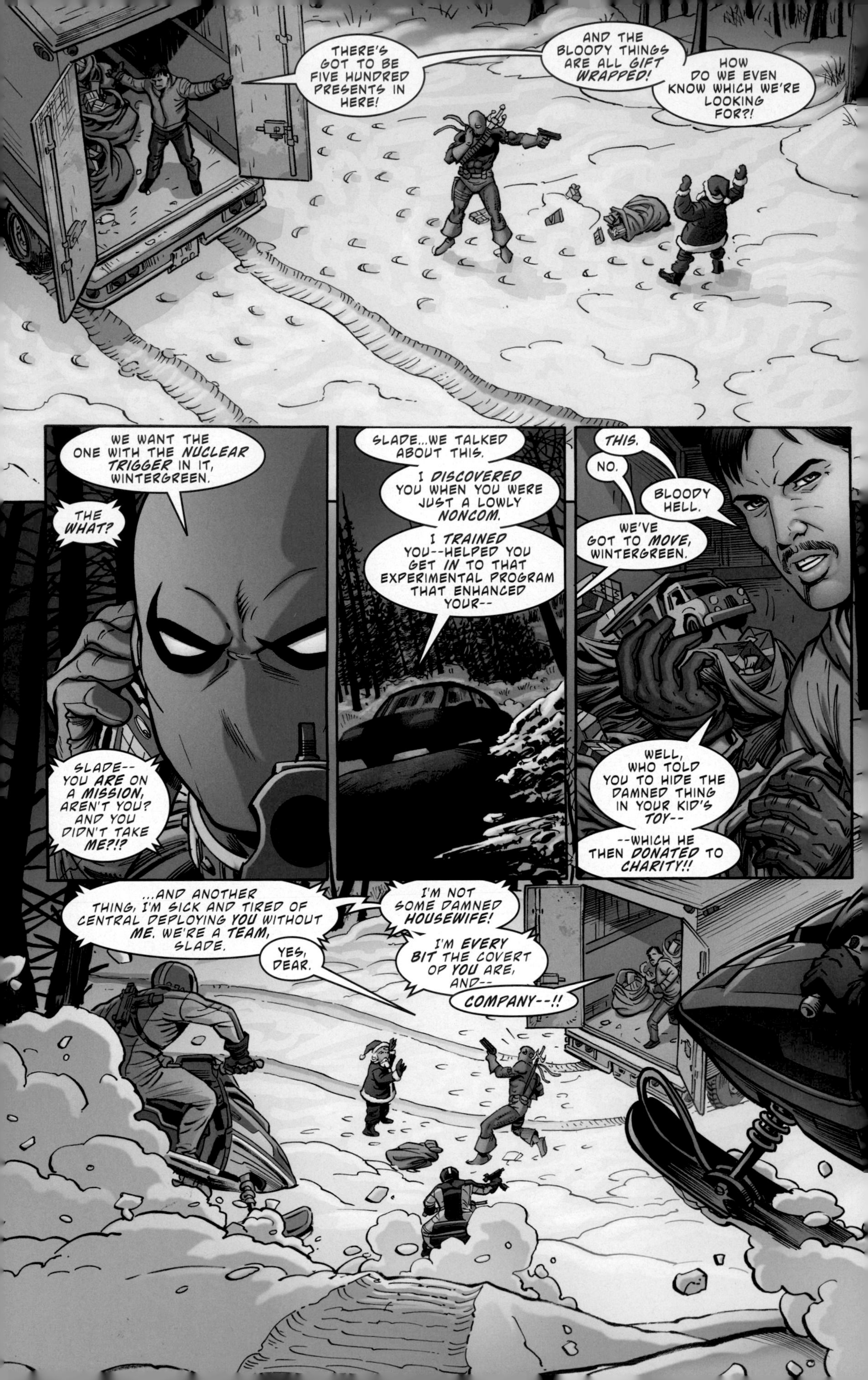
THERE'S GOT TO BE FIVE HUNDRED PRESENTS IN HERE!
AND THE BLOODY THINGS ARE ALL GIFT WRAPPED!
HOW DO WE EVEN KNOW WHICH WE'RE LOOKING FOR?!
WE WANT THE ONE WITH THE NUCLEAR TRIGGER IN IT, WINTERGREEN.
THE WHAT?
SLADE-- YOU ARE ON A MISSION, AREN'T YOU? AND YOU DIDN'T TAKE ME?!?
SLADE...WE TALKED ABOUT THIS.
I DISCOVERED YOU WHEN YOU WERE JUST A LOWLY NONCOM.
I TRAINED YOU--HELPED YOU GET IN TO THAT EXPERIMENTAL PROGRAM THAT ENHANCED YOUR--
THIS.
NO.
BLOODY HELL.
WE'VE GOT TO MOVE, WINTERGREEN.
WELL, WHO TOLD YOU TO HIDE THE DAMNED THING IN YOUR KID'S TOY--
--WHICH HE THEN DONATED TO CHARITY!!
...AND ANOTHER THING, I'M SICK AND TIRED OF CENTRAL DEPLOYING YOU WITHOUT ME. WE'RE A TEAM, SLADE.
I'M NOT SOME DAMNED HOUSEWIFE!
YES, DEAR.
I'M EVERY BIT THE COVERT OP YOU ARE, AND--
COMPANY--!!

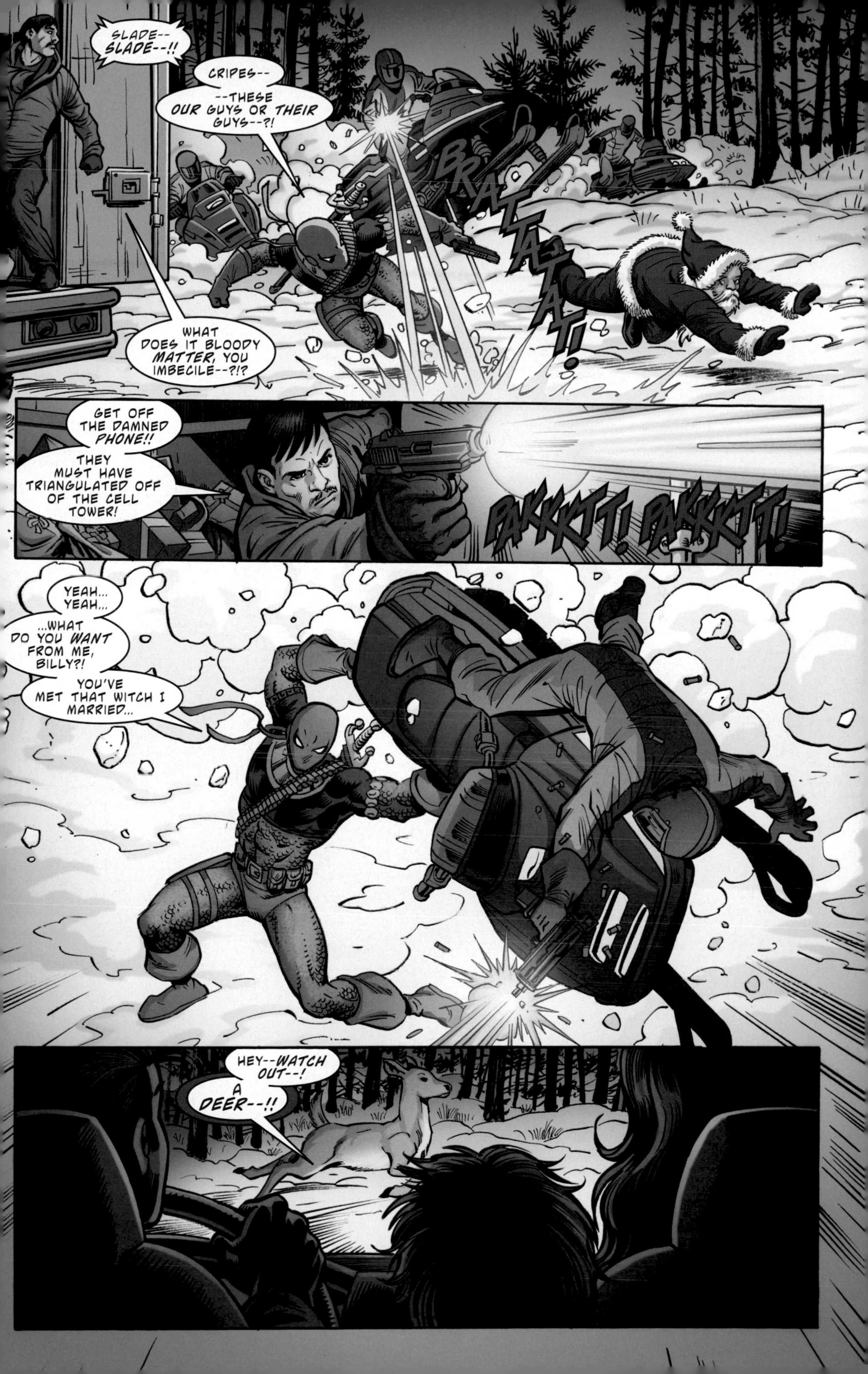
SLADE-- SLADE--!!
CRIPES--
--THESE OUR GUYS OR THEIR GUYS--?!
BRATATATAT!
WHAT DOES IT BLOODY MATTER, YOU IMBECILE--?!?
GET OFF THE DAMNED PHONE!!
THEY MUST HAVE TRIANGULATED OFF OF THE CELL TOWER!
PAKKKTT! PAKKKTT!
YEAH... YEAH...
...WHAT DO YOU WANT FROM ME, BILLY?!
YOU'VE MET THAT WITCH I MARRIED...
HEY--WATCH OUT--!
A DEER--!!

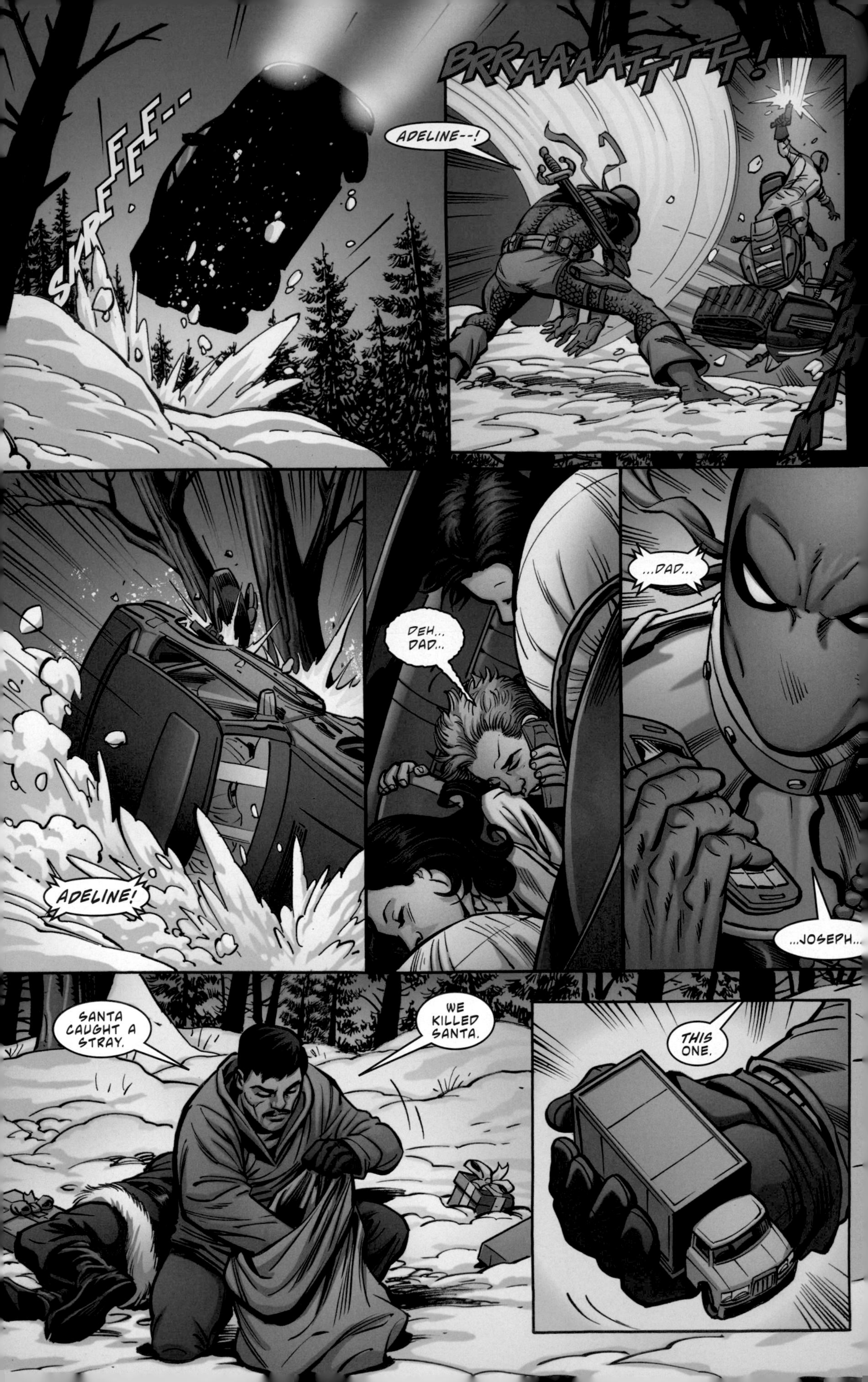
SKREEEEE--
BRRAAAATTTTT!
ADELINE--!
ADELINE!
DEH... DAD...
...DAD...
...JOSEPH...
SANTA CAUGHT A STRAY.
WE KILLED SANTA.
THIS ONE.

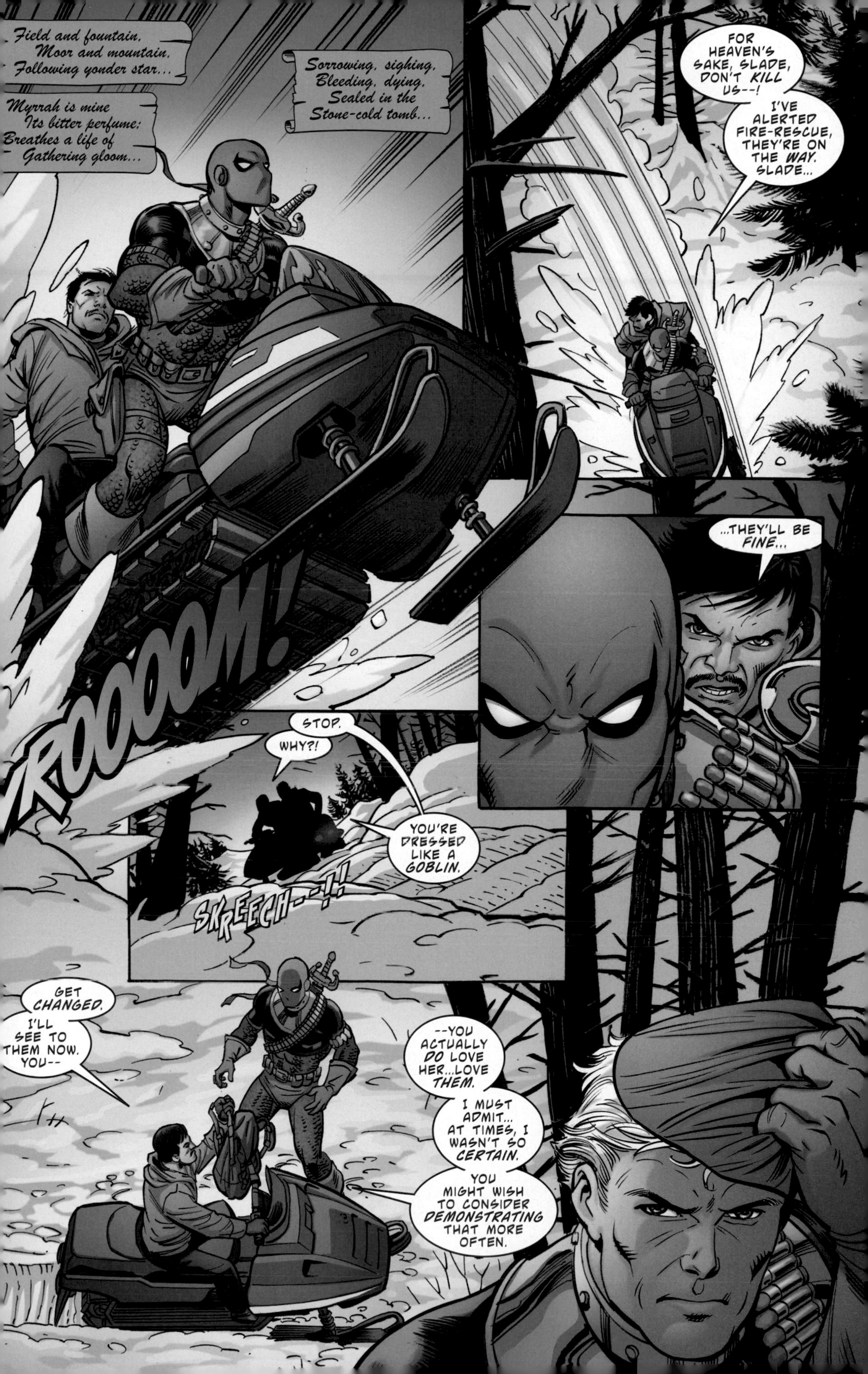

Field and fountain, Moor and mountain, Following yonder star...
Myrrah is mine Its bitter perfume: Breathes a life of Gathering gloom...
Sorrowing, sighing, Bleeding, dying, Sealed in the Stone-cold tomb...
FOR HEAVEN'S SAKE, SLADE, DON'T KILL US--!
I'VE ALERTED FIRE-RESCUE, THEY'RE ON THE WAY. SLADE...
VROOOOM!
...THEY'LL BE FINE...
STOP.
WHY?!
YOU'RE DRESSED LIKE A GOBLIN.
SKREECH--!!
GET CHANGED.
I'LL SEE TO THEM NOW. YOU--
--YOU ACTUALLY DO LOVE HER...LOVE THEM.
I MUST ADMIT... AT TIMES, I WASN'T SO CERTAIN.
YOU MIGHT WISH TO CONSIDER DEMONSTRATING THAT MORE OFTEN.

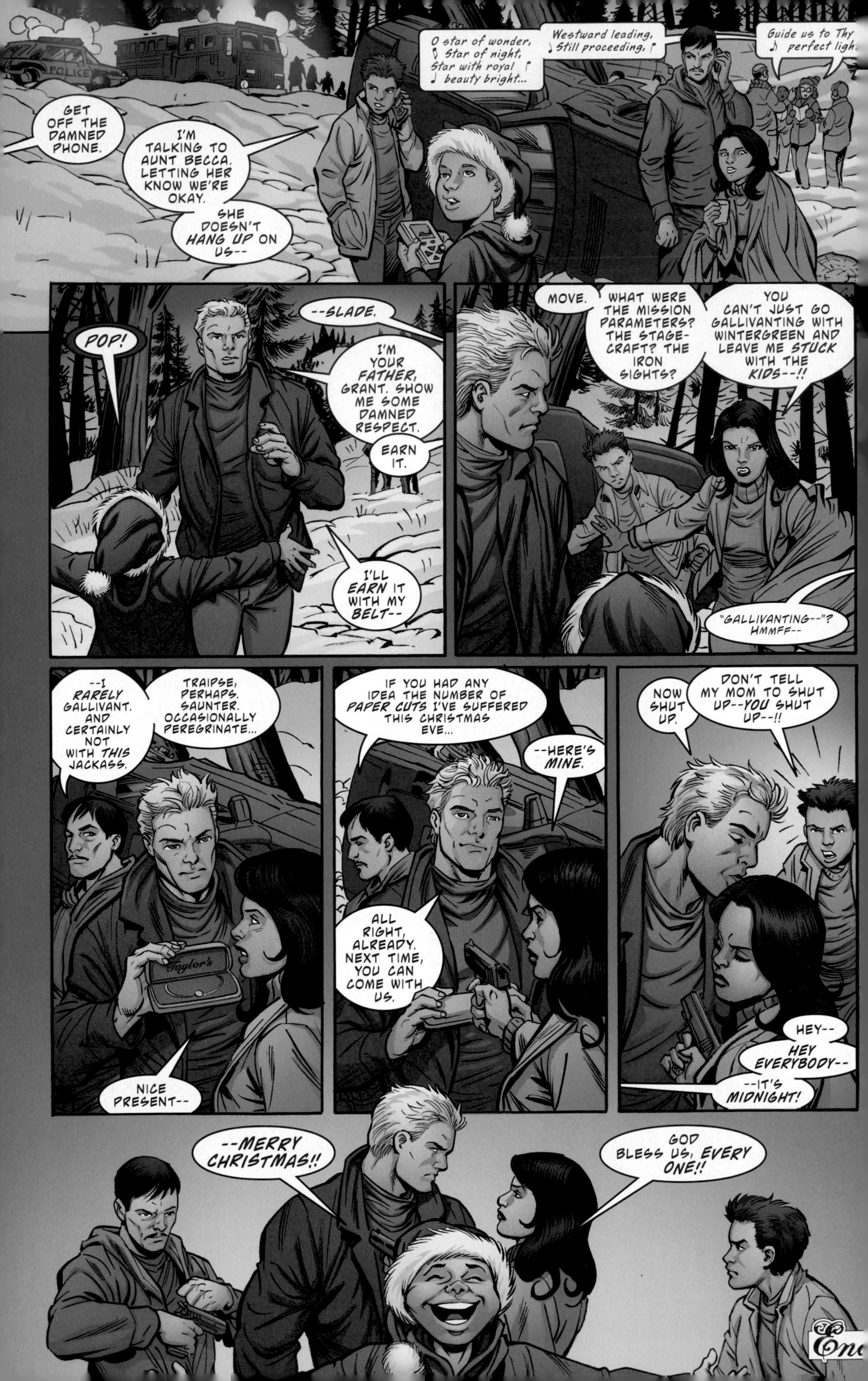
O star of wonder, Star of night, Star with royal beauty bright...
Westward leading, Still proceeding,
Guide us to Thy perfect ligh
GET OFF THE DAMNED PHONE.
I'M TALKING TO AUNT BECCA. LETTING HER KNOW WE'RE OKAY.
SHE DOESN'T HANG UP ON US--
POP!
--SLADE.
I'M YOUR FATHER, GRANT. SHOW ME SOME DAMNED RESPECT.
EARN IT.
I'LL EARN IT WITH MY BELT--
MOVE.
WHAT WERE THE MISSION PARAMETERS? THE STAGE-CRAFT? THE IRON SIGHTS?
YOU CAN'T JUST GO GALLIVANTING WITH WINTERGREEN AND LEAVE ME STUCK WITH THE KIDS--!!
"GALLIVANTING--"? HMMFF--
--I RARELY GALLIVANT. AND CERTAINLY NOT WITH THIS JACKASS.
TRAIPSE, PERHAPS. SAUNTER. OCCASIONALLY PEREGRINATE...
Taylor's
NICE PRESENT--
IF YOU HAD ANY IDEA THE NUMBER OF PAPER CUTS I'VE SUFFERED THIS CHRISTMAS EVE...
--HERE'S MINE.
ALL RIGHT, ALREADY. NEXT TIME, YOU CAN COME WITH US.
NOW SHUT UP.
DON'T TELL MY MOM TO SHUT UP--YOU SHUT UP--!!
HEY--
HEY EVERYBODY--
--IT'S MIDNIGHT!
--MERRY CHRISTMAS!!
GOD BLESS US, EVERY ONE!!

SILENT NIGHT

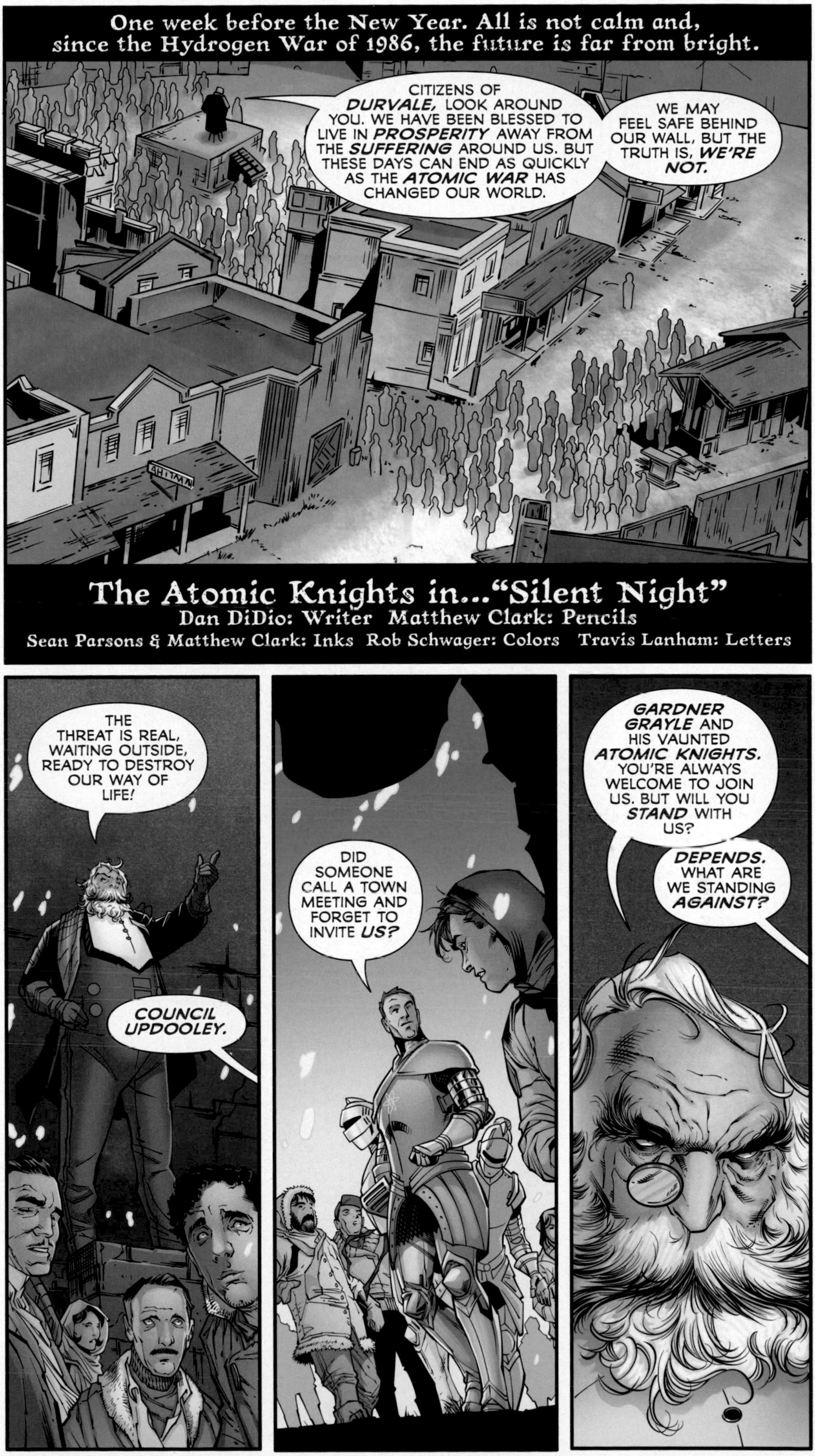
One week before the New Year. All is not calm and, since the Hydrogen War of 1986, the future is far from bright.
CITIZENS OF DURVALE, LOOK AROUND YOU. WE HAVE BEEN BLESSED TO LIVE IN PROSPERITY AWAY FROM THE SUFFERING AROUND US. BUT THESE DAYS CAN END AS QUICKLY AS THE ATOMIC WAR HAS CHANGED OUR WORLD.
WE MAY FEEL SAFE BEHIND OUR WALL, BUT THE TRUTH IS, WE'RE NOT.
The Atomic Knights in..."Silent Night"
Dan DiDio: Writer Matthew Clark: Pencils
Sean Parsons & Matthew Clark: Inks Rob Schwager: Colors Travis Lanham: Letters
THE THREAT IS REAL, WAITING OUTSIDE, READY TO DESTROY OUR WAY OF LIFE!
COUNCIL UPDOOLEY.
DID SOMEONE CALL A TOWN MEETING AND FORGET TO INVITE US?
GARDNER GRAYLE AND HIS VAUNTED ATOMIC KNIGHTS. YOU'RE ALWAYS WELCOME TO JOIN US. BUT WILL YOU STAND WITH US?
DEPENDS. WHAT ARE WE STANDING AGAINST?

ATOMIC KNIGHTS

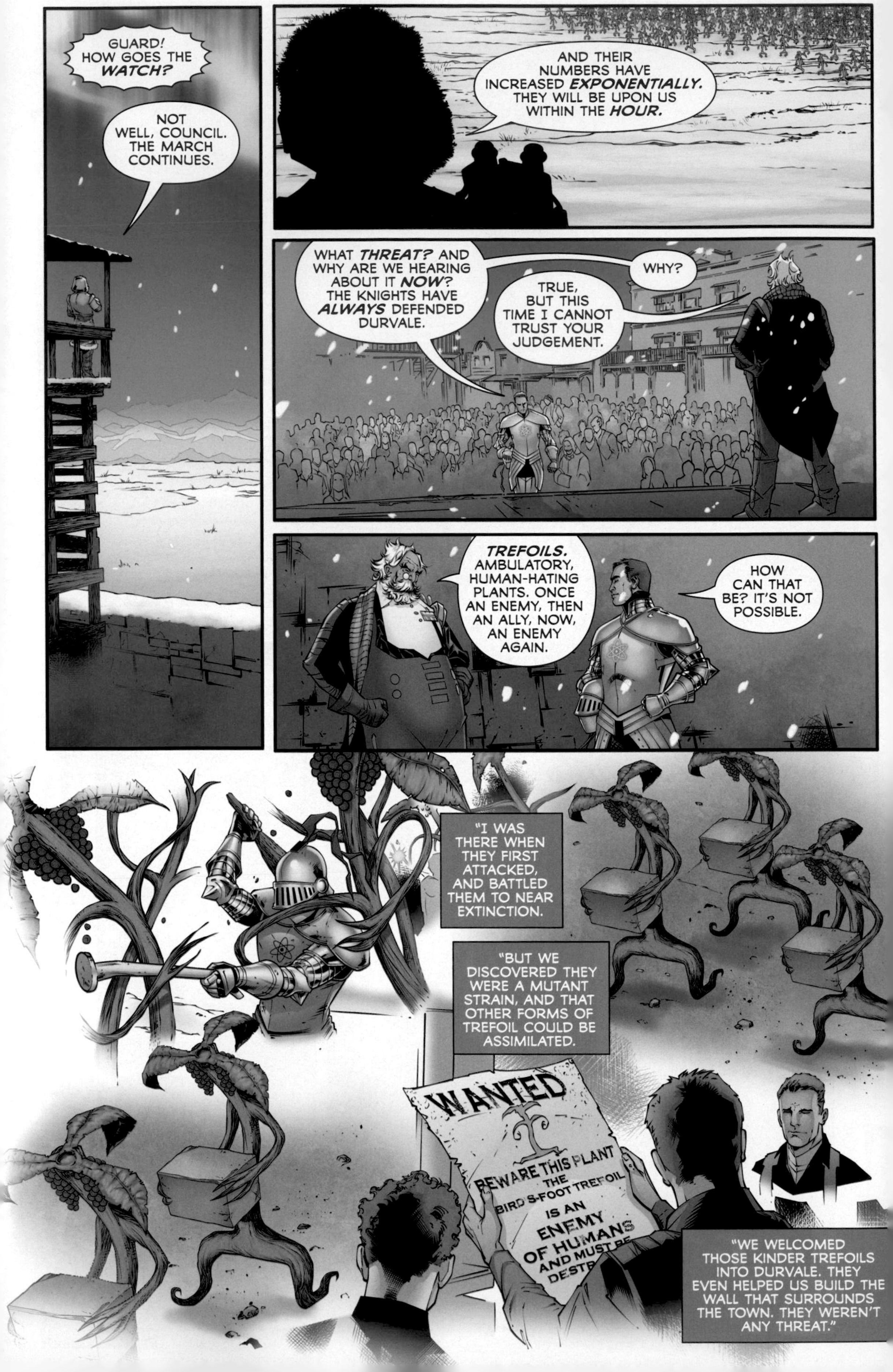
GUARD! HOW GOES THE WATCH?
NOT WELL, COUNCIL. THE MARCH CONTINUES.
AND THEIR NUMBERS HAVE INCREASED EXPONENTIALLY. THEY WILL BE UPON US WITHIN THE HOUR.
WHAT THREAT? AND WHY ARE WE HEARING ABOUT IT NOW? THE KNIGHTS HAVE ALWAYS DEFENDED DURVALE.
WHY?
TRUE, BUT THIS TIME I CANNOT TRUST YOUR JUDGEMENT.
TREFOILS. AMBULATORY, HUMAN-HATING PLANTS. ONCE AN ENEMY, THEN AN ALLY, NOW, AN ENEMY AGAIN.
HOW CAN THAT BE? IT'S NOT POSSIBLE.
"I WAS THERE WHEN THEY FIRST ATTACKED, AND BATTLED THEM TO NEAR EXTINCTION.
"BUT WE DISCOVERED THEY WERE A MUTANT STRAIN, AND THAT OTHER FORMS OF TREFOIL COULD BE ASSIMILATED.
WANTED
BEWARE THIS PLANT THE BIRD'S-FOOT TREFOIL IS AN ENEMY OF HUMANS AND MUST BE DESTR
"WE WELCOMED THOSE KINDER TREFOILS INTO DURVALE. THEY EVEN HELPED US BUILD THE WALL THAT SURROUNDS THE TOWN. THEY WEREN'T ANY THREAT."

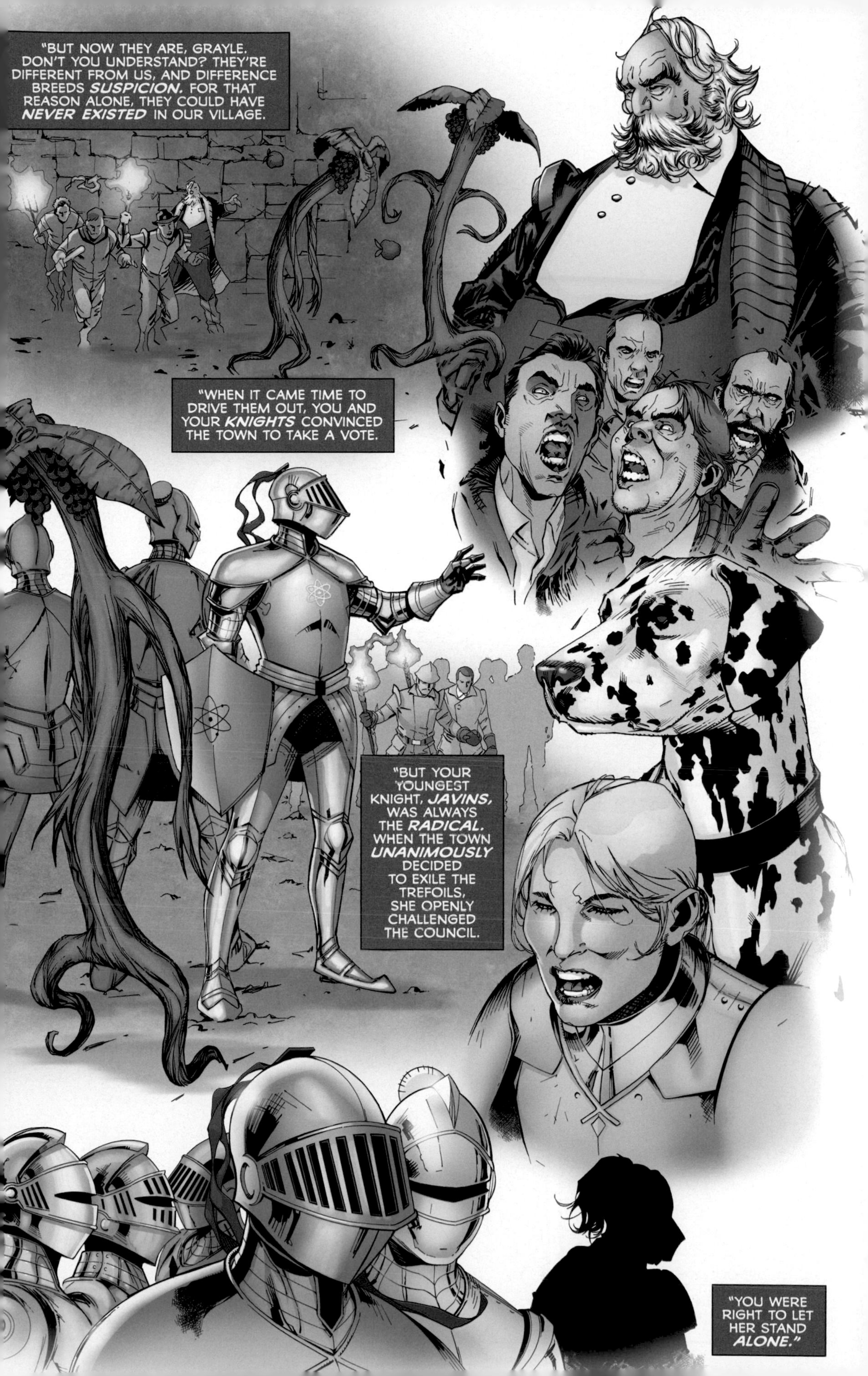
"BUT NOW THEY ARE, GRAYLE. DON'T YOU UNDERSTAND? THEY'RE DIFFERENT FROM US, AND DIFFERENCE BREEDS SUSPICION. FOR THAT REASON ALONE, THEY COULD HAVE NEVER EXISTED IN OUR VILLAGE.
"WHEN IT CAME TIME TO DRIVE THEM OUT, YOU AND YOUR KNIGHTS CONVINCED THE TOWN TO TAKE A VOTE.
"BUT YOUR YOUNGEST KNIGHT, JAVINS, WAS ALWAYS THE RADICAL. WHEN THE TOWN UNANIMOUSLY DECIDED TO EXILE THE TREFOILS, SHE OPENLY CHALLENGED THE COUNCIL.
"YOU WERE RIGHT TO LET HER STAND ALONE."

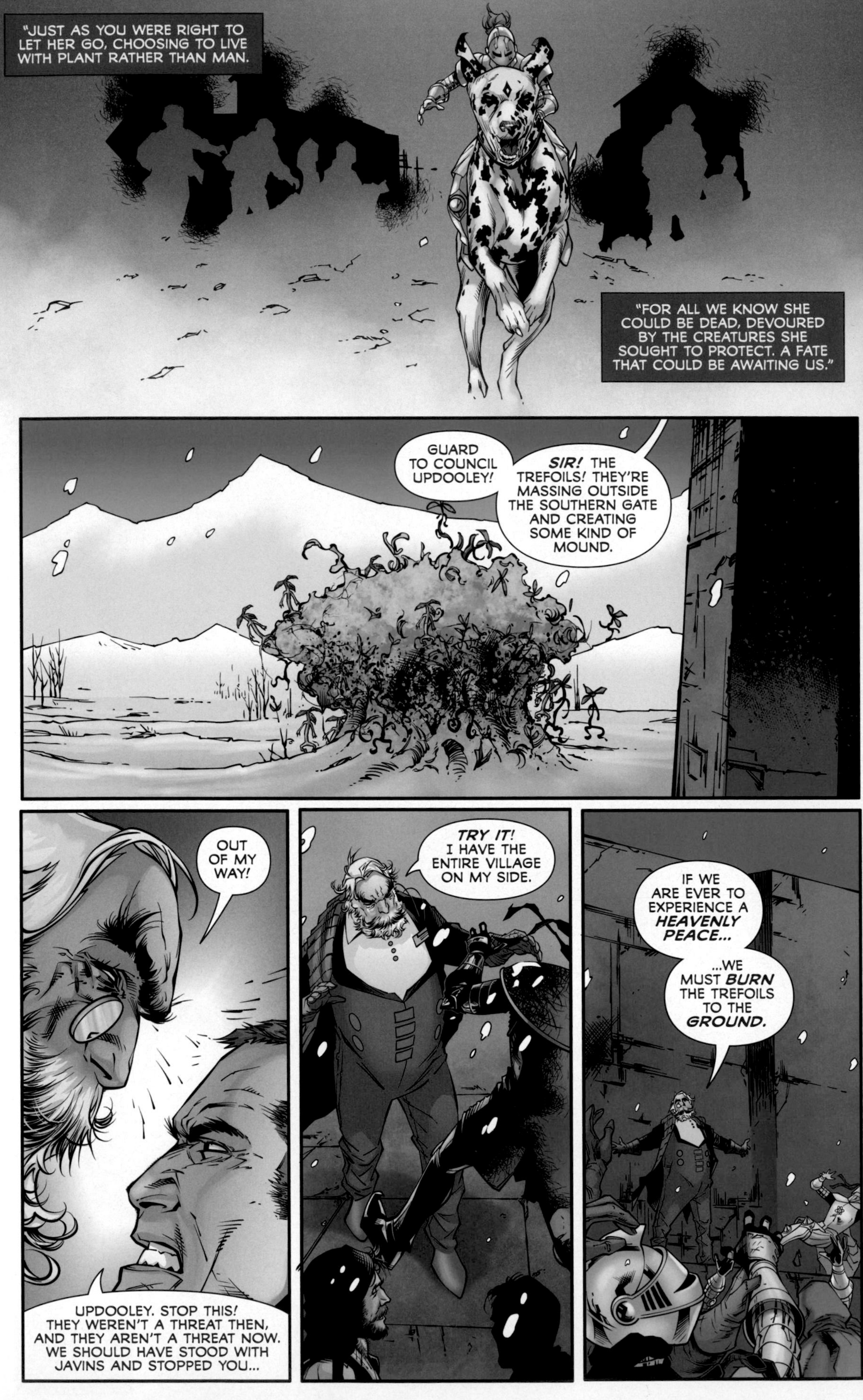
"JUST AS YOU WERE RIGHT TO LET HER GO, CHOOSING TO LIVE WITH PLANT RATHER THAN MAN.
"FOR ALL WE KNOW SHE COULD BE DEAD, DEVOURED BY THE CREATURES SHE SOUGHT TO PROTECT. A FATE THAT COULD BE AWAITING US."
GUARD TO COUNCIL UPDOOLEY!
SIR! THE TREFOILS! THEY'RE MASSING OUTSIDE THE SOUTHERN GATE AND CREATING SOME KIND OF MOUND.
OUT OF MY WAY!
UPDOOLEY. STOP THIS! THEY WEREN'T A THREAT THEN, AND THEY AREN'T A THREAT NOW. WE SHOULD HAVE STOOD WITH JAVINS AND STOPPED YOU...
TRY IT! I HAVE THE ENTIRE VILLAGE ON MY SIDE.
IF WE ARE EVER TO EXPERIENCE A HEAVENLY PEACE...
...WE MUST BURN THE TREFOILS TO THE GROUND.

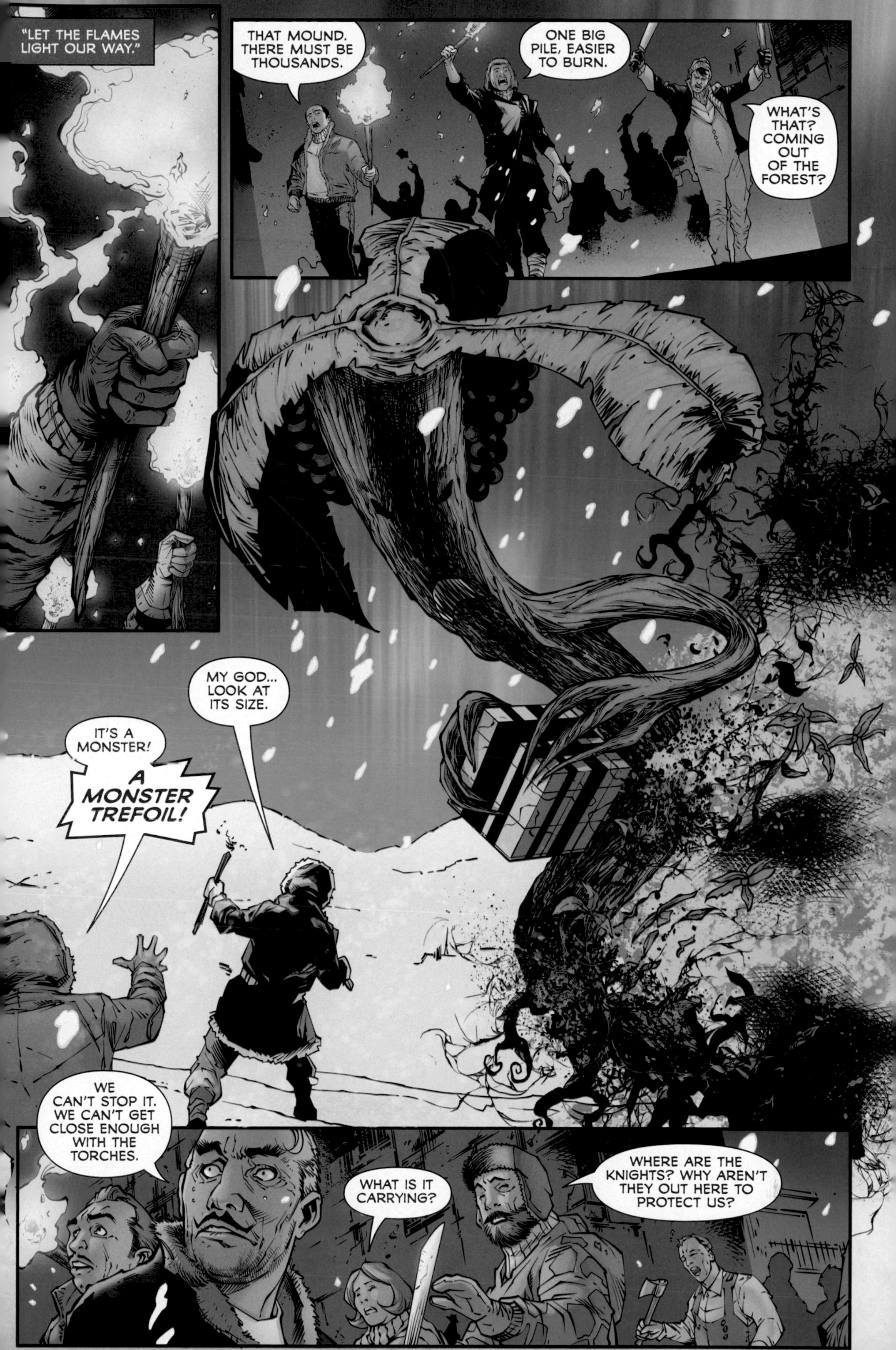
"LET THE FLAMES LIGHT OUR WAY."
THAT MOUND. THERE MUST BE THOUSANDS.
ONE BIG PILE, EASIER TO BURN.
WHAT'S THAT? COMING OUT OF THE FOREST?
MY GOD... LOOK AT ITS SIZE.
IT'S A MONSTER!
A MONSTER TREFOIL!
WE CAN'T STOP IT. WE CAN'T GET CLOSE ENOUGH WITH THE TORCHES.
WHAT IS IT CARRYING?
WHERE ARE THE KNIGHTS? WHY AREN'T THEY OUT HERE TO PROTECT US?

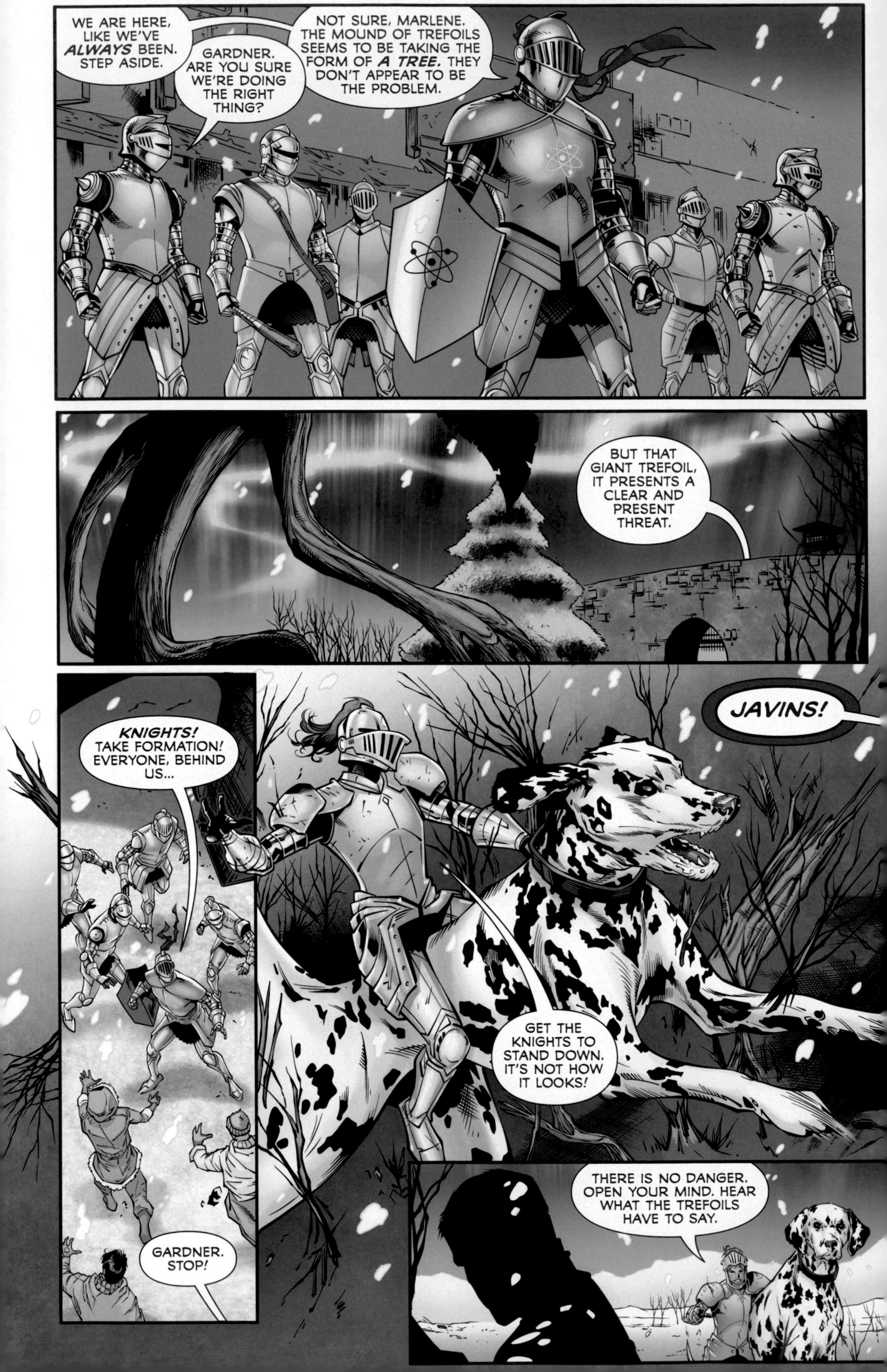

WE ARE HERE, LIKE WE'VE ALWAYS BEEN. STEP ASIDE.
GARDNER. ARE YOU SURE WE'RE DOING THE RIGHT THING?
NOT SURE, MARLENE. THE MOUND OF TREFOILS SEEMS TO BE TAKING THE FORM OF A TREE. THEY DON'T APPEAR TO BE THE PROBLEM.
BUT THAT GIANT TREFOIL, IT PRESENTS A CLEAR AND PRESENT THREAT.
KNIGHTS! TAKE FORMATION! EVERYONE, BEHIND US...
GARDNER. STOP!
JAVINS!
GET THE KNIGHTS TO STAND DOWN. IT'S NOT HOW IT LOOKS!
THERE IS NO DANGER. OPEN YOUR MIND. HEAR WHAT THE TREFOILS HAVE TO SAY.

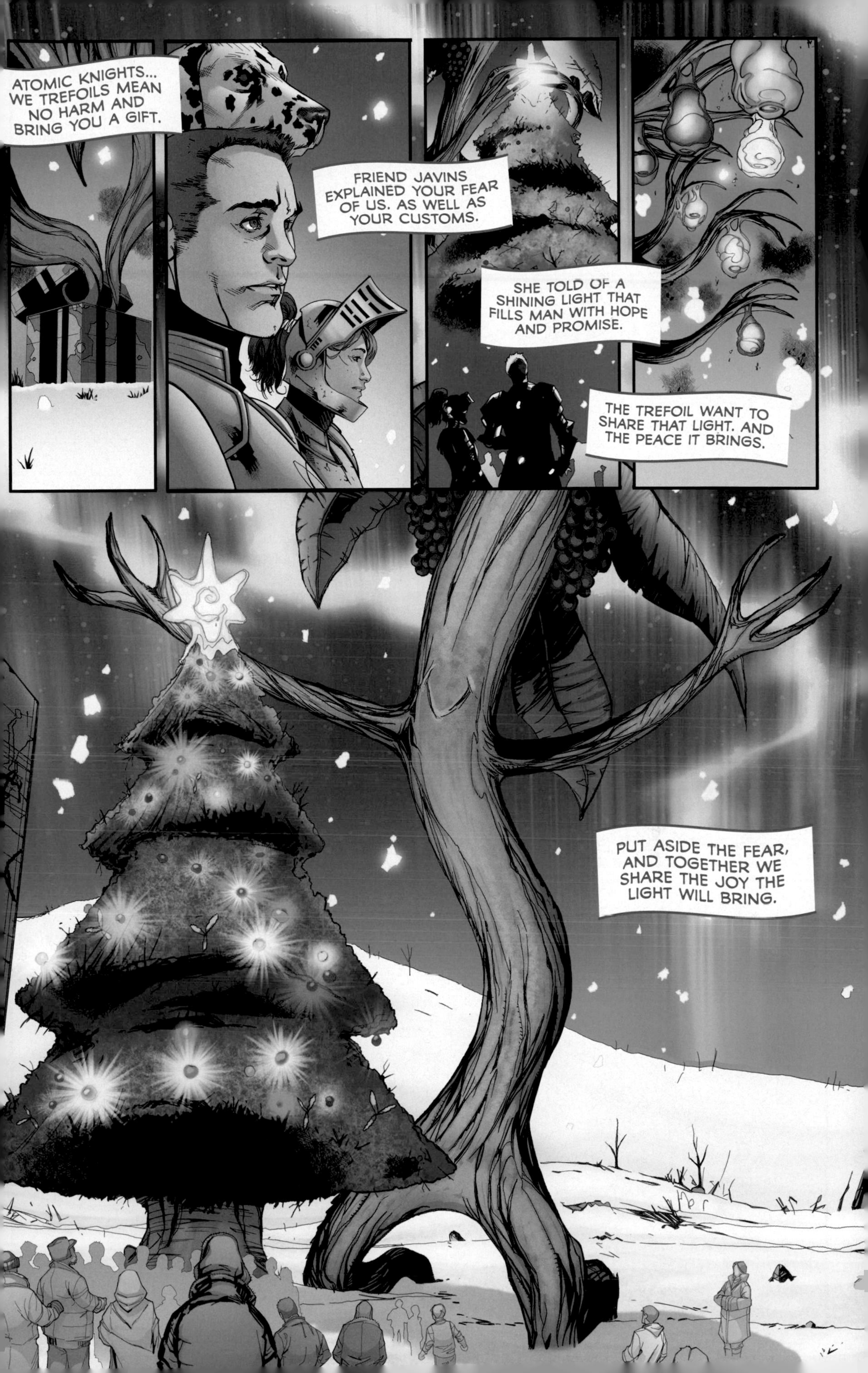
ATOMIC KNIGHTS... WE TREFOILS MEAN NO HARM AND BRING YOU A GIFT.
FRIEND JAVINS EXPLAINED YOUR FEAR OF US. AS WELL AS YOUR CUSTOMS.
SHE TOLD OF A SHINING LIGHT THAT FILLS MAN WITH HOPE AND PROMISE.
THE TREFOIL WANT TO SHARE THAT LIGHT. AND THE PEACE IT BRINGS.
PUT ASIDE THE FEAR, AND TOGETHER WE SHARE THE JOY THE LIGHT WILL BRING.

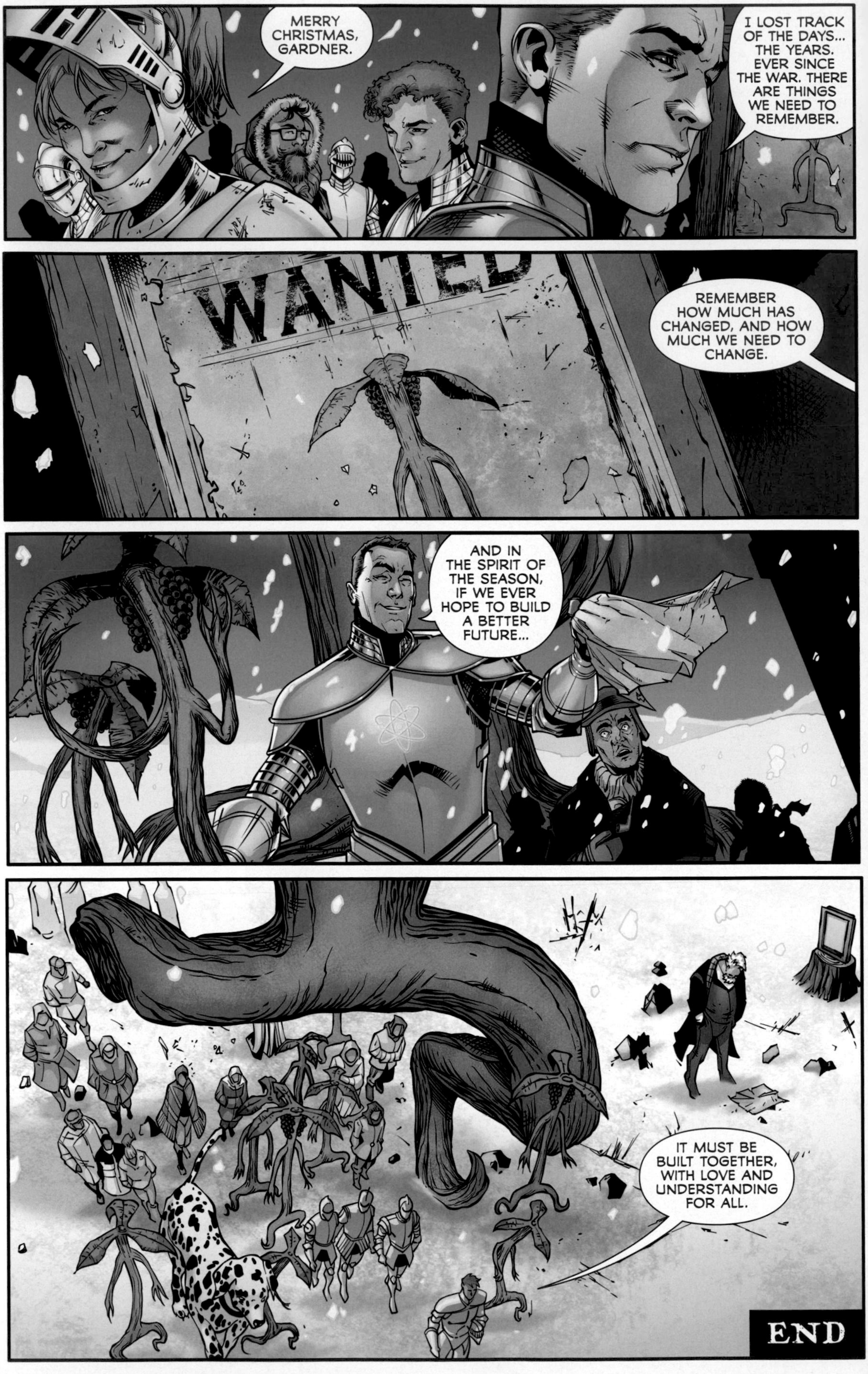
MERRY CHRISTMAS, GARDNER.
I LOST TRACK OF THE DAYS... THE YEARS. EVER SINCE THE WAR. THERE ARE THINGS WE NEED TO REMEMBER.
WANTED
REMEMBER HOW MUCH HAS CHANGED, AND HOW MUCH WE NEED TO CHANGE.
AND IN THE SPIRIT OF THE SEASON, IF WE EVER HOPE TO BUILD A BETTER FUTURE...
IT MUST BE BUILT TOGETHER, WITH LOVE AND UNDERSTANDING FOR ALL.
END

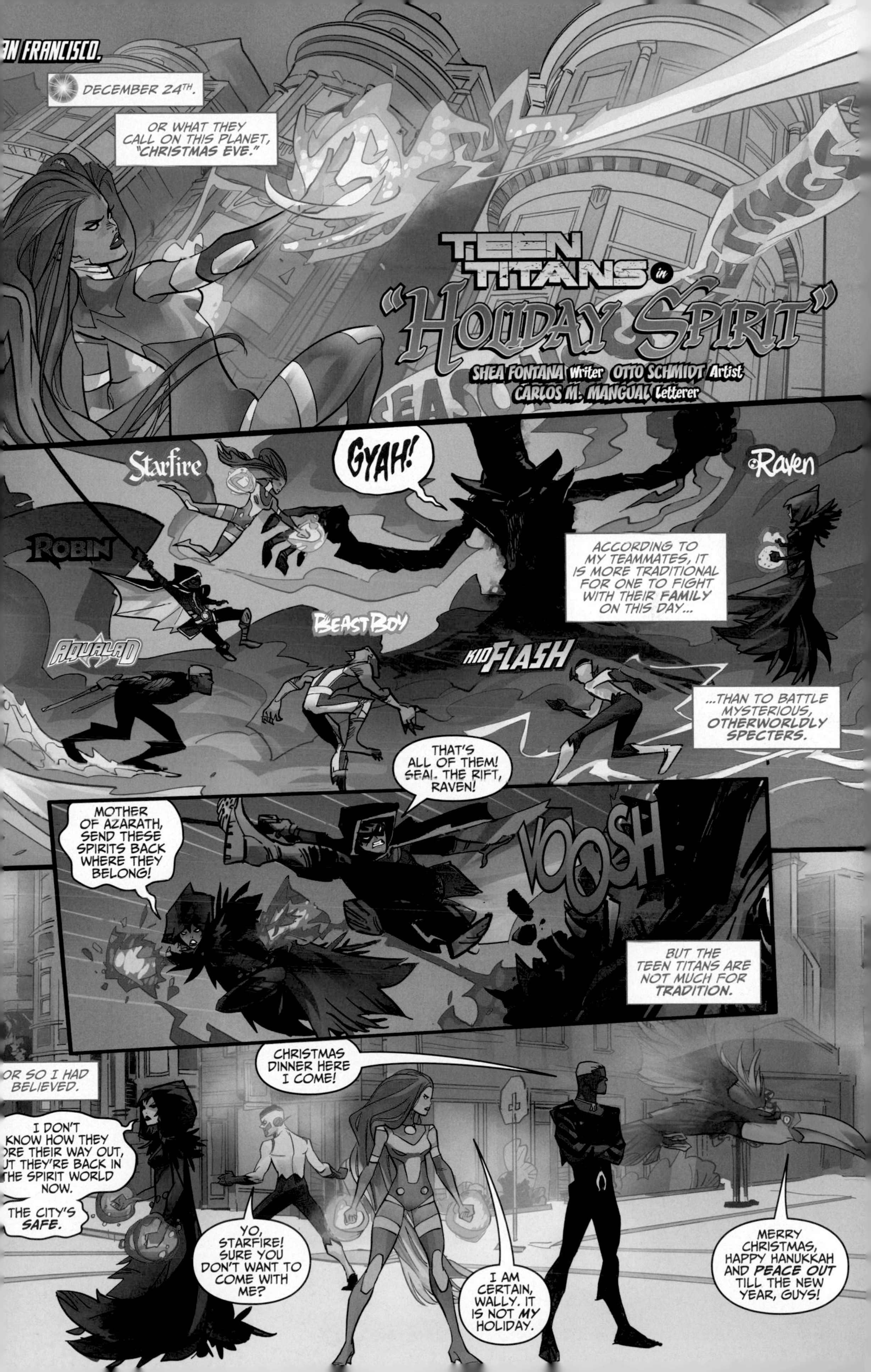

AN FRANCISCO.
DECEMBER 24TH.
OR WHAT THEY CALL ON THIS PLANET, "CHRISTMAS EVE."
TEEN TITANS in "HOLIDAY SPIRIT"
SHEA FONTANA Writer OTTO SCHMIDT Artist
CARLOS M. MANGUAL Letterer
Starfire
GYAH!
Raven
ROBIN
ACCORDING TO MY TEAMMATES, IT IS MORE TRADITIONAL FOR ONE TO FIGHT WITH THEIR FAMILY ON THIS DAY...
BEAST BOY
AQUALAD
KID FLASH
...THAN TO BATTLE MYSTERIOUS, OTHERWORLDLY SPECTERS.
THAT'S ALL OF THEM! SEAL THE RIFT, RAVEN!
MOTHER OF AZARATH, SEND THESE SPIRITS BACK WHERE THEY BELONG!
VOOSH
BUT THE TEEN TITANS ARE NOT MUCH FOR TRADITION.
OR SO I HAD BELIEVED.
CHRISTMAS DINNER HERE I COME!
I DON'T KNOW HOW THEY ORE THEIR WAY OUT, UT THEY'RE BACK IN THE SPIRIT WORLD NOW.
THE CITY'S SAFE.
YO, STARFIRE! SURE YOU DON'T WANT TO COME WITH ME?
I AM CERTAIN, WALLY. IT IS NOT MY HOLIDAY.
MERRY CHRISTMAS, HAPPY HANUKKAH AND PEACE OUT TILL THE NEW YEAR, GUYS!

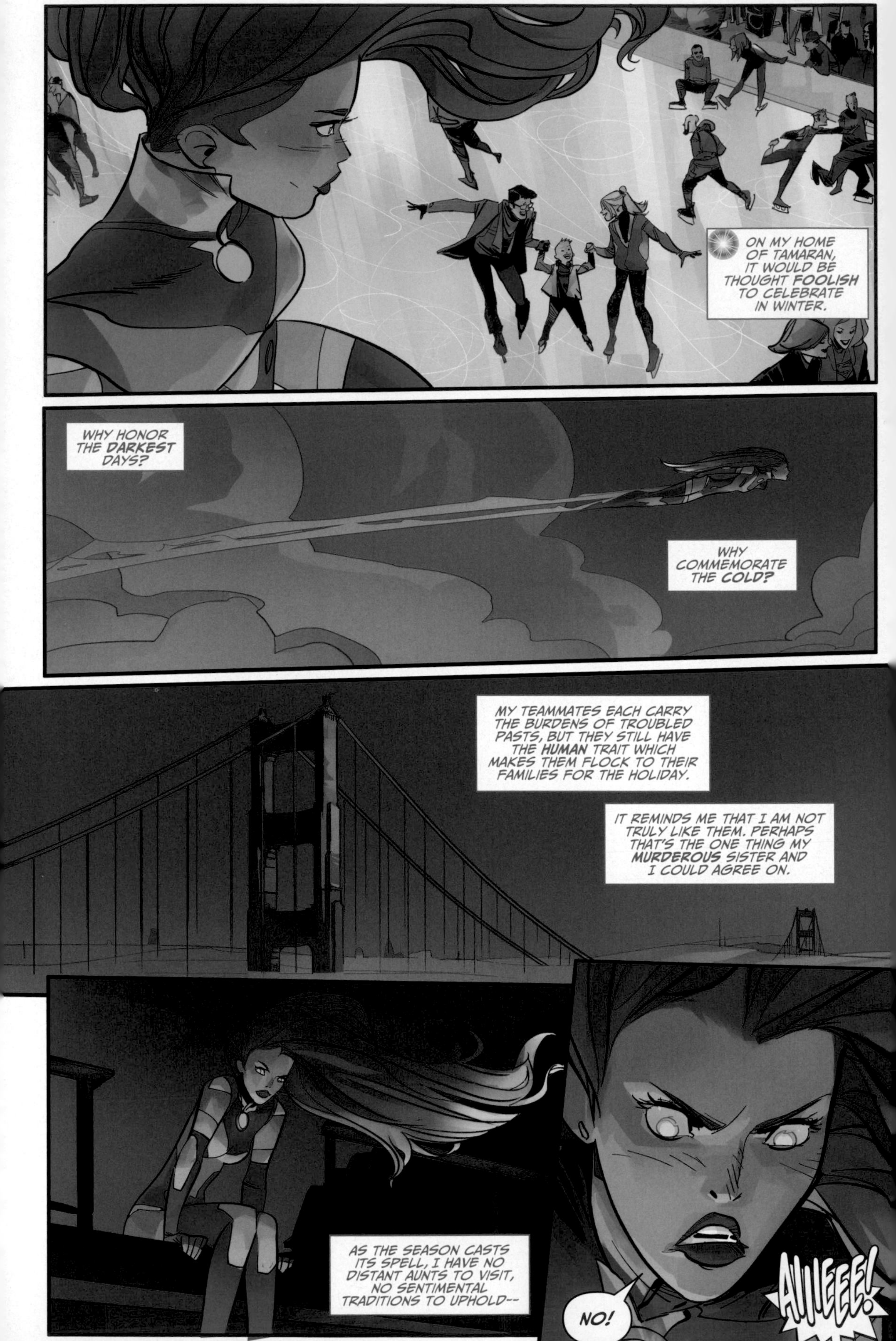
ON MY HOME OF TAMARAN, IT WOULD BE THOUGHT FOOLISH TO CELEBRATE IN WINTER.
WHY HONOR THE DARKEST DAYS?
WHY COMMEMORATE THE COLD?
MY TEAMMATES EACH CARRY THE BURDENS OF TROUBLED PASTS, BUT THEY STILL HAVE THE HUMAN TRAIT WHICH MAKES THEM FLOCK TO THEIR FAMILIES FOR THE HOLIDAY.
IT REMINDS ME THAT I AM NOT TRULY LIKE THEM. PERHAPS THAT'S THE ONE THING MY MURDEROUS SISTER AND I COULD AGREE ON.
AS THE SEASON CASTS ITS SPELL, I HAVE NO DISTANT AUNTS TO VISIT, NO SENTIMENTAL TRADITIONS TO UPHOLD--
NO!
AIIIEEE!

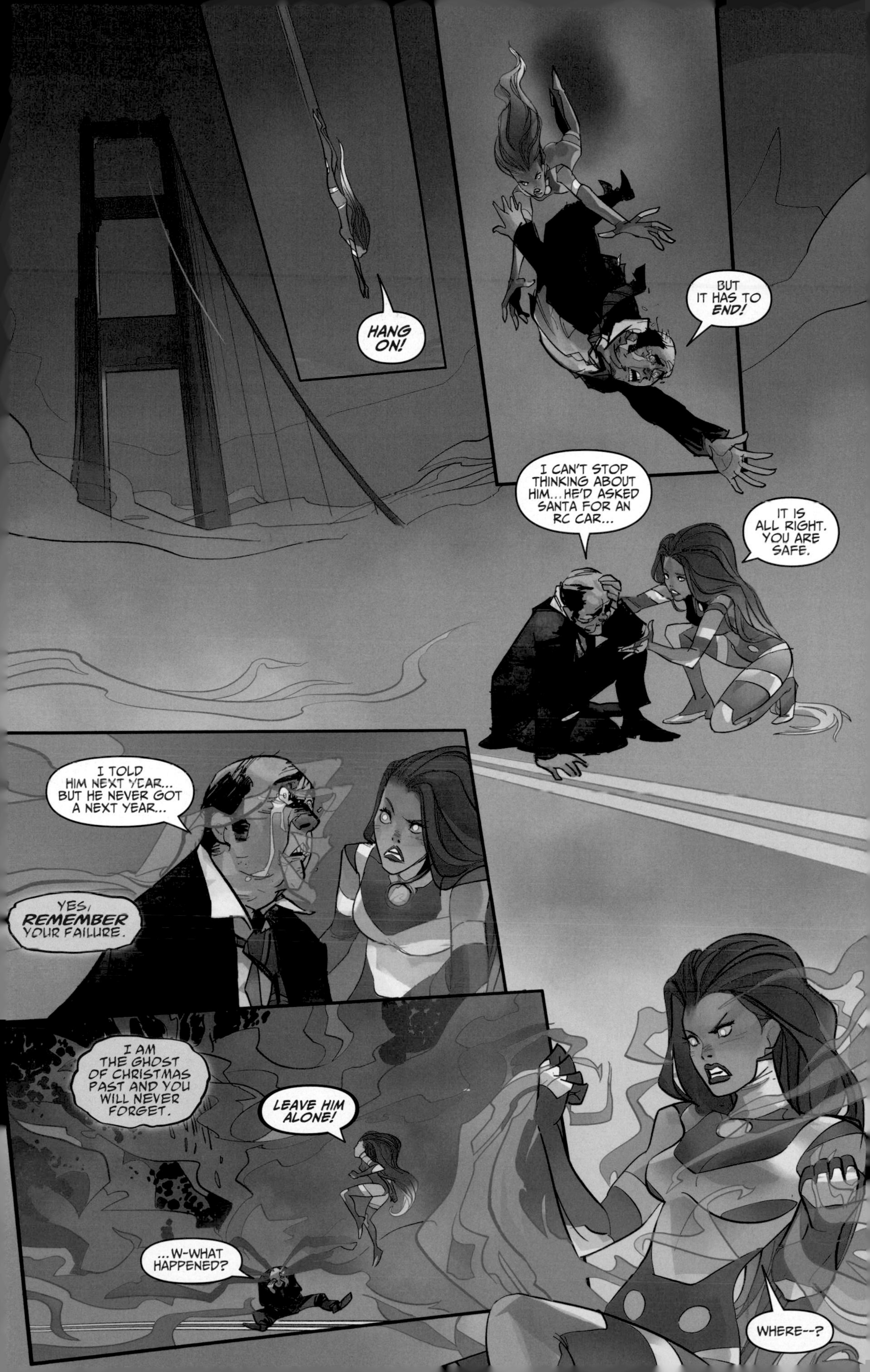
HANG ON!
BUT IT HAS TO END!
I CAN'T STOP THINKING ABOUT HIM... HE'D ASKED SANTA FOR AN RC CAR...
IT IS ALL RIGHT. YOU ARE SAFE.
I TOLD HIM NEXT YEAR... BUT HE NEVER GOT A NEXT YEAR...
YES, REMEMBER YOUR FAILURE.
I AM THE GHOST OF CHRISTMAS PAST AND YOU WILL NEVER FORGET.
LEAVE HIM ALONE!
...W-WHAT HAPPENED?
WHERE--?

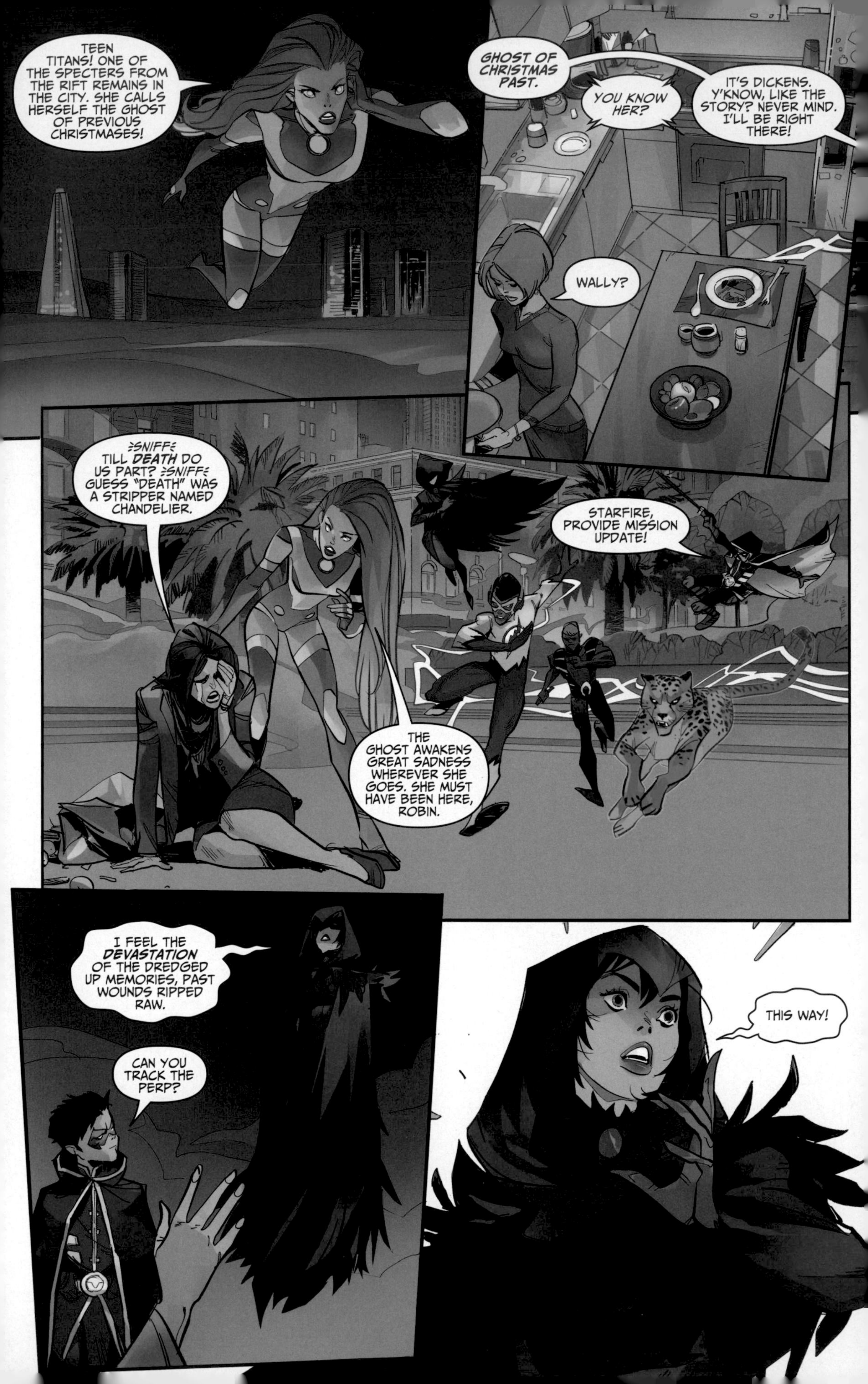

TEEN TITANS! ONE OF THE SPECTERS FROM THE RIFT REMAINS IN THE CITY. SHE CALLS HERSELF THE GHOST OF PREVIOUS CHRISTMASES!
GHOST OF CHRISTMAS PAST.
YOU KNOW HER?
IT'S DICKENS. Y'KNOW, LIKE THE STORY? NEVER MIND. I'LL BE RIGHT THERE!
WALLY?
SNIFF TILL DEATH DO US PART? SNIFF GUESS "DEATH" WAS A STRIPPER NAMED CHANDELIER.
STARFIRE, PROVIDE MISSION UPDATE!
THE GHOST AWAKENS GREAT SADNESS WHEREVER SHE GOES. SHE MUST HAVE BEEN HERE, ROBIN.
I FEEL THE DEVASTATION OF THE DREDGED UP MEMORIES, PAST WOUNDS RIPPED RAW.
CAN YOU TRACK THE PERP?
THIS WAY!

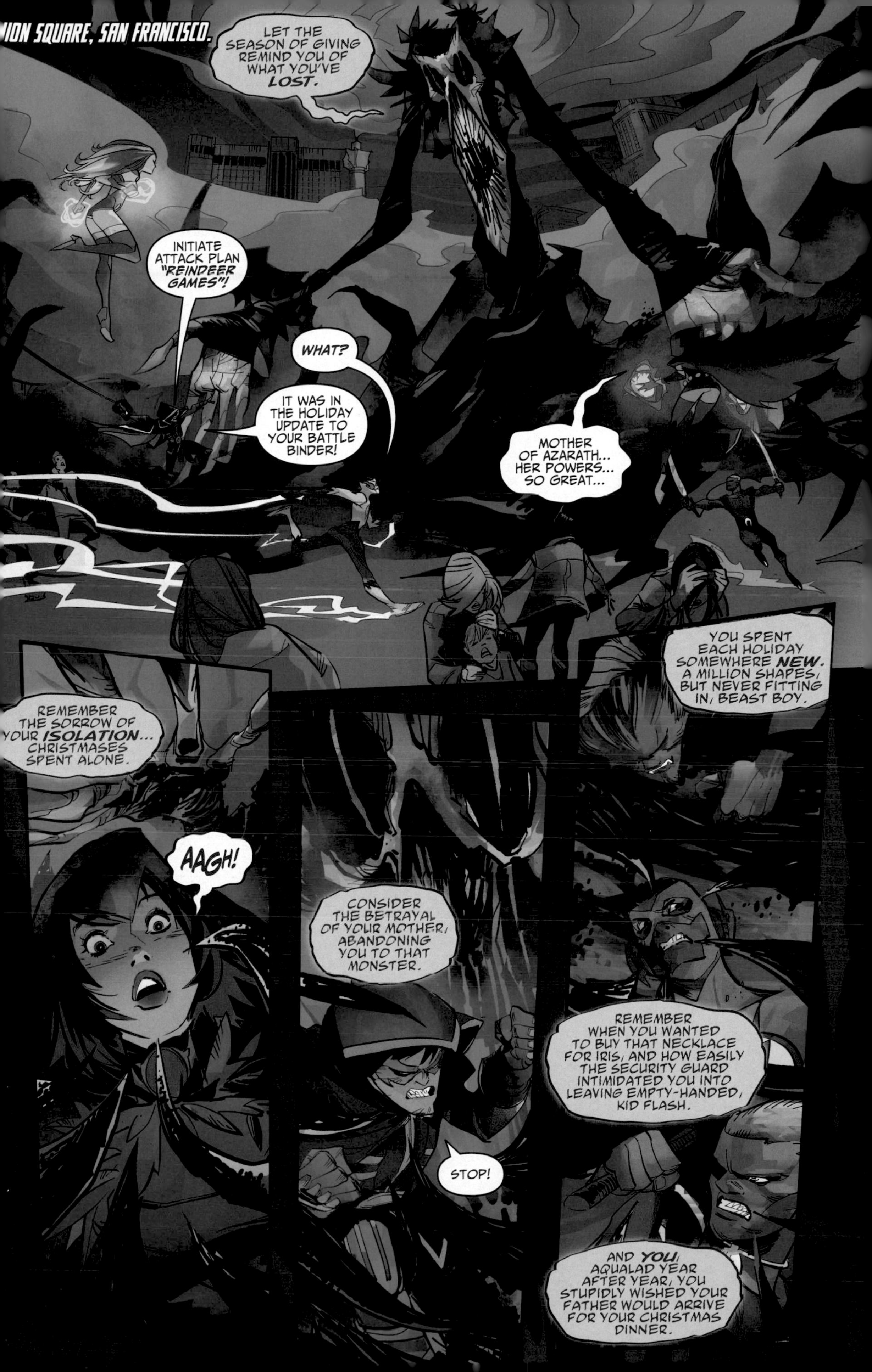
ION SQUARE, SAN FRANCISCO.
LET THE SEASON OF GIVING REMIND YOU OF WHAT YOU'VE LOST.
INITIATE ATTACK PLAN "REINDEER GAMES"!
WHAT?
IT WAS IN THE HOLIDAY UPDATE TO YOUR BATTLE BINDER!
MOTHER OF AZARATH... HER POWERS... SO GREAT...
REMEMBER THE SORROW OF YOUR ISOLATION... CHRISTMASES SPENT ALONE.
AAGH!
CONSIDER THE BETRAYAL OF YOUR MOTHER, ABANDONING YOU TO THAT MONSTER.
STOP!
YOU SPENT EACH HOLIDAY SOMEWHERE NEW. A MILLION SHAPES, BUT NEVER FITTING IN, BEAST BOY.
REMEMBER WHEN YOU WANTED TO BUY THAT NECKLACE FOR IRIS, AND HOW EASILY THE SECURITY GUARD INTIMIDATED YOU INTO LEAVING EMPTY-HANDED, KID FLASH.
AND YOU, AQUALAD YEAR AFTER YEAR, YOU STUPIDLY WISHED YOUR FATHER WOULD ARRIVE FOR YOUR CHRISTMAS DINNER.

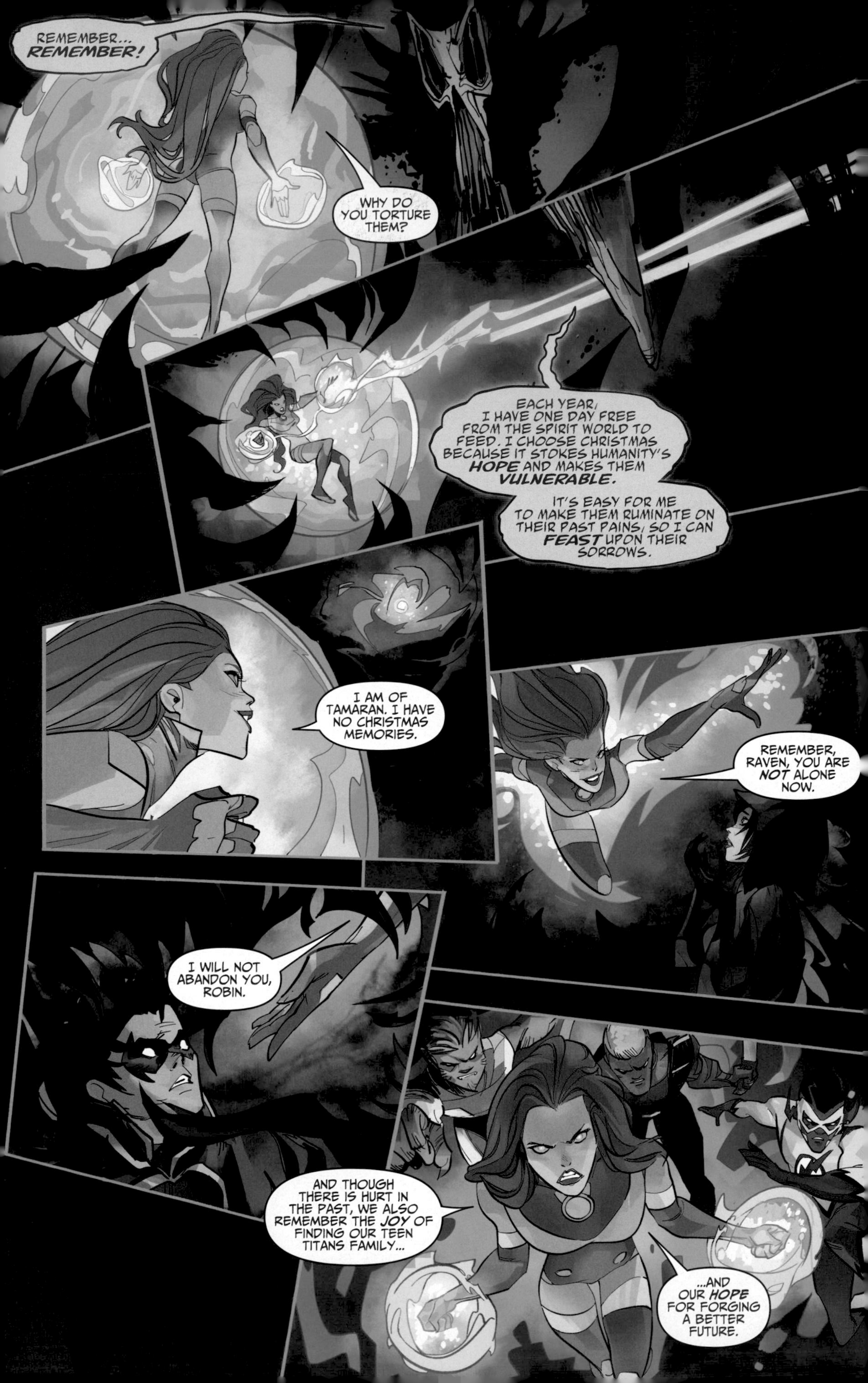
REMEMBER... REMEMBER!
WHY DO YOU TORTURE THEM?
EACH YEAR, I HAVE ONE DAY FREE FROM THE SPIRIT WORLD TO FEED. I CHOOSE CHRISTMAS BECAUSE IT STOKES HUMANITY'S HOPE AND MAKES THEM VULNERABLE.
IT'S EASY FOR ME TO MAKE THEM RUMINATE ON THEIR PAST PAINS, SO I CAN FEAST UPON THEIR SORROWS.
I AM OF TAMARAN. I HAVE NO CHRISTMAS MEMORIES.
REMEMBER, RAVEN, YOU ARE NOT ALONE NOW.
I WILL NOT ABANDON YOU, ROBIN.
AND THOUGH THERE IS HURT IN THE PAST, WE ALSO REMEMBER THE JOY OF FINDING OUR TEEN TITANS FAMILY...
...AND OUR HOPE FOR FORGING A BETTER FUTURE.

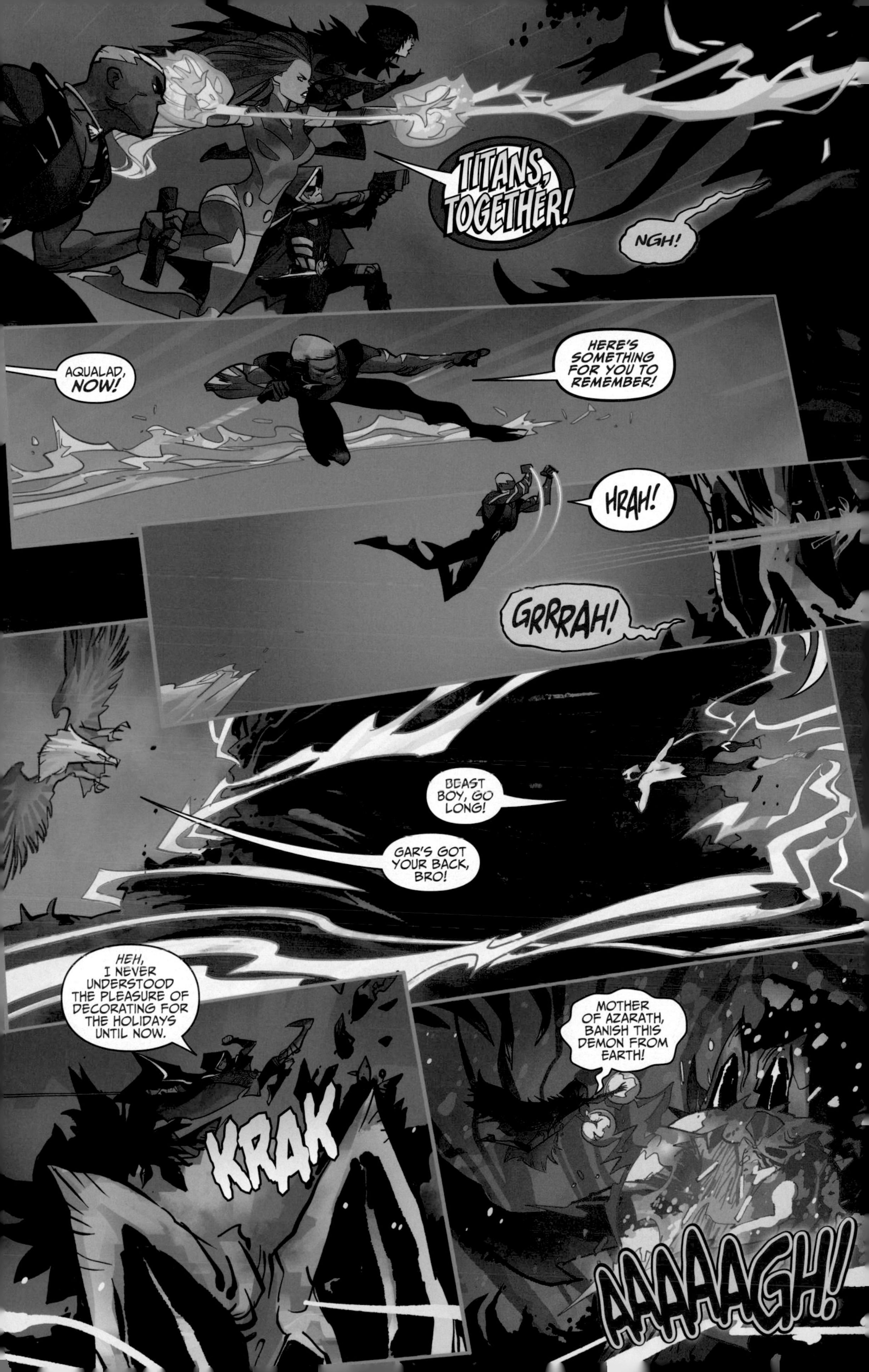
TITANS, TOGETHER!
NGH!
AQUALAD, NOW!
HERE'S SOMETHING FOR YOU TO REMEMBER!
HRAH!
GRRRAH!
BEAST BOY, GO LONG!
GAR'S GOT YOUR BACK, BRO!
HEH, I NEVER UNDERSTOOD THE PLEASURE OF DECORATING FOR THE HOLIDAYS UNTIL NOW.
KRAK
MOTHER OF AZARATH, BANISH THIS DEMON FROM EARTH!
AAAAAGH!

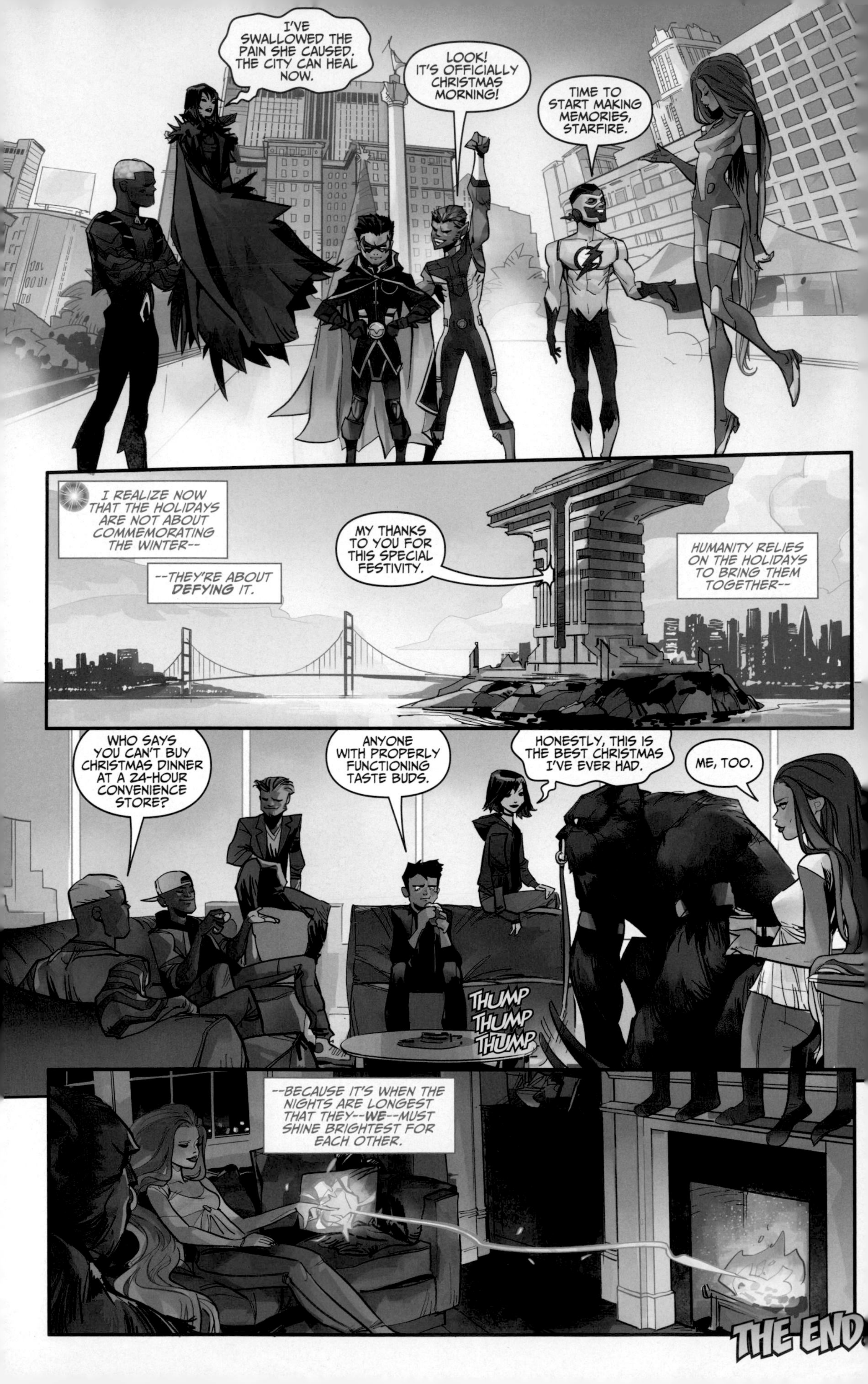
I'VE SWALLOWED THE PAIN SHE CAUSED. THE CITY CAN HEAL NOW.
LOOK! IT'S OFFICIALLY CHRISTMAS MORNING!
TIME TO START MAKING MEMORIES, STARFIRE.
I REALIZE NOW THAT THE HOLIDAYS ARE NOT ABOUT COMMEMORATING THE WINTER--
--THEY'RE ABOUT DEFYING IT.
MY THANKS TO YOU FOR THIS SPECIAL FESTIVITY.
HUMANITY RELIES ON THE HOLIDAYS TO BRING THEM TOGETHER--
WHO SAYS YOU CAN'T BUY CHRISTMAS DINNER AT A 24-HOUR CONVENIENCE STORE?
ANYONE WITH PROPERLY FUNCTIONING TASTE BUDS.
HONESTLY, THIS IS THE BEST CHRISTMAS I'VE EVER HAD.
ME, TOO.
THUMP THUMP THUMP
--BECAUSE IT'S WHEN THE NIGHTS ARE LONGEST THAT THEY--WE--MUST SHINE BRIGHTEST FOR EACH OTHER.
THE END

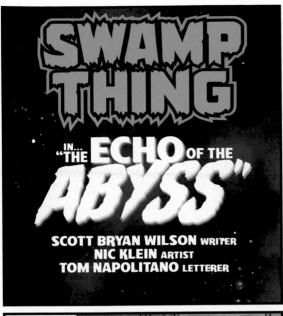

SWAMP THING

IN... "THE ECHO OF THE ABYSS"

SCOTT BRYAN WILSON WRITER
NIC KLEIN ARTIST
TOM NAPOLITANO LETTERER

THE SPACE STATION *ARCHER.* SIX MONTHS INTO RADIATION QUARANTINE.

CREW: SIX.

ANYBODY?

HERNDON? BERNHARD? SLATER? *ANYBODY?*

KEPT THIS FROZEN FOR SIX MONTHS, AND NOW NOBODY'S IN THE HOLIDAY SPIRIT.

GUESS KNOWING YOU'RE A *DEAD MAN* WILL DO THAT!

NO ONE IS IN THE MOOD, *CIAMPO,* AND ALL DUE RESPECT...

--ESCALATION IN THE TWO-MONTH STANDOFF.

NUCLEAR WAR IS NOW INEVITABLE, WITH *SEVEN COUNTRIES* ARMED TO *STRIKE* AND *REFUSING--*

THEY'RE GONNA LEAVE US UP HERE TO DIE! WHY DON'T THEY DO SOMETHING?

IF THE BILLIONS ON EARTH ARE DOOMED--

--WHAT DOES THAT MEAN FOR US?

WE'RE THE LAST?

IS THAT A TORCH WE CAN CARRY?!

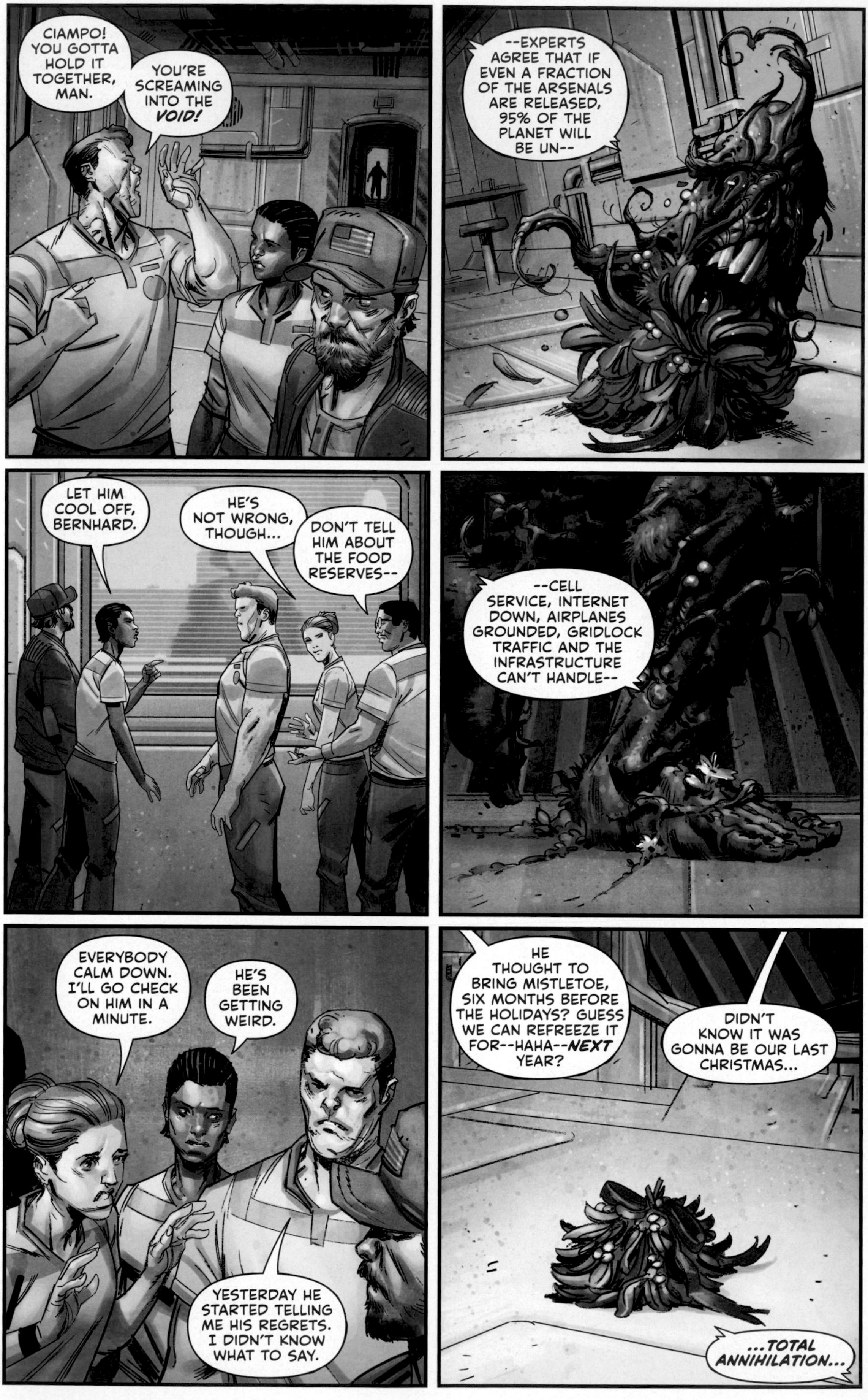
CIAMPO! YOU GOTTA HOLD IT TOGETHER, MAN.
YOU'RE SCREAMING INTO THE *VOID!*
--EXPERTS AGREE THAT IF EVEN A FRACTION OF THE ARSENALS ARE RELEASED, 95% OF THE PLANET WILL BE UN--
LET HIM COOL OFF, BERNHARD.
HE'S NOT WRONG, THOUGH...
DON'T TELL HIM ABOUT THE FOOD RESERVES--
--CELL SERVICE, INTERNET DOWN, AIRPLANES GROUNDED, GRIDLOCK TRAFFIC AND THE INFRASTRUCTURE CAN'T HANDLE--
EVERYBODY CALM DOWN. I'LL GO CHECK ON HIM IN A MINUTE.
HE'S BEEN GETTING WEIRD.
YESTERDAY HE STARTED TELLING ME HIS REGRETS. I DIDN'T KNOW WHAT TO SAY.
HE THOUGHT TO BRING MISTLETOE, SIX MONTHS BEFORE THE HOLIDAYS? GUESS WE CAN REFREEZE IT FOR--HAHA--*NEXT* YEAR?
DIDN'T KNOW IT WAS GONNA BE OUR LAST CHRISTMAS...
...TOTAL ANNIHILATION...

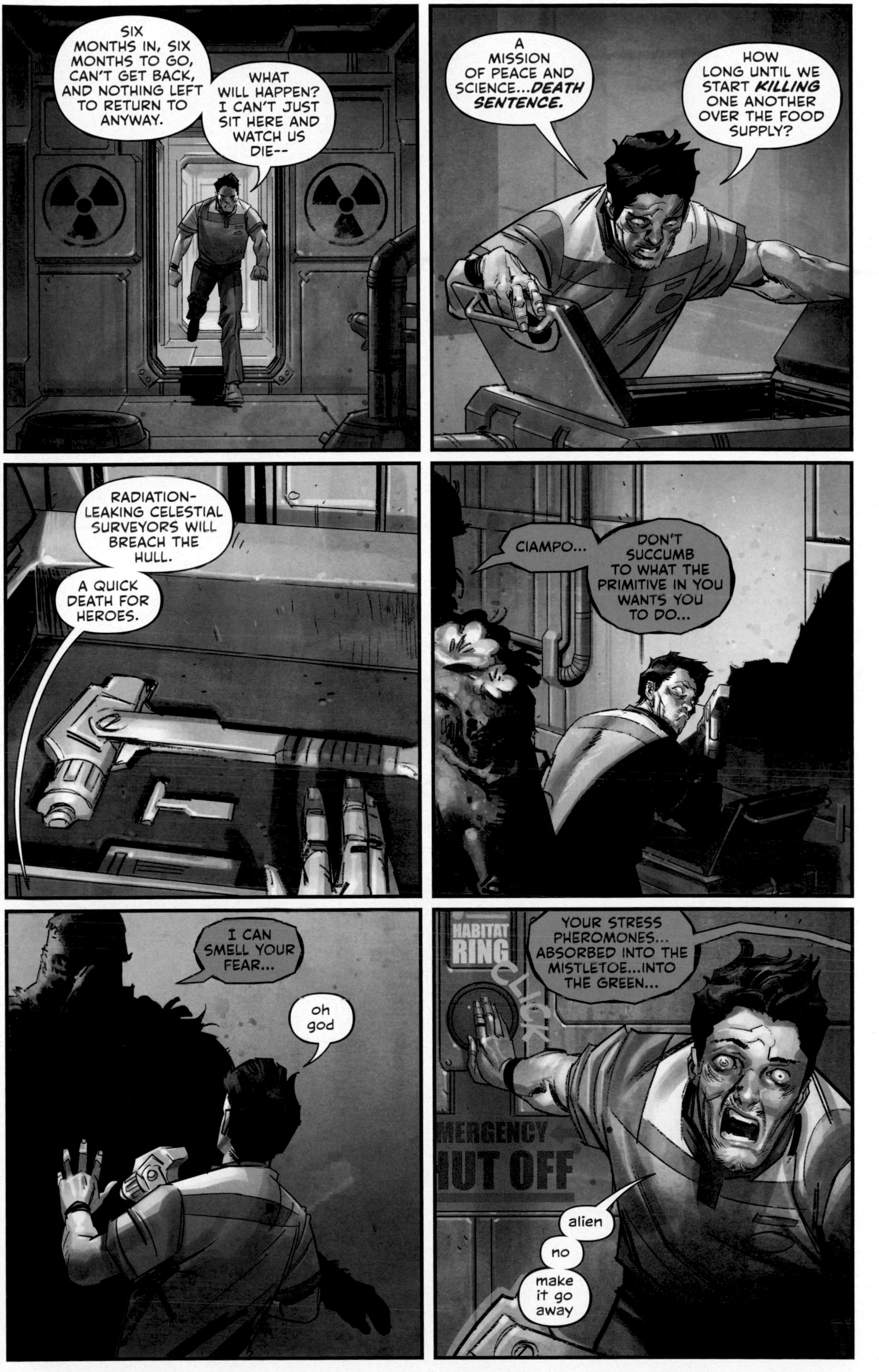
SIX MONTHS IN, SIX MONTHS TO GO, CAN'T GET BACK, AND NOTHING LEFT TO RETURN TO ANYWAY.
WHAT WILL HAPPEN? I CAN'T JUST SIT HERE AND WATCH US DIE--
A MISSION OF PEACE AND SCIENCE...DEATH SENTENCE.
HOW LONG UNTIL WE START KILLING ONE ANOTHER OVER THE FOOD SUPPLY?
RADIATION-LEAKING CELESTIAL SURVEYORS WILL BREACH THE HULL.
A QUICK DEATH FOR HEROES.
CIAMPO...
DON'T SUCCUMB TO WHAT THE PRIMITIVE IN YOU WANTS YOU TO DO...
I CAN SMELL YOUR FEAR...
oh god
HABITAT RING
CLICK
YOUR STRESS PHEROMONES... ABSORBED INTO THE MISTLETOE...INTO THE GREEN...
MERGENCY
HUT OFF
alien
no
make it go away

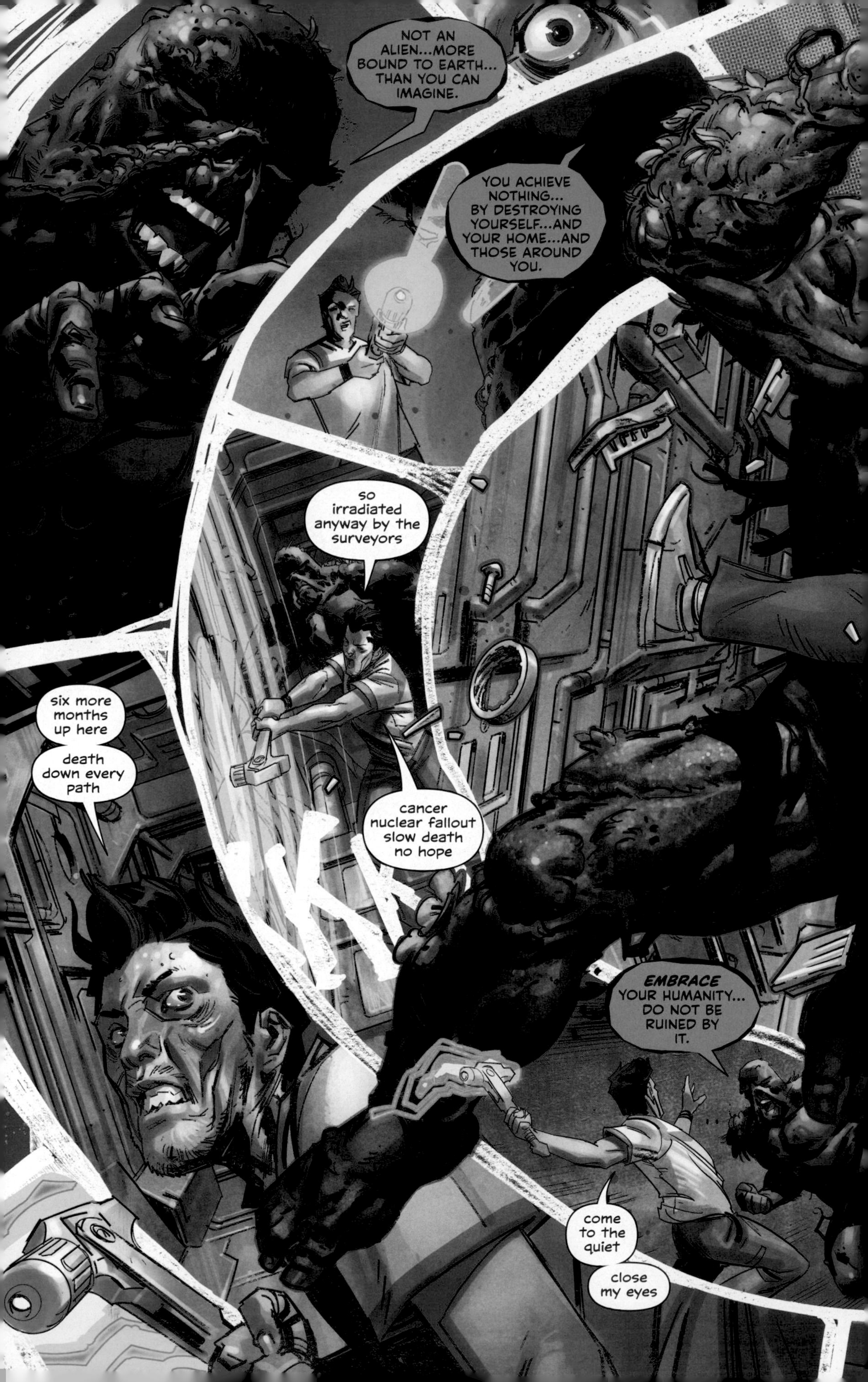
NOT AN ALIEN...MORE BOUND TO EARTH... THAN YOU CAN IMAGINE.
YOU ACHIEVE NOTHING... BY DESTROYING YOURSELF...AND YOUR HOME...AND THOSE AROUND YOU.
so irradiated anyway by the surveyors
six more months up here
death down every path
cancer nuclear fallout slow death no hope
EMBRACE YOUR HUMANITY... DO NOT BE RUINED BY IT.
come to the quiet
close my eyes

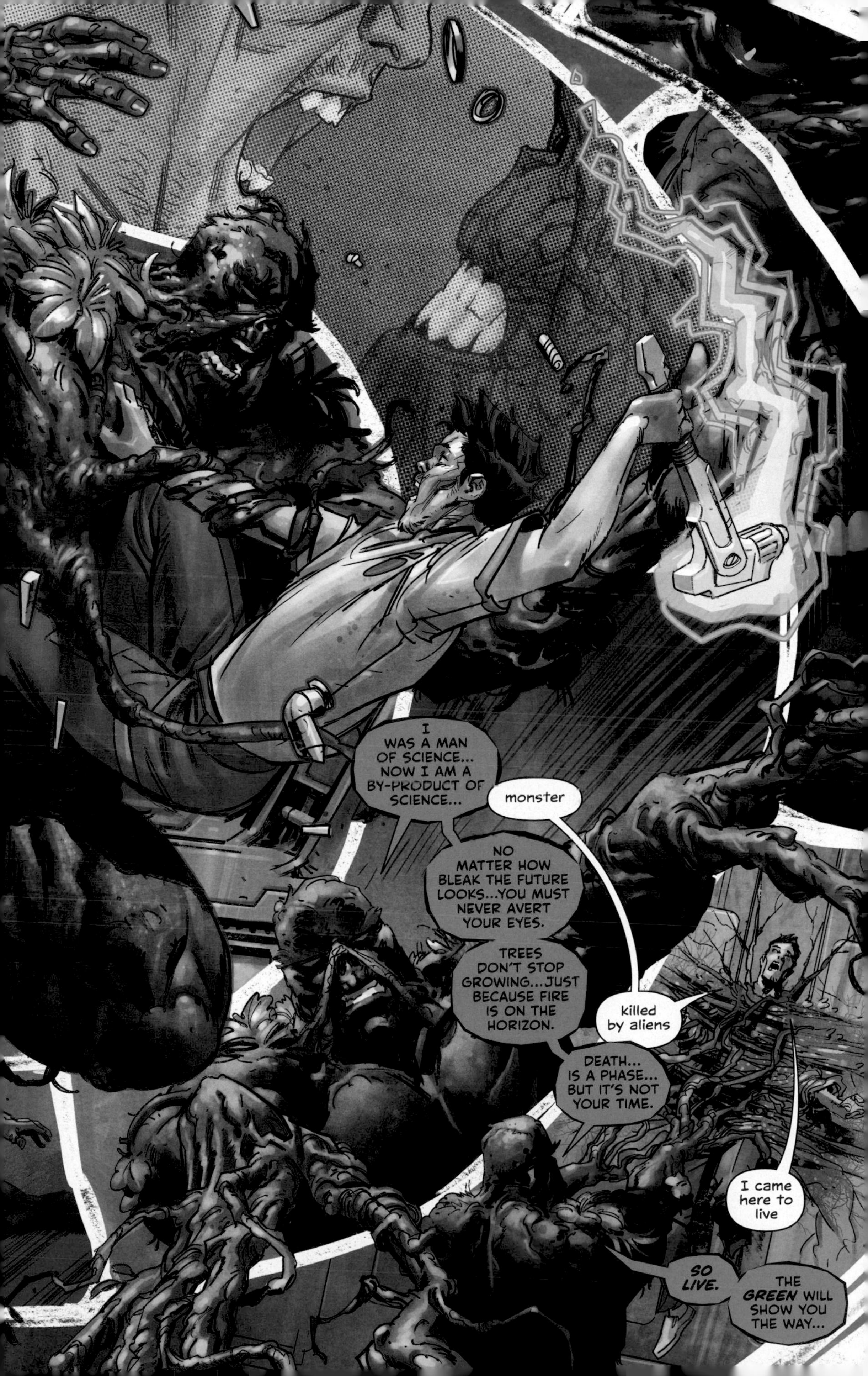
I WAS A MAN OF SCIENCE... NOW I AM A BY-PRODUCT OF SCIENCE...
monster
NO MATTER HOW BLEAK THE FUTURE LOOKS...YOU MUST NEVER AVERT YOUR EYES.
TREES DON'T STOP GROWING...JUST BECAUSE FIRE IS ON THE HORIZON.
killed by aliens
DEATH... IS A PHASE... BUT IT'S NOT YOUR TIME.
I came here to live
SO LIVE.
THE GREEN WILL SHOW YOU THE WAY...

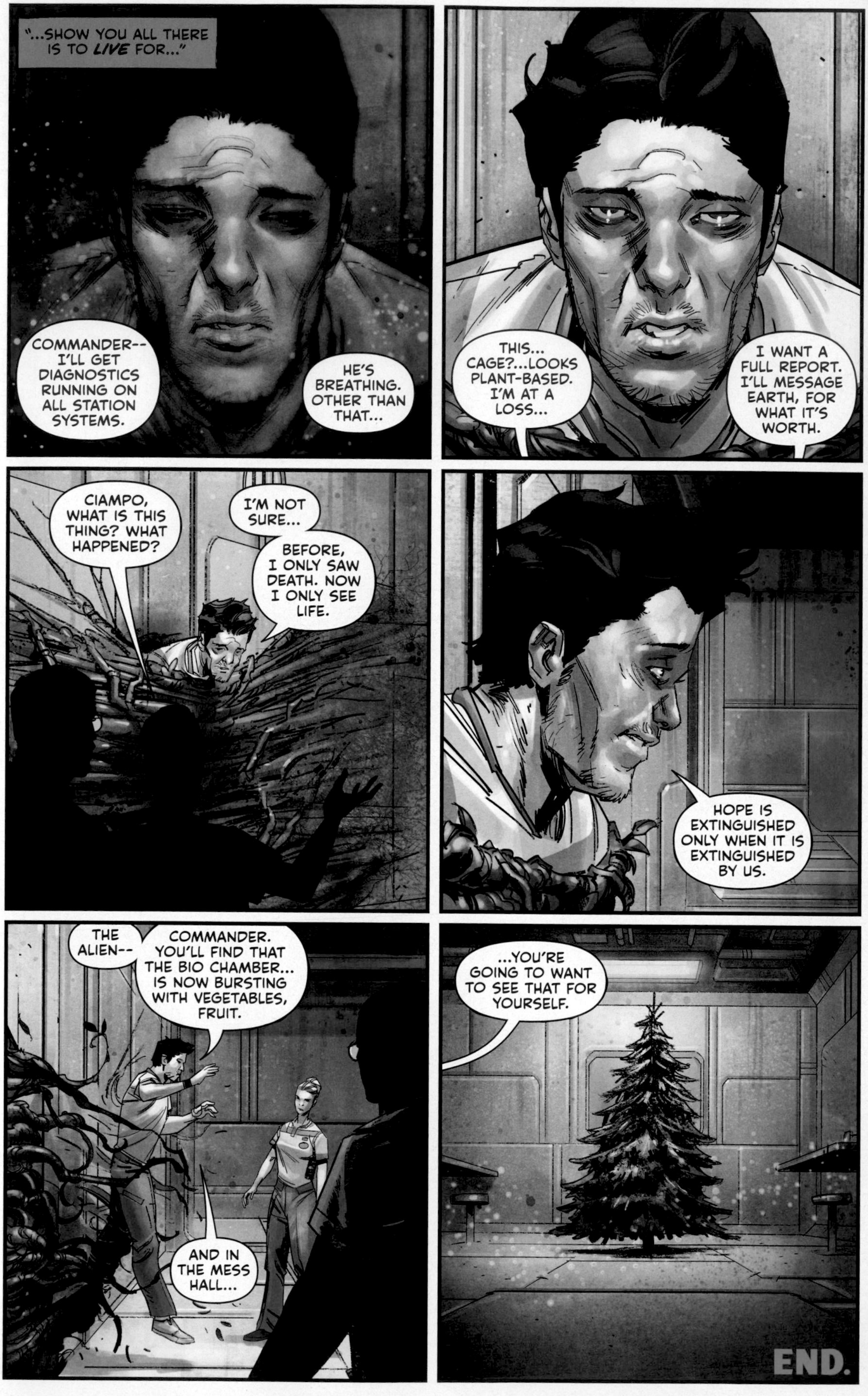
"...SHOW YOU ALL THERE IS TO LIVE FOR..."
COMMANDER-- I'LL GET DIAGNOSTICS RUNNING ON ALL STATION SYSTEMS.
HE'S BREATHING. OTHER THAN THAT...
THIS... CAGE?...LOOKS PLANT-BASED. I'M AT A LOSS...
I WANT A FULL REPORT. I'LL MESSAGE EARTH, FOR WHAT IT'S WORTH.
CIAMPO, WHAT IS THIS THING? WHAT HAPPENED?
I'M NOT SURE...
BEFORE, I ONLY SAW DEATH. NOW I ONLY SEE LIFE.
HOPE IS EXTINGUISHED ONLY WHEN IT IS EXTINGUISHED BY US.
THE ALIEN--
COMMANDER. YOU'LL FIND THAT THE BIO CHAMBER... IS NOW BURSTING WITH VEGETABLES, FRUIT.
AND IN THE MESS HALL...
...YOU'RE GOING TO WANT TO SEE THAT FOR YOURSELF.
END.

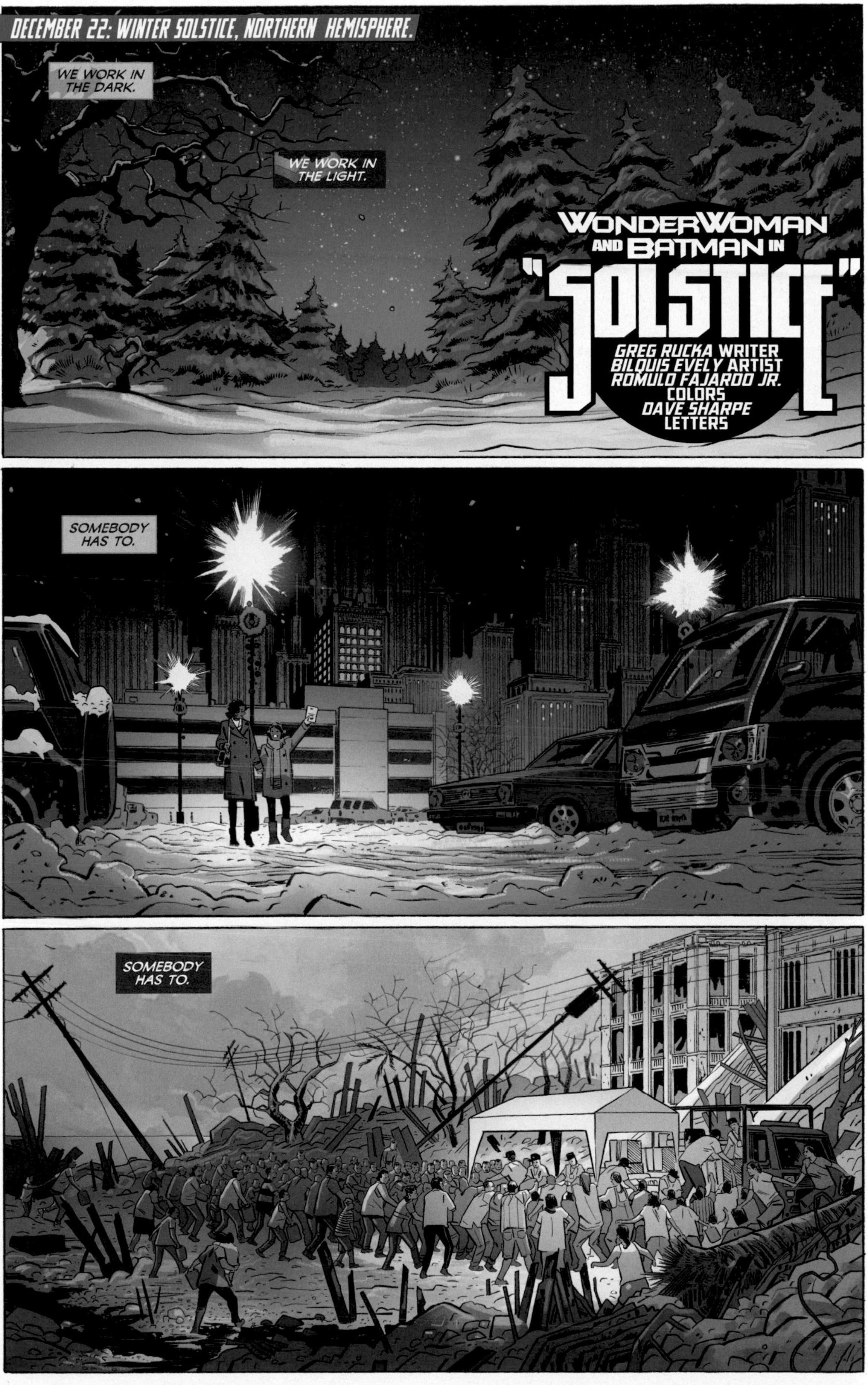

DECEMBER 22: WINTER SOLSTICE, NORTHERN HEMISPHERE.
WE WORK IN THE DARK.
WE WORK IN THE LIGHT.
WONDER WOMAN AND BATMAN IN
"SOLSTICE"
GREG RUCKA WRITER
BILQUIS EVELY ARTIST
ROMULO FAJARDO JR. COLORS
DAVE SHARPE LETTERS
SOMEBODY HAS TO.
SOMEBODY HAS TO.

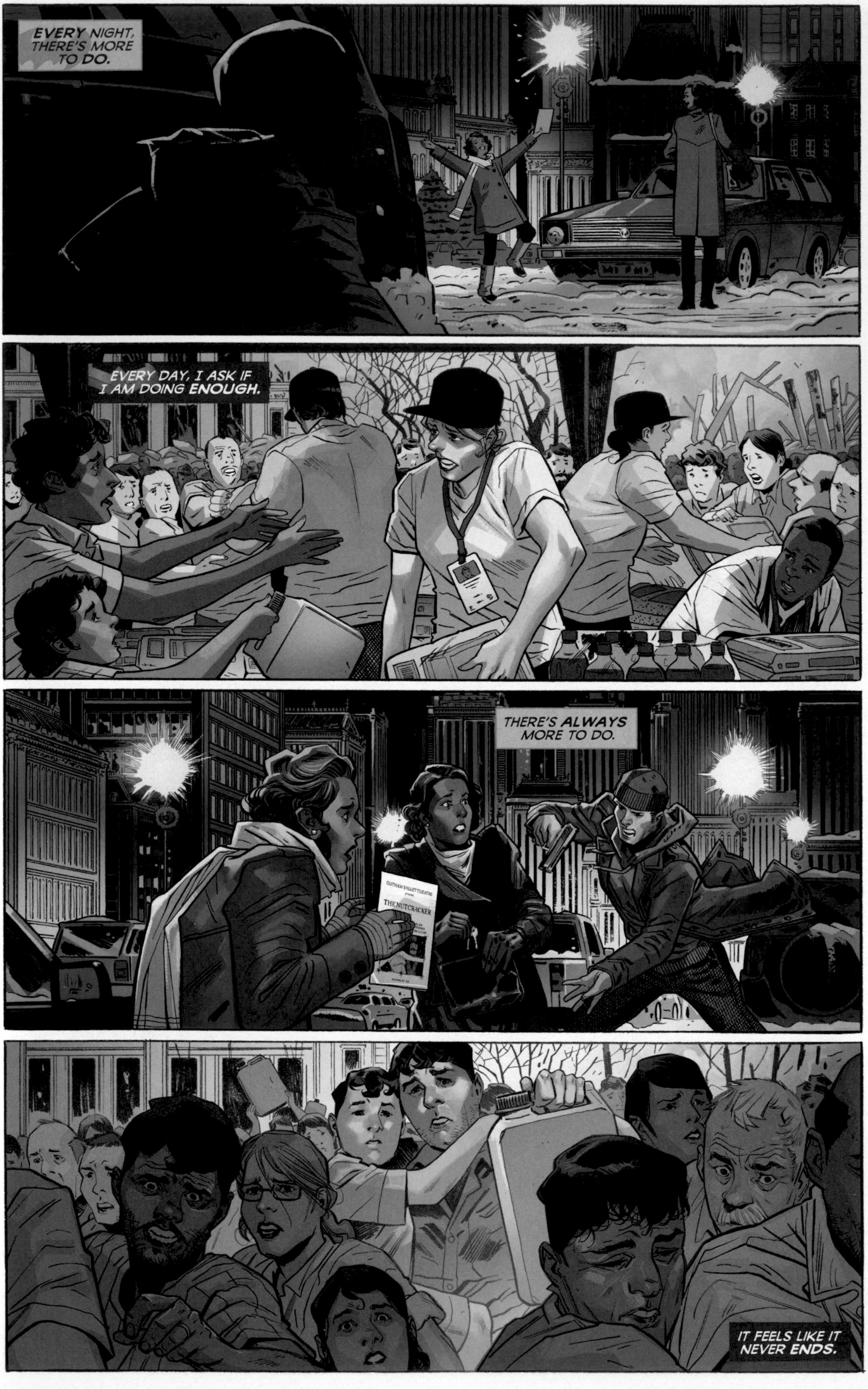
EVERY NIGHT, THERE'S MORE TO DO.
EVERY DAY, I ASK IF I AM DOING ENOUGH.
THERE'S ALWAYS MORE TO DO.
THE NUTCRACKER
IT FEELS LIKE IT NEVER ENDS.

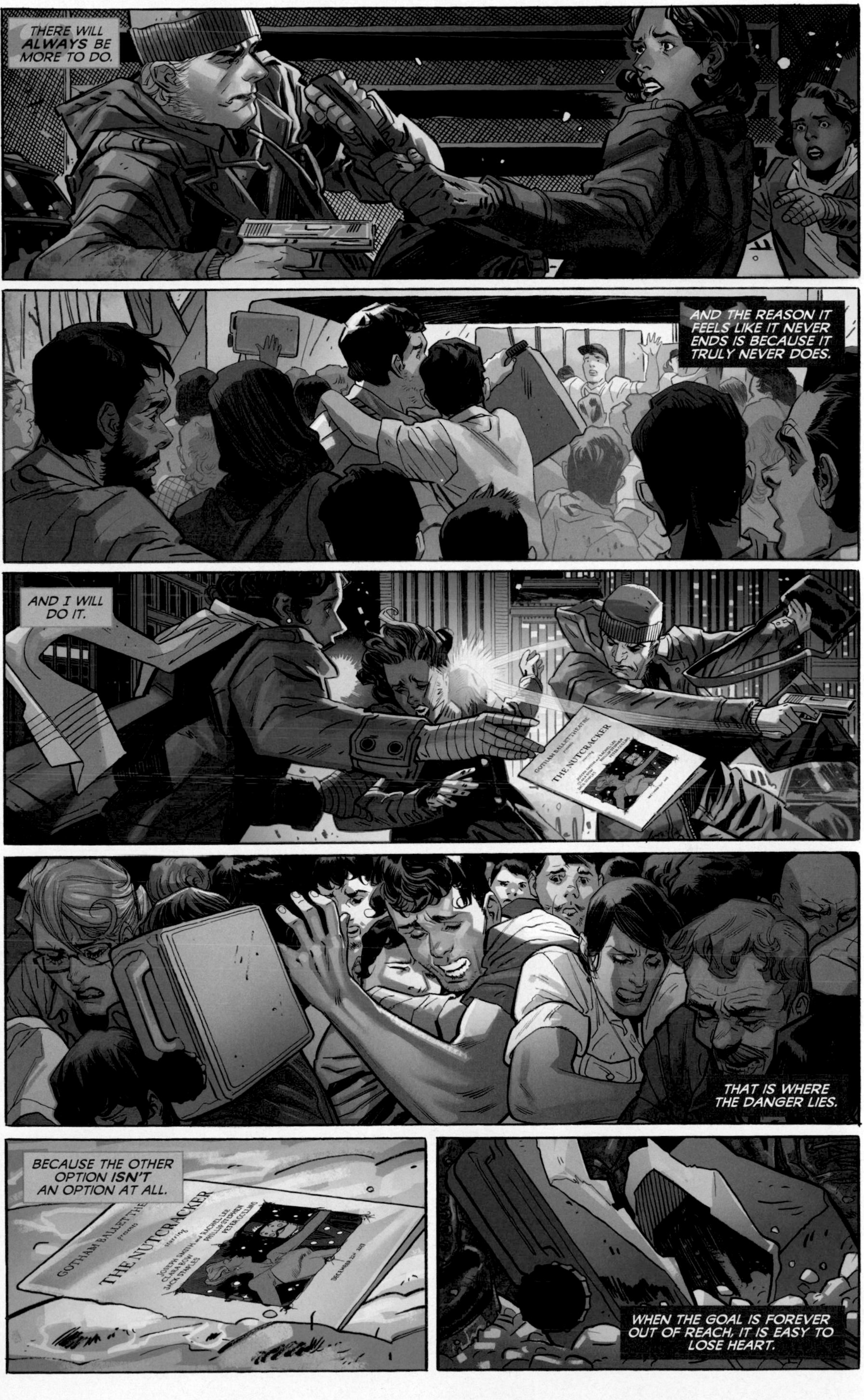
THERE WILL ALWAYS BE MORE TO DO.
AND THE REASON IT FEELS LIKE IT NEVER ENDS IS BECAUSE IT TRULY NEVER DOES.
AND I WILL DO IT.
THE NUTCRACKER
THAT IS WHERE THE DANGER LIES.
BECAUSE THE OTHER OPTION ISN'T AN OPTION AT ALL.
THE NUTCRACKER
WHEN THE GOAL IS FOREVER OUT OF REACH, IT IS EASY TO LOSE HEART.

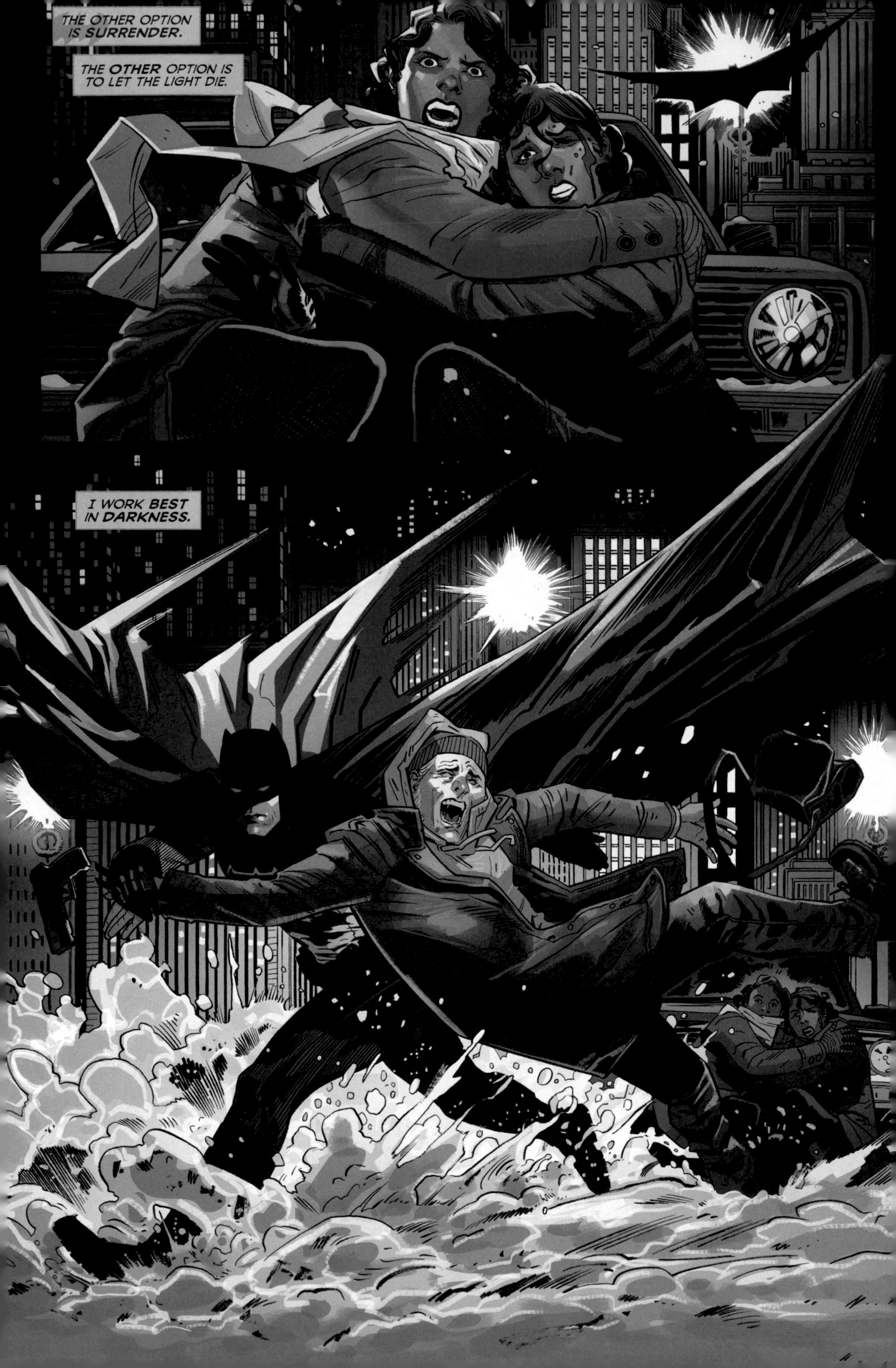
THE OTHER OPTION IS SURRENDER.
THE OTHER OPTION IS TO LET THE LIGHT DIE.
I WORK BEST IN DARKNESS.

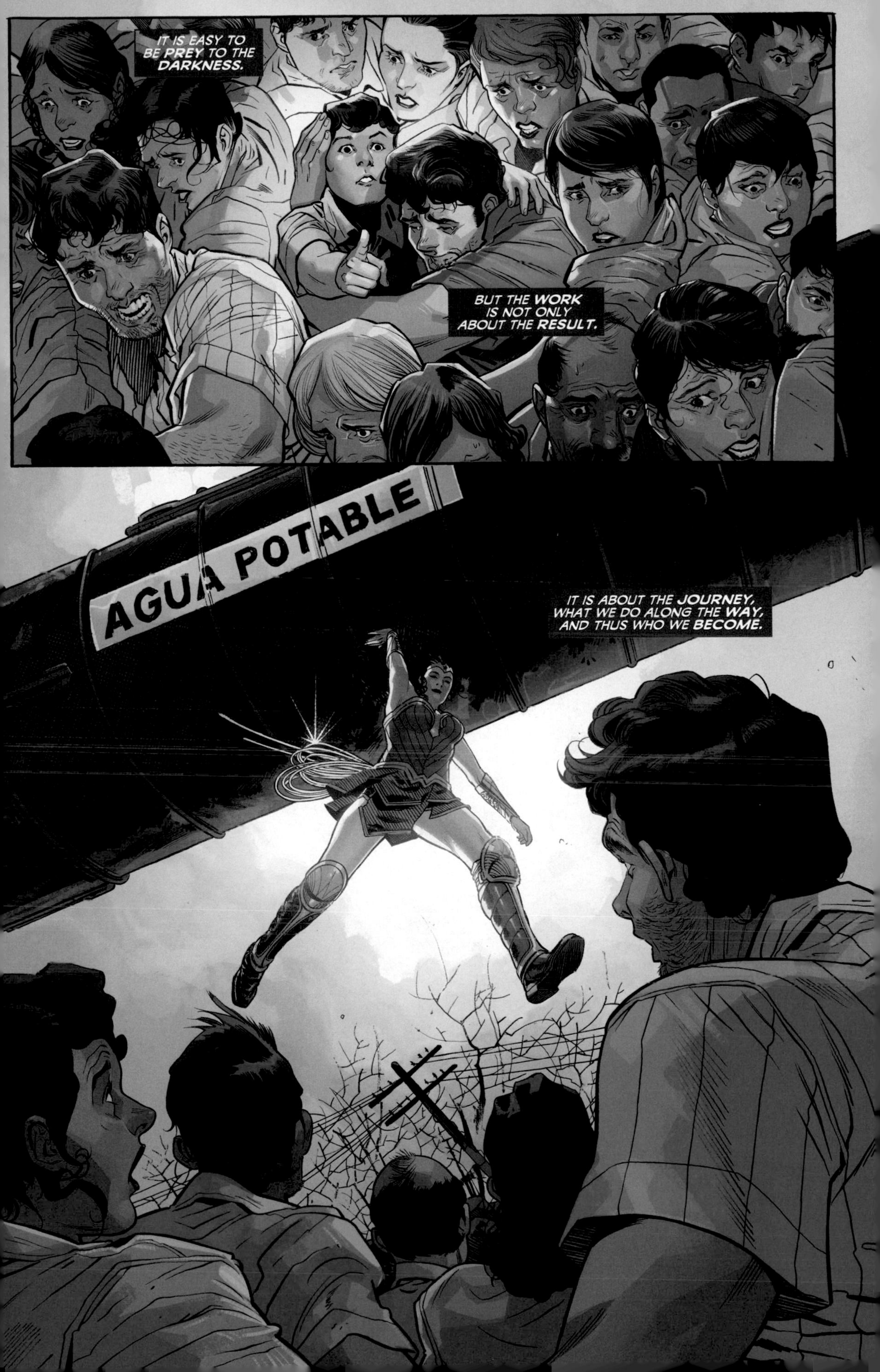
IT IS EASY TO BE PREY TO THE DARKNESS.
BUT THE WORK IS NOT ONLY ABOUT THE RESULT.
AGUA POTABLE
IT IS ABOUT THE JOURNEY, WHAT WE DO ALONG THE WAY, AND THUS WHO WE BECOME.

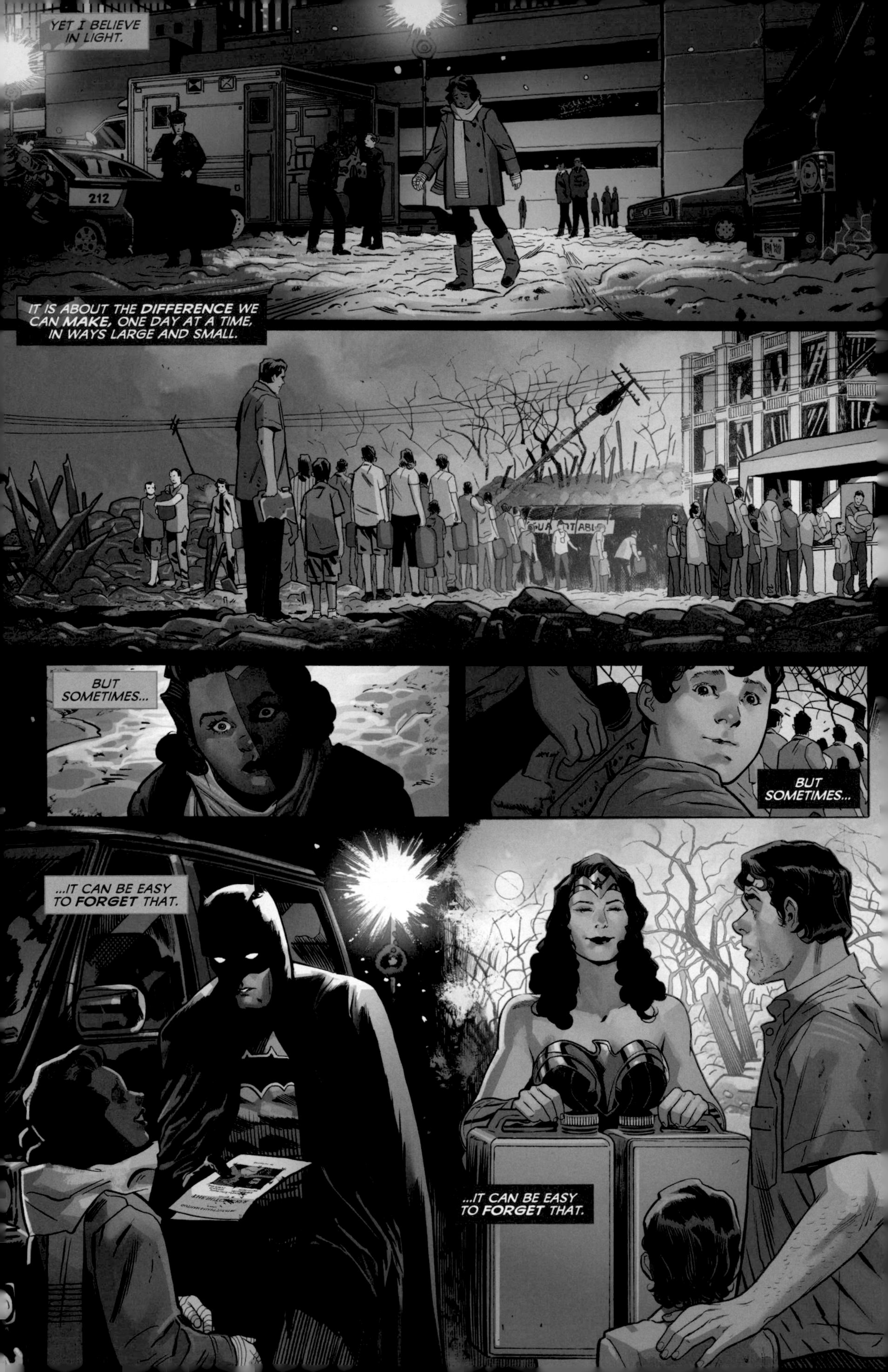
YET I BELIEVE IN LIGHT.
IT IS ABOUT THE DIFFERENCE WE CAN MAKE, ONE DAY AT A TIME, IN WAYS LARGE AND SMALL.
BUT SOMETIMES...
BUT SOMETIMES...
...IT CAN BE EASY TO FORGET THAT.
...IT CAN BE EASY TO FORGET THAT.

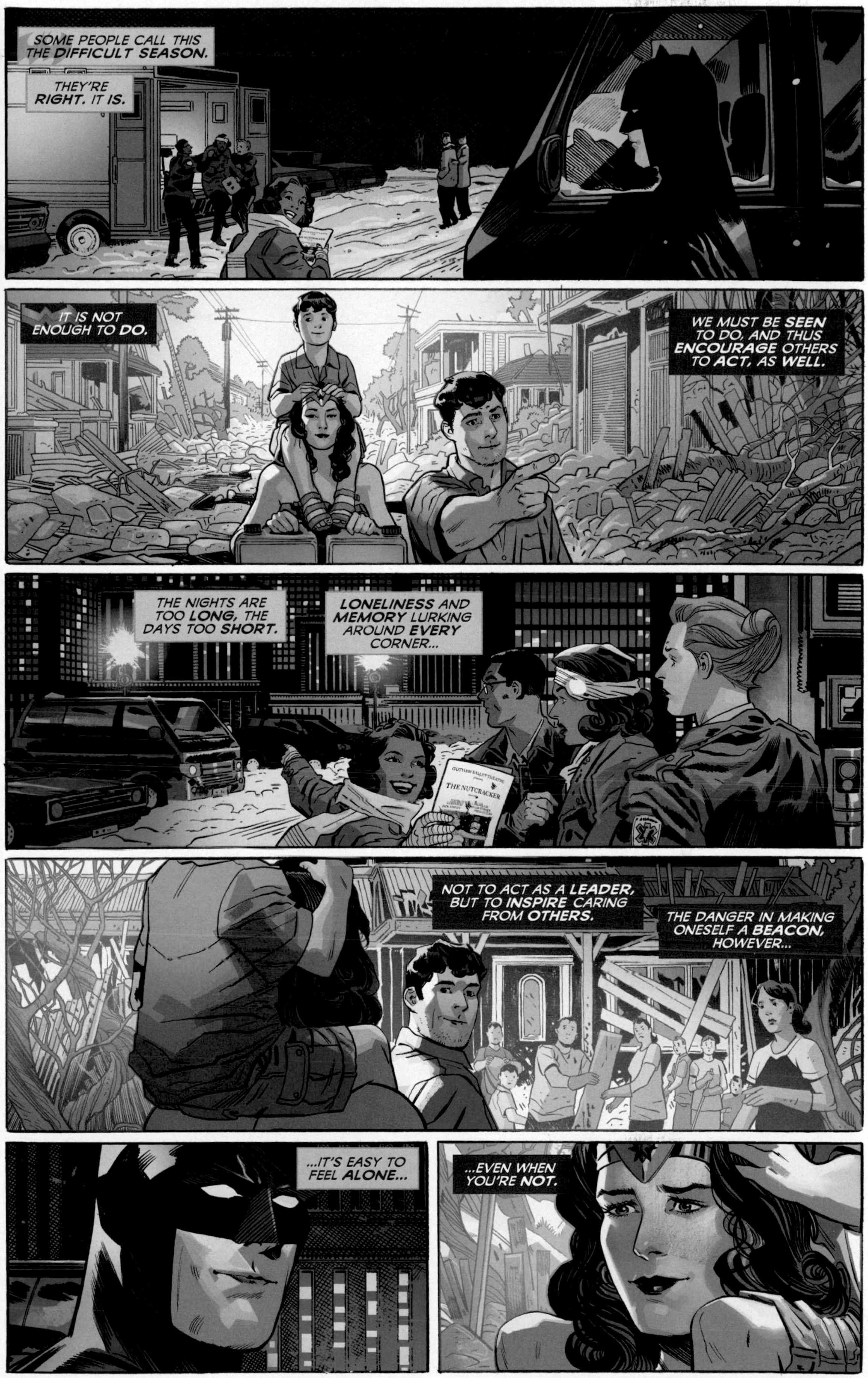

SOME PEOPLE CALL THIS THE DIFFICULT SEASON.
THEY'RE RIGHT. IT IS.
IT IS NOT ENOUGH TO DO.
WE MUST BE SEEN TO DO, AND THUS ENCOURAGE OTHERS TO ACT, AS WELL.
THE NIGHTS ARE TOO LONG, THE DAYS TOO SHORT.
LONELINESS AND MEMORY LURKING AROUND EVERY CORNER...
GOTHAM BALLET THEATRE
THE NUTCRACKER
NOT TO ACT AS A LEADER, BUT TO INSPIRE CARING FROM OTHERS.
THE DANGER IN MAKING ONESELF A BEACON, HOWEVER...
...IT'S EASY TO FEEL ALONE...
...EVEN WHEN YOU'RE NOT.

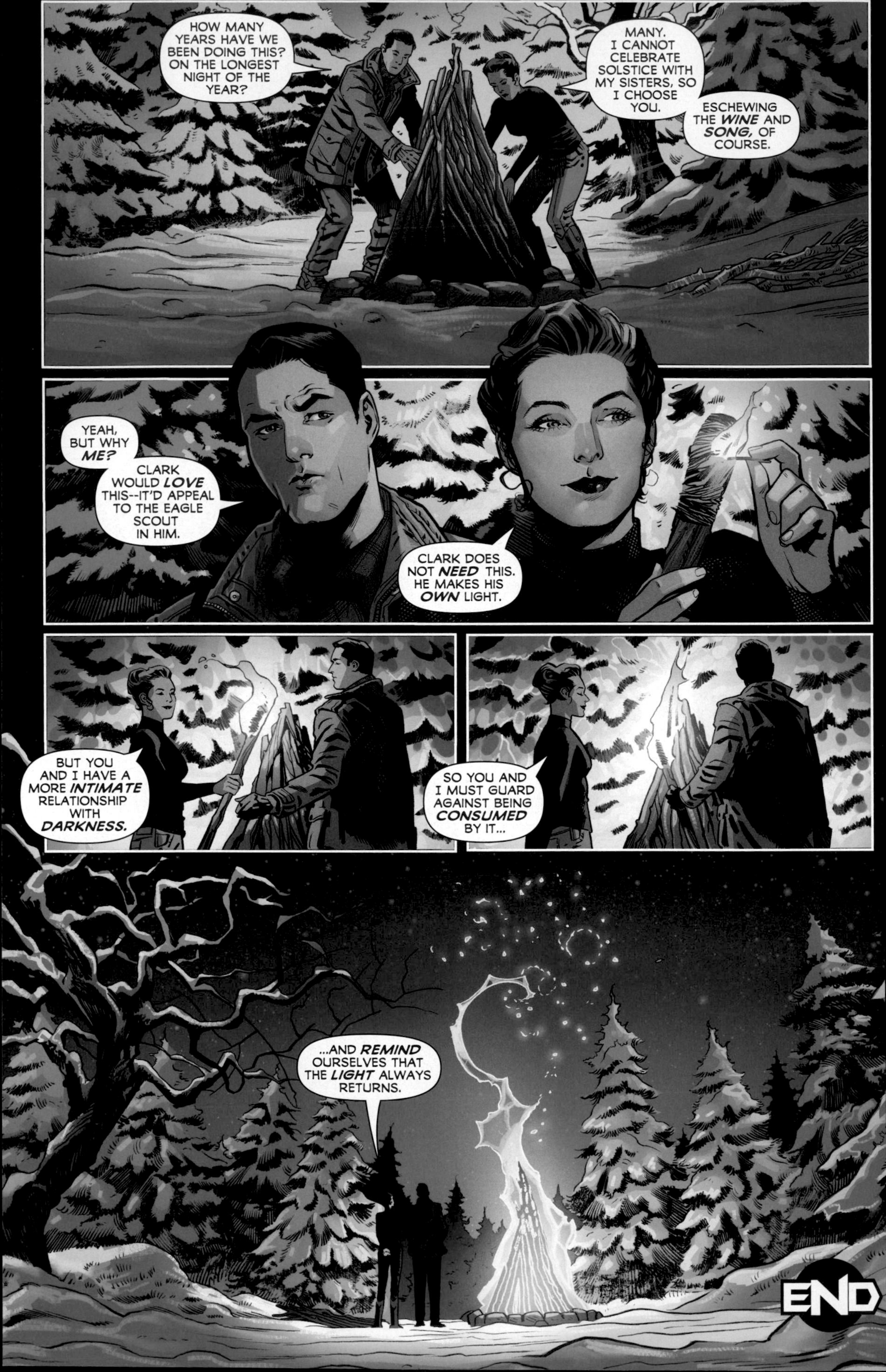
HOW MANY YEARS HAVE WE BEEN DOING THIS? ON THE LONGEST NIGHT OF THE YEAR?
MANY. I CANNOT CELEBRATE SOLSTICE WITH MY SISTERS, SO I CHOOSE YOU.
ESCHEWING THE WINE AND SONG, OF COURSE.
YEAH, BUT WHY ME?
CLARK WOULD LOVE THIS--IT'D APPEAL TO THE EAGLE SCOUT IN HIM.
CLARK DOES NOT NEED THIS. HE MAKES HIS OWN LIGHT.
BUT YOU AND I HAVE A MORE INTIMATE RELATIONSHIP WITH DARKNESS.
SO YOU AND I MUST GUARD AGAINST BEING CONSUMED BY IT...
...AND REMIND OURSELVES THAT THE LIGHT ALWAYS RETURNS.
END

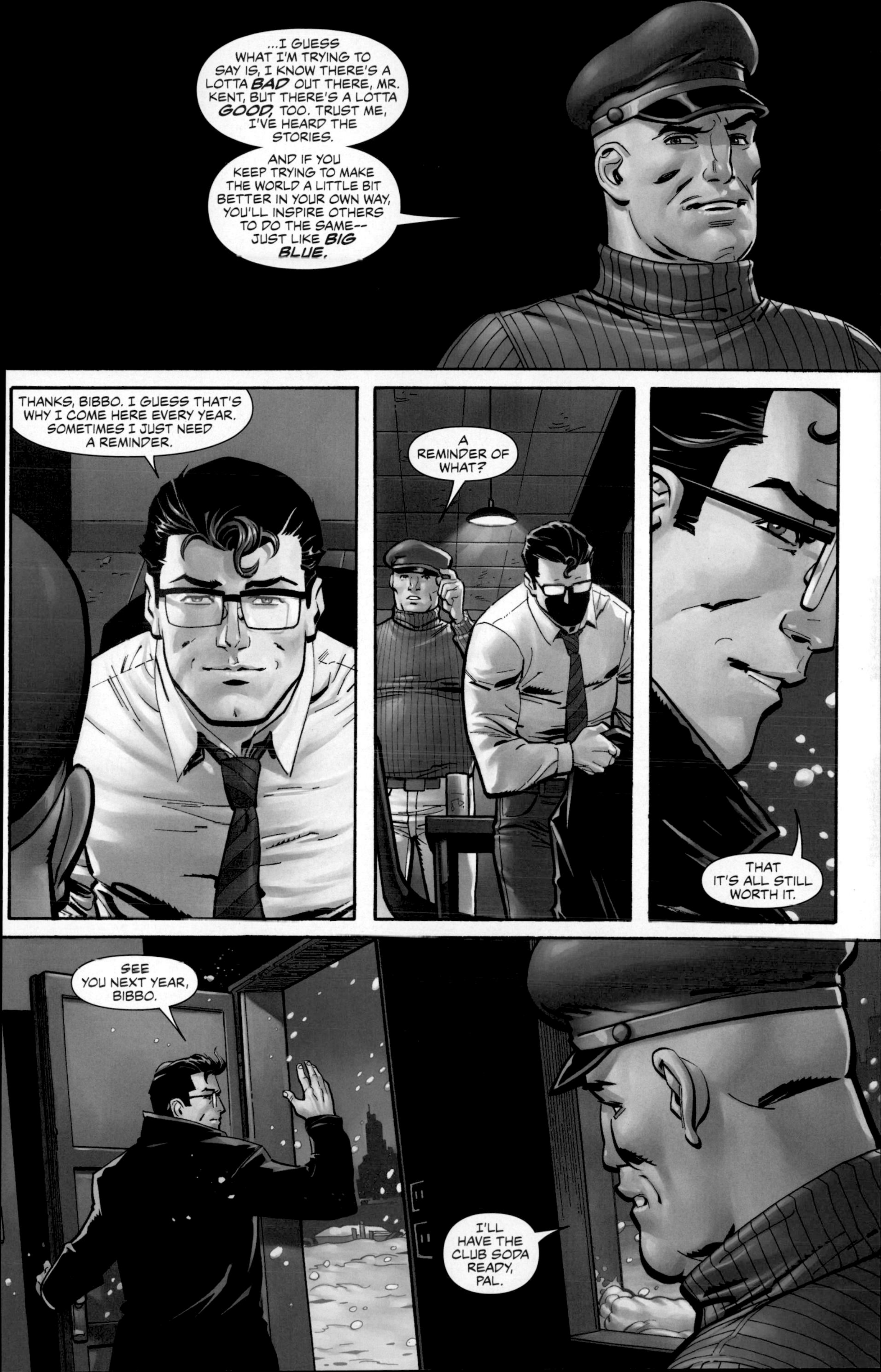

...I GUESS WHAT I'M TRYING TO SAY IS, I KNOW THERE'S A LOTTA BAD OUT THERE, MR. KENT, BUT THERE'S A LOTTA GOOD, TOO. TRUST ME, I'VE HEARD THE STORIES.
AND IF YOU KEEP TRYING TO MAKE THE WORLD A LITTLE BIT BETTER IN YOUR OWN WAY, YOU'LL INSPIRE OTHERS TO DO THE SAME-- JUST LIKE BIG BLUE.
THANKS, BIBBO. I GUESS THAT'S WHY I COME HERE EVERY YEAR. SOMETIMES I JUST NEED A REMINDER.
A REMINDER OF WHAT?
THAT IT'S ALL STILL WORTH IT.
SEE YOU NEXT YEAR, BIBBO.
I'LL HAVE THE CLUB SODA READY, PAL.

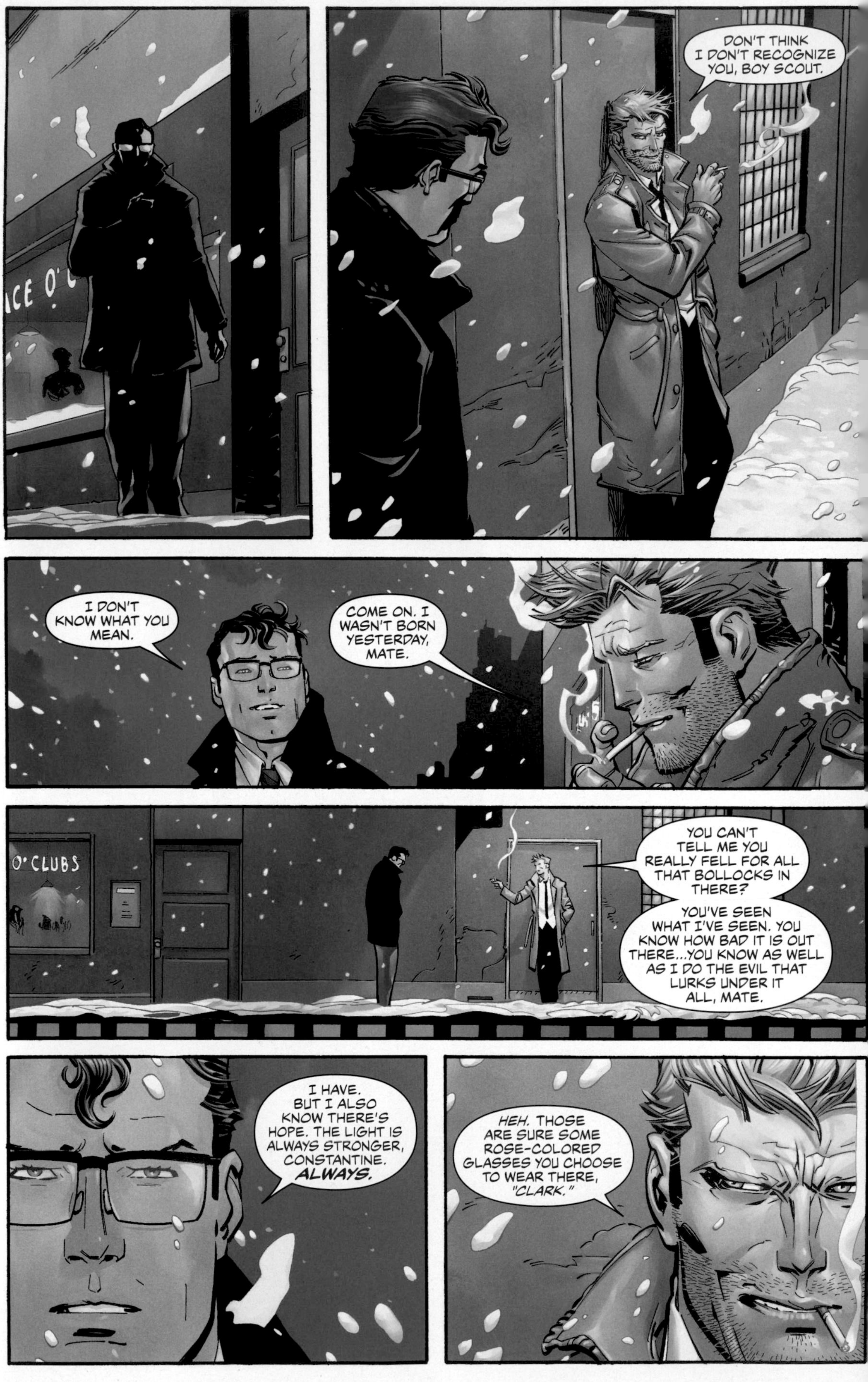
ACE O'C
DON'T THINK I DON'T RECOGNIZE YOU, BOY SCOUT.
I DON'T KNOW WHAT YOU MEAN.
COME ON. I WASN'T BORN YESTERDAY, MATE.
O'CLUBS
YOU CAN'T TELL ME YOU REALLY FELL FOR ALL THAT BOLLOCKS IN THERE?
YOU'VE SEEN WHAT I'VE SEEN. YOU KNOW HOW BAD IT IS OUT THERE...YOU KNOW AS WELL AS I DO THE EVIL THAT LURKS UNDER IT ALL, MATE.
I HAVE. BUT I ALSO KNOW THERE'S HOPE. THE LIGHT IS ALWAYS STRONGER, CONSTANTINE. ***ALWAYS.***
HEH. THOSE ARE SURE SOME ROSE-COLORED GLASSES YOU CHOOSE TO WEAR THERE, *"CLARK."*

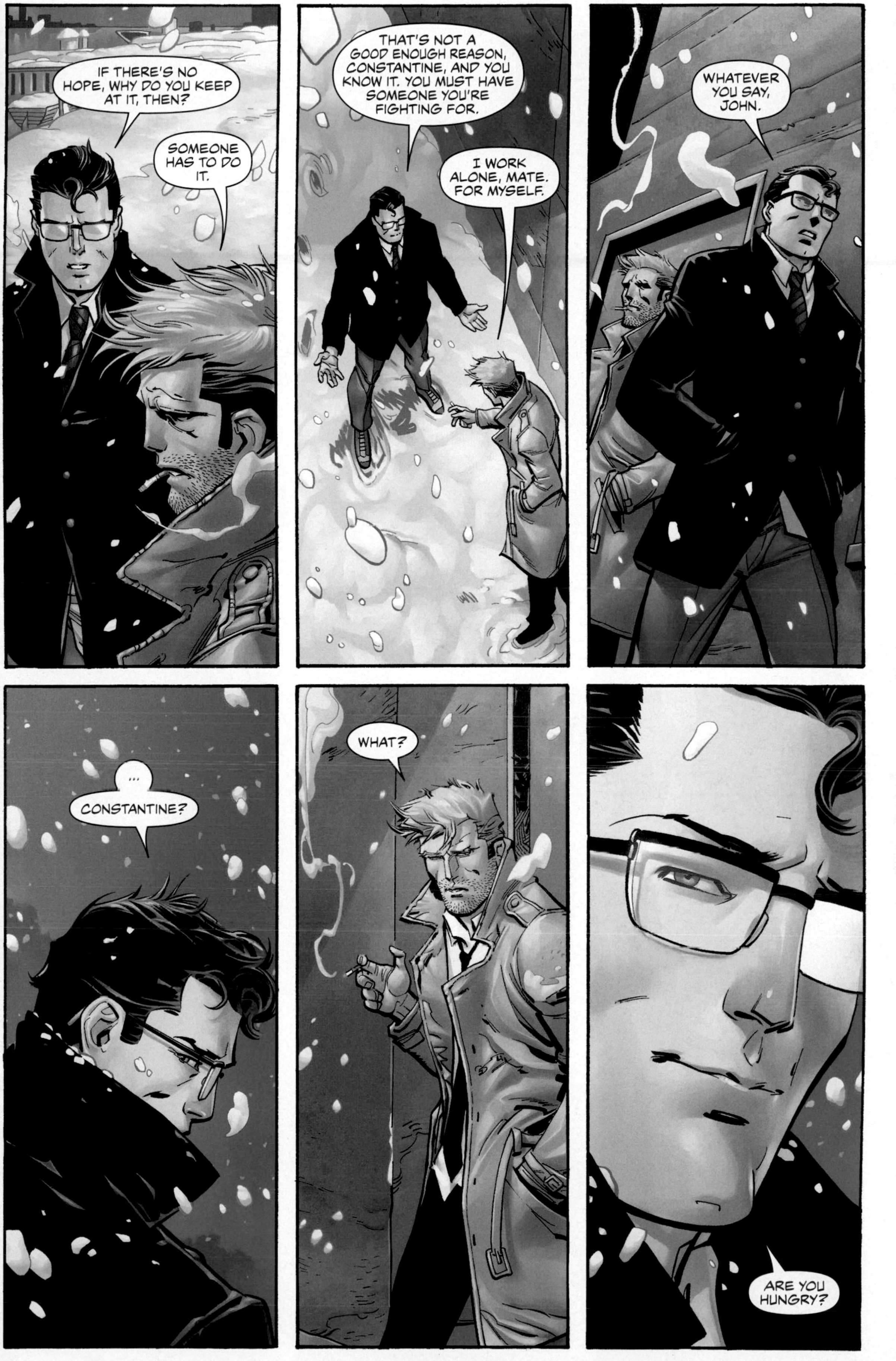
IF THERE'S NO HOPE, WHY DO YOU KEEP AT IT, THEN?
SOMEONE HAS TO DO IT.
THAT'S NOT A GOOD ENOUGH REASON, CONSTANTINE, AND YOU KNOW IT. YOU MUST HAVE SOMEONE YOU'RE FIGHTING FOR.
I WORK ALONE, MATE. FOR MYSELF.
WHATEVER YOU SAY, JOHN.
...
CONSTANTINE?
WHAT?
ARE YOU HUNGRY?

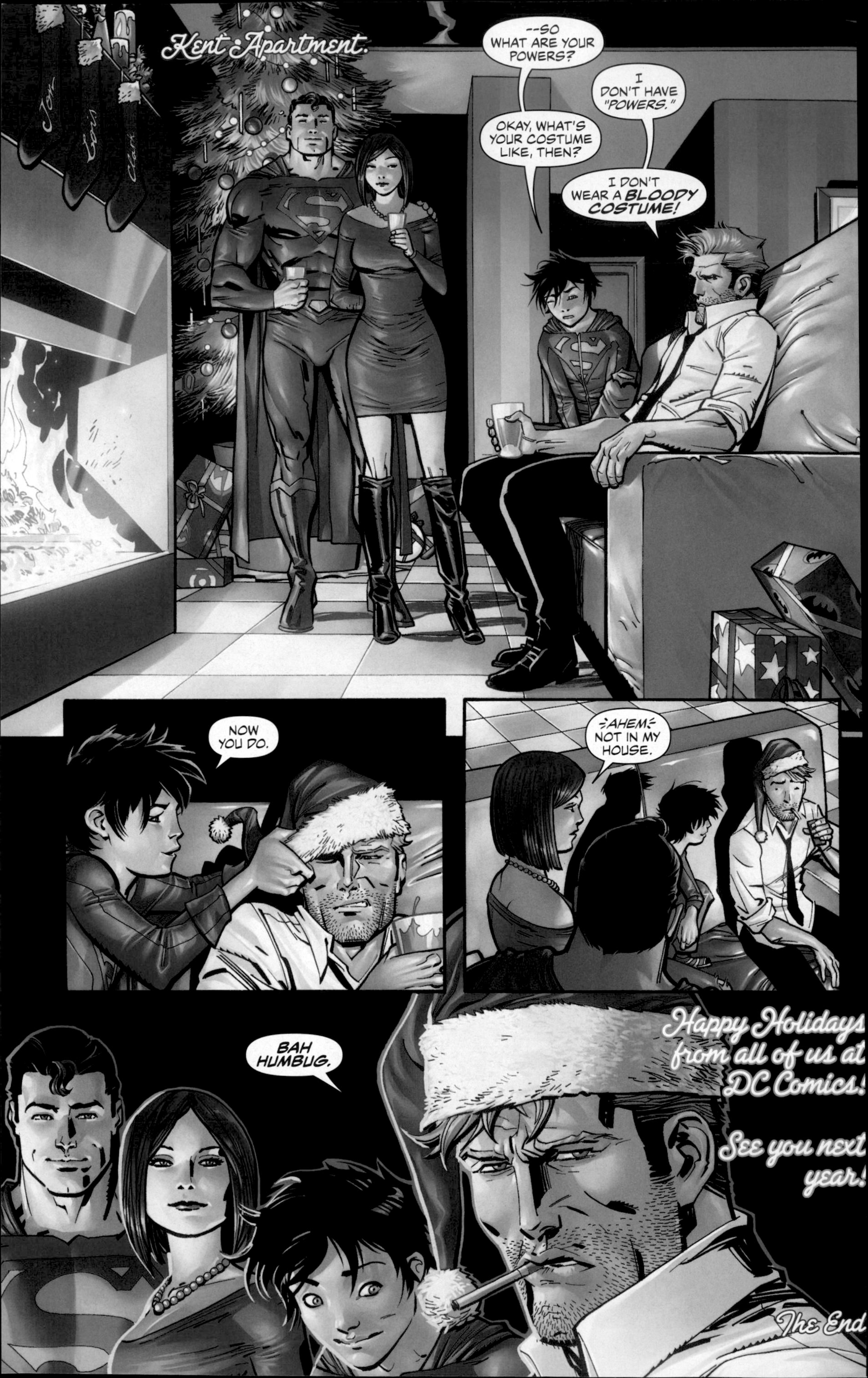
Kent Apartment.
Jon
Lois
Clark
--SO WHAT ARE YOUR POWERS?
I DON'T HAVE "POWERS."
OKAY, WHAT'S YOUR COSTUME LIKE, THEN?
I DON'T WEAR A BLOODY COSTUME!
NOW YOU DO.
AHEM. NOT IN MY HOUSE.
BAH HUMBUG.
Happy Holidays from all of us at DC Comics!
See you next year!
The End

Encore Holiday Classic

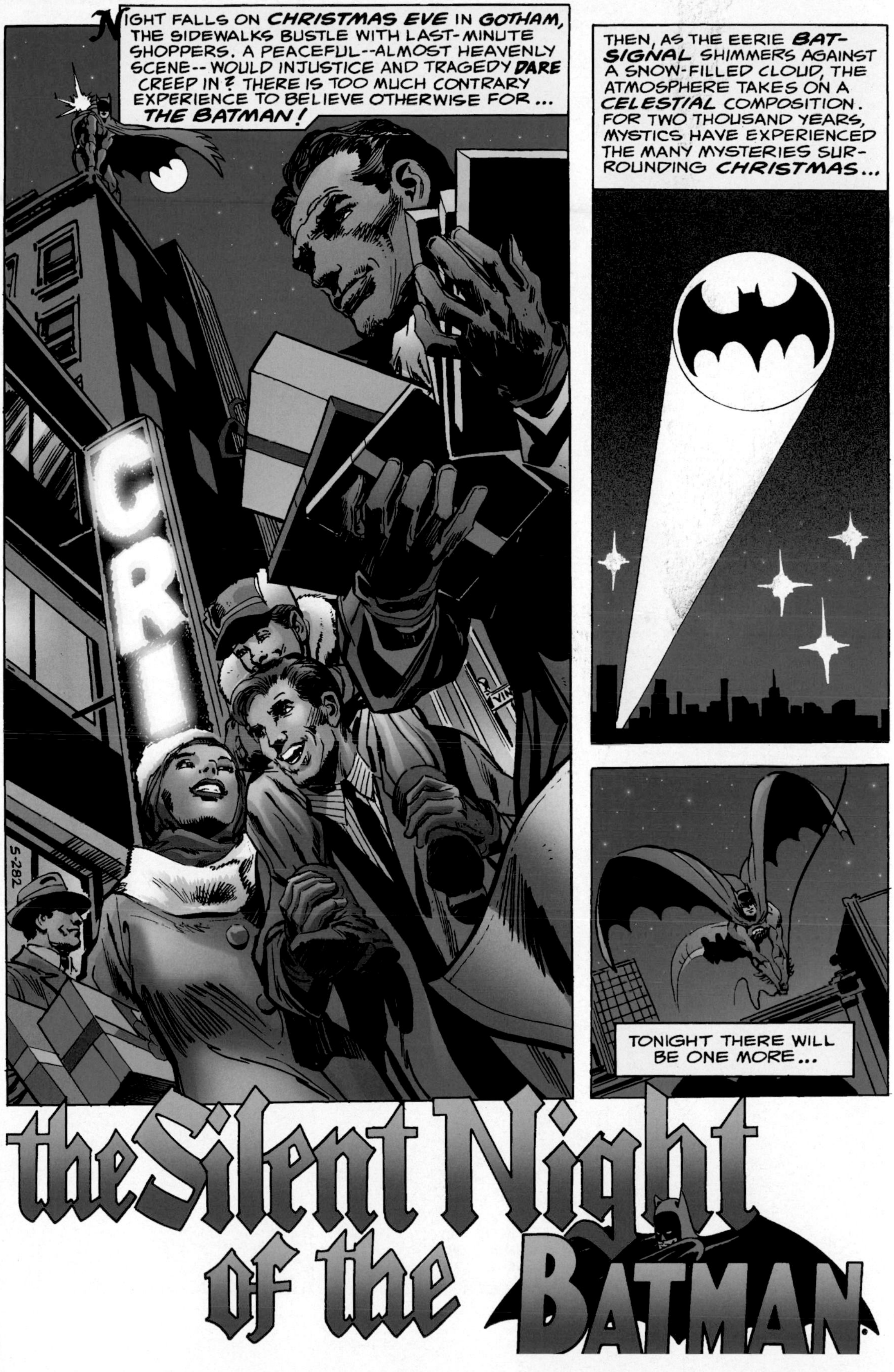
NIGHT FALLS ON CHRISTMAS EVE IN GOTHAM, THE SIDEWALKS BUSTLE WITH LAST-MINUTE SHOPPERS. A PEACEFUL--ALMOST HEAVENLY SCENE-- WOULD INJUSTICE AND TRAGEDY DARE CREEP IN? THERE IS TOO MUCH CONTRARY EXPERIENCE TO BELIEVE OTHERWISE FOR... THE BATMAN!
CRI
THEN, AS THE EERIE BAT-SIGNAL SHIMMERS AGAINST A SNOW-FILLED CLOUD, THE ATMOSPHERE TAKES ON A CELESTIAL COMPOSITION. FOR TWO THOUSAND YEARS, MYSTICS HAVE EXPERIENCED THE MANY MYSTERIES SURROUNDING CHRISTMAS...
TONIGHT THERE WILL BE ONE MORE...
the Silent Night of the BATMAN

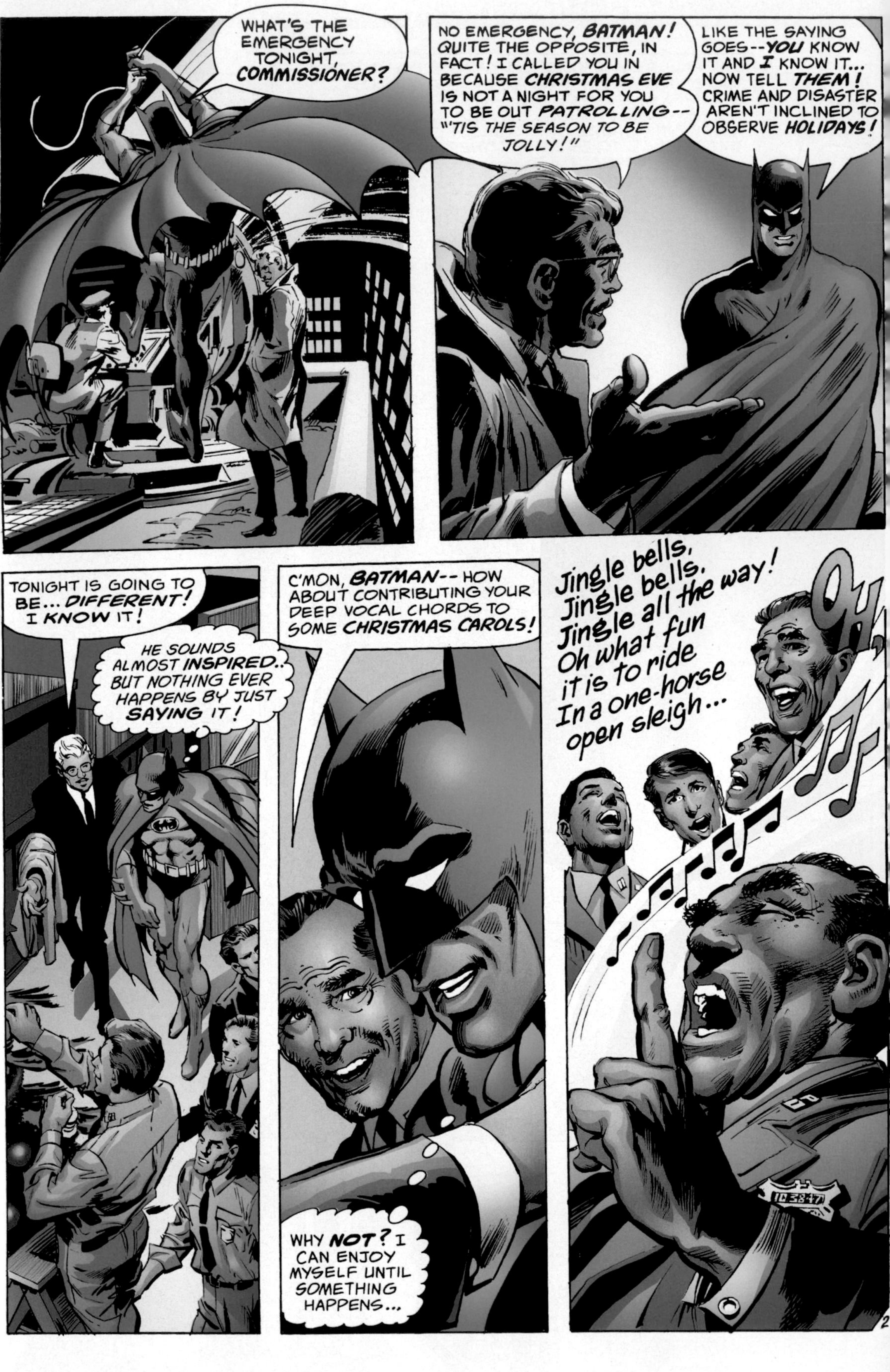
WHAT'S THE EMERGENCY TONIGHT, COMMISSIONER?
NO EMERGENCY, BATMAN! QUITE THE OPPOSITE, IN FACT! I CALLED YOU IN BECAUSE CHRISTMAS EVE IS NOT A NIGHT FOR YOU TO BE OUT PATROLLING-- "'TIS THE SEASON TO BE JOLLY!"
LIKE THE SAYING GOES--YOU KNOW IT AND I KNOW IT... NOW TELL THEM! CRIME AND DISASTER AREN'T INCLINED TO OBSERVE HOLIDAYS!
TONIGHT IS GOING TO BE... DIFFERENT! I KNOW IT!
HE SOUNDS ALMOST INSPIRED.. BUT NOTHING EVER HAPPENS BY JUST SAYING IT!
C'MON, BATMAN-- HOW ABOUT CONTRIBUTING YOUR DEEP VOCAL CHORDS TO SOME CHRISTMAS CAROLS!
WHY NOT? I CAN ENJOY MYSELF UNTIL SOMETHING HAPPENS...
Jingle bells, Jingle bells, Jingle all the way! Oh what fun it is to ride In a one-horse open sleigh...
OH,

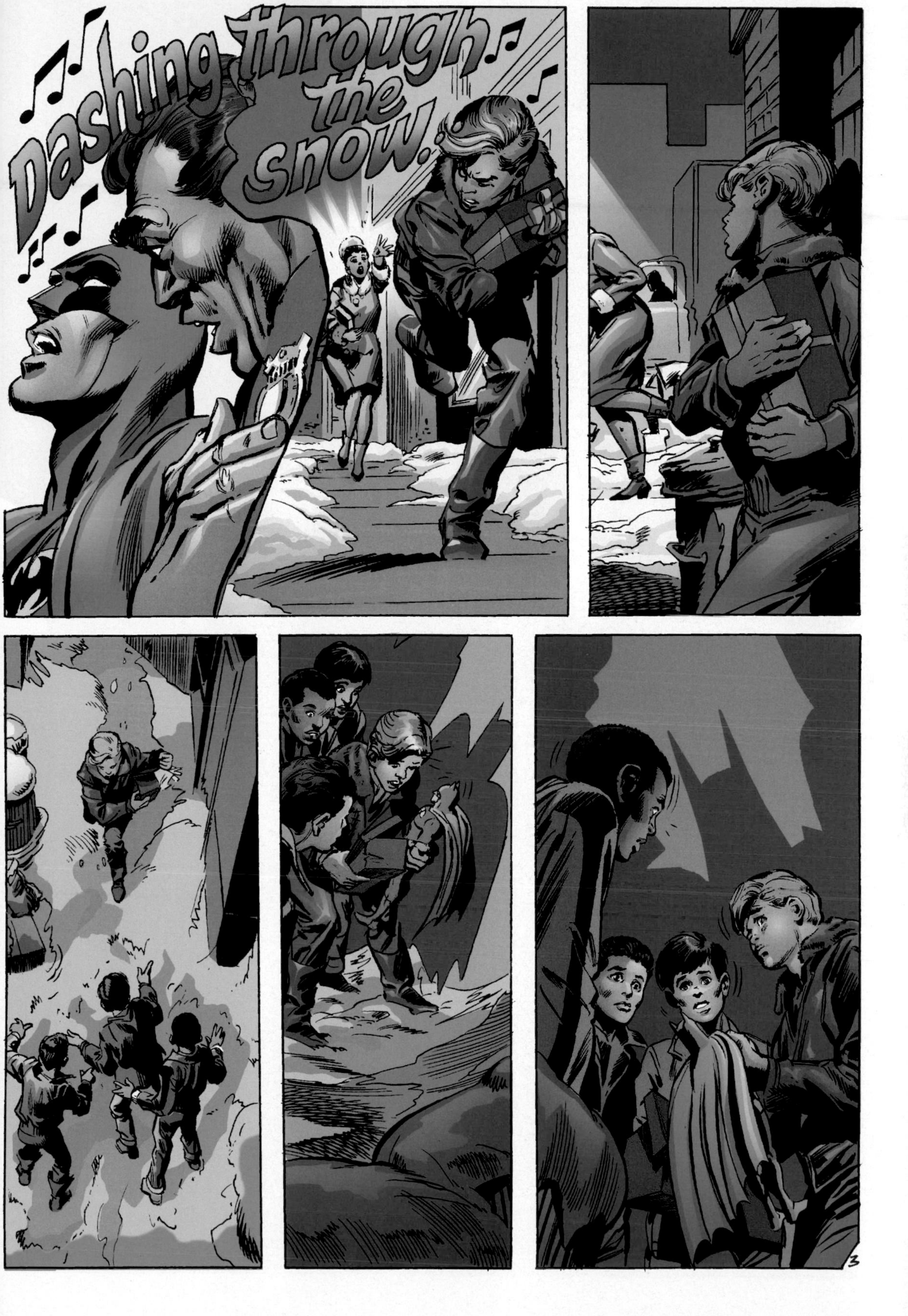
Dashing through the snow.

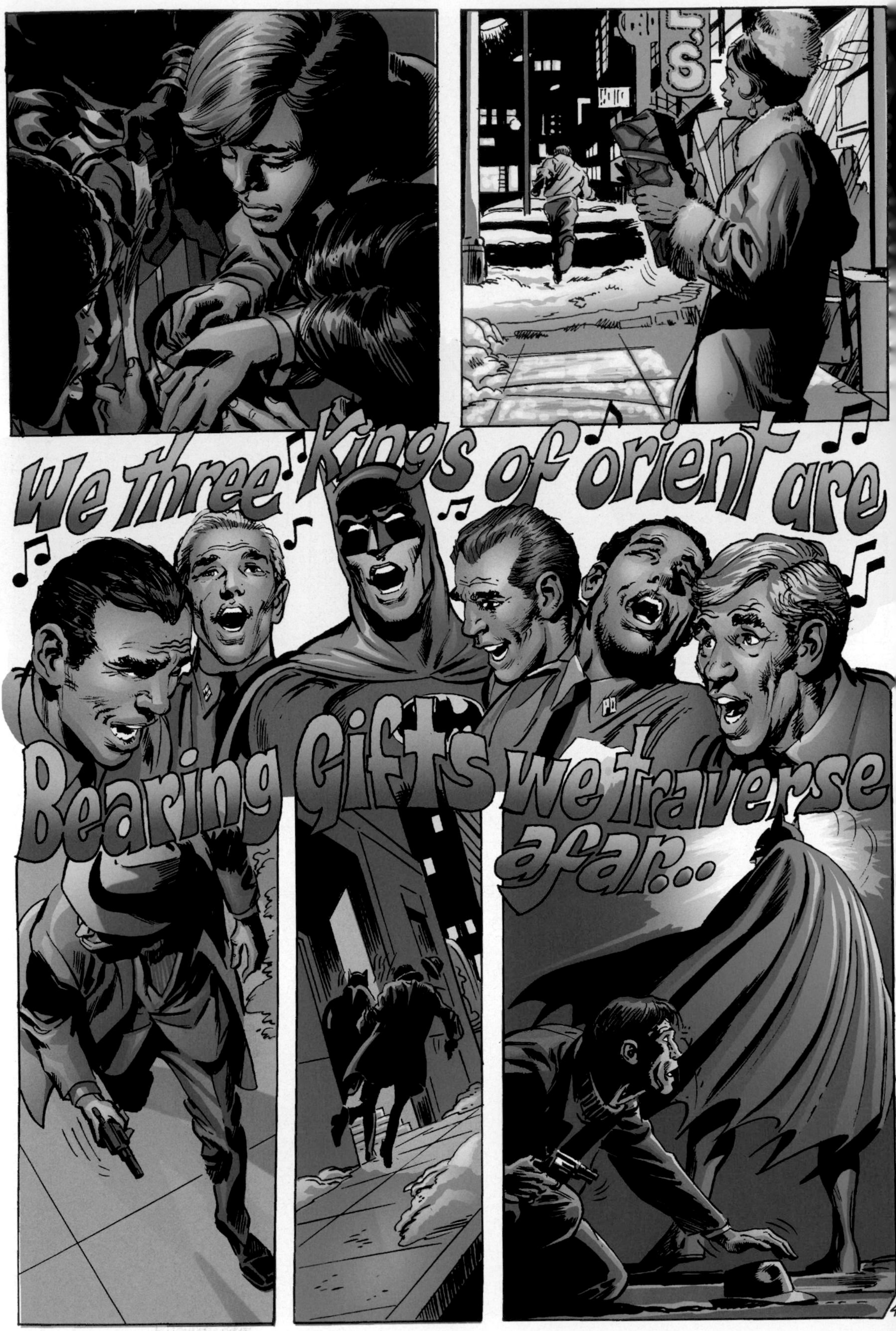
We three Kings of orient are
Bearing Gifts we traverse afar...

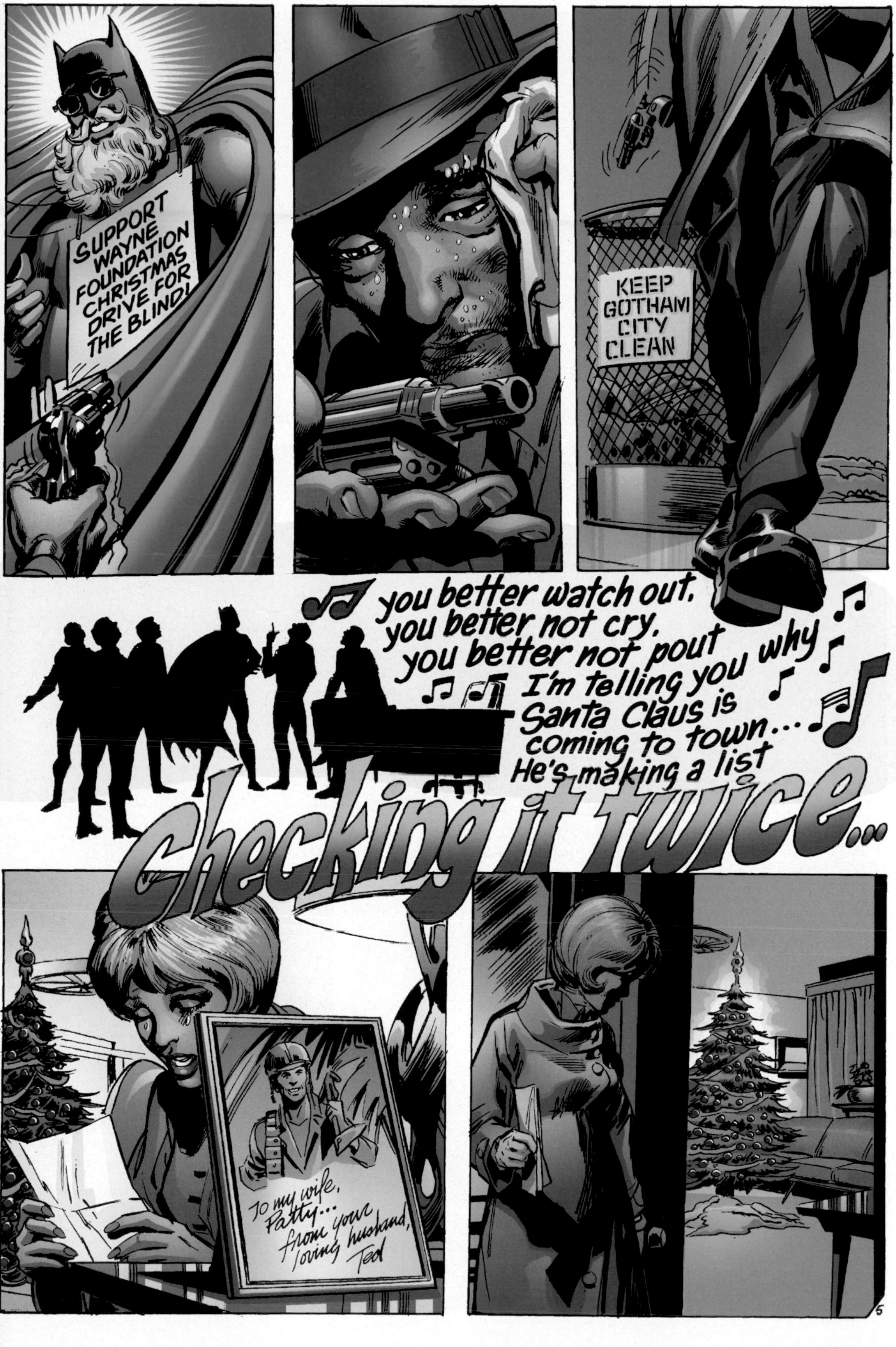
SUPPORT WAYNE FOUNDATION CHRISTMAS DRIVE FOR THE BLIND!
KEEP GOTHAM CITY CLEAN
you better watch out, you better not cry, you better not pout I'm telling you why Santa Claus is coming to town... He's making a list
Checking it twice...
To my wife, Patty... from your loving husband, Ted

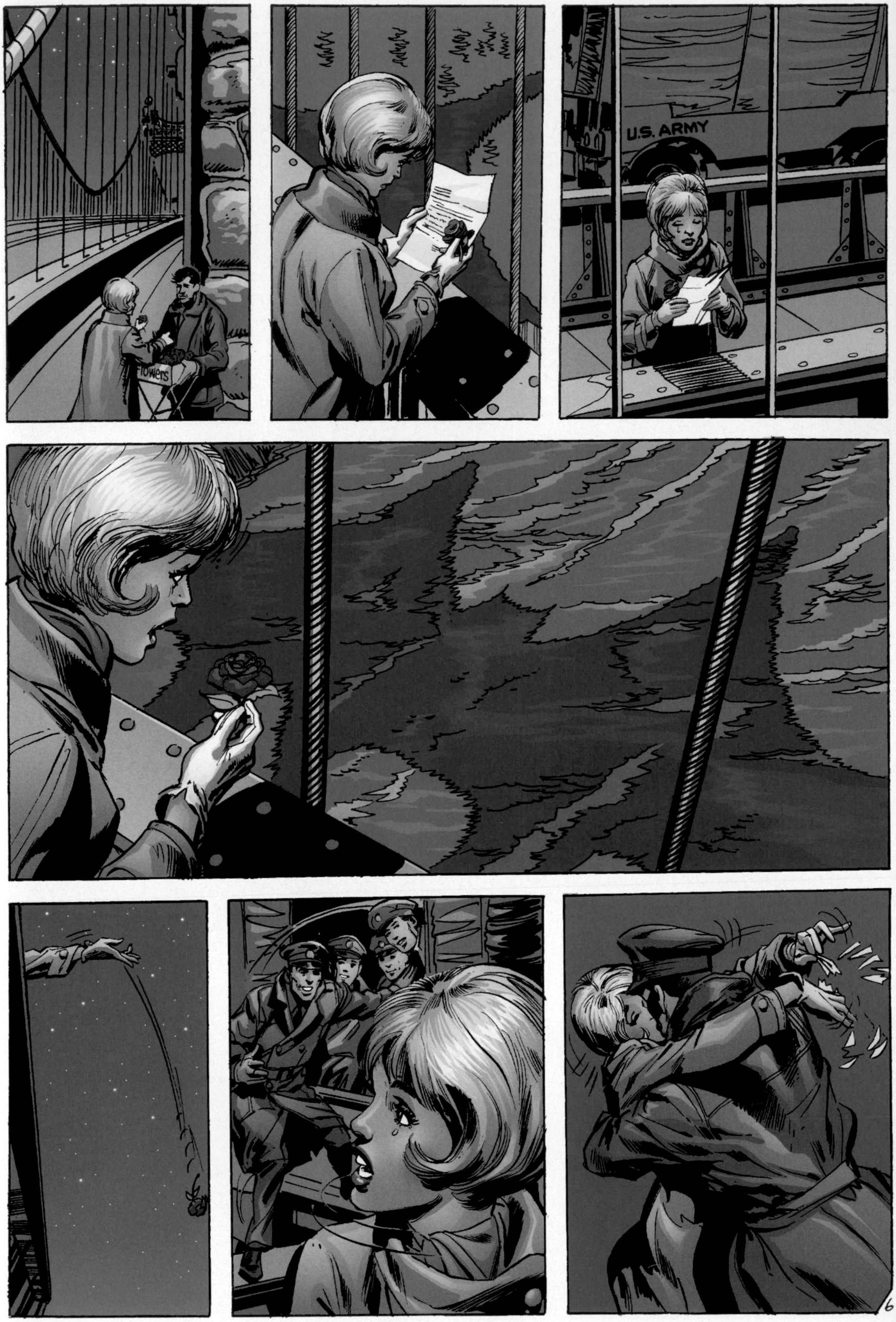
Flowers
U.S. ARMY

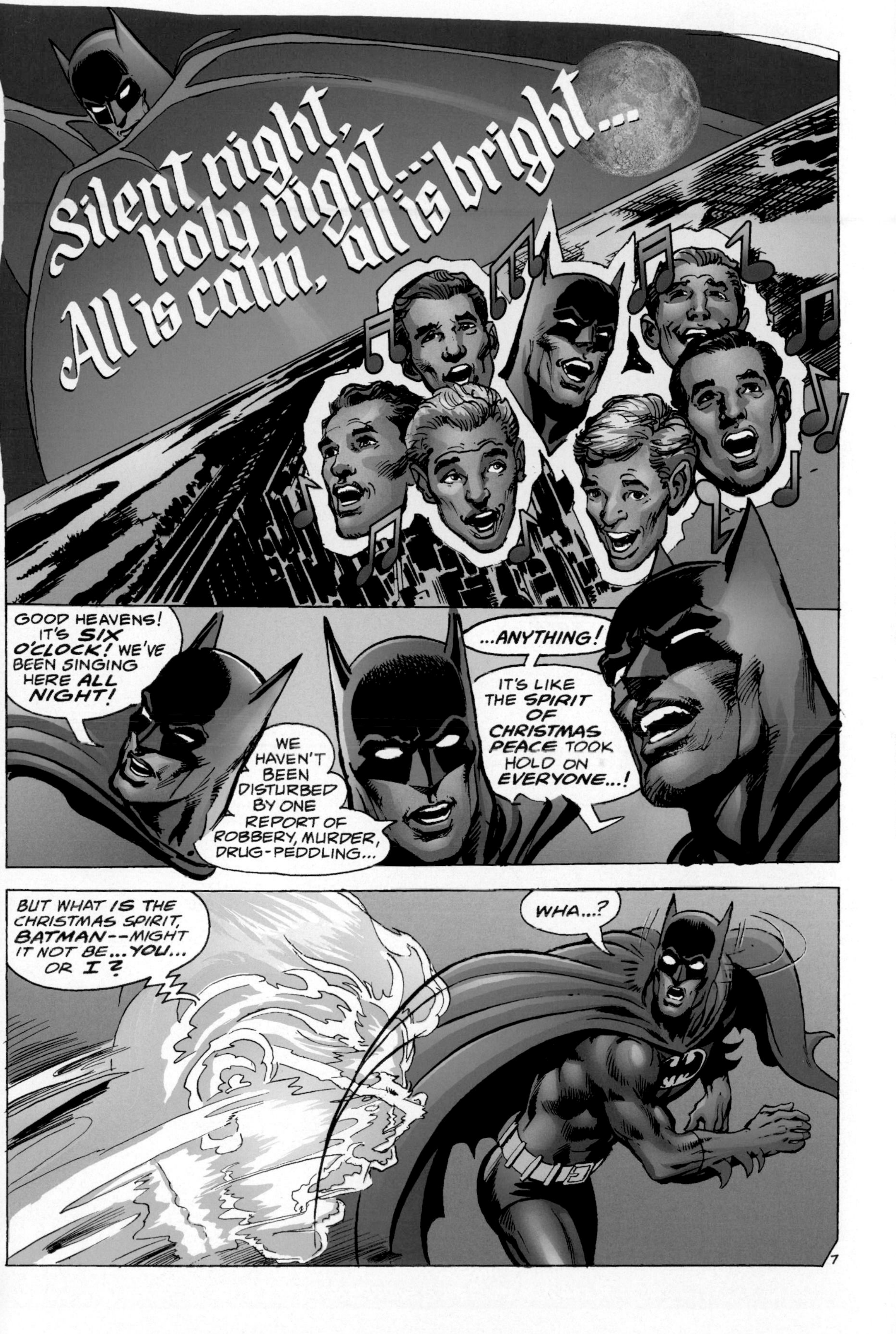
Silent night, holy night... All is calm, all is bright...
GOOD HEAVENS! IT'S SIX O'CLOCK! WE'VE BEEN SINGING HERE ALL NIGHT!
WE HAVEN'T BEEN DISTURBED BY ONE REPORT OF ROBBERY, MURDER, DRUG-PEDDLING...
...ANYTHING!
IT'S LIKE THE SPIRIT OF CHRISTMAS PEACE TOOK HOLD ON EVERYONE...!
BUT WHAT IS THE CHRISTMAS SPIRIT, BATMAN--MIGHT IT NOT BE...YOU... OR I?
WHA...?

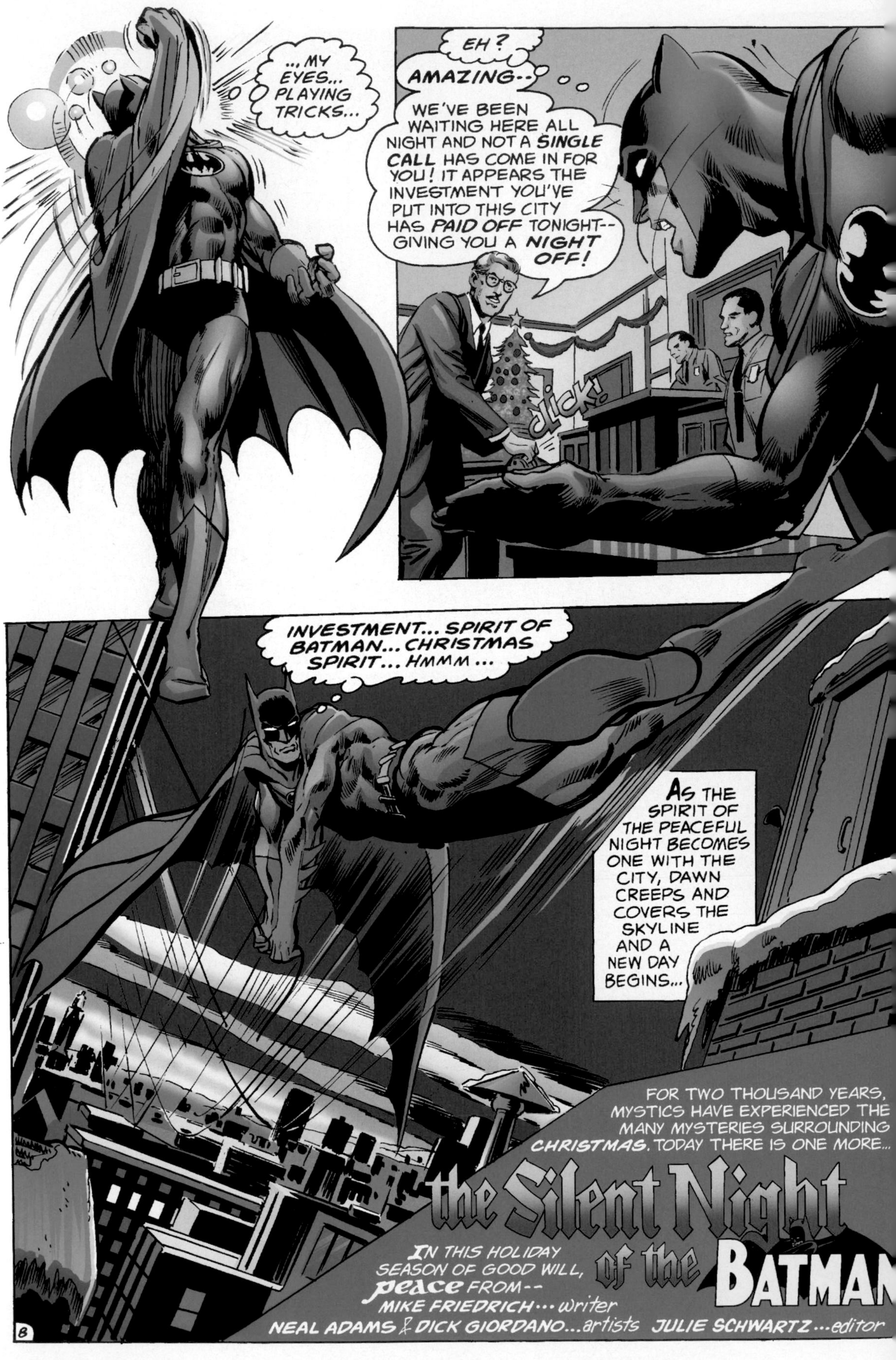
...MY EYES... PLAYING TRICKS...
EH? AMAZING--
WE'VE BEEN WAITING HERE ALL NIGHT AND NOT A SINGLE CALL HAS COME IN FOR YOU! IT APPEARS THE INVESTMENT YOU'VE PUT INTO THIS CITY HAS PAID OFF TONIGHT-- GIVING YOU A NIGHT OFF!
CLICK!
INVESTMENT... SPIRIT OF BATMAN... CHRISTMAS SPIRIT... HMMM...
AS THE SPIRIT OF THE PEACEFUL NIGHT BECOMES ONE WITH THE CITY, DAWN CREEPS AND COVERS THE SKYLINE AND A NEW DAY BEGINS...
FOR TWO THOUSAND YEARS, MYSTICS HAVE EXPERIENCED THE MANY MYSTERIES SURROUNDING CHRISTMAS. TODAY THERE IS ONE MORE...
the Silent Night of the BATMAN
IN THIS HOLIDAY SEASON OF GOOD WILL, peace FROM--
MIKE FRIEDRICH... writer
NEAL ADAMS & DICK GIORDANO...artists JULIE SCHWARTZ...editor
8

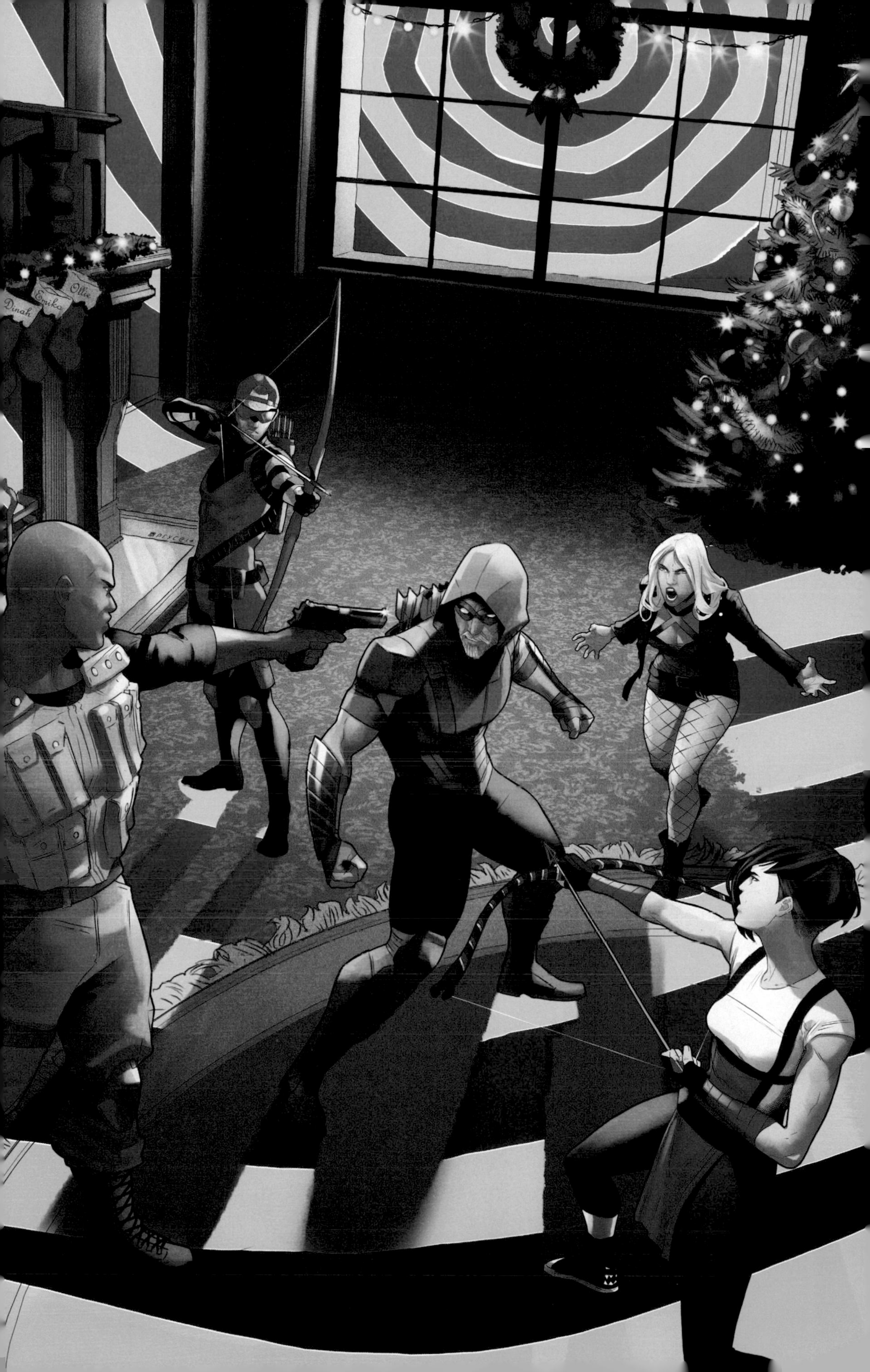
Dinah
Emiko
Ollie

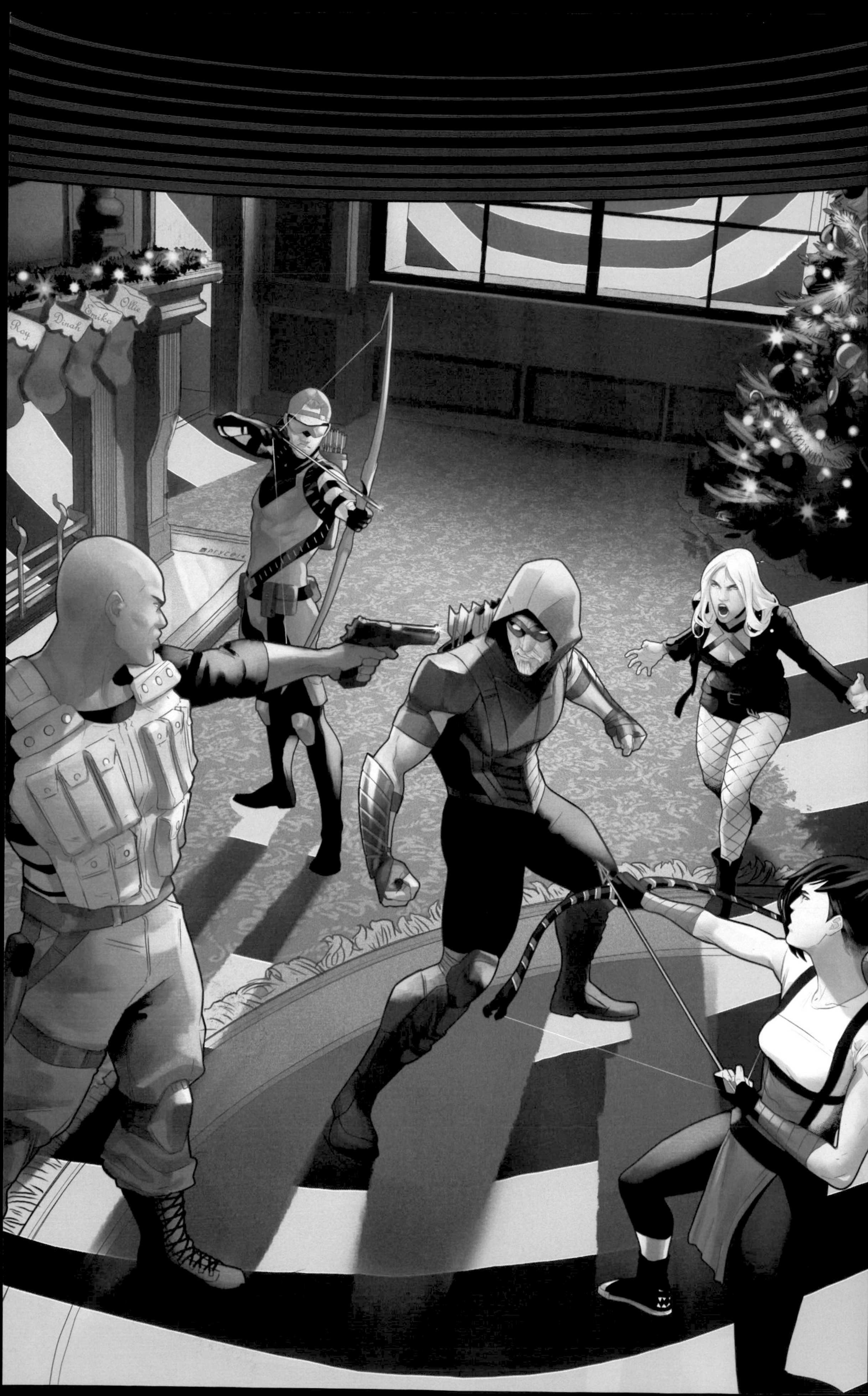
Roy
Dinah
Emiko
Ollie

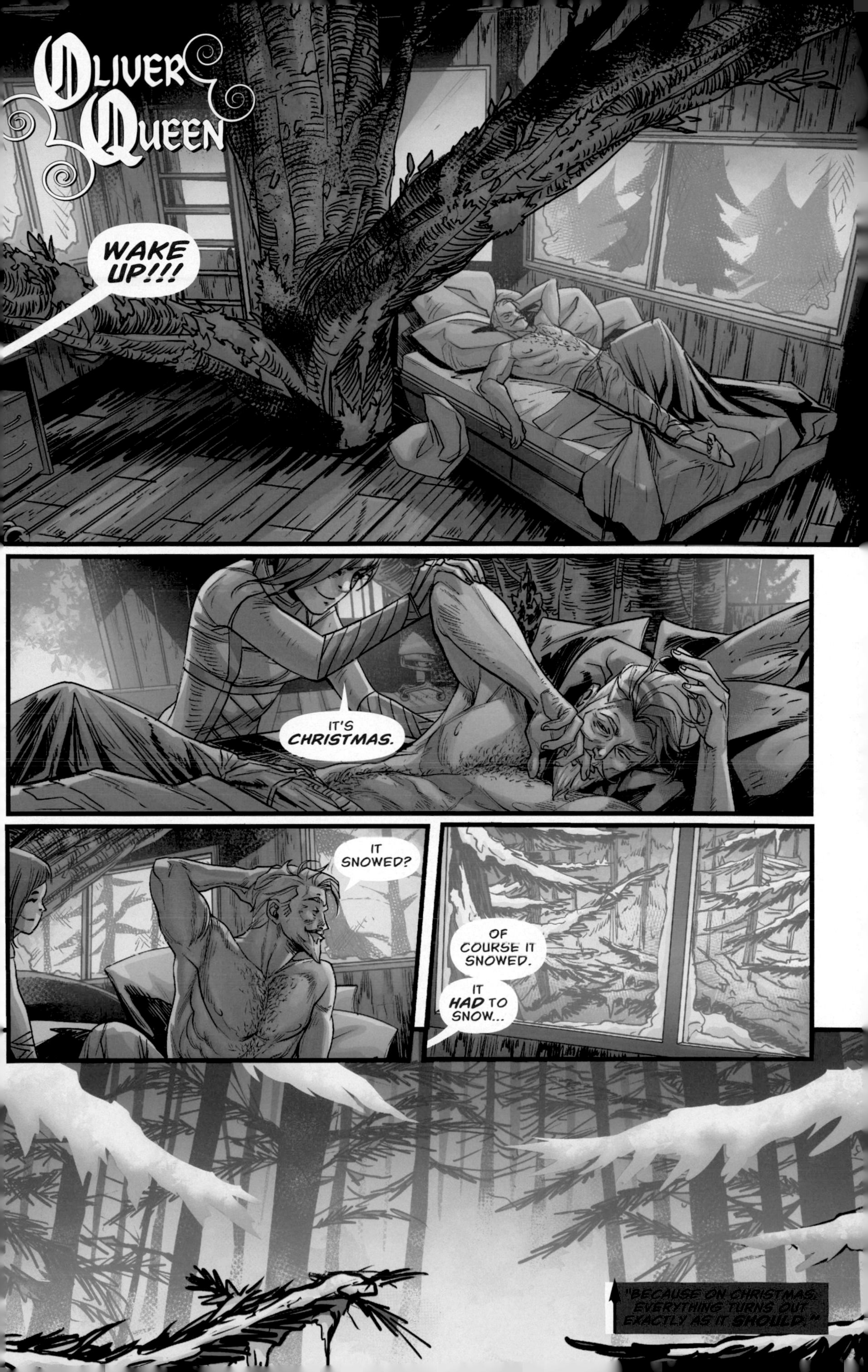
Oliver Queen
WAKE UP!!!
IT'S CHRISTMAS.
IT SNOWED?
OF COURSE IT SNOWED.
IT HAD TO SNOW...
"BECAUSE ON CHRISTMAS, EVERYTHING TURNS OUT EXACTLY AS IT SHOULD."

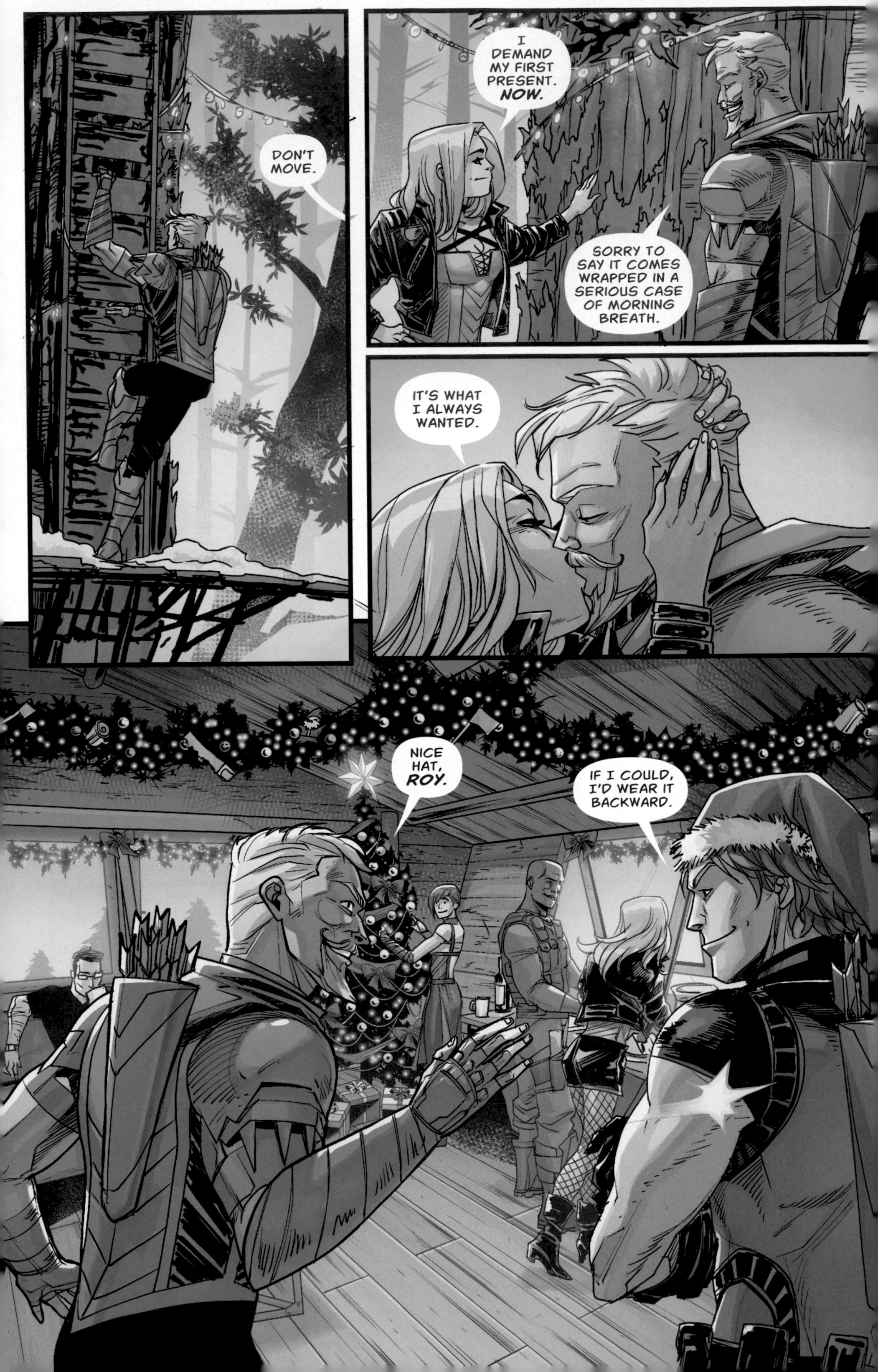
DON'T MOVE.
I DEMAND MY FIRST PRESENT. NOW.
SORRY TO SAY IT COMES WRAPPED IN A SERIOUS CASE OF MORNING BREATH.
IT'S WHAT I ALWAYS WANTED.
NICE HAT, ROY.
IF I COULD, I'D WEAR IT BACKWARD.

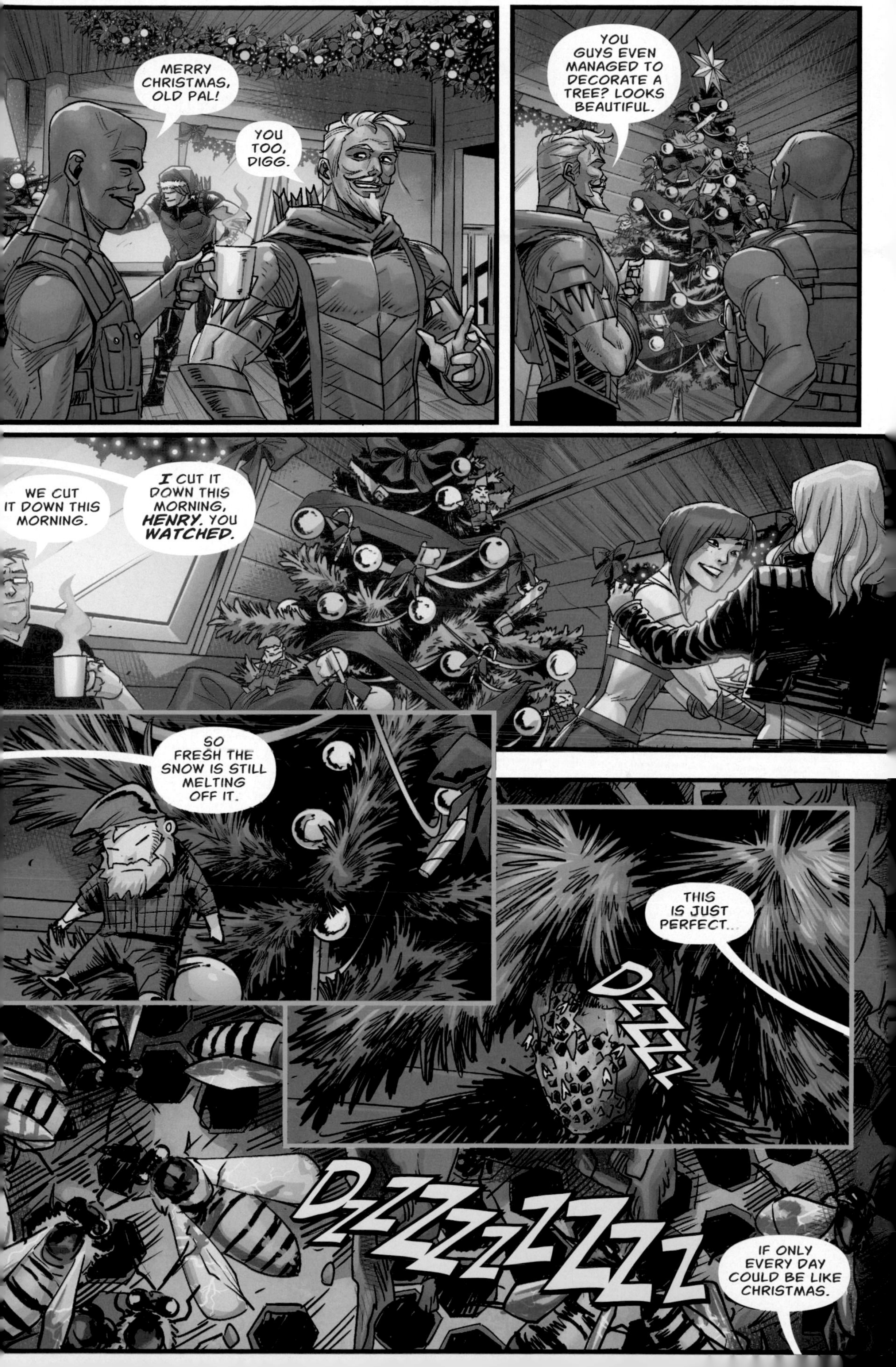
MERRY CHRISTMAS, OLD PAL!
YOU TOO, DIGG.
YOU GUYS EVEN MANAGED TO DECORATE A TREE? LOOKS BEAUTIFUL.
WE CUT IT DOWN THIS MORNING.
I CUT IT DOWN THIS MORNING, HENRY. YOU WATCHED.
SO FRESH THE SNOW IS STILL MELTING OFF IT.
THIS IS JUST PERFECT...
DZZZZ
DZZZZZZZZZ
IF ONLY EVERY DAY COULD BE LIKE CHRISTMAS.

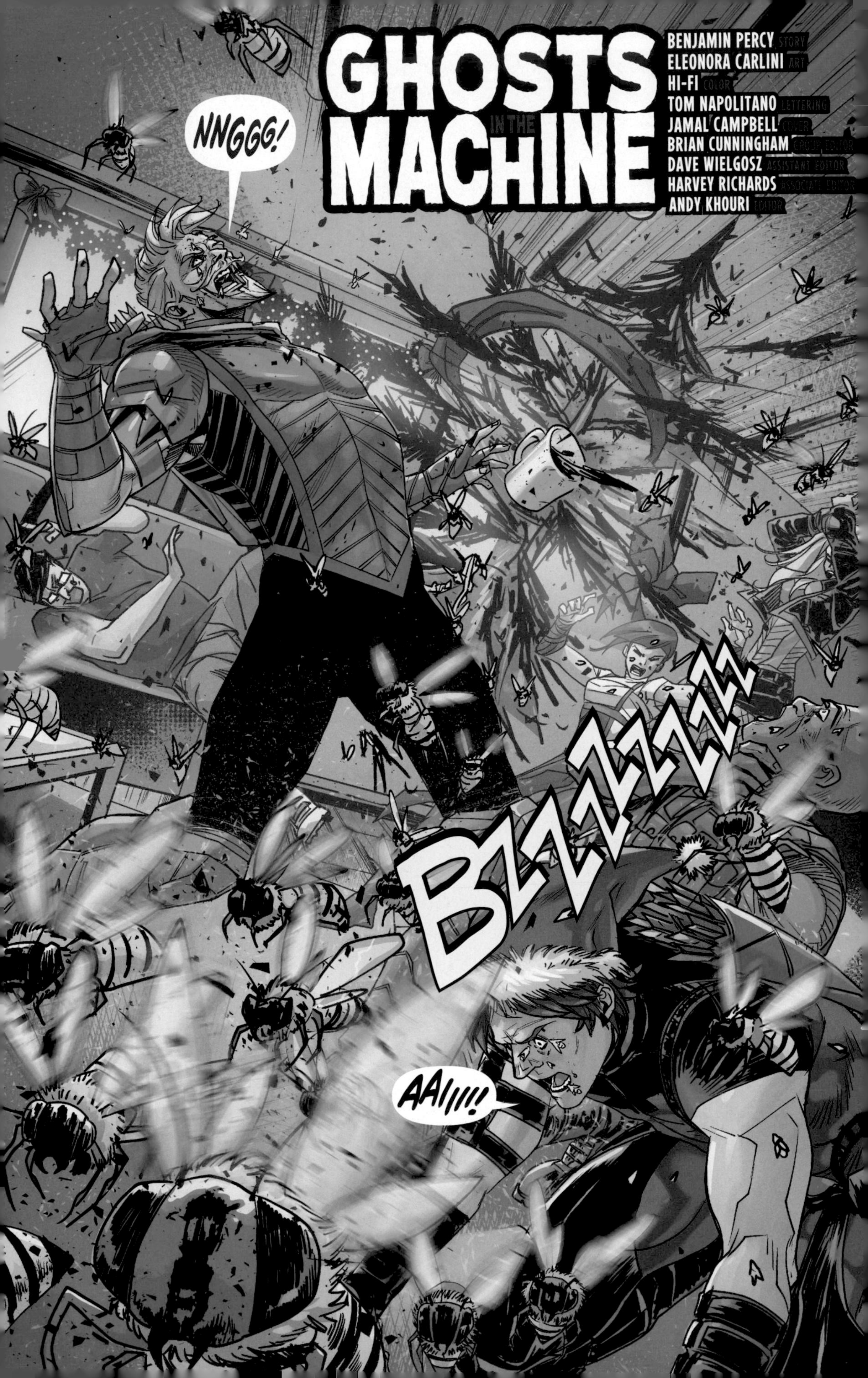
GHOSTS IN THE MACHINE
BENJAMIN PERCY STORY
ELEONORA CARLINI ART
HI-FI COLOR
TOM NAPOLITANO LETTERING
JAMAL CAMPBELL COVER
BRIAN CUNNINGHAM GROUP EDITOR
DAVE WIELGOSZ ASSISTANT EDITOR
HARVEY RICHARDS ASSOCIATE EDITOR
ANDY KHOURI EDITOR
NNGGG!
BZZZZZZZ
AAIIII!

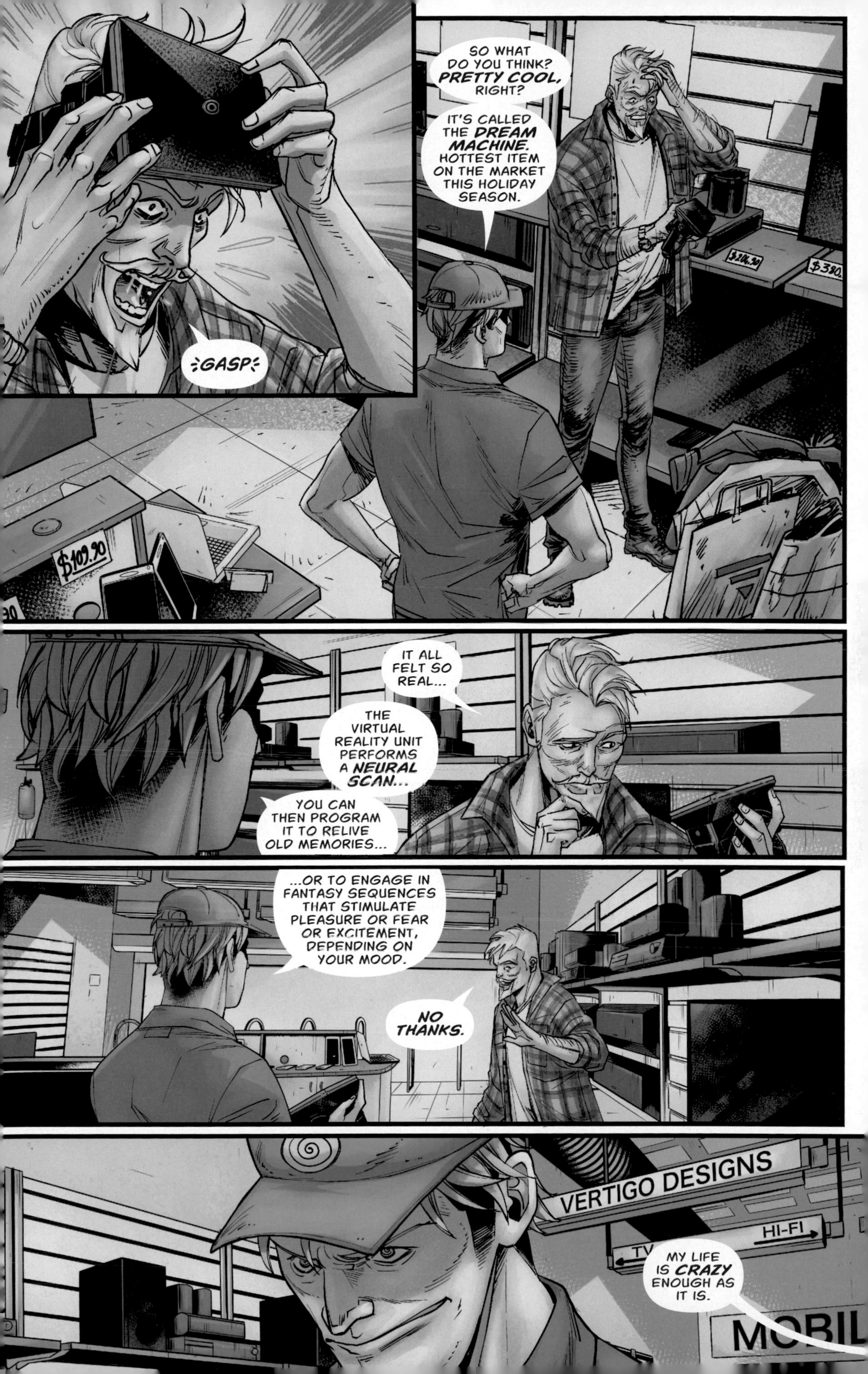

:GASP:
SO WHAT DO YOU THINK? PRETTY COOL, RIGHT?
IT'S CALLED THE DREAM MACHINE. HOTTEST ITEM ON THE MARKET THIS HOLIDAY SEASON.
$204.90
$380.
$109.90
IT ALL FELT SO REAL...
THE VIRTUAL REALITY UNIT PERFORMS A NEURAL SCAN...
YOU CAN THEN PROGRAM IT TO RELIVE OLD MEMORIES...
...OR TO ENGAGE IN FANTASY SEQUENCES THAT STIMULATE PLEASURE OR FEAR OR EXCITEMENT, DEPENDING ON YOUR MOOD.
NO THANKS.
VERTIGO DESIGNS
HI-FI
TV
MY LIFE IS CRAZY ENOUGH AS IT IS.
MOBIL

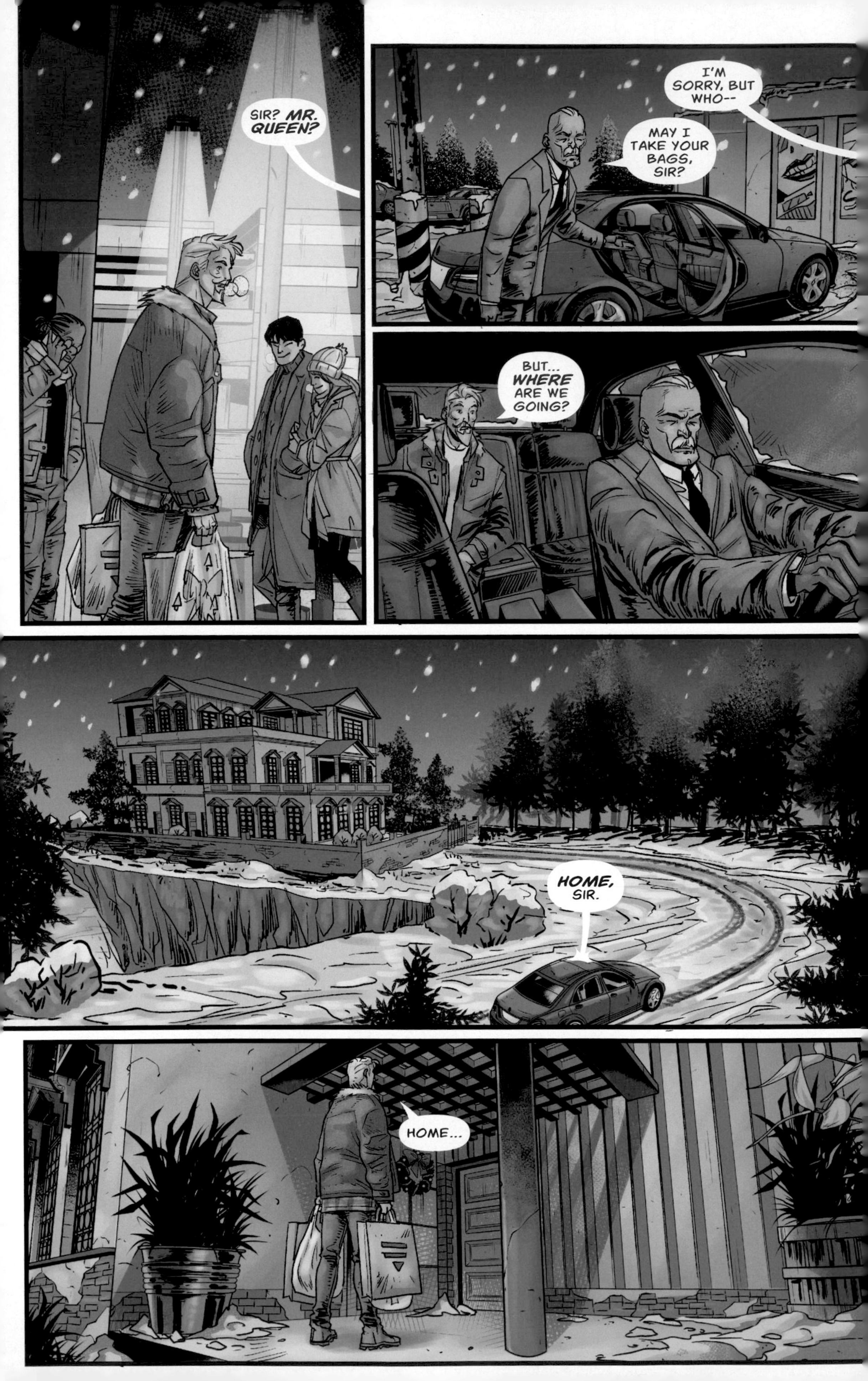
SIR? MR. QUEEN?
I'M SORRY, BUT WHO--
MAY I TAKE YOUR BAGS, SIR?
BUT... WHERE ARE WE GOING?
HOME, SIR.
HOME...

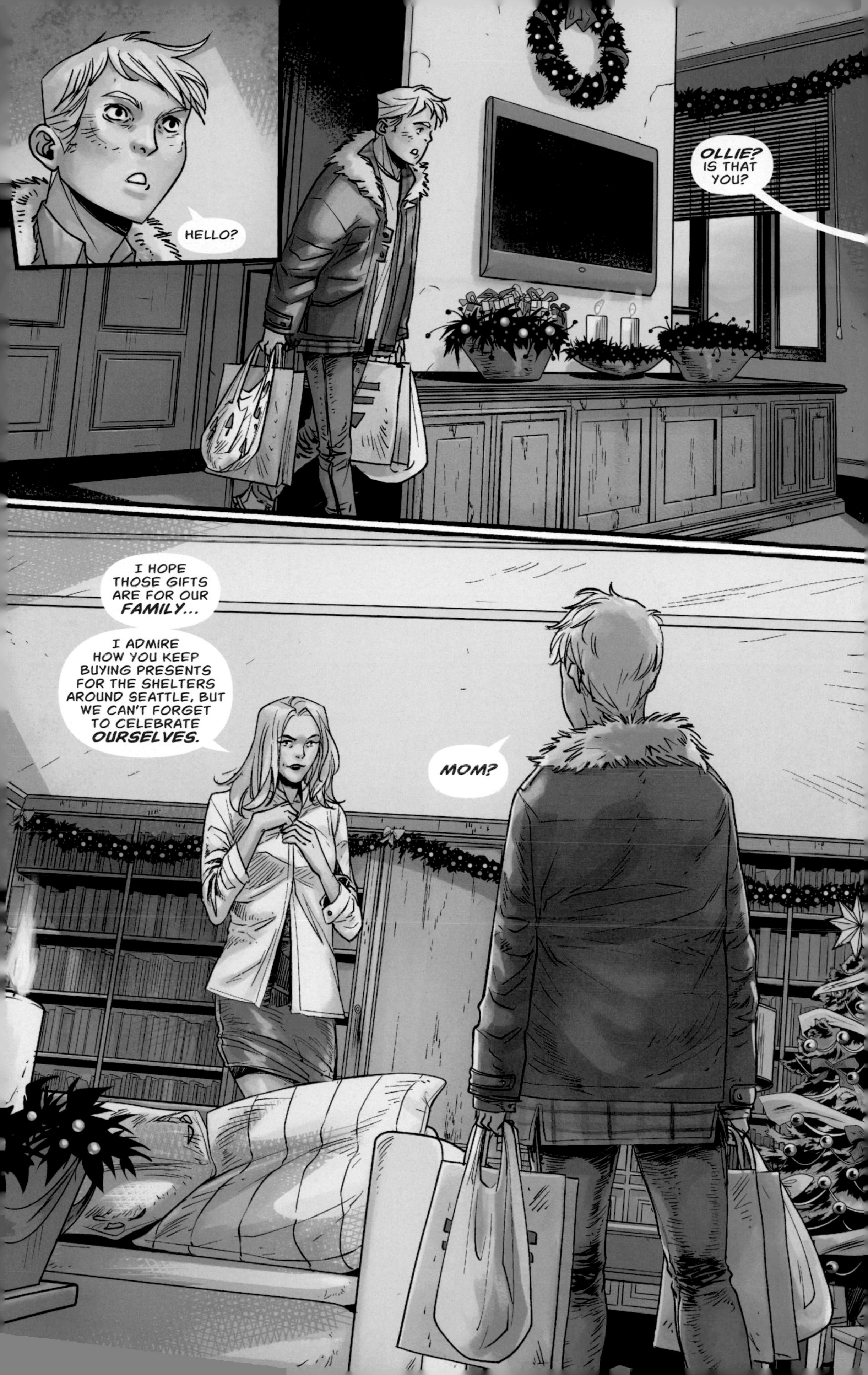
HELLO?
OLLIE? IS THAT YOU?
I HOPE THOSE GIFTS ARE FOR OUR FAMILY...
I ADMIRE HOW YOU KEEP BUYING PRESENTS FOR THE SHELTERS AROUND SEATTLE, BUT WE CAN'T FORGET TO CELEBRATE OURSELVES.
MOM?

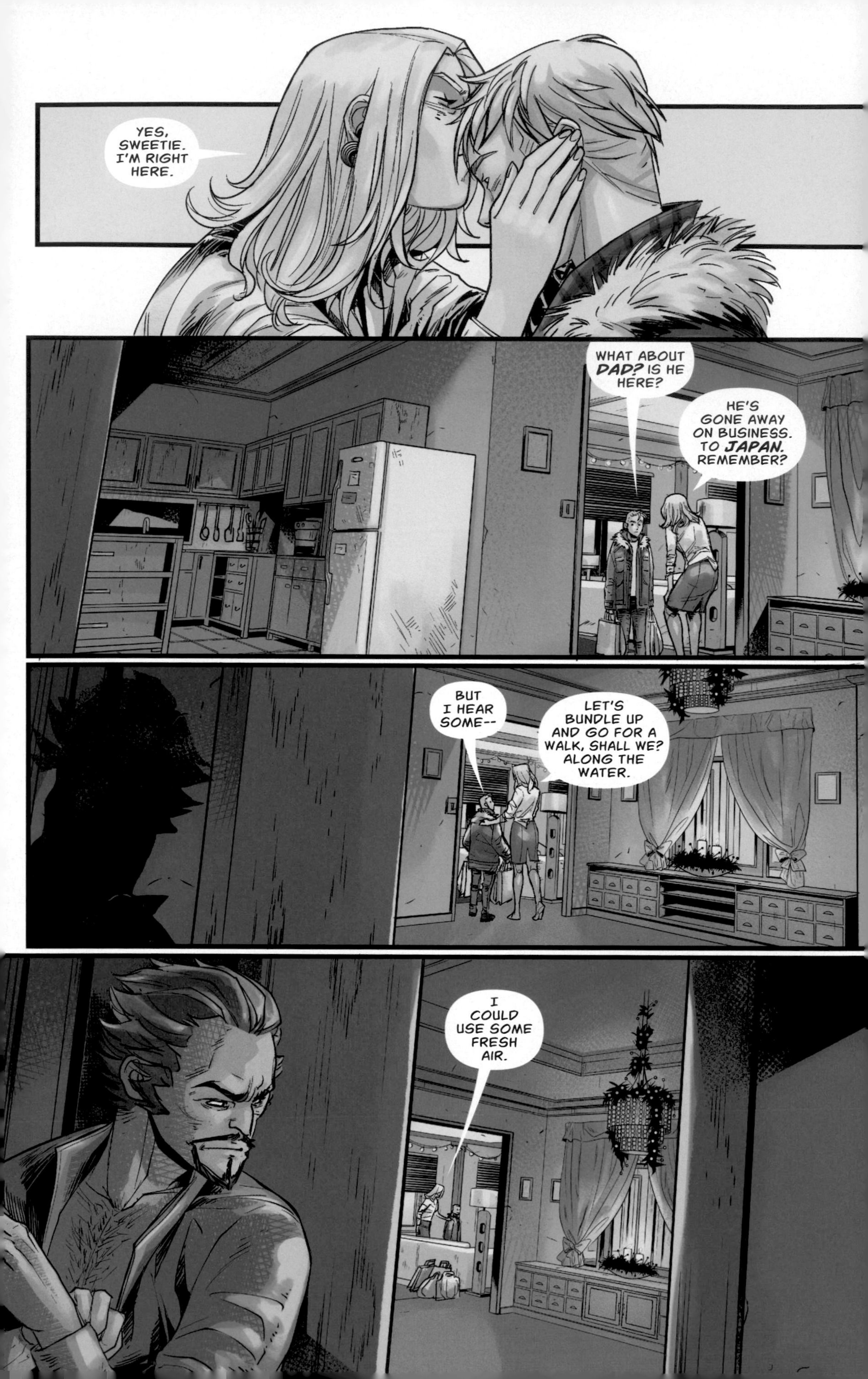
YES, SWEETIE. I'M RIGHT HERE.
WHAT ABOUT DAD? IS HE HERE?
HE'S GONE AWAY ON BUSINESS. TO JAPAN. REMEMBER?
BUT I HEAR SOME--
LET'S BUNDLE UP AND GO FOR A WALK, SHALL WE? ALONG THE WATER.
I COULD USE SOME FRESH AIR.

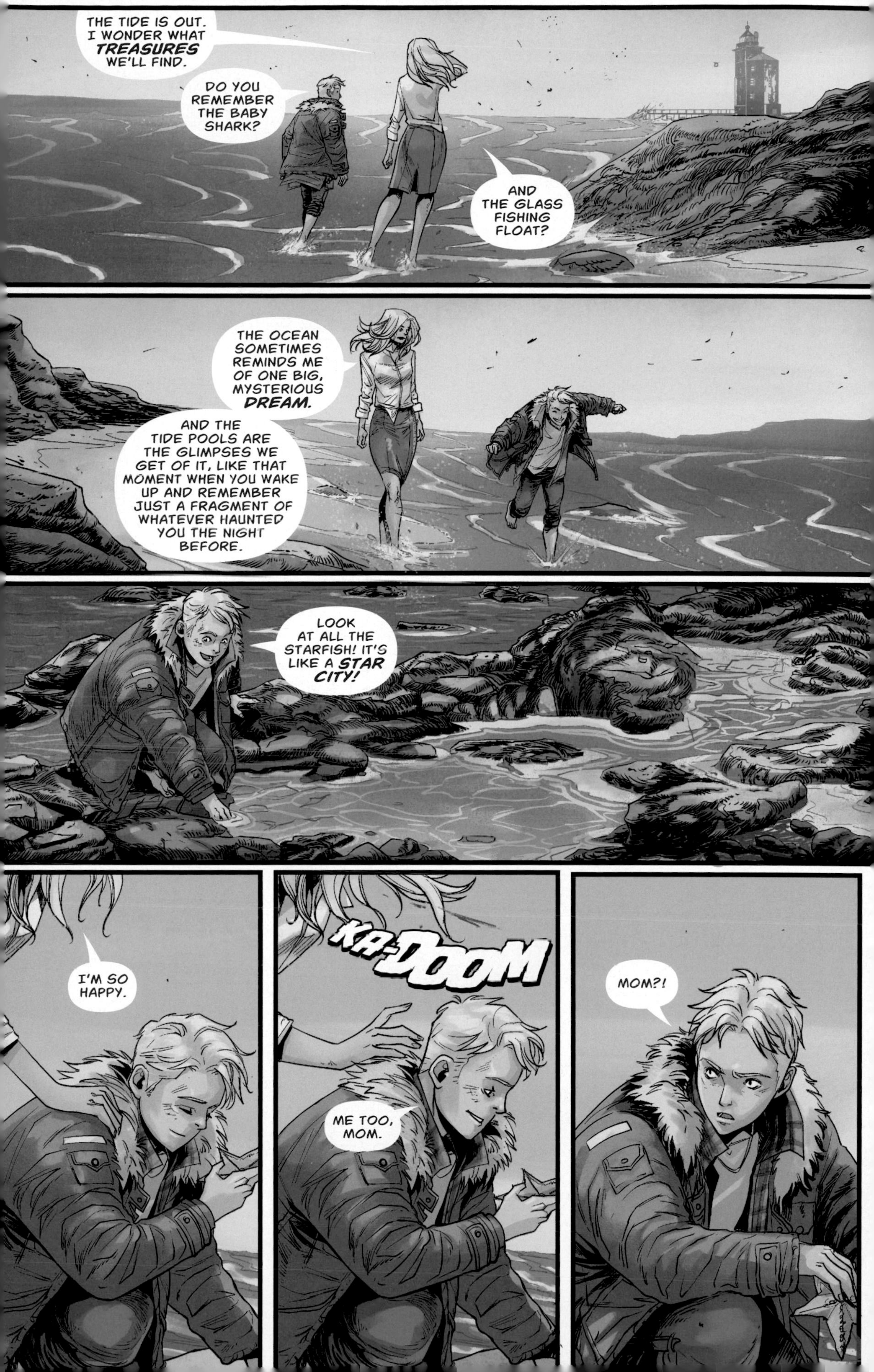
THE TIDE IS OUT. I WONDER WHAT TREASURES WE'LL FIND.
DO YOU REMEMBER THE BABY SHARK?
AND THE GLASS FISHING FLOAT?
THE OCEAN SOMETIMES REMINDS ME OF ONE BIG, MYSTERIOUS DREAM.
AND THE TIDE POOLS ARE THE GLIMPSES WE GET OF IT, LIKE THAT MOMENT WHEN YOU WAKE UP AND REMEMBER JUST A FRAGMENT OF WHATEVER HAUNTED YOU THE NIGHT BEFORE.
LOOK AT ALL THE STARFISH! IT'S LIKE A STAR CITY!
I'M SO HAPPY.
KA-DOOM
ME TOO, MOM.
MOM?!

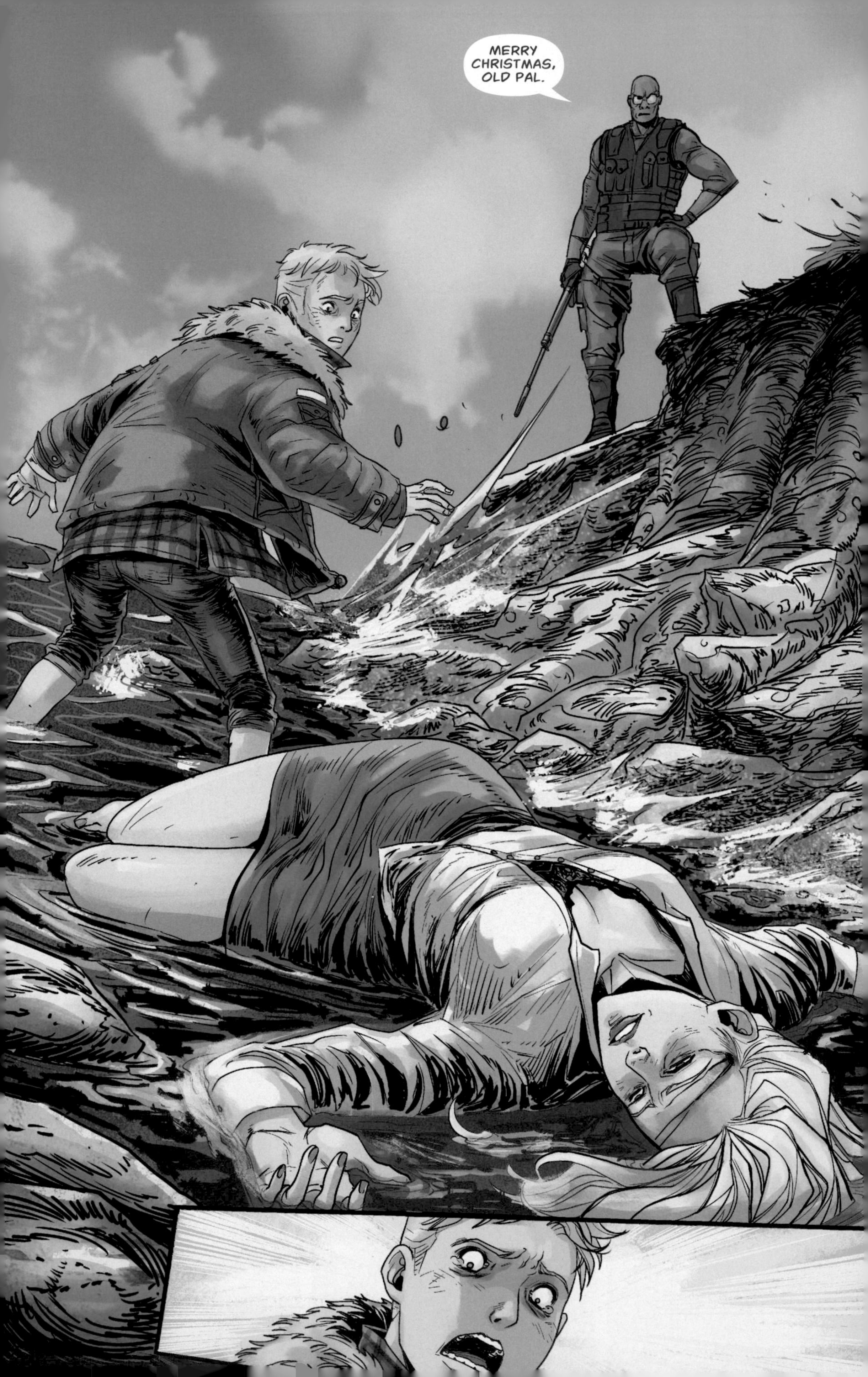
MERRY CHRISTMAS, OLD PAL.

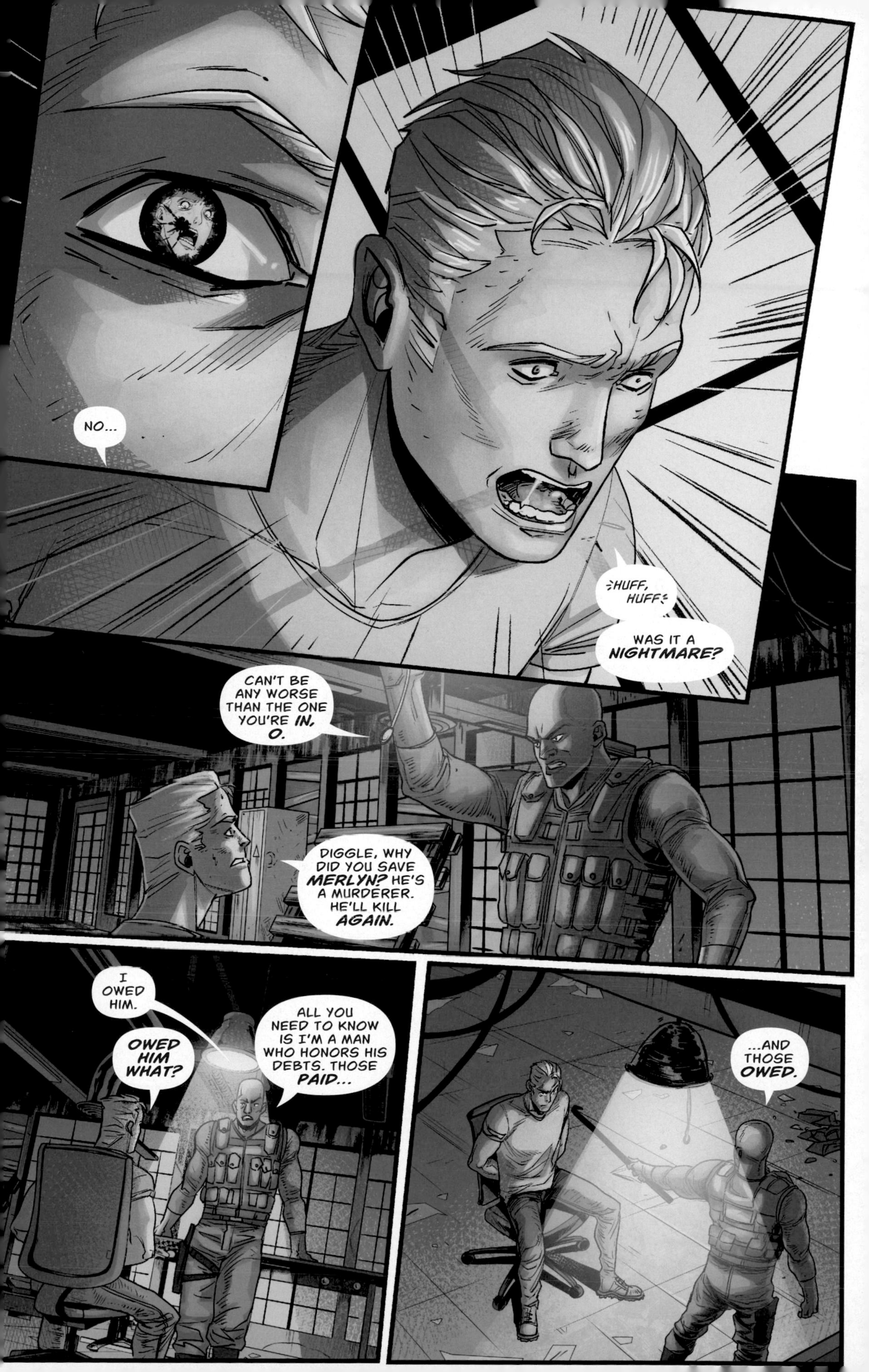
NO...
HUFF, HUFF
WAS IT A NIGHTMARE?
CAN'T BE ANY WORSE THAN THE ONE YOU'RE IN, O.
DIGGLE, WHY DID YOU SAVE MERLYN? HE'S A MURDERER. HE'LL KILL AGAIN.
I OWED HIM.
OWED HIM WHAT?
ALL YOU NEED TO KNOW IS I'M A MAN WHO HONORS HIS DEBTS. THOSE PAID...
...AND THOSE OWED.

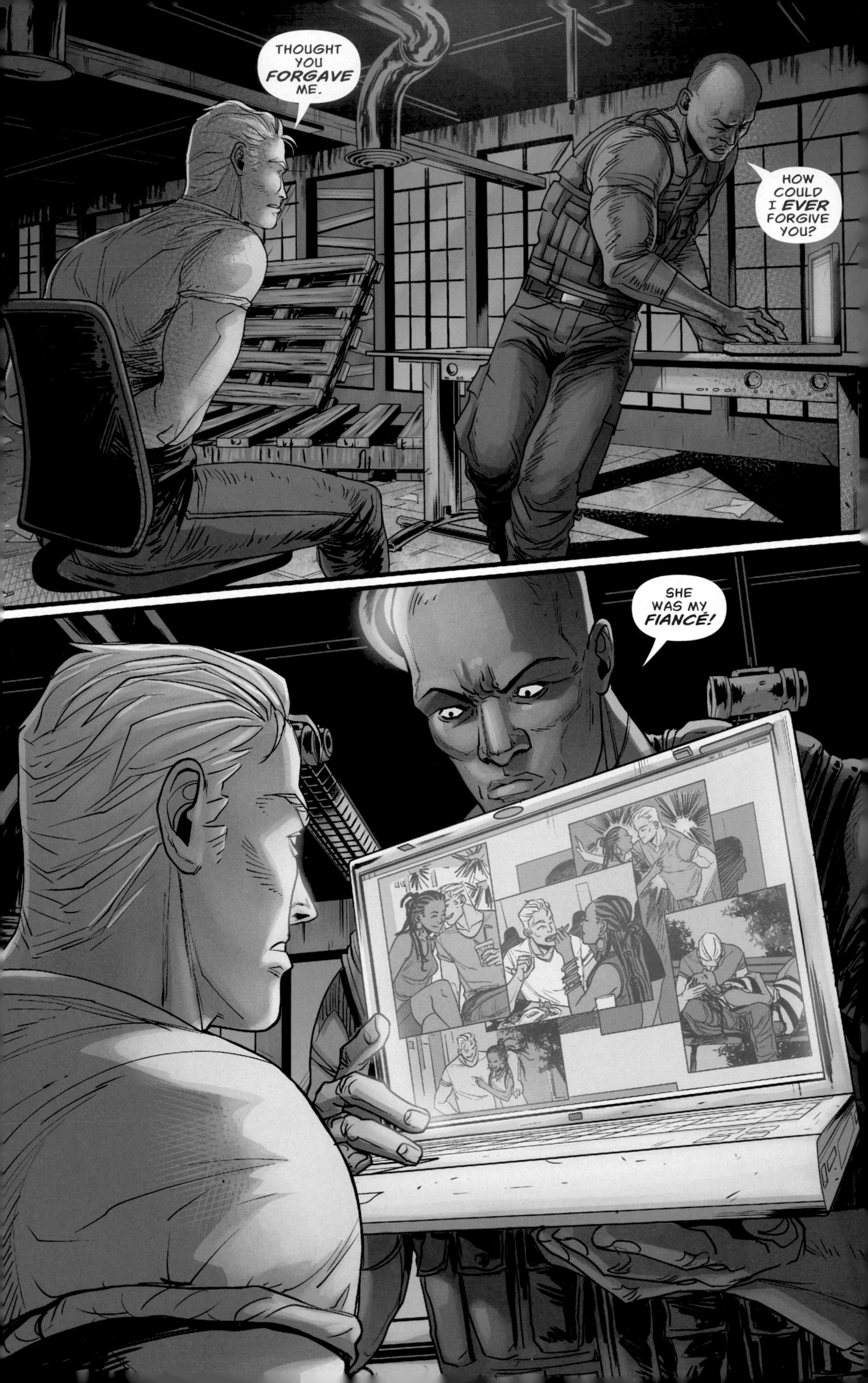
THOUGHT YOU FORGAVE ME.
HOW COULD I EVER FORGIVE YOU?
SHE WAS MY FIANCÉ!

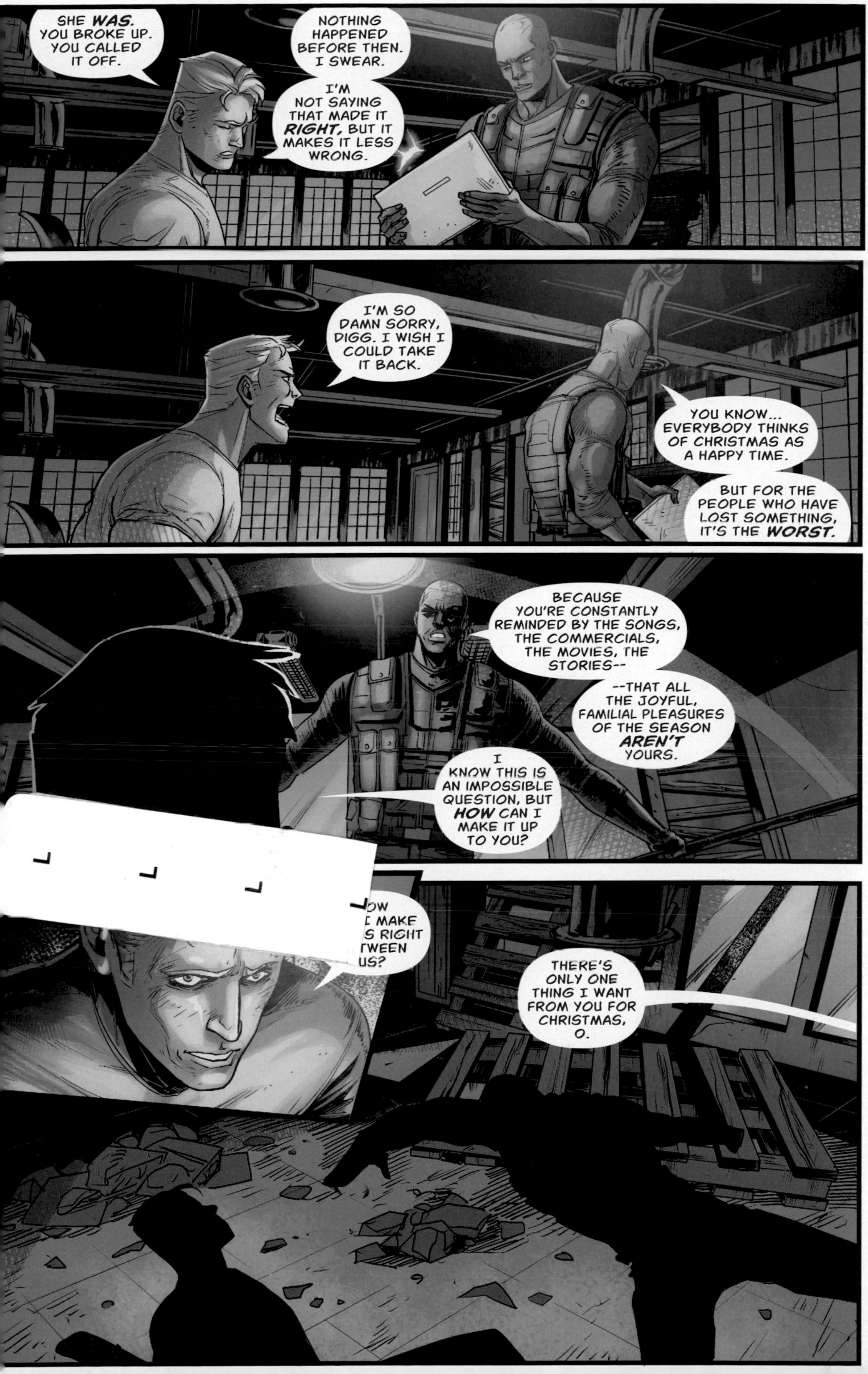
SHE WAS. YOU BROKE UP. YOU CALLED IT OFF.
NOTHING HAPPENED BEFORE THEN. I SWEAR.
I'M NOT SAYING THAT MADE IT RIGHT, BUT IT MAKES IT LESS WRONG.
I'M SO DAMN SORRY, DIGG. I WISH I COULD TAKE IT BACK.
YOU KNOW... EVERYBODY THINKS OF CHRISTMAS AS A HAPPY TIME.
BUT FOR THE PEOPLE WHO HAVE LOST SOMETHING, IT'S THE WORST.
BECAUSE YOU'RE CONSTANTLY REMINDED BY THE SONGS, THE COMMERCIALS, THE MOVIES, THE STORIES--
--THAT ALL THE JOYFUL, FAMILIAL PLEASURES OF THE SEASON AREN'T YOURS.
I KNOW THIS IS AN IMPOSSIBLE QUESTION, BUT HOW CAN I MAKE IT UP TO YOU?
THERE'S ONLY ONE THING I WANT FROM YOU FOR CHRISTMAS, O.

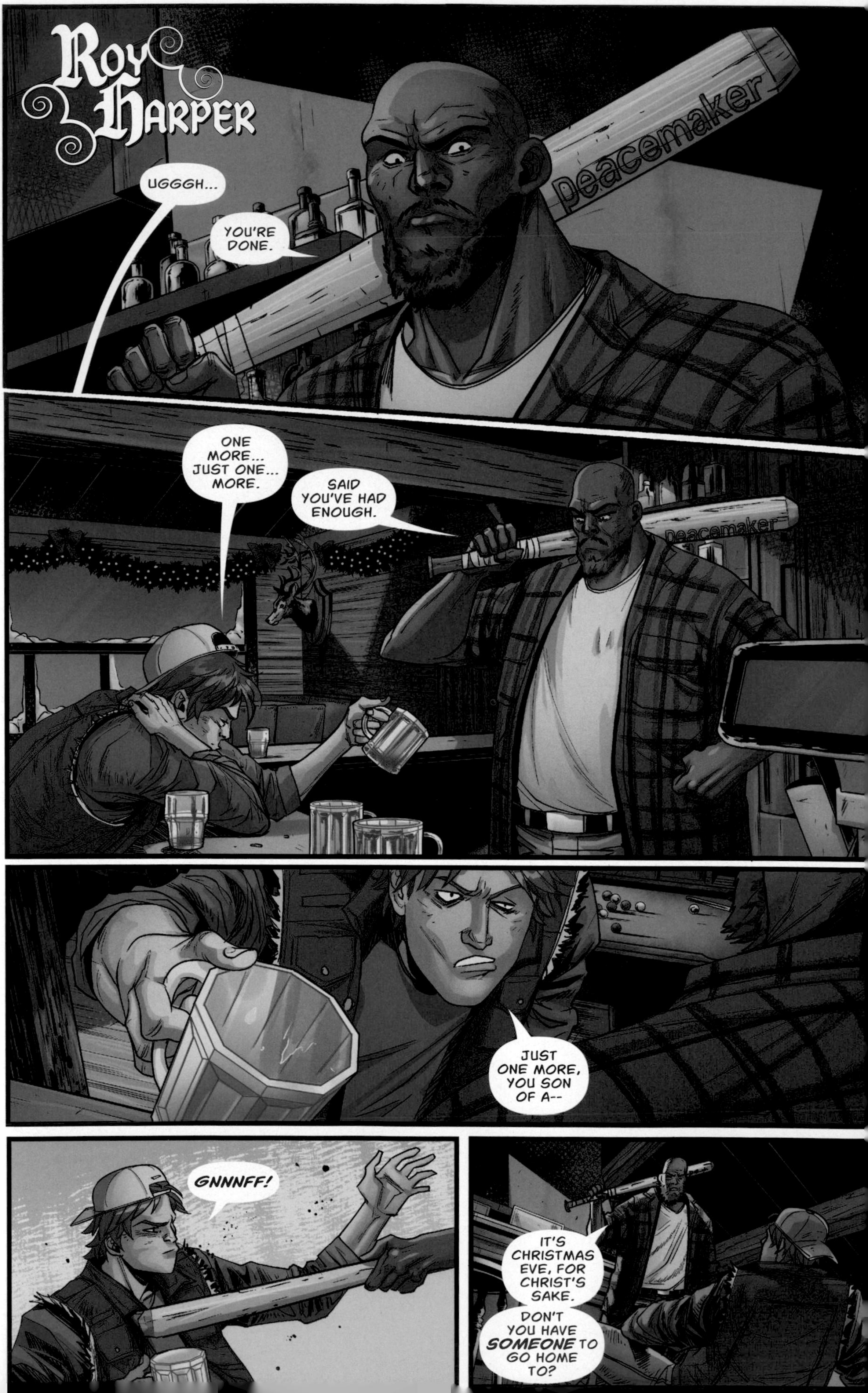
Roy Harper
UGGGH...
YOU'RE DONE.
peacemaker
ONE MORE... JUST ONE... MORE.
SAID YOU'VE HAD ENOUGH.
peacemaker
JUST ONE MORE, YOU SON OF A--
GNNNFF!
IT'S CHRISTMAS EVE, FOR CHRIST'S SAKE.
DON'T YOU HAVE SOMEONE TO GO HOME TO?

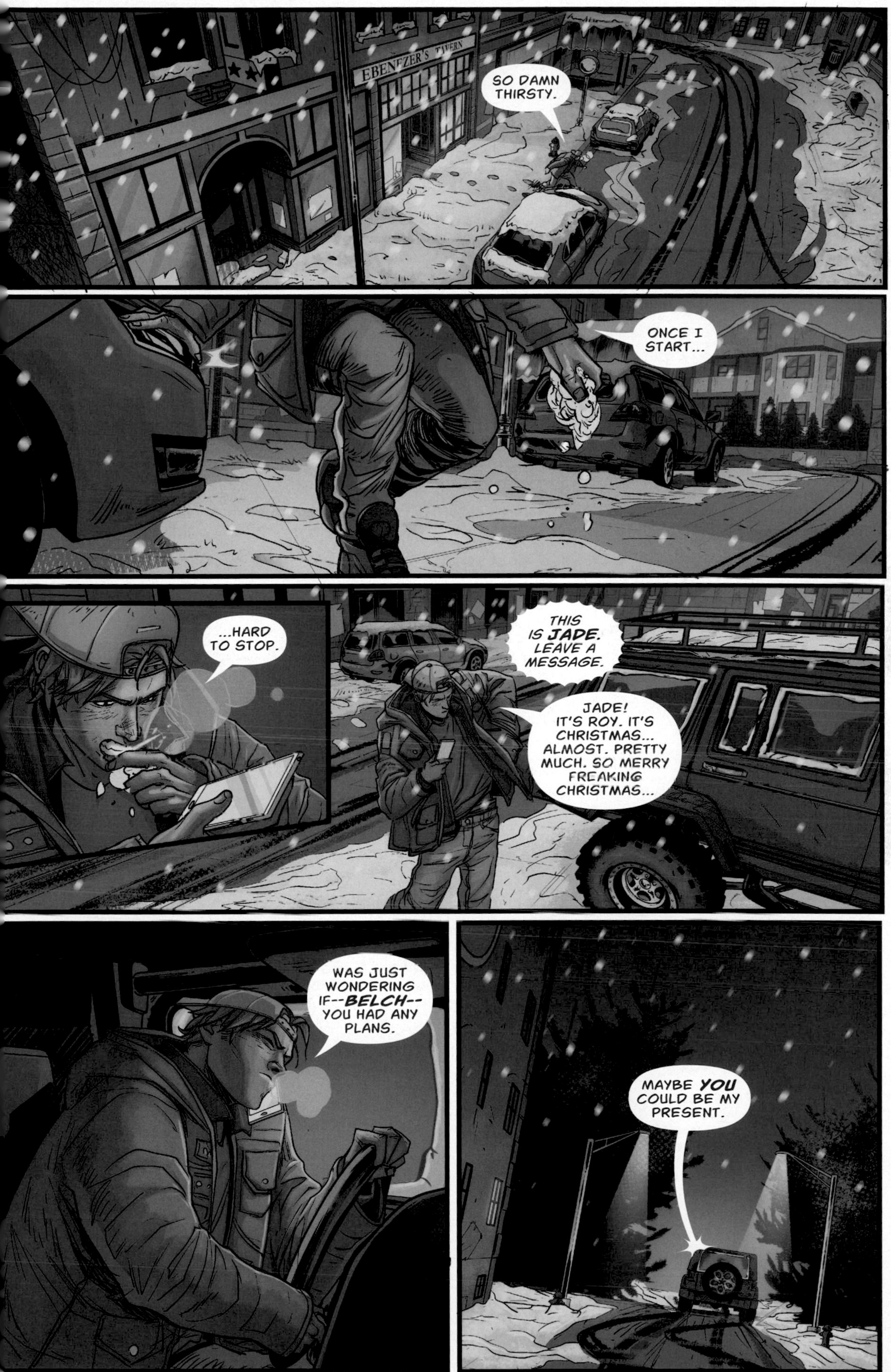

EBENEZER'S TAVERN
SO DAMN THIRSTY.
ONCE I START...
...HARD TO STOP.
THIS IS JADE. LEAVE A MESSAGE.
JADE! IT'S ROY. IT'S CHRISTMAS... ALMOST. PRETTY MUCH. SO MERRY FREAKING CHRISTMAS...
WAS JUST WONDERING IF--BELCH--YOU HAD ANY PLANS.
MAYBE YOU COULD BE MY PRESENT.

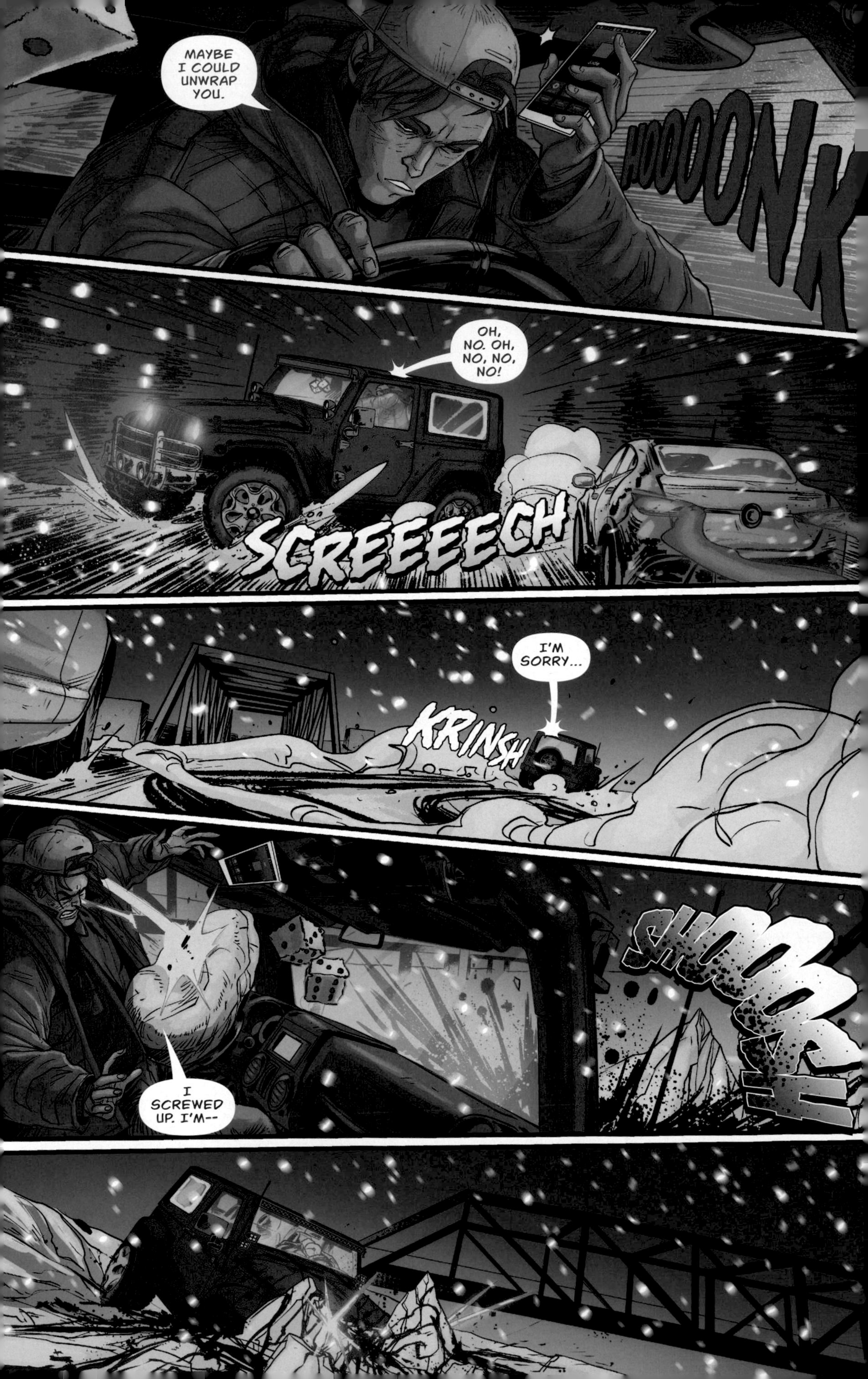
MAYBE I COULD UNWRAP YOU.
HOOOONK
OH, NO. OH, NO, NO, NO!
SCREEEEECH
I'M SORRY...
KRINSH
SHOOOM
I SCREWED UP. I'M--

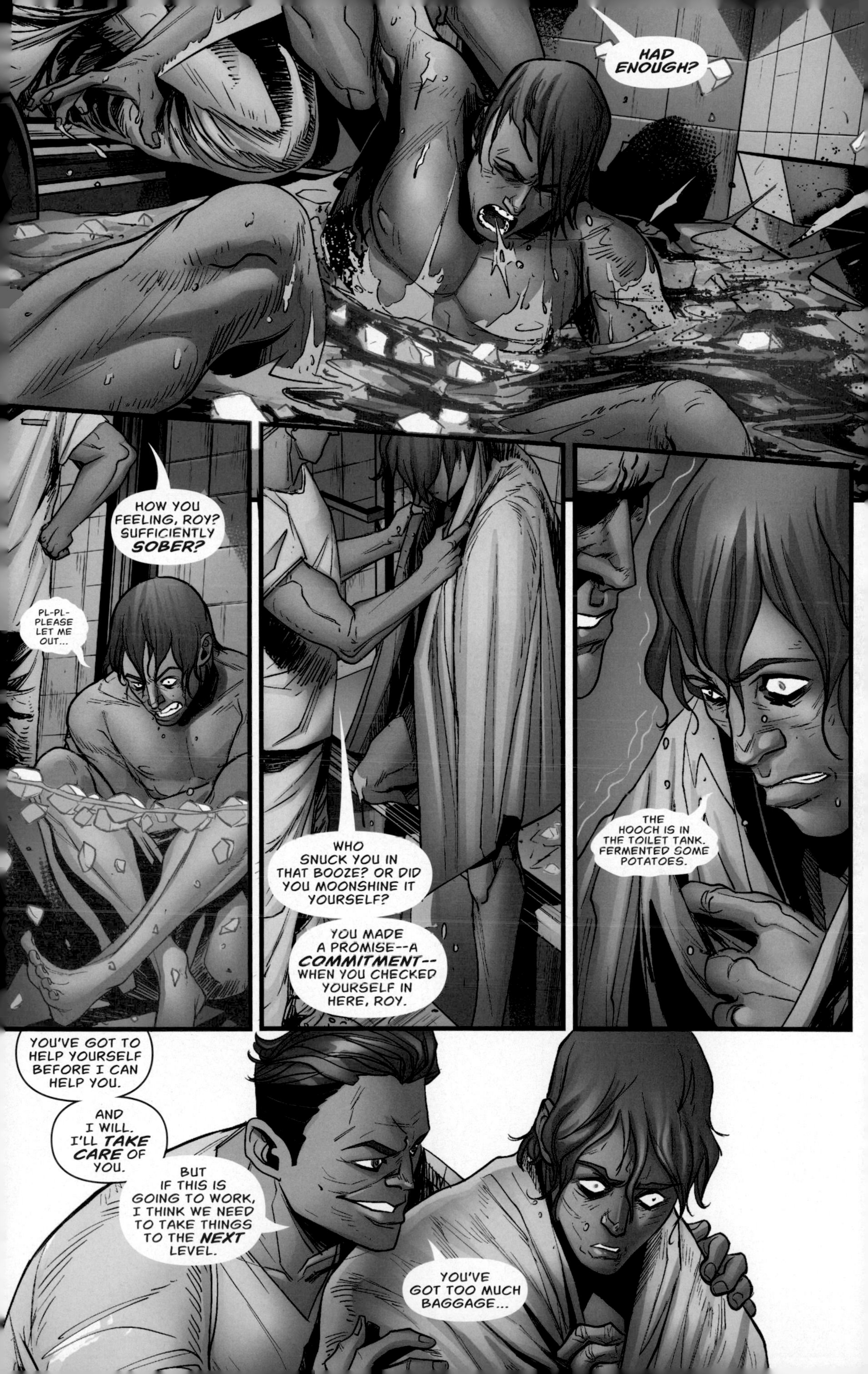
HAD ENOUGH?
HOW YOU FEELING, ROY? SUFFICIENTLY SOBER?
PL-PL-PLEASE LET ME OUT...
WHO SNUCK YOU IN THAT BOOZE? OR DID YOU MOONSHINE IT YOURSELF?
YOU MADE A PROMISE--A COMMITMENT--WHEN YOU CHECKED YOURSELF IN HERE, ROY.
THE HOOCH IS IN THE TOILET TANK. FERMENTED SOME POTATOES.
YOU'VE GOT TO HELP YOURSELF BEFORE I CAN HELP YOU.
AND I WILL. I'LL TAKE CARE OF YOU.
BUT IF THIS IS GOING TO WORK, I THINK WE NEED TO TAKE THINGS TO THE NEXT LEVEL.
YOU'VE GOT TOO MUCH BAGGAGE...

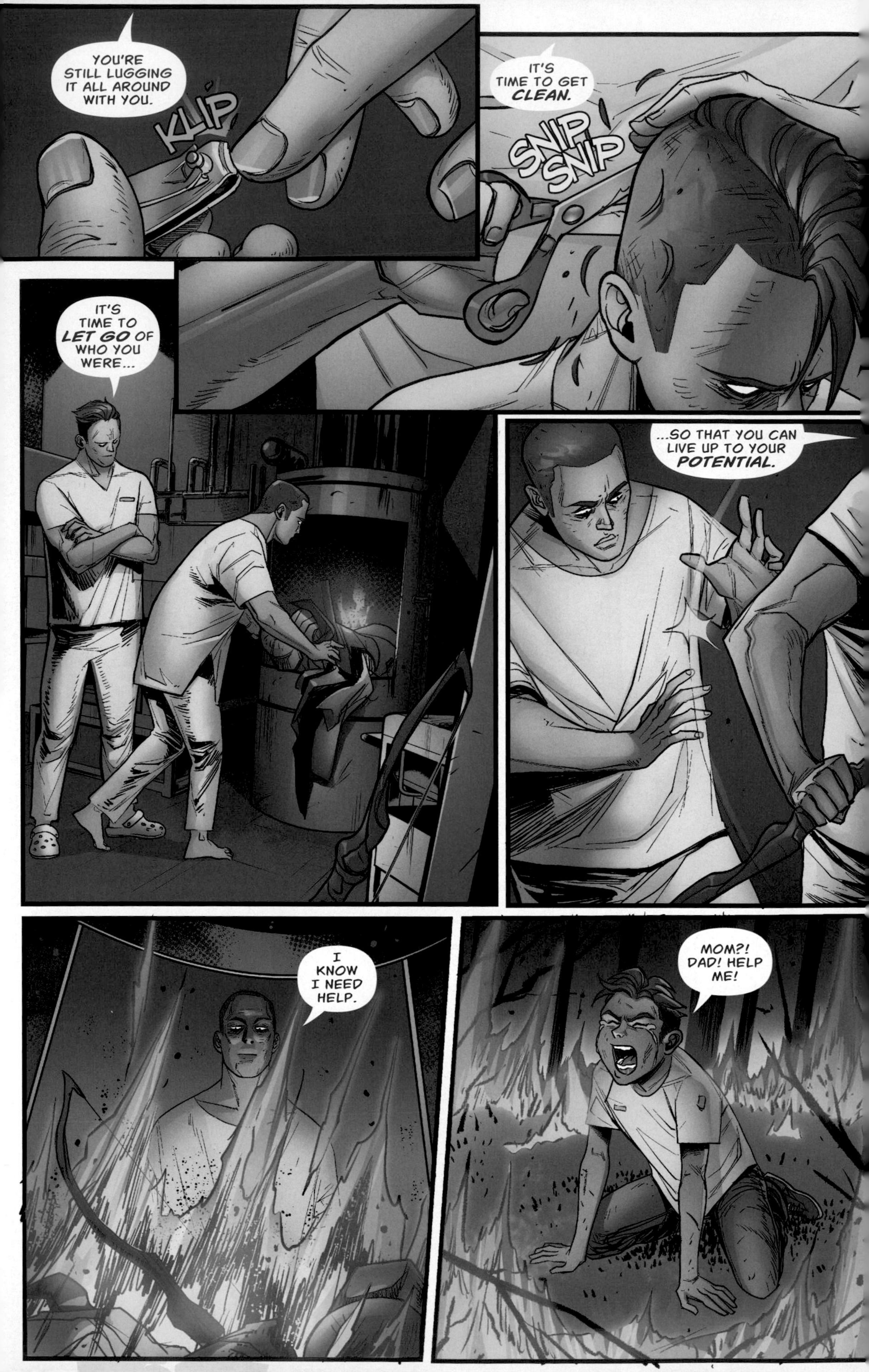
YOU'RE STILL LUGGING IT ALL AROUND WITH YOU.
KLIP
IT'S TIME TO GET CLEAN.
SNIP SNIP
IT'S TIME TO LET GO OF WHO YOU WERE...
...SO THAT YOU CAN LIVE UP TO YOUR POTENTIAL.
I KNOW I NEED HELP.
MOM?! DAD! HELP ME!

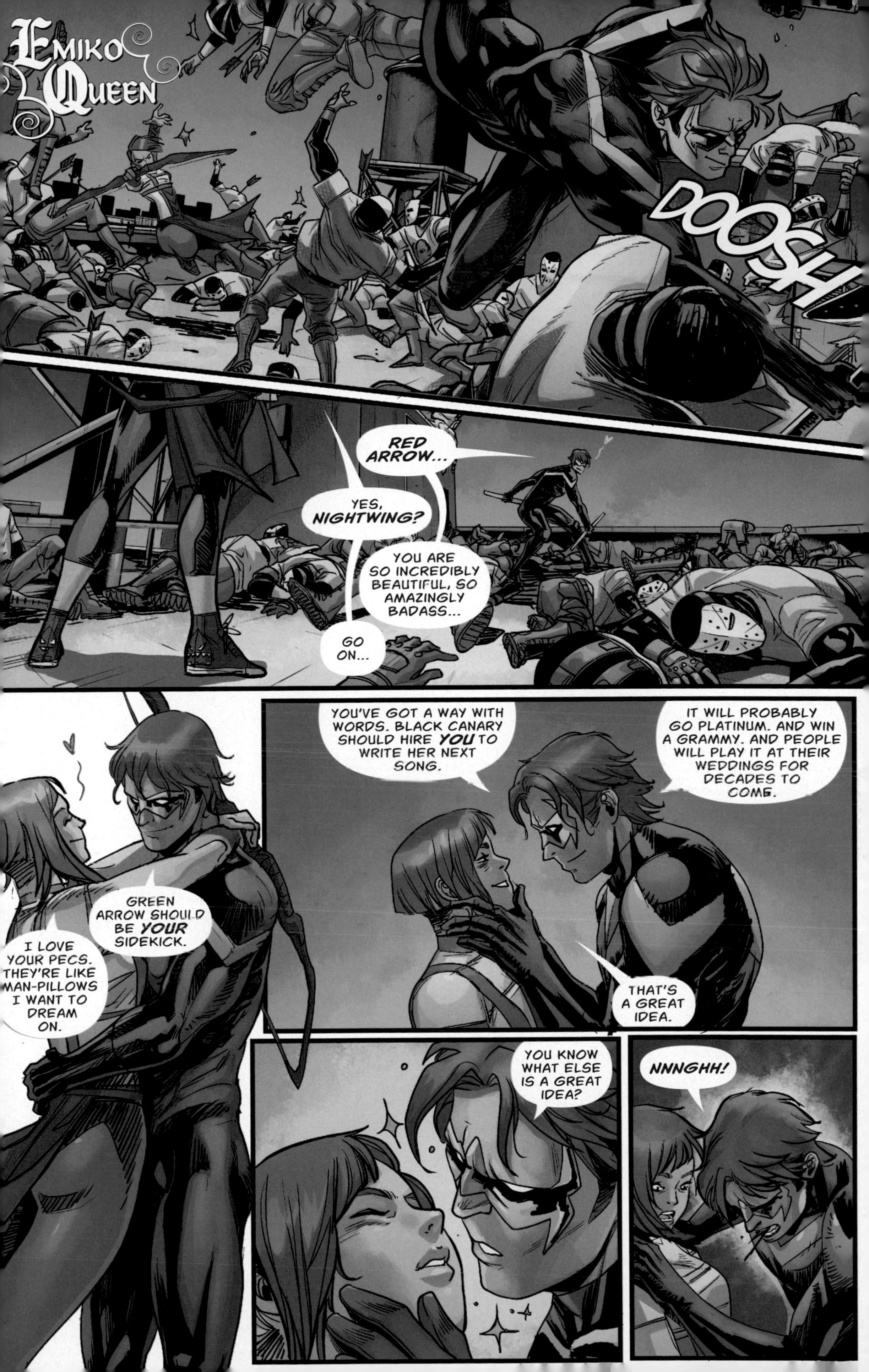
EMIKO QUEEN
DOOSH
RED ARROW...
YES, NIGHTWING?
YOU ARE SO INCREDIBLY BEAUTIFUL, SO AMAZINGLY BADASS...
GO ON...
YOU'VE GOT A WAY WITH WORDS. BLACK CANARY SHOULD HIRE YOU TO WRITE HER NEXT SONG.
IT WILL PROBABLY GO PLATINUM. AND WIN A GRAMMY. AND PEOPLE WILL PLAY IT AT THEIR WEDDINGS FOR DECADES TO COME.
THAT'S A GREAT IDEA.
GREEN ARROW SHOULD BE YOUR SIDEKICK.
I LOVE YOUR PECS. THEY'RE LIKE MAN-PILLOWS I WANT TO DREAM ON.
YOU KNOW WHAT ELSE IS A GREAT IDEA?
NNNGHH!

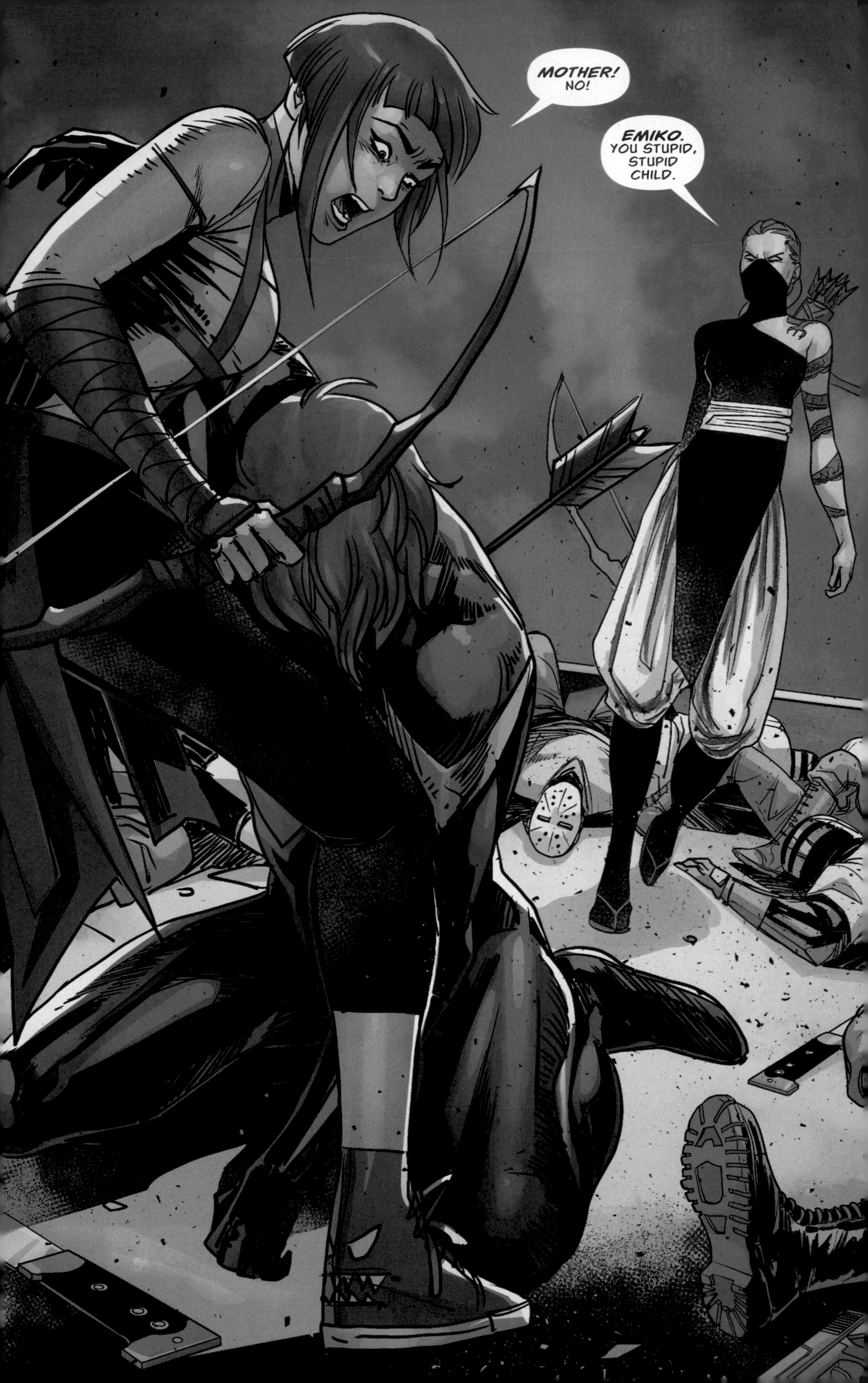
MOTHER! NO!
EMIKO. YOU STUPID, STUPID CHILD.

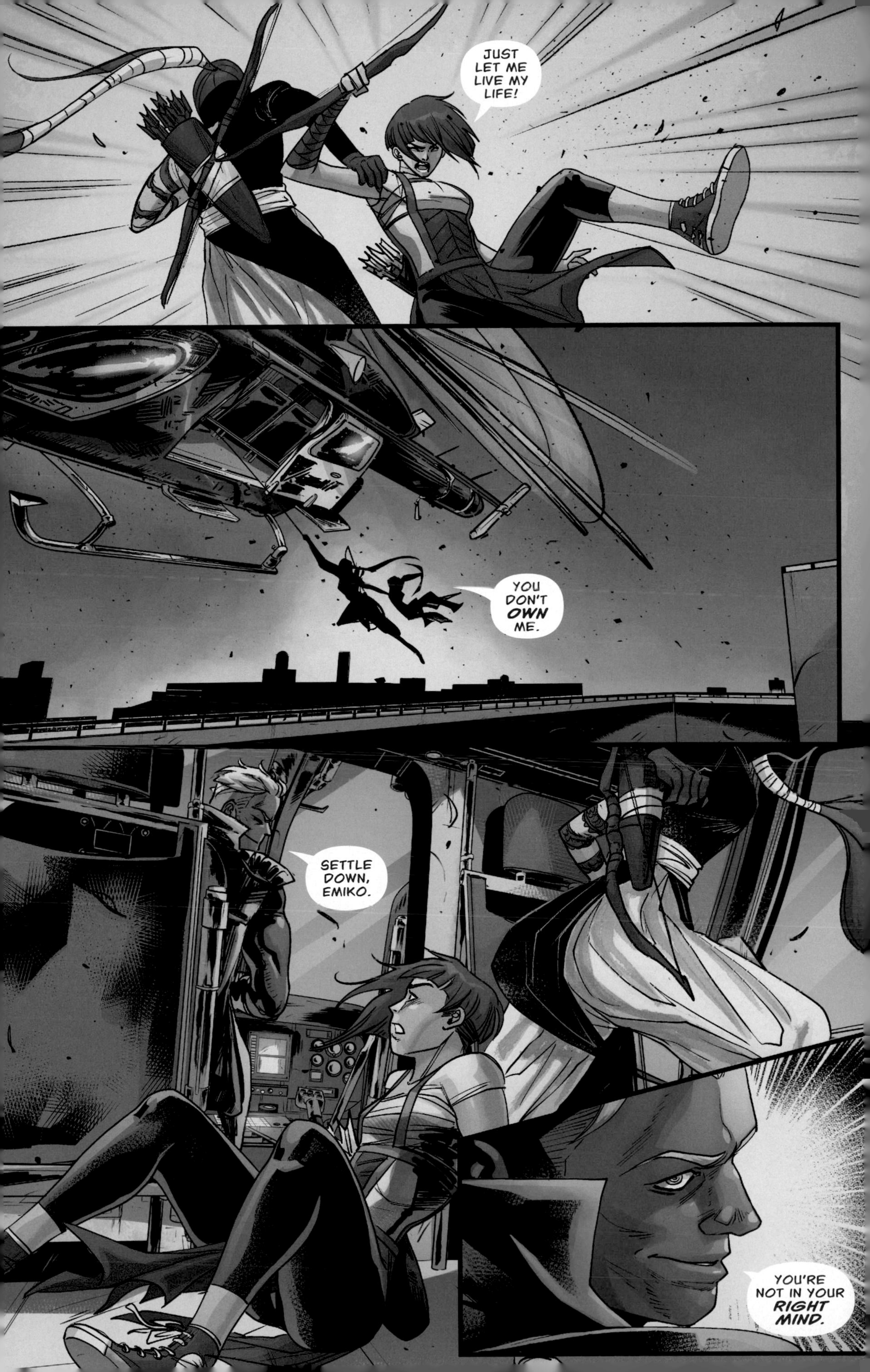
JUST LET ME LIVE MY LIFE!
YOU DON'T OWN ME.
SETTLE DOWN, EMIKO.
YOU'RE NOT IN YOUR RIGHT MIND.

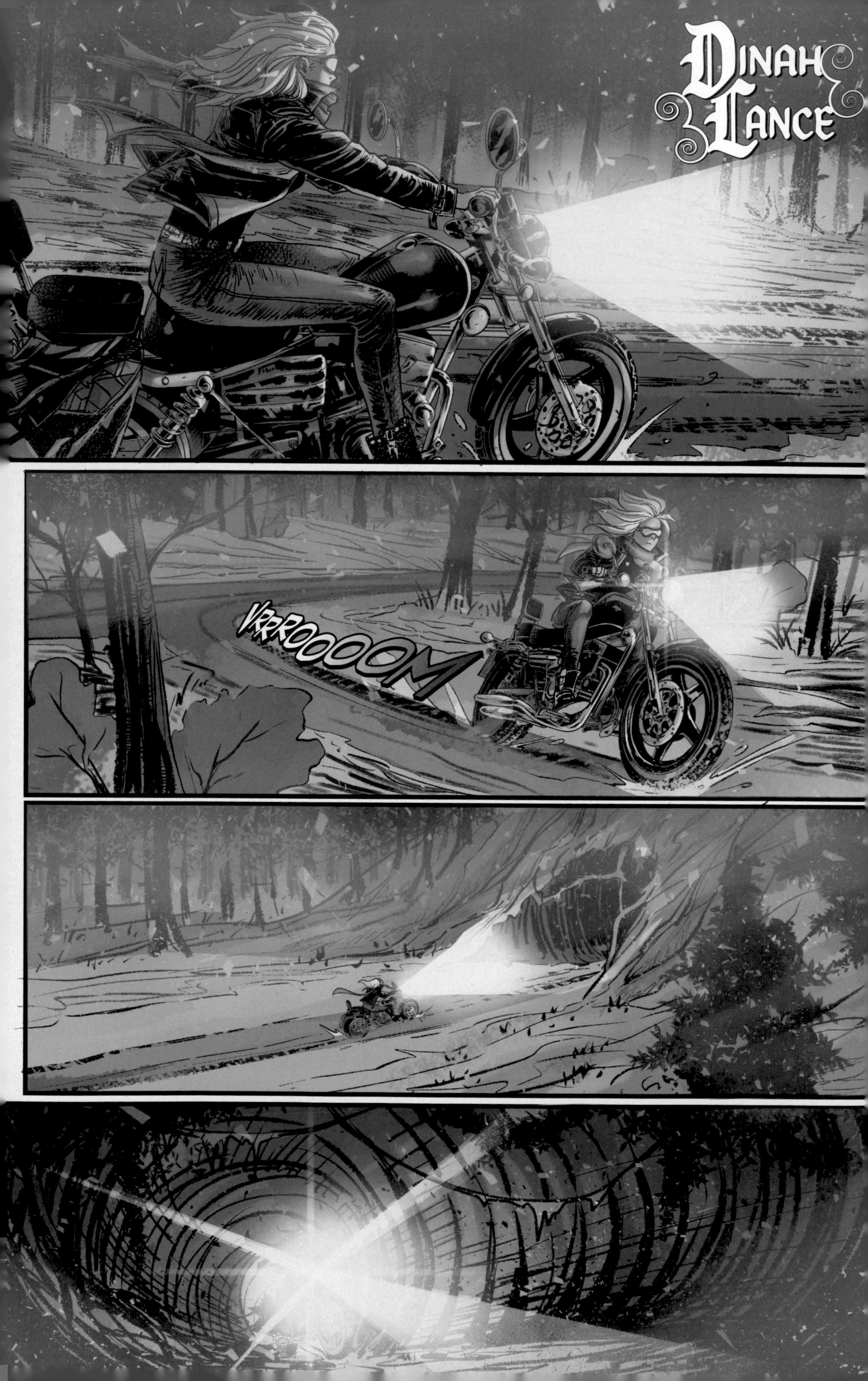
DINAH LANCE
VRRROOOOM

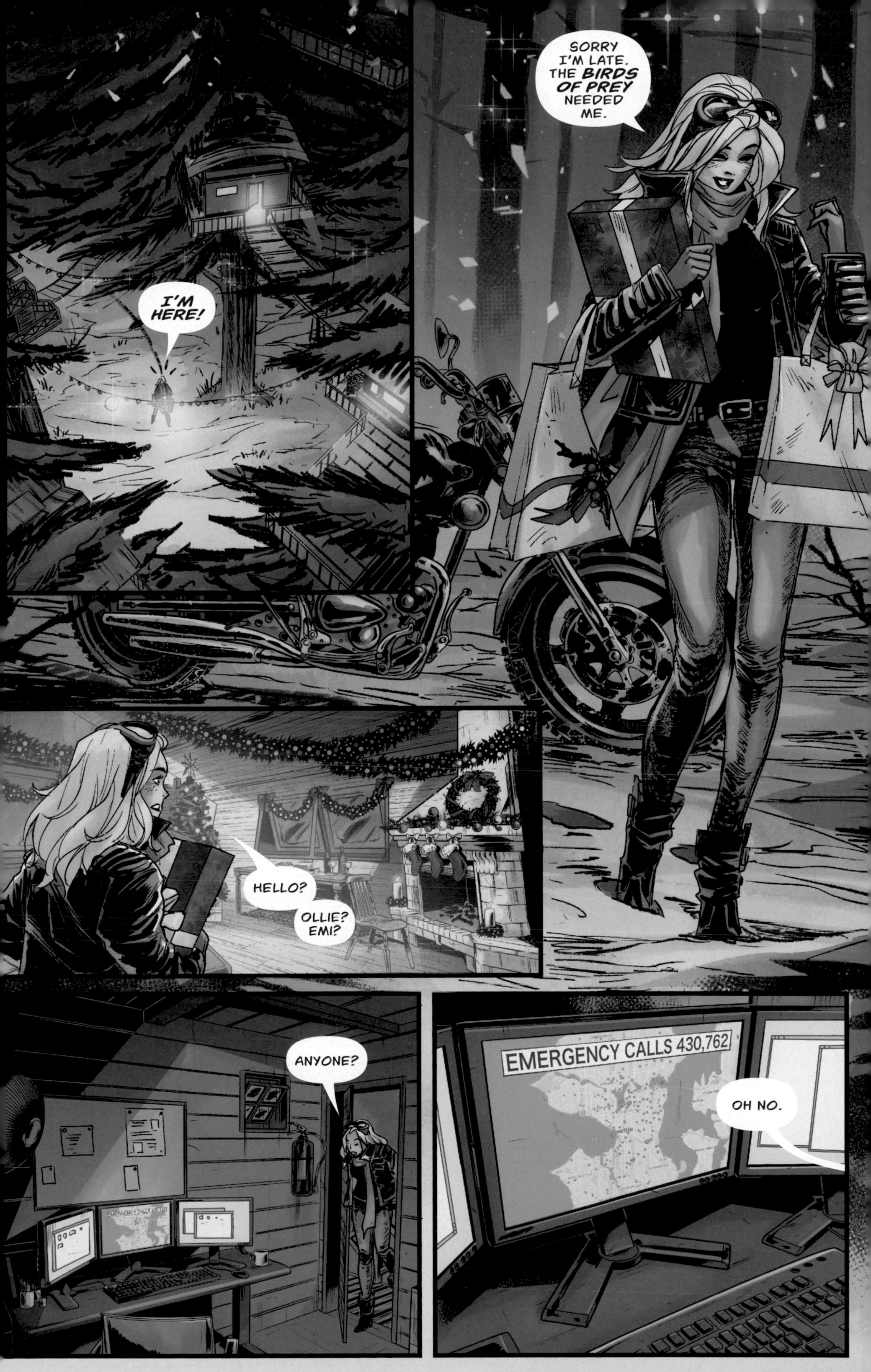
I'M HERE!
SORRY I'M LATE. THE BIRDS OF PREY NEEDED ME.
HELLO?
OLLIE? EMI?
ANYONE?
EMERGENCY CALLS 430,762
OH NO.

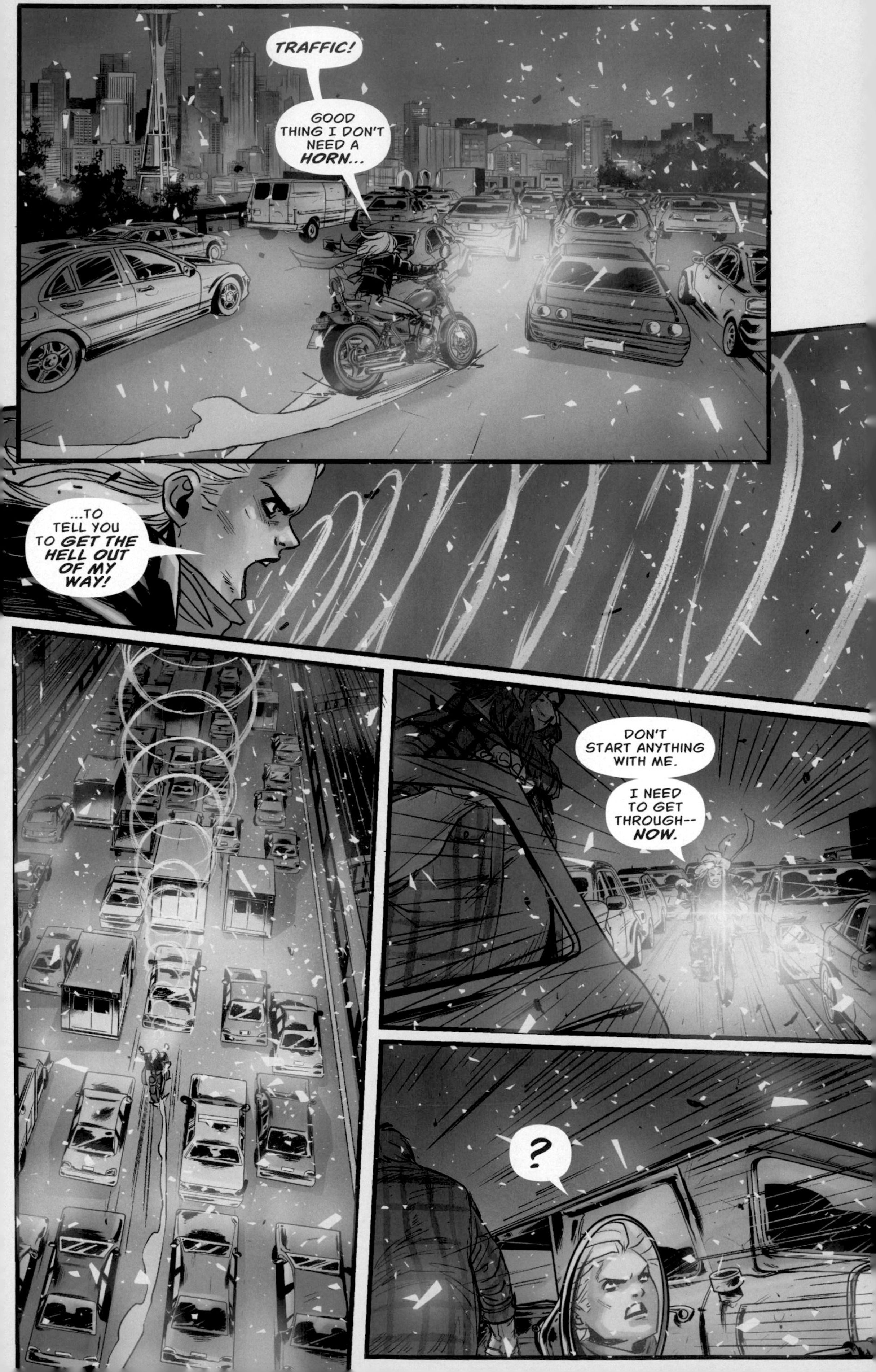
TRAFFIC!
GOOD THING I DON'T NEED A HORN...
...TO TELL YOU TO GET THE HELL OUT OF MY WAY!
DON'T START ANYTHING WITH ME.
I NEED TO GET THROUGH-- NOW.
?

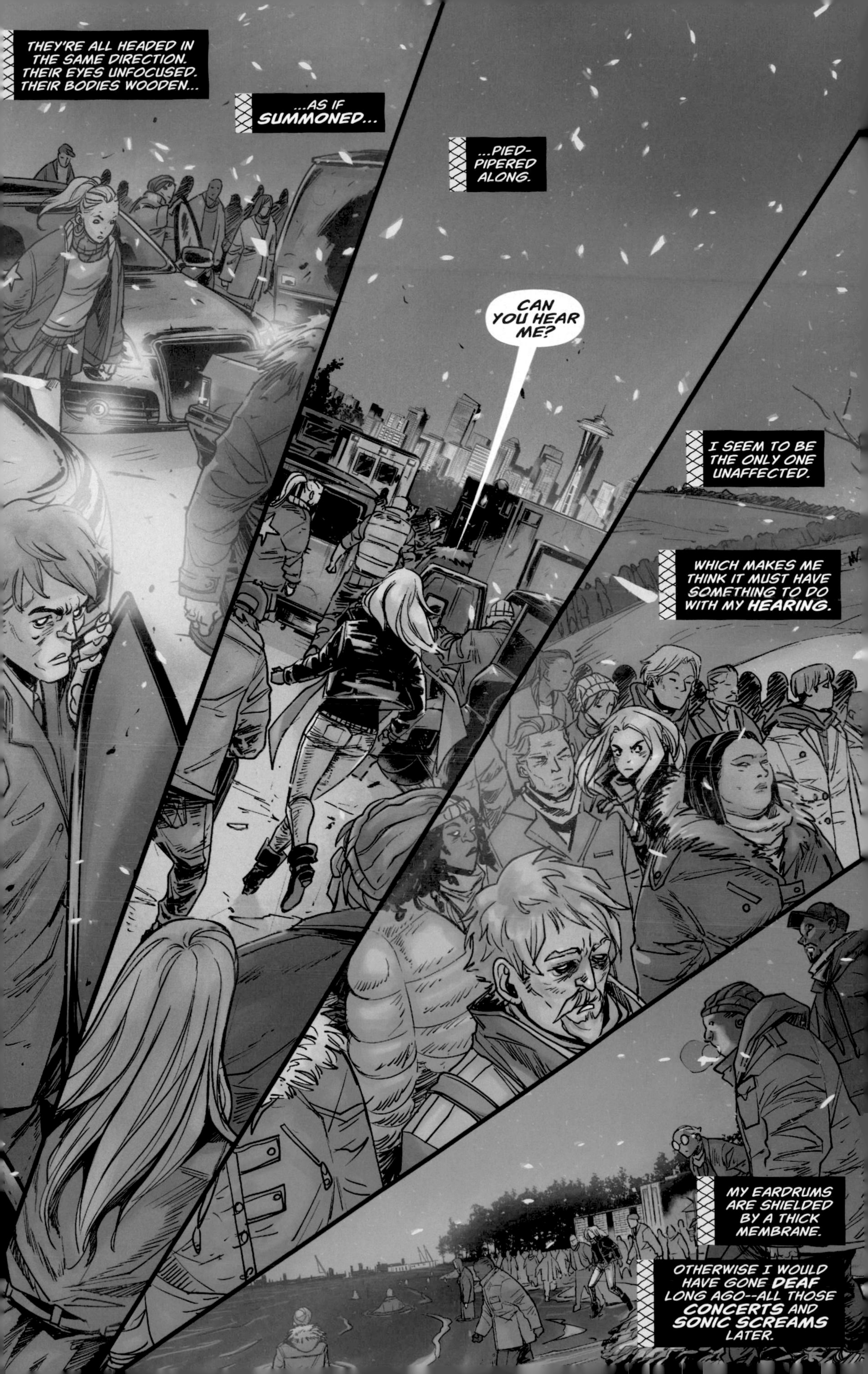

THEY'RE ALL HEADED IN THE SAME DIRECTION. THEIR EYES UNFOCUSED. THEIR BODIES WOODEN...
...AS IF SUMMONED...
...PIED-PIPERED ALONG.
CAN YOU HEAR ME?
I SEEM TO BE THE ONLY ONE UNAFFECTED.
WHICH MAKES ME THINK IT MUST HAVE SOMETHING TO DO WITH MY HEARING.
MY EARDRUMS ARE SHIELDED BY A THICK MEMBRANE.
OTHERWISE I WOULD HAVE GONE DEAF LONG AGO--ALL THOSE CONCERTS AND SONIC SCREAMS LATER.

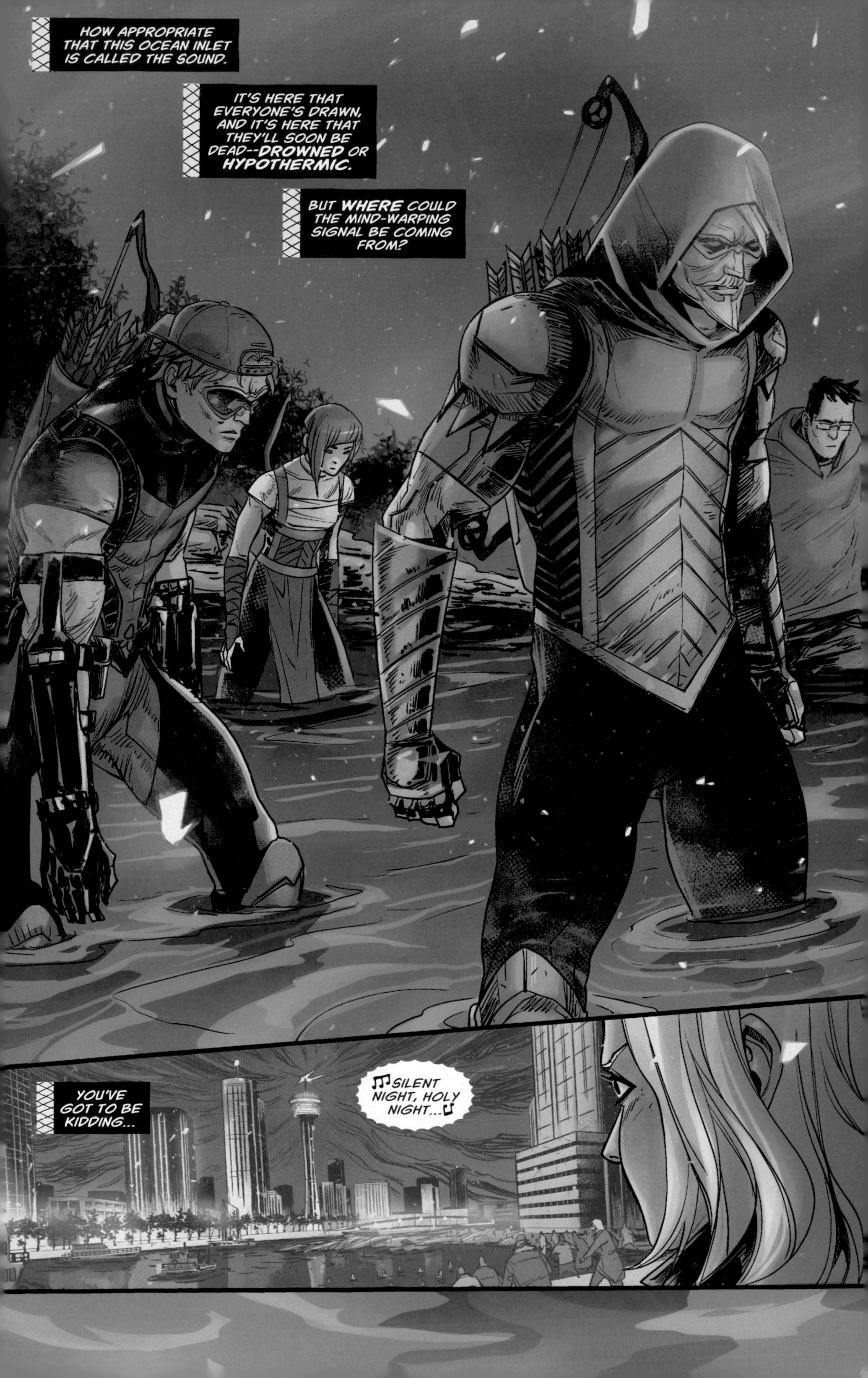
HOW APPROPRIATE THAT THIS OCEAN INLET IS CALLED THE SOUND.
IT'S HERE THAT EVERYONE'S DRAWN, AND IT'S HERE THAT THEY'LL SOON BE DEAD--**DROWNED** OR **HYPOTHERMIC.**
BUT **WHERE** COULD THE MIND-WARPING SIGNAL BE COMING FROM?
YOU'VE GOT TO BE KIDDING...
♫SILENT NIGHT, HOLY NIGHT...♫

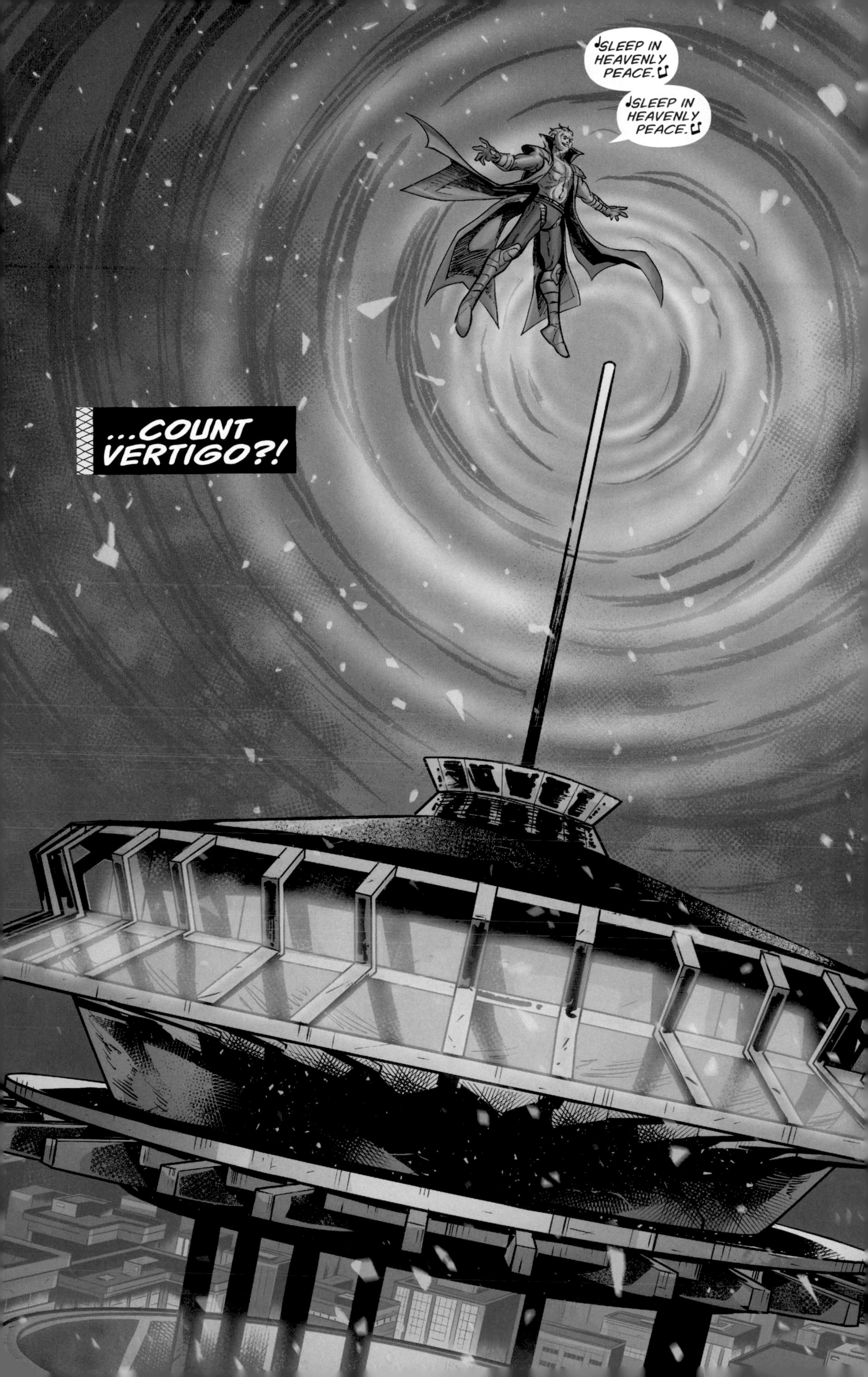
♪SLEEP IN HEAVENLY PEACE.♫
♪SLEEP IN HEAVENLY PEACE.♫
...COUNT VERTIGO?!

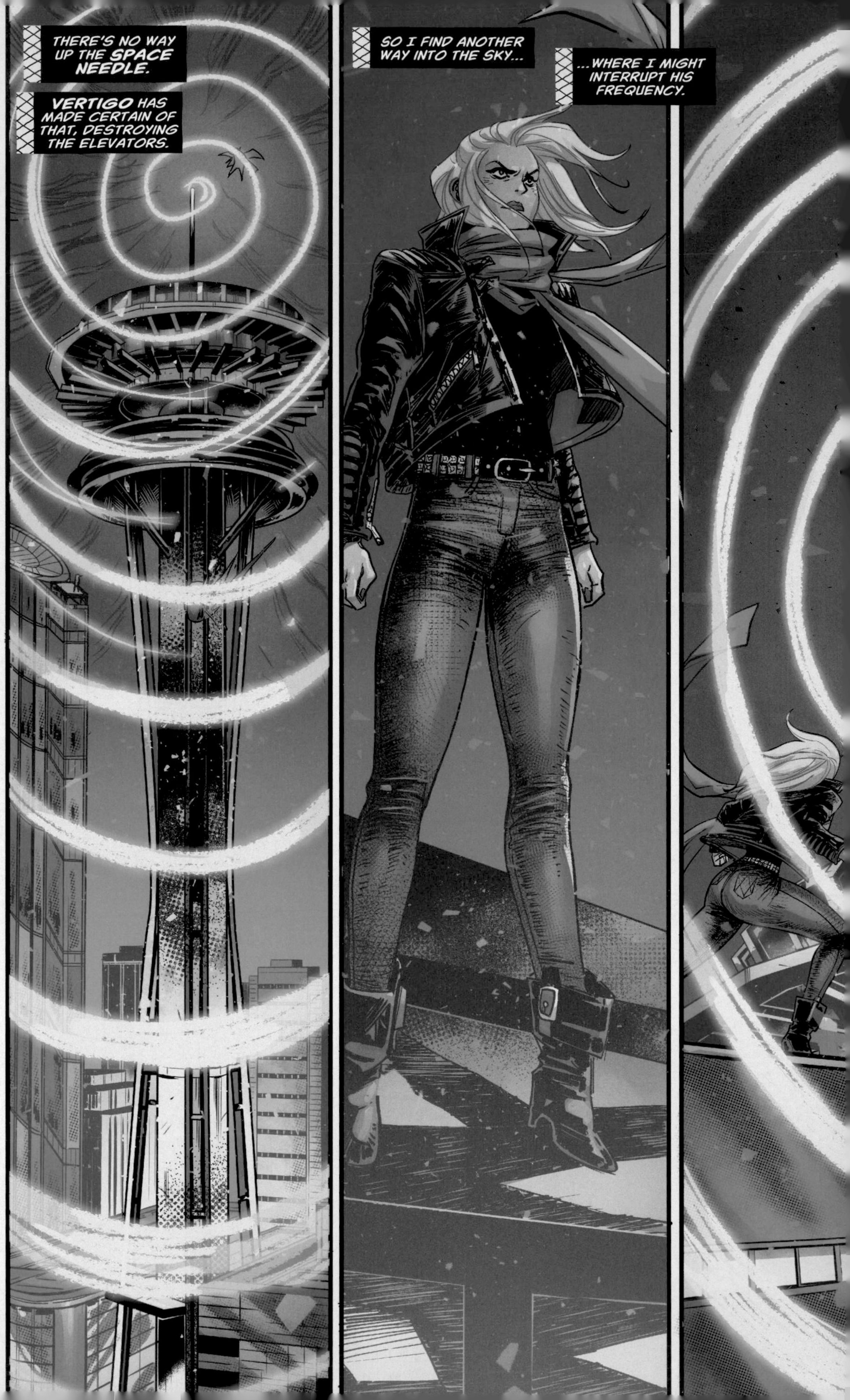
THERE'S NO WAY UP THE SPACE NEEDLE.
VERTIGO HAS MADE CERTAIN OF THAT, DESTROYING THE ELEVATORS.
SO I FIND ANOTHER WAY INTO THE SKY...
...WHERE I MIGHT INTERRUPT HIS FREQUENCY.

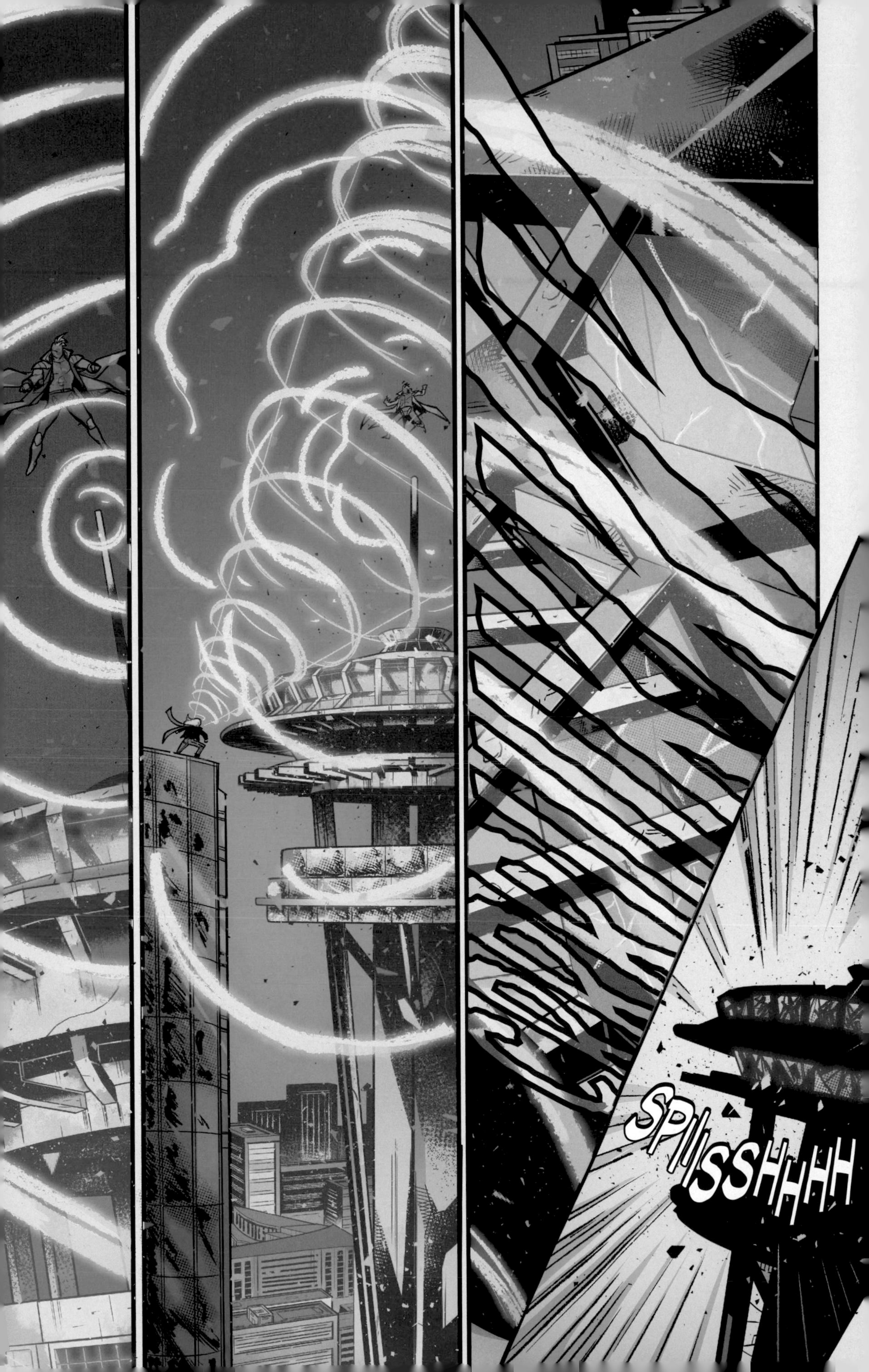
SPIIISSHHHHH

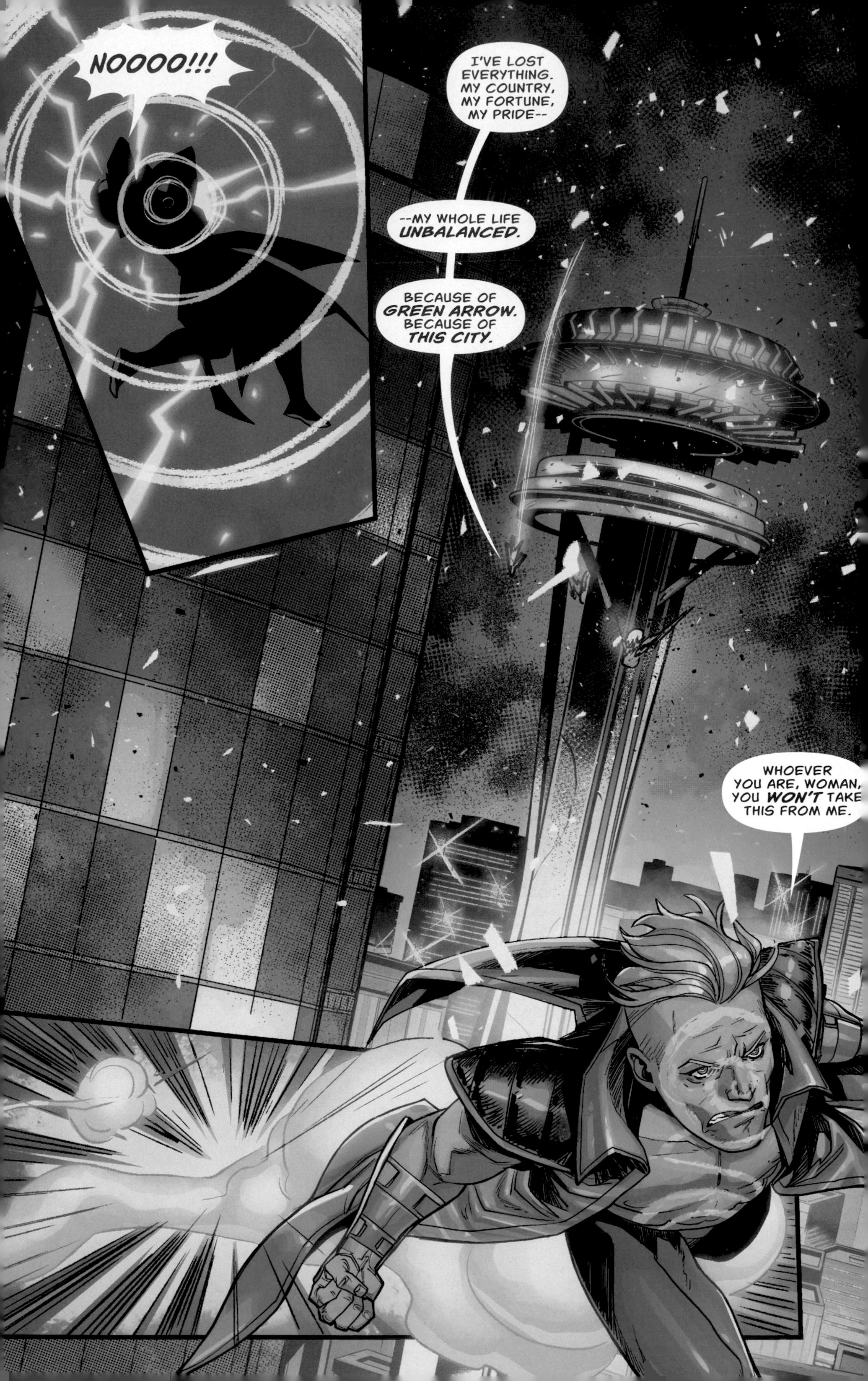
NOOOO!!!
I'VE LOST EVERYTHING. MY COUNTRY, MY FORTUNE, MY PRIDE--
--MY WHOLE LIFE UNBALANCED.
BECAUSE OF GREEN ARROW. BECAUSE OF THIS CITY.
WHOEVER YOU ARE, WOMAN, YOU WON'T TAKE THIS FROM ME.

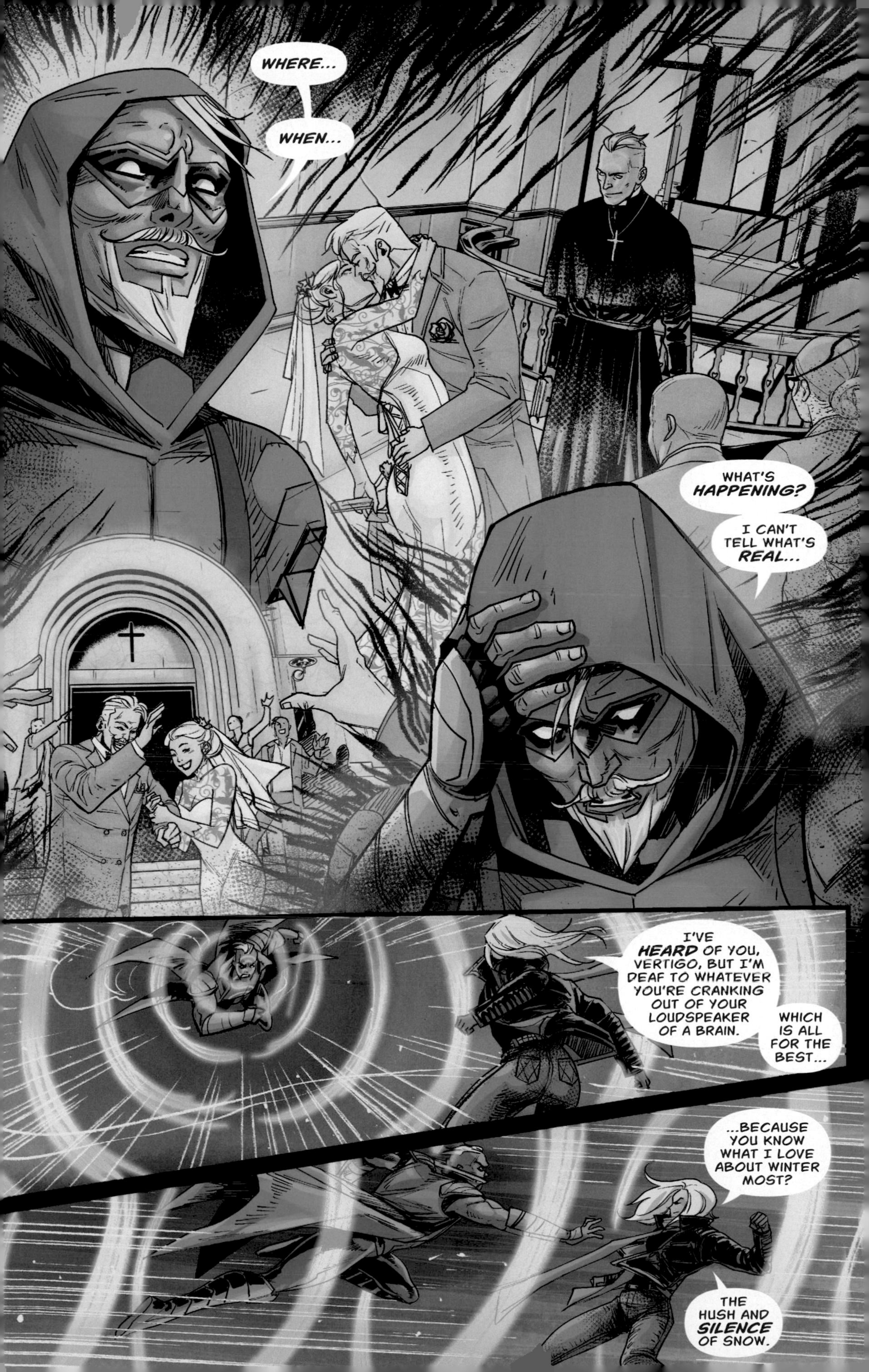

WHERE...
WHEN...
WHAT'S HAPPENING?
I CAN'T TELL WHAT'S REAL...
I'VE HEARD OF YOU, VERTIGO, BUT I'M DEAF TO WHATEVER YOU'RE CRANKING OUT OF YOUR LOUDSPEAKER OF A BRAIN.
WHICH IS ALL FOR THE BEST...
...BECAUSE YOU KNOW WHAT I LOVE ABOUT WINTER MOST?
THE HUSH AND SILENCE OF SNOW.

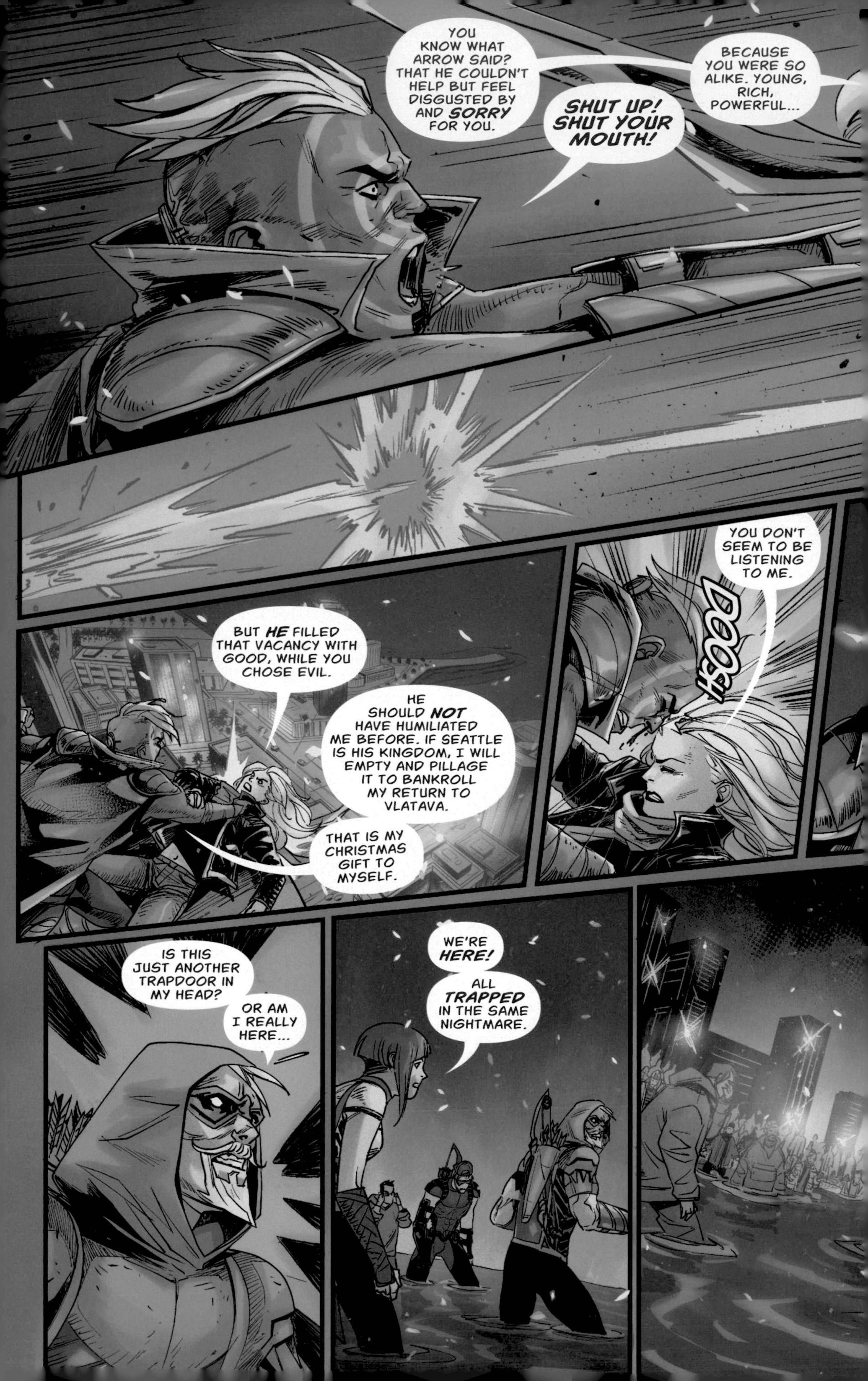
YOU KNOW WHAT ARROW SAID? THAT HE COULDN'T HELP BUT FEEL DISGUSTED BY AND SORRY FOR YOU.
BECAUSE YOU WERE SO ALIKE. YOUNG, RICH, POWERFUL...
SHUT UP! SHUT YOUR MOUTH!
YOU DON'T SEEM TO BE LISTENING TO ME.
BOOSH!
BUT HE FILLED THAT VACANCY WITH GOOD, WHILE YOU CHOSE EVIL.
HE SHOULD NOT HAVE HUMILIATED ME BEFORE. IF SEATTLE IS HIS KINGDOM, I WILL EMPTY AND PILLAGE IT TO BANKROLL MY RETURN TO VLATAVA.
THAT IS MY CHRISTMAS GIFT TO MYSELF.
IS THIS JUST ANOTHER TRAPDOOR IN MY HEAD?
OR AM I REALLY HERE...
WE'RE HERE!
ALL TRAPPED IN THE SAME NIGHTMARE.

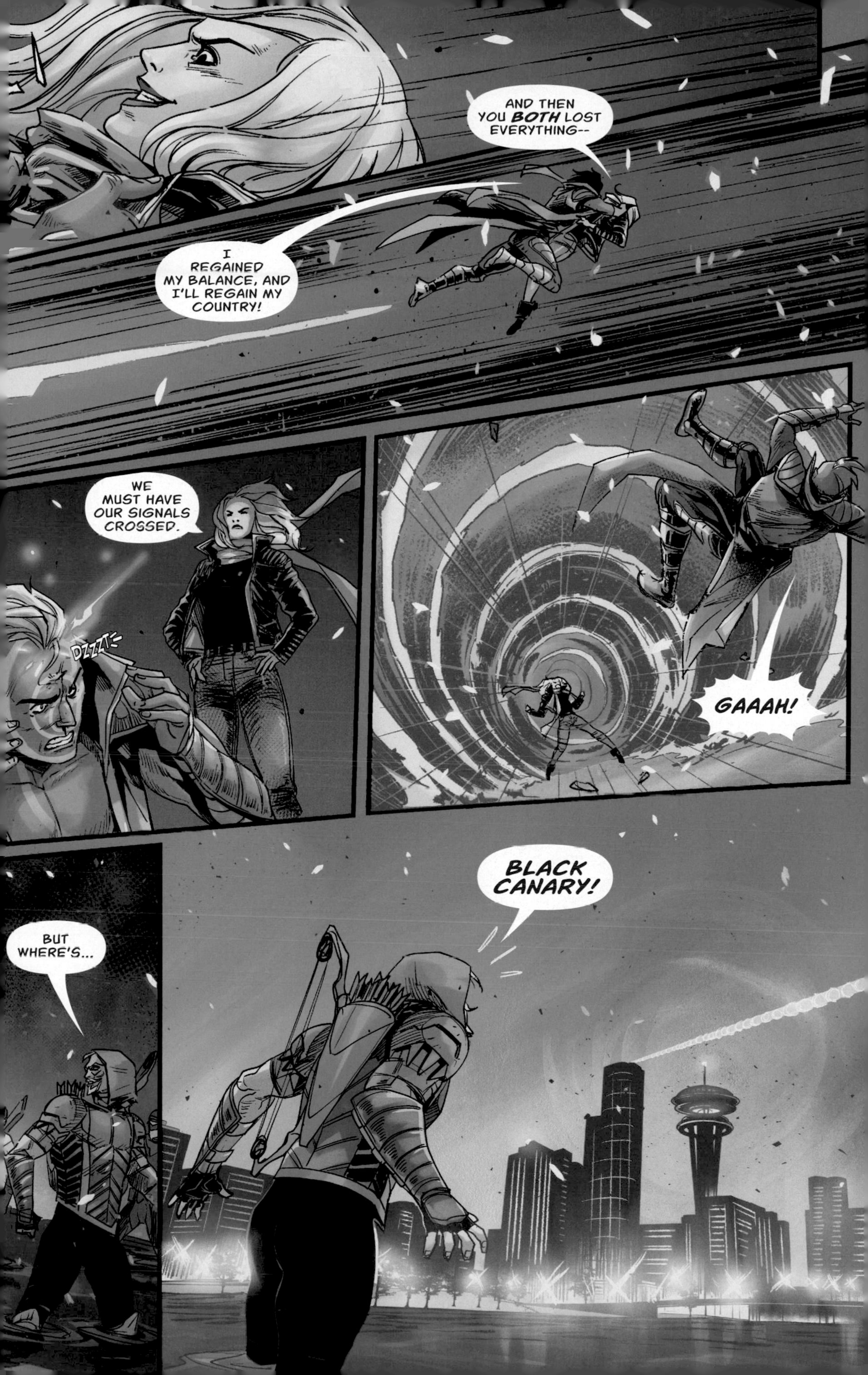
AND THEN YOU BOTH LOST EVERYTHING--
I REGAINED MY BALANCE, AND I'LL REGAIN MY COUNTRY!
WE MUST HAVE OUR SIGNALS CROSSED.
DZZZT
GAAAH!
BUT WHERE'S...
BLACK CANARY!

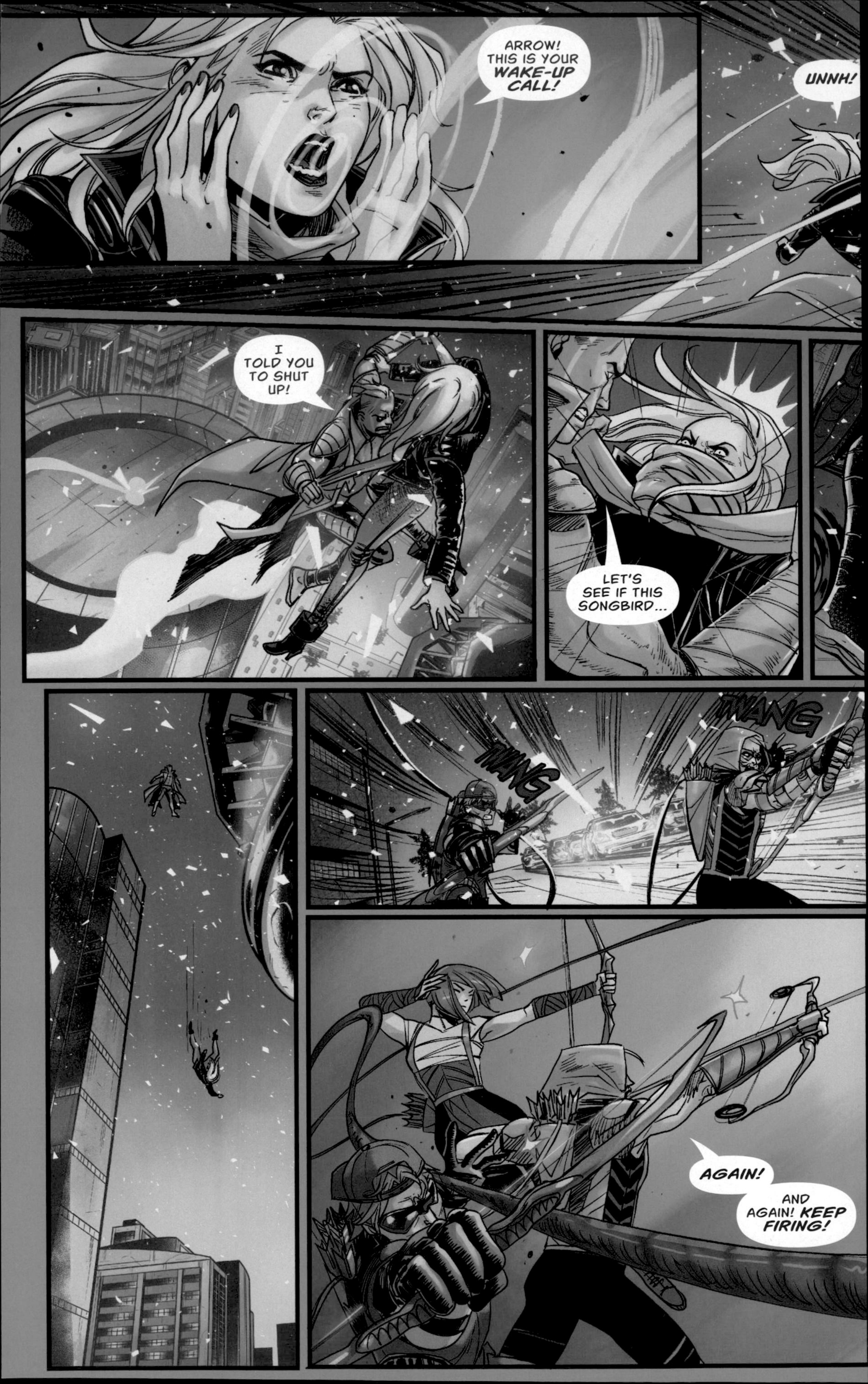
ARROW! THIS IS YOUR WAKE-UP CALL!
UNNH!
I TOLD YOU TO SHUT UP!
LET'S SEE IF THIS SONGBIRD...
TWANG
TWANG
AGAIN!
AND AGAIN! KEEP FIRING!

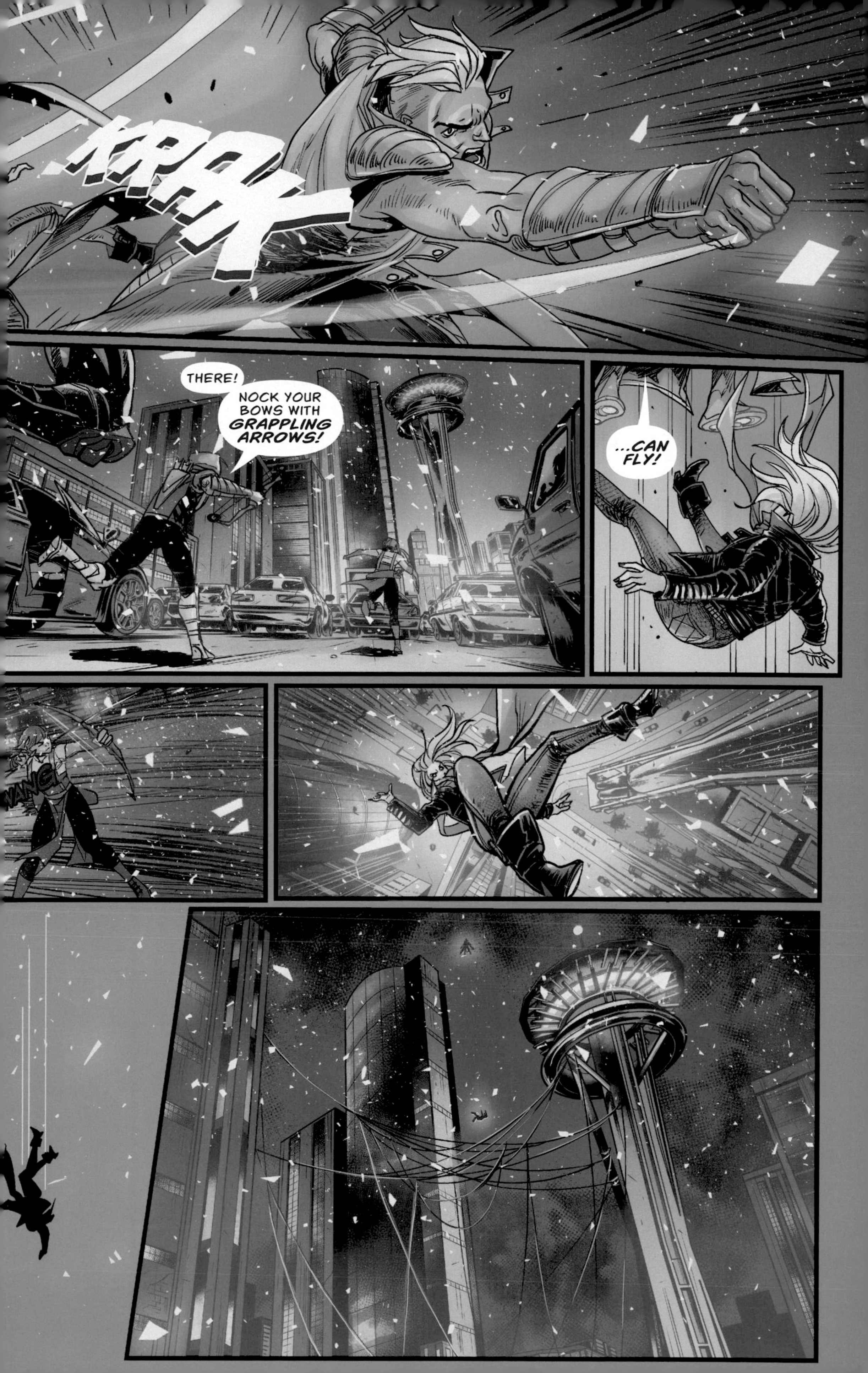
KRAK
THERE!
NOCK YOUR BOWS WITH GRAPPLING ARROWS!
...CAN FLY!
VANG!

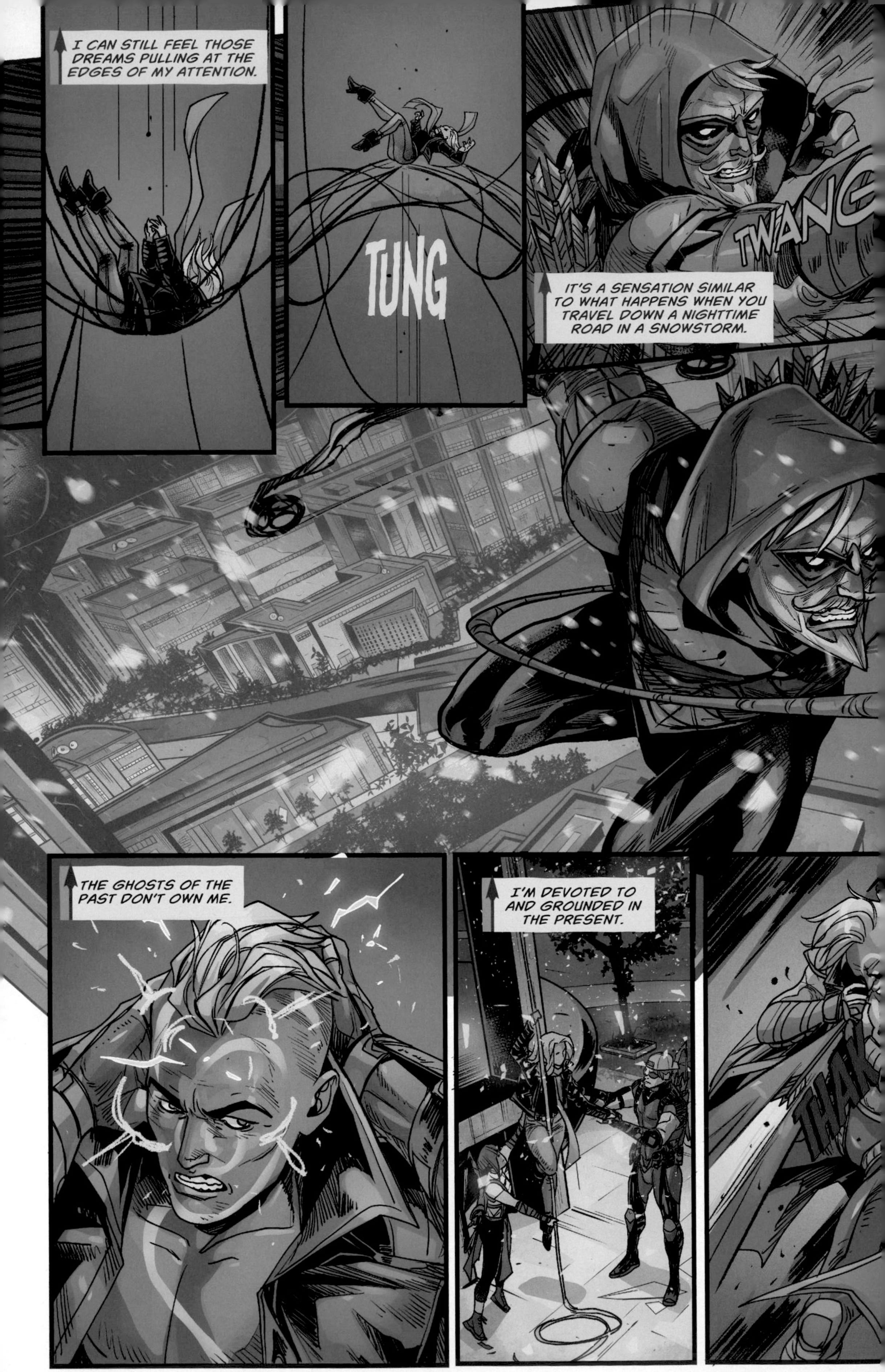

I CAN STILL FEEL THOSE DREAMS PULLING AT THE EDGES OF MY ATTENTION.
TUNG
TWANG
IT'S A SENSATION SIMILAR TO WHAT HAPPENS WHEN YOU TRAVEL DOWN A NIGHTTIME ROAD IN A SNOWSTORM.
THE GHOSTS OF THE PAST DON'T OWN ME.
I'M DEVOTED TO AND GROUNDED IN THE PRESENT.

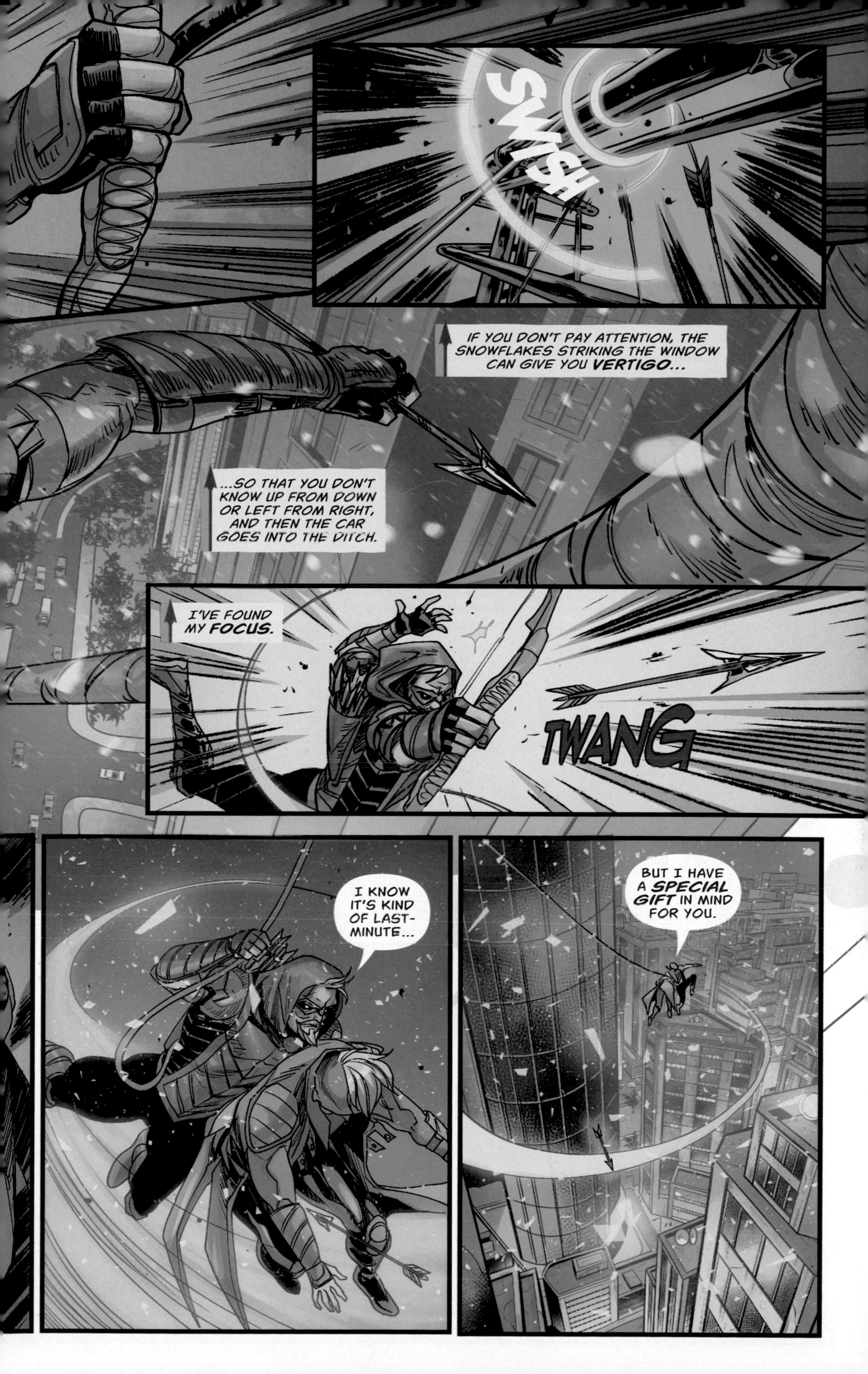
SWISH
IF YOU DON'T PAY ATTENTION, THE SNOWFLAKES STRIKING THE WINDOW CAN GIVE YOU VERTIGO...
...SO THAT YOU DON'T KNOW UP FROM DOWN OR LEFT FROM RIGHT, AND THEN THE CAR GOES INTO THE DITCH.
I'VE FOUND MY FOCUS.
TWANG
I KNOW IT'S KIND OF LAST-MINUTE...
BUT I HAVE A SPECIAL GIFT IN MIND FOR YOU.

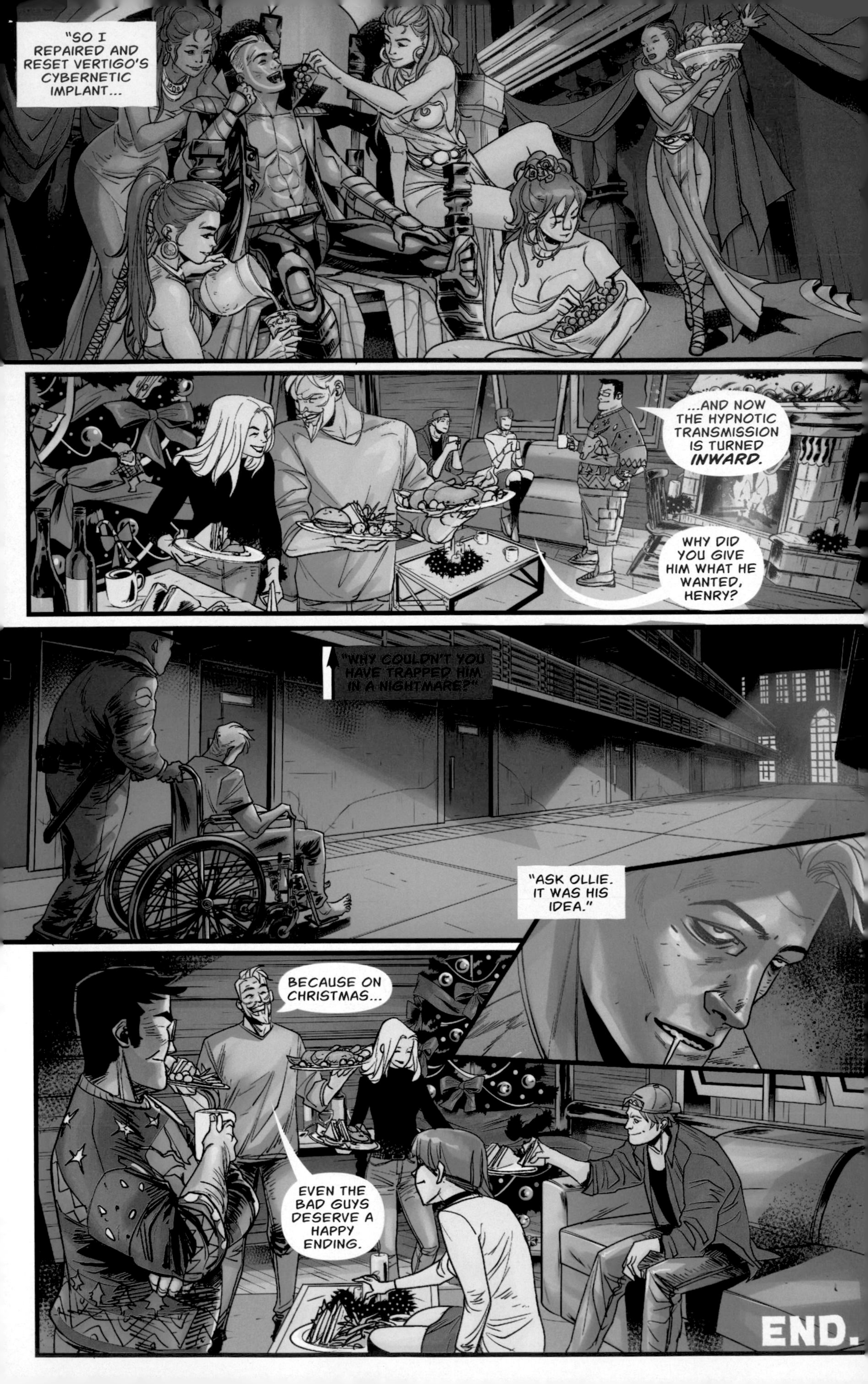
"SO I REPAIRED AND RESET VERTIGO'S CYBERNETIC IMPLANT...
...AND NOW THE HYPNOTIC TRANSMISSION IS TURNED *INWARD.*
WHY DID YOU GIVE HIM WHAT HE WANTED, HENRY?
"WHY COULDN'T YOU HAVE TRAPPED HIM IN A NIGHTMARE?"
"ASK OLLIE. IT WAS HIS IDEA."
BECAUSE ON CHRISTMAS...
EVEN THE BAD GUYS DESERVE A HAPPY ENDING.
END.

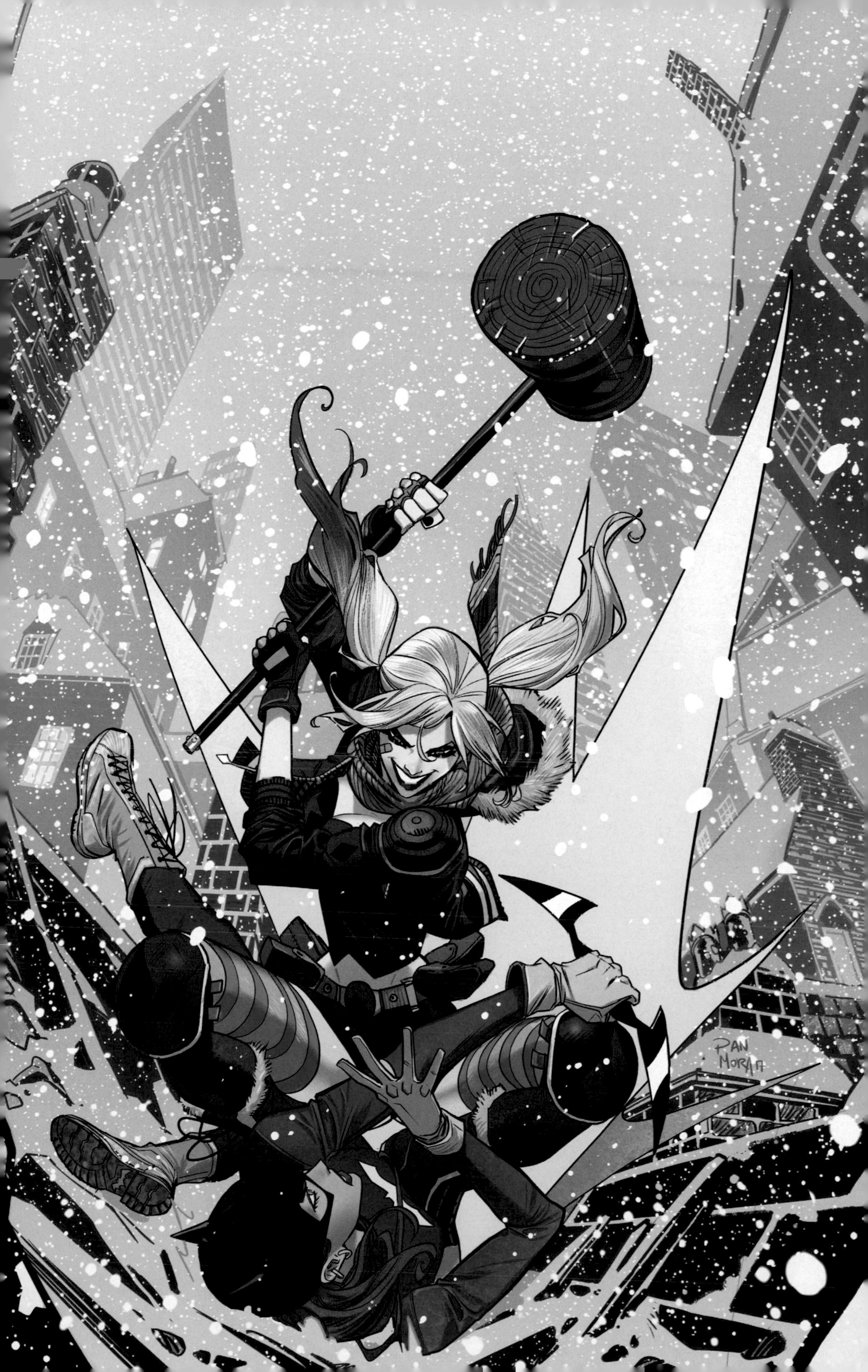
DAN
MORA 17

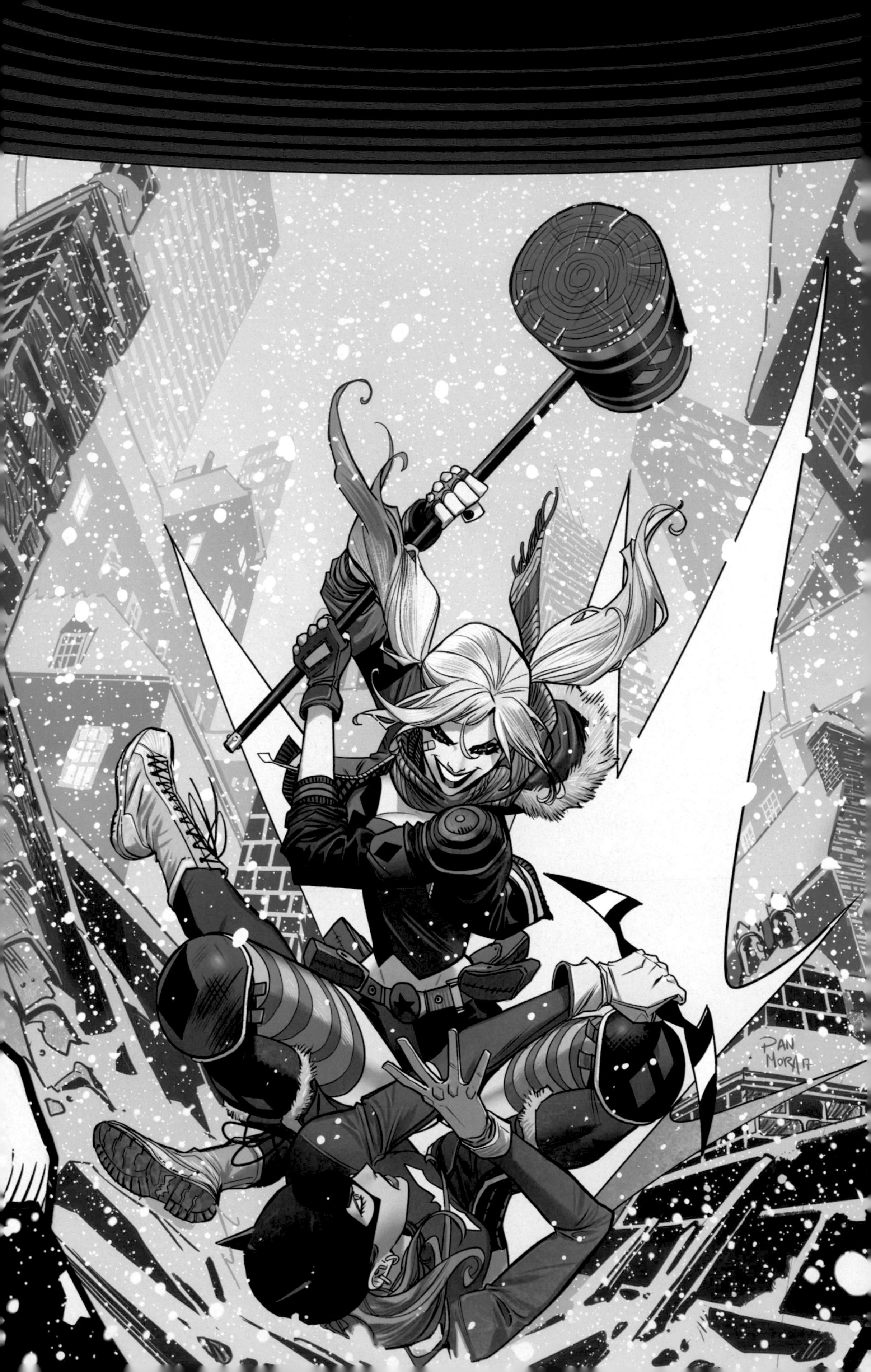
DAN MORA 17

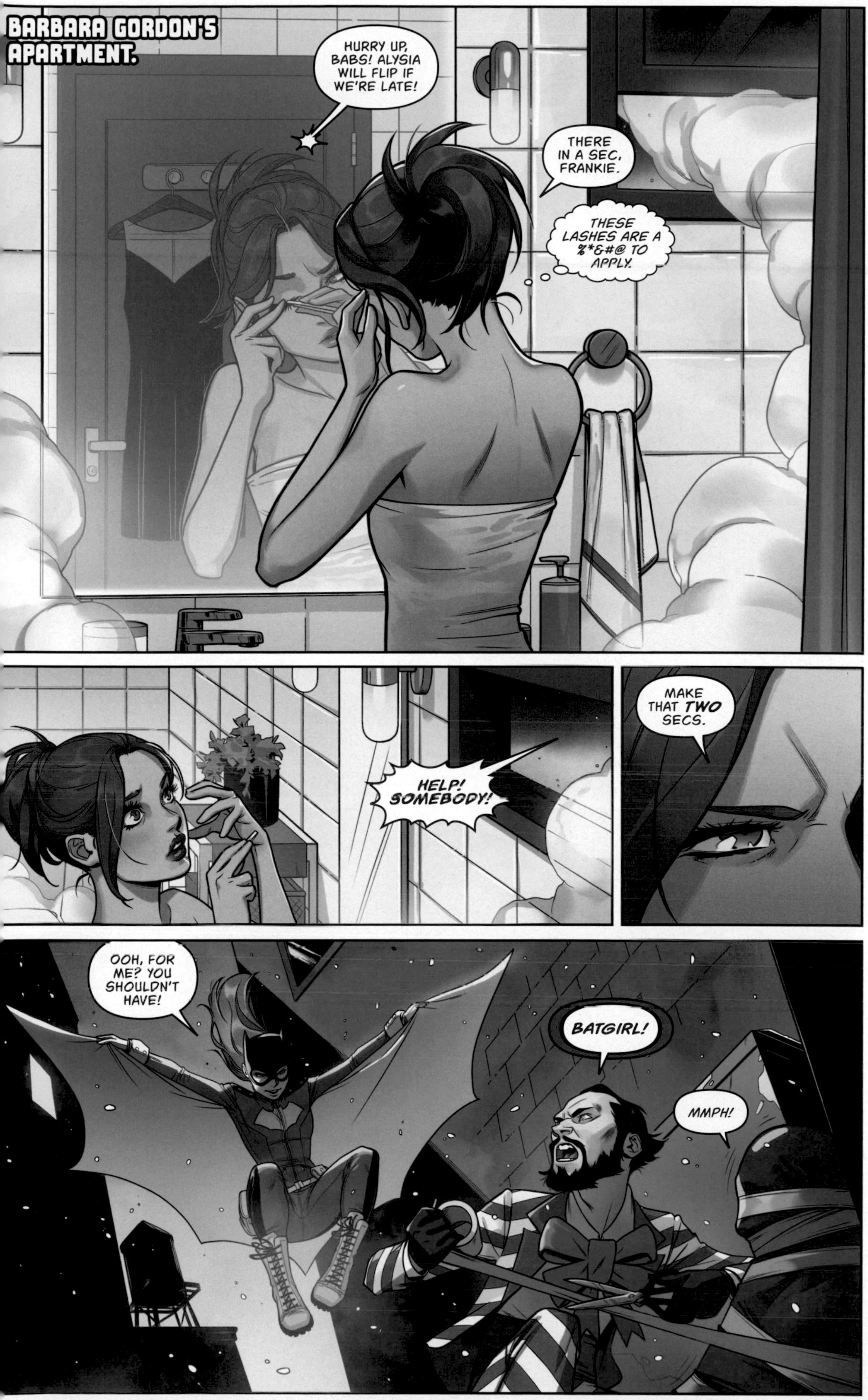
BARBARA GORDON'S APARTMENT.
HURRY UP, BABS! ALYSIA WILL FLIP IF WE'RE LATE!
THERE IN A SEC, FRANKIE.
THESE LASHES ARE A %*&#@ TO APPLY.
HELP! SOMEBODY!
MAKE THAT TWO SECS.
OOH, FOR ME? YOU SHOULDN'T HAVE!
BATGIRL!
MMPH!

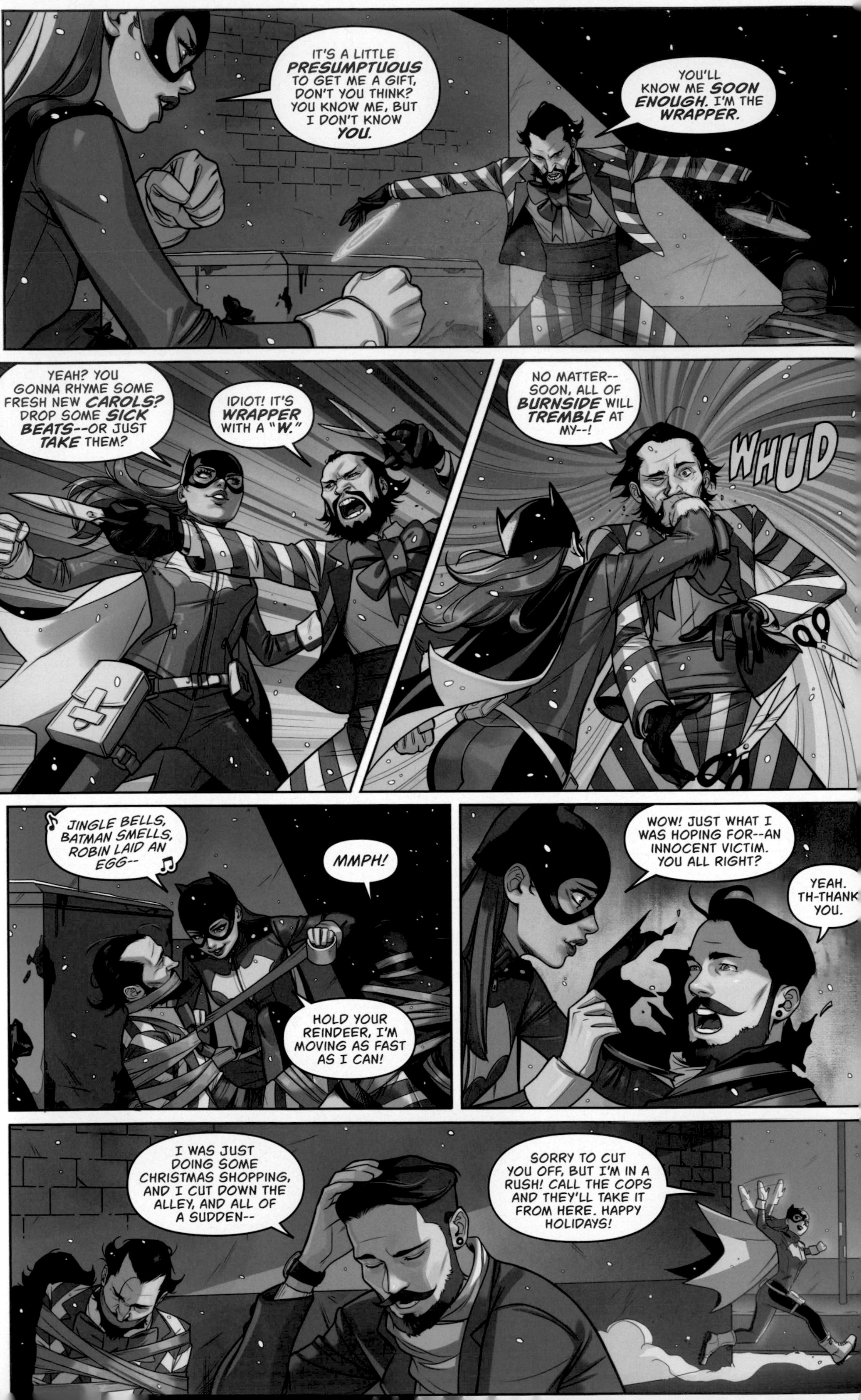

IT'S A LITTLE PRESUMPTUOUS TO GET ME A GIFT, DON'T YOU THINK? YOU KNOW ME, BUT I DON'T KNOW YOU.
YOU'LL KNOW ME SOON ENOUGH. I'M THE WRAPPER.
YEAH? YOU GONNA RHYME SOME FRESH NEW CAROLS? DROP SOME SICK BEATS--OR JUST TAKE THEM?
IDIOT! IT'S WRAPPER WITH A "W."
NO MATTER--SOON, ALL OF BURNSIDE WILL TREMBLE AT MY--!
WHUD
JINGLE BELLS, BATMAN SMELLS, ROBIN LAID AN EGG--
MMPH!
HOLD YOUR REINDEER, I'M MOVING AS FAST AS I CAN!
WOW! JUST WHAT I WAS HOPING FOR--AN INNOCENT VICTIM. YOU ALL RIGHT?
YEAH. TH-THANK YOU.
I WAS JUST DOING SOME CHRISTMAS SHOPPING, AND I CUT DOWN THE ALLEY, AND ALL OF A SUDDEN--
SORRY TO CUT YOU OFF, BUT I'M IN A RUSH! CALL THE COPS AND THEY'LL TAKE IT FROM HERE. HAPPY HOLIDAYS!

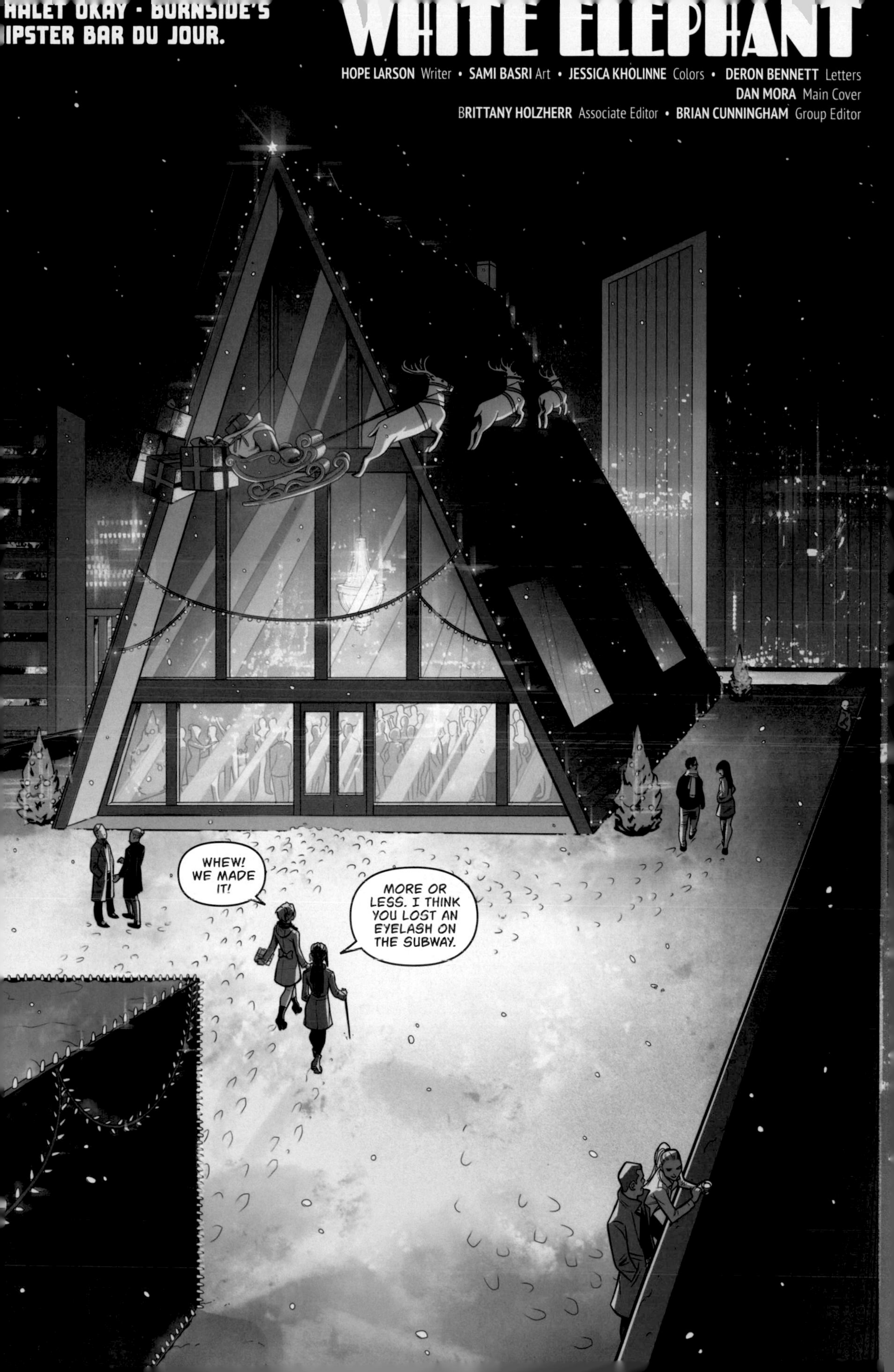

HALET OKAY • BURNSIDE'S
IPSTER BAR DU JOUR.
WHITE ELEPHANT
HOPE LARSON Writer • SAMI BASRI Art • JESSICA KHOLINNE Colors • DERON BENNETT Letters
DAN MORA Main Cover
BRITTANY HOLZHERR Associate Editor • BRIAN CUNNINGHAM Group Editor
WHEW! WE MADE IT!
MORE OR LESS. I THINK YOU LOST AN EYELASH ON THE SUBWAY.

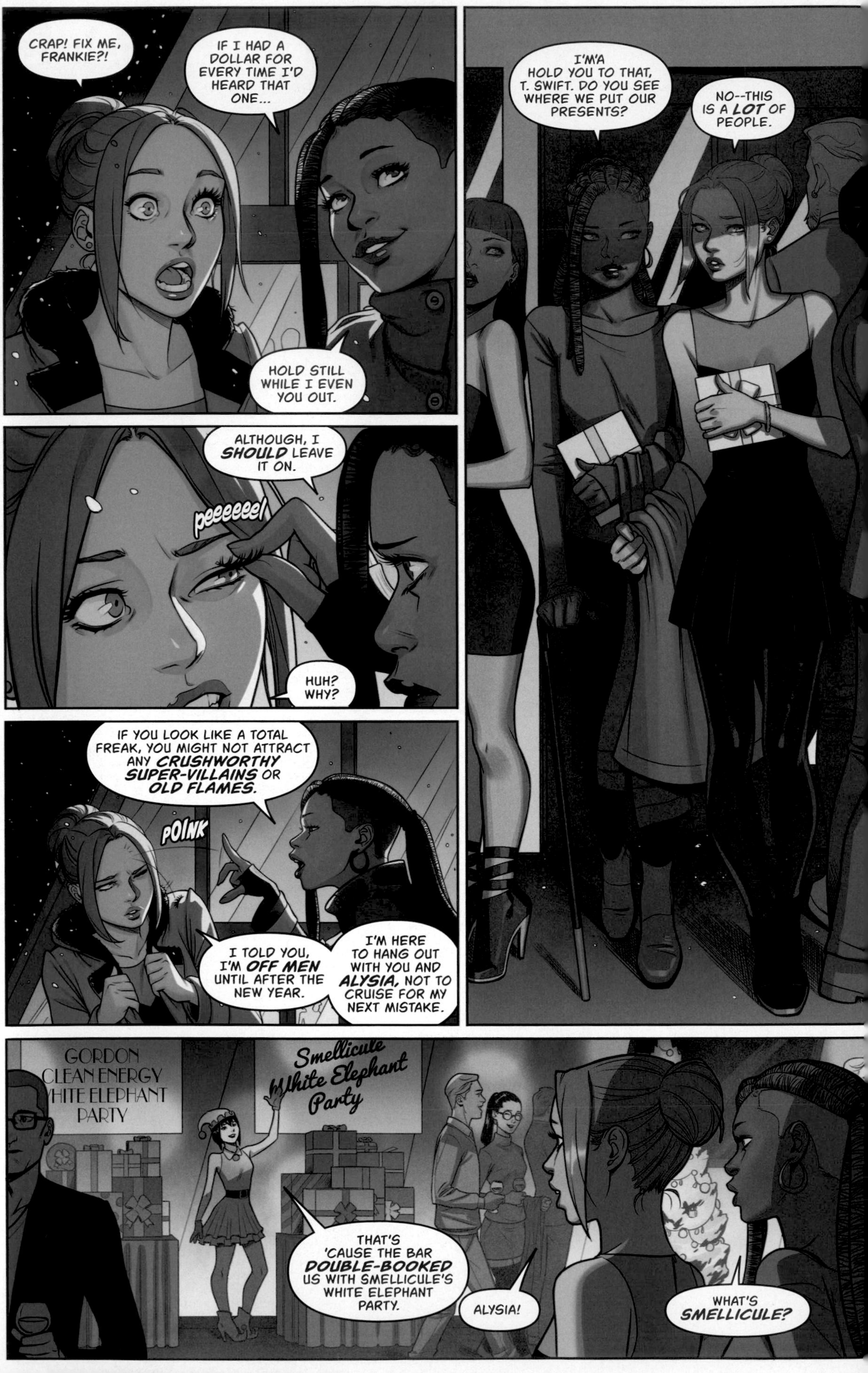
CRAP! FIX ME, FRANKIE?!
IF I HAD A DOLLAR FOR EVERY TIME I'D HEARD THAT ONE...
HOLD STILL WHILE I EVEN YOU OUT.
ALTHOUGH, I SHOULD LEAVE IT ON.
peeeeeel
HUH? WHY?
IF YOU LOOK LIKE A TOTAL FREAK, YOU MIGHT NOT ATTRACT ANY CRUSHWORTHY SUPER-VILLAINS OR OLD FLAMES.
POINK
I TOLD YOU, I'M OFF MEN UNTIL AFTER THE NEW YEAR.
I'M HERE TO HANG OUT WITH YOU AND ALYSIA, NOT TO CRUISE FOR MY NEXT MISTAKE.
I'M'A HOLD YOU TO THAT, T. SWIFT. DO YOU SEE WHERE WE PUT OUR PRESENTS?
NO--THIS IS A LOT OF PEOPLE.
GORDON CLEAN ENERGY WHITE ELEPHANT PARTY
Smellicule White Elephant Party
THAT'S 'CAUSE THE BAR DOUBLE-BOOKED US WITH SMELLICULE'S WHITE ELEPHANT PARTY.
ALYSIA!
WHAT'S SMELLICULE?

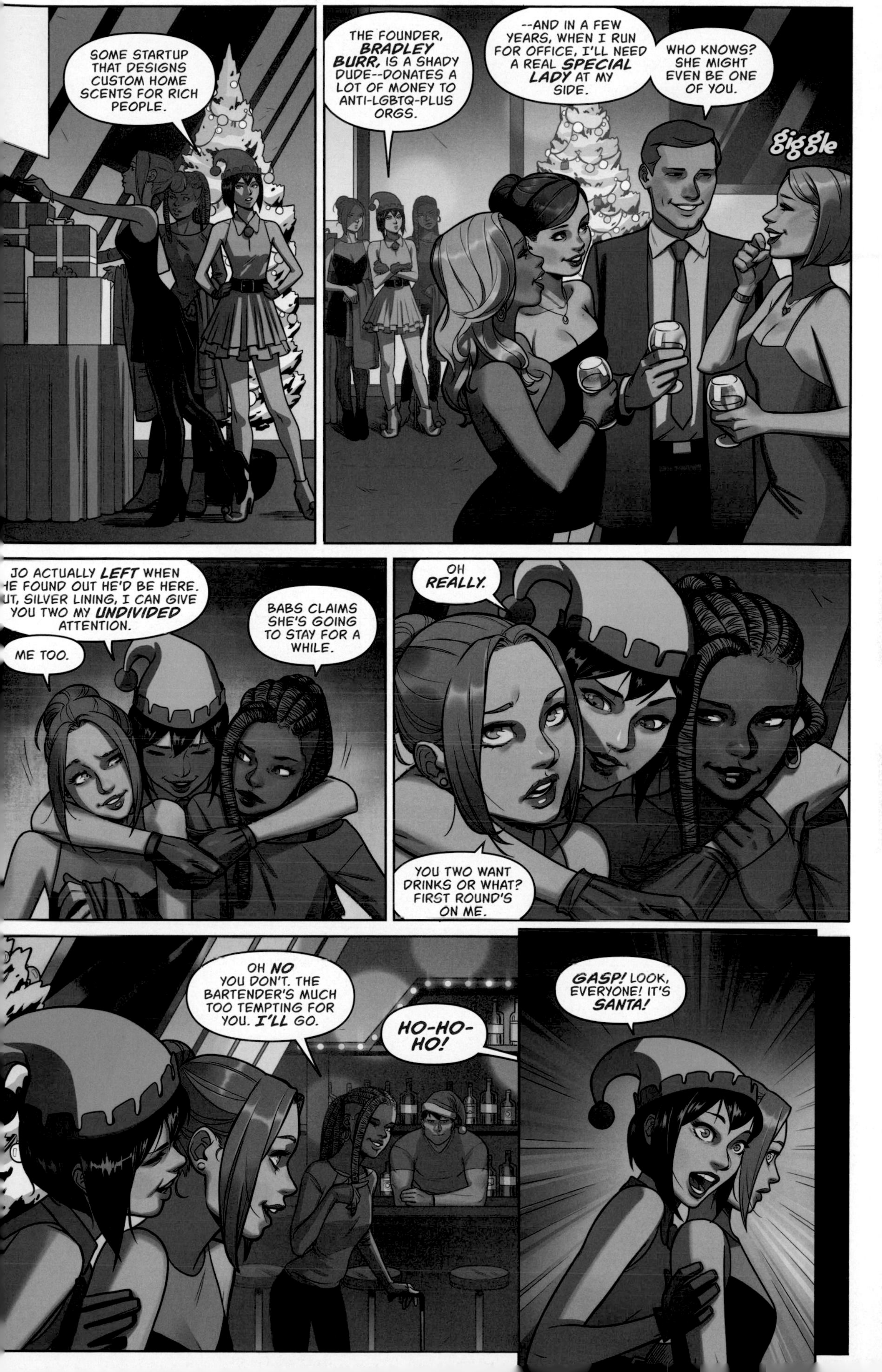
SOME STARTUP THAT DESIGNS CUSTOM HOME SCENTS FOR RICH PEOPLE.
THE FOUNDER, BRADLEY BURR, IS A SHADY DUDE--DONATES A LOT OF MONEY TO ANTI-LGBTQ-PLUS ORGS.
--AND IN A FEW YEARS, WHEN I RUN FOR OFFICE, I'LL NEED A REAL SPECIAL LADY AT MY SIDE.
WHO KNOWS? SHE MIGHT EVEN BE ONE OF YOU.
giggle
JO ACTUALLY LEFT WHEN E FOUND OUT HE'D BE HERE. UT, SILVER LINING, I CAN GIVE YOU TWO MY UNDIVIDED ATTENTION.
ME TOO.
BABS CLAIMS SHE'S GOING TO STAY FOR A WHILE.
OH REALLY.
YOU TWO WANT DRINKS OR WHAT? FIRST ROUND'S ON ME.
OH NO YOU DON'T. THE BARTENDER'S MUCH TOO TEMPTING FOR YOU. I'LL GO.
HO-HO-HO!
GASP! LOOK, EVERYONE! IT'S SANTA!

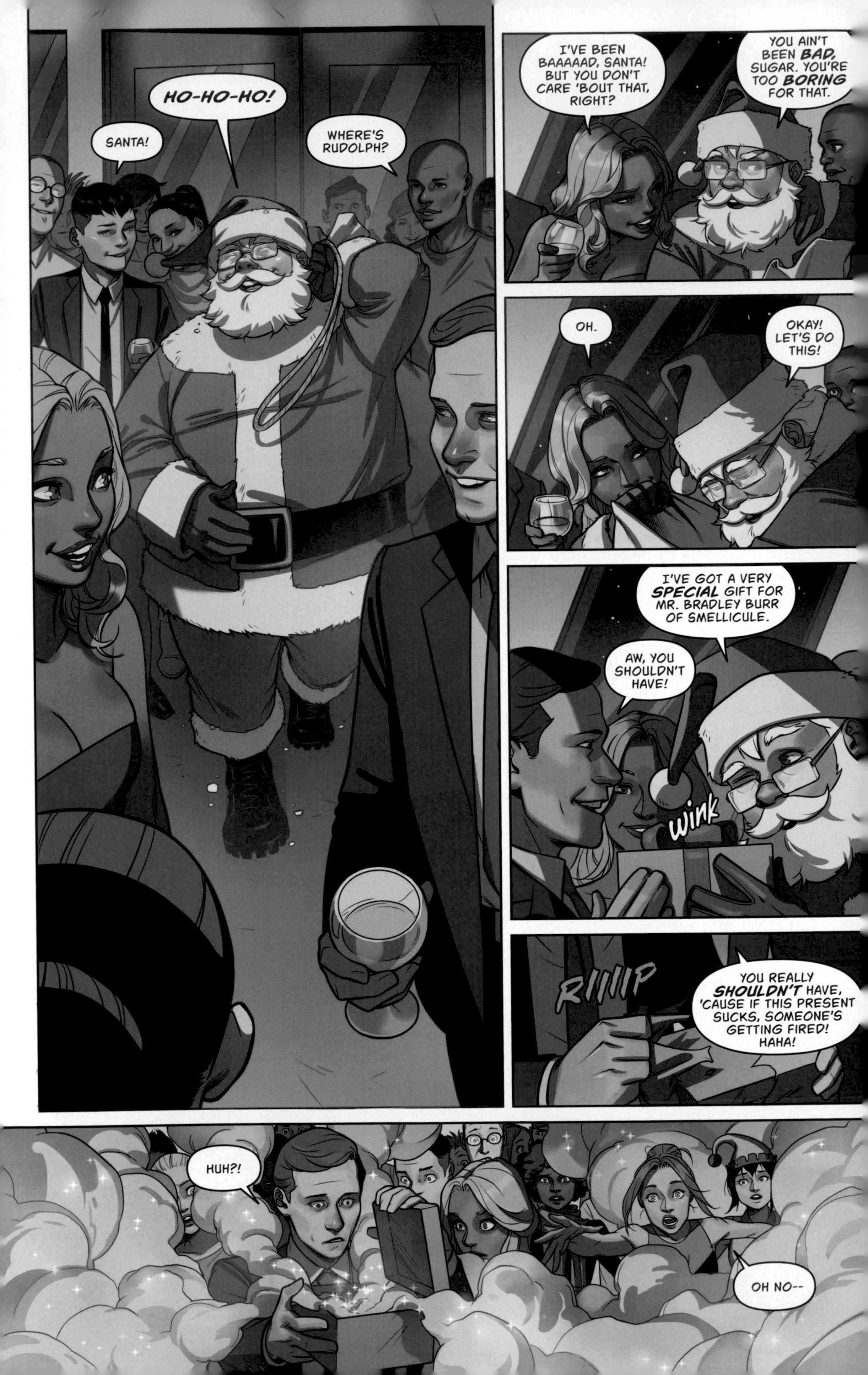

HO-HO-HO!
SANTA!
WHERE'S RUDOLPH?
I'VE BEEN BAAAAAD, SANTA! BUT YOU DON'T CARE 'BOUT THAT, RIGHT?
YOU AIN'T BEEN BAD, SUGAR. YOU'RE TOO BORING FOR THAT.
OH.
OKAY! LET'S DO THIS!
I'VE GOT A VERY SPECIAL GIFT FOR MR. BRADLEY BURR OF SMELLICULE.
AW, YOU SHOULDN'T HAVE!
wink
RIIIIP
YOU REALLY SHOULDN'T HAVE, 'CAUSE IF THIS PRESENT SUCKS, SOMEONE'S GETTING FIRED! HAHA!
HUH?!
OH NO--

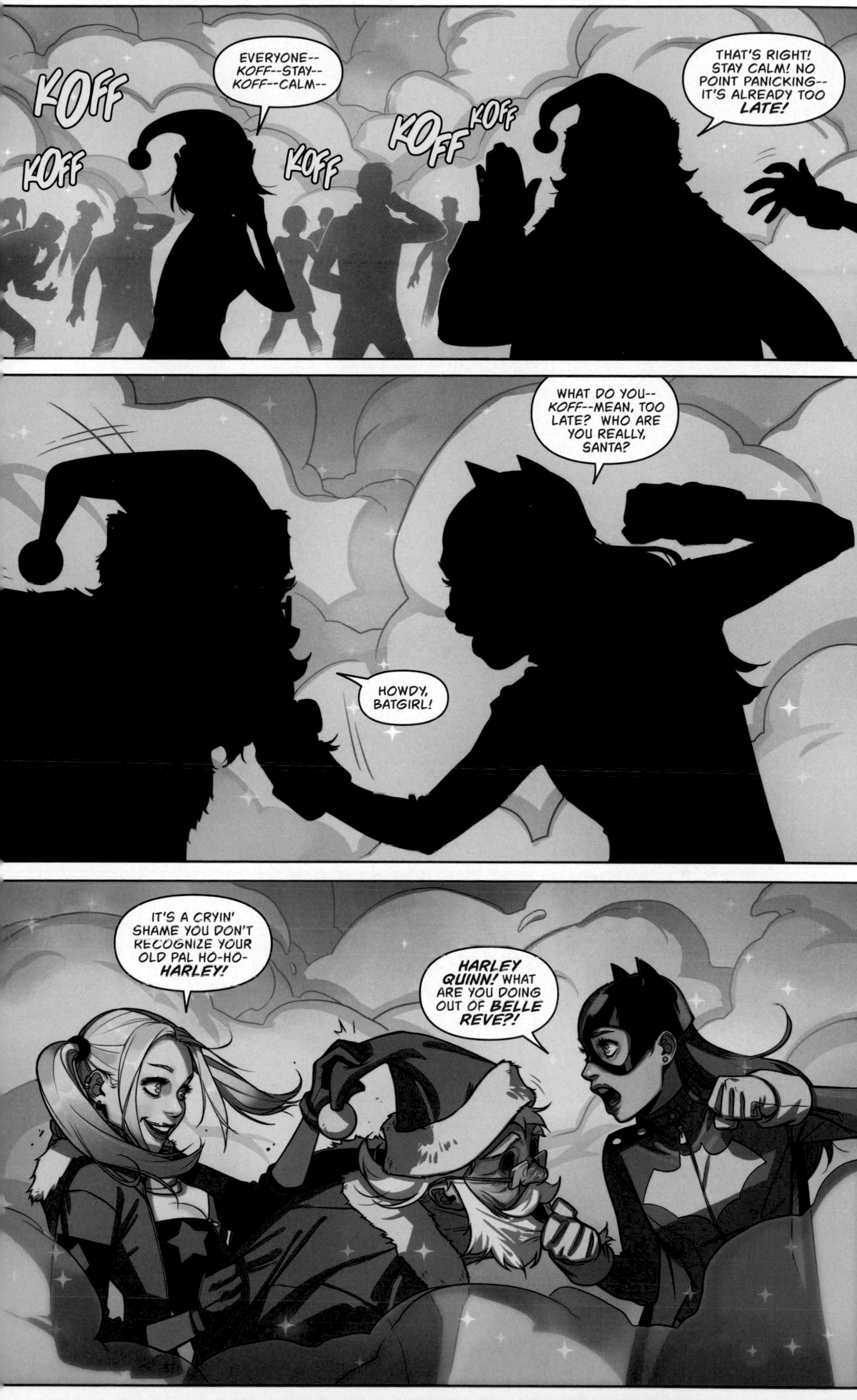
KOFF
KOFF
EVERYONE-- KOFF--STAY-- KOFF--CALM--
KOFF
KOFF
KOFF
THAT'S RIGHT! STAY CALM! NO POINT PANICKING-- IT'S ALREADY TOO LATE!
WHAT DO YOU-- KOFF--MEAN, TOO LATE? WHO ARE YOU REALLY, SANTA?
HOWDY, BATGIRL!
IT'S A CRYIN' SHAME YOU DON'T RECOGNIZE YOUR OLD PAL HO-HO-HARLEY!
HARLEY QUINN! WHAT ARE YOU DOING OUT OF BELLE REVE?!

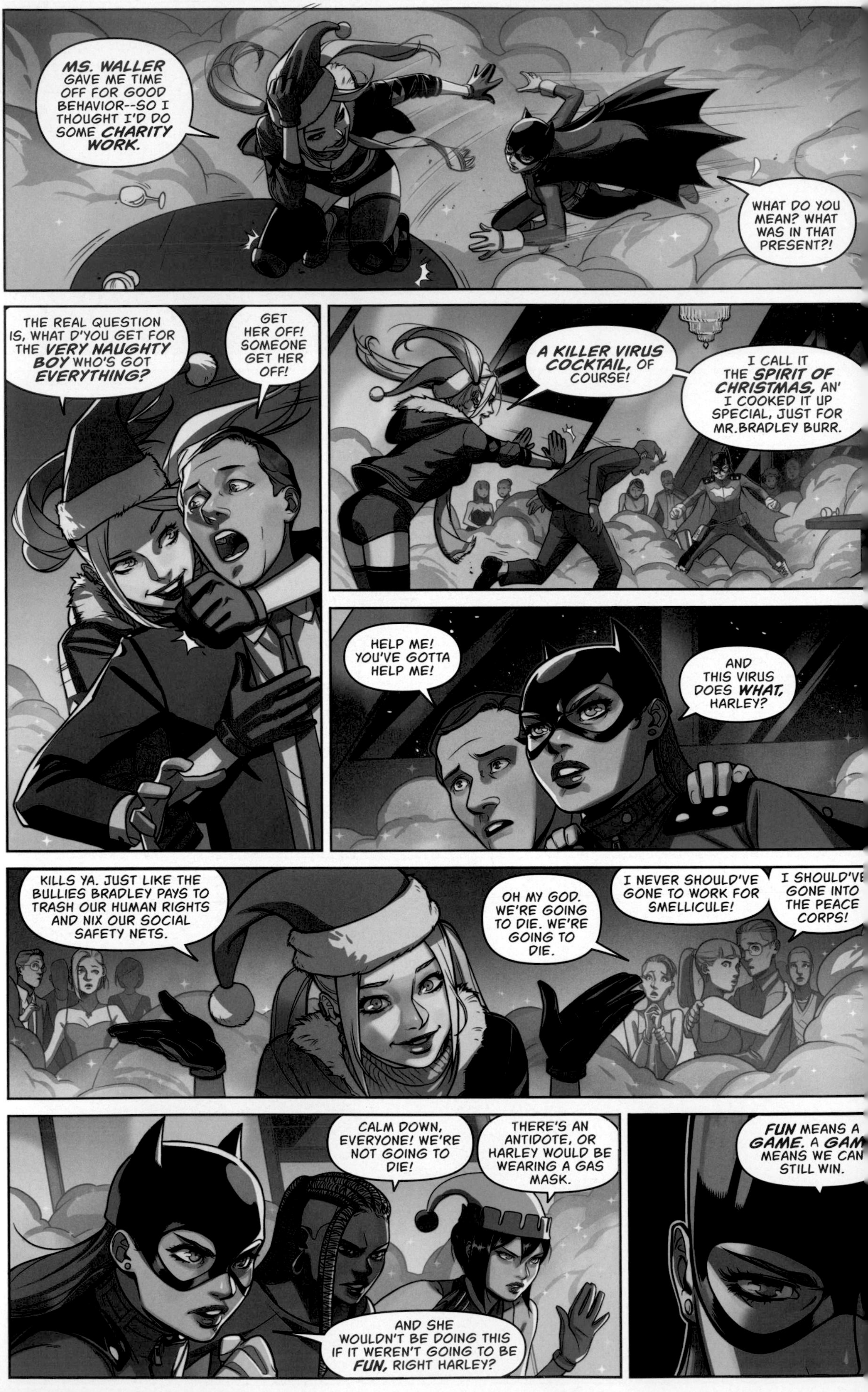
MS. WALLER GAVE ME TIME OFF FOR GOOD BEHAVIOR--SO I THOUGHT I'D DO SOME CHARITY WORK.
WHAT DO YOU MEAN? WHAT WAS IN THAT PRESENT?!
THE REAL QUESTION IS, WHAT D'YOU GET FOR THE VERY NAUGHTY BOY WHO'S GOT EVERYTHING?
GET HER OFF! SOMEONE GET HER OFF!
A KILLER VIRUS COCKTAIL, OF COURSE!
I CALL IT THE SPIRIT OF CHRISTMAS, AN' I COOKED IT UP SPECIAL, JUST FOR MR.BRADLEY BURR.
HELP ME! YOU'VE GOTTA HELP ME!
AND THIS VIRUS DOES WHAT, HARLEY?
KILLS YA. JUST LIKE THE BULLIES BRADLEY PAYS TO TRASH OUR HUMAN RIGHTS AND NIX OUR SOCIAL SAFETY NETS.
OH MY GOD. WE'RE GOING TO DIE. WE'RE GOING TO DIE.
I NEVER SHOULD'VE GONE TO WORK FOR SMELLICULE!
I SHOULD'VE GONE INTO THE PEACE CORPS!
CALM DOWN, EVERYONE! WE'RE NOT GOING TO DIE!
THERE'S AN ANTIDOTE, OR HARLEY WOULD BE WEARING A GAS MASK.
AND SHE WOULDN'T BE DOING THIS IF IT WEREN'T GOING TO BE FUN, RIGHT HARLEY?
FUN MEANS A GAME. A GAM MEANS WE CAN STILL WIN.

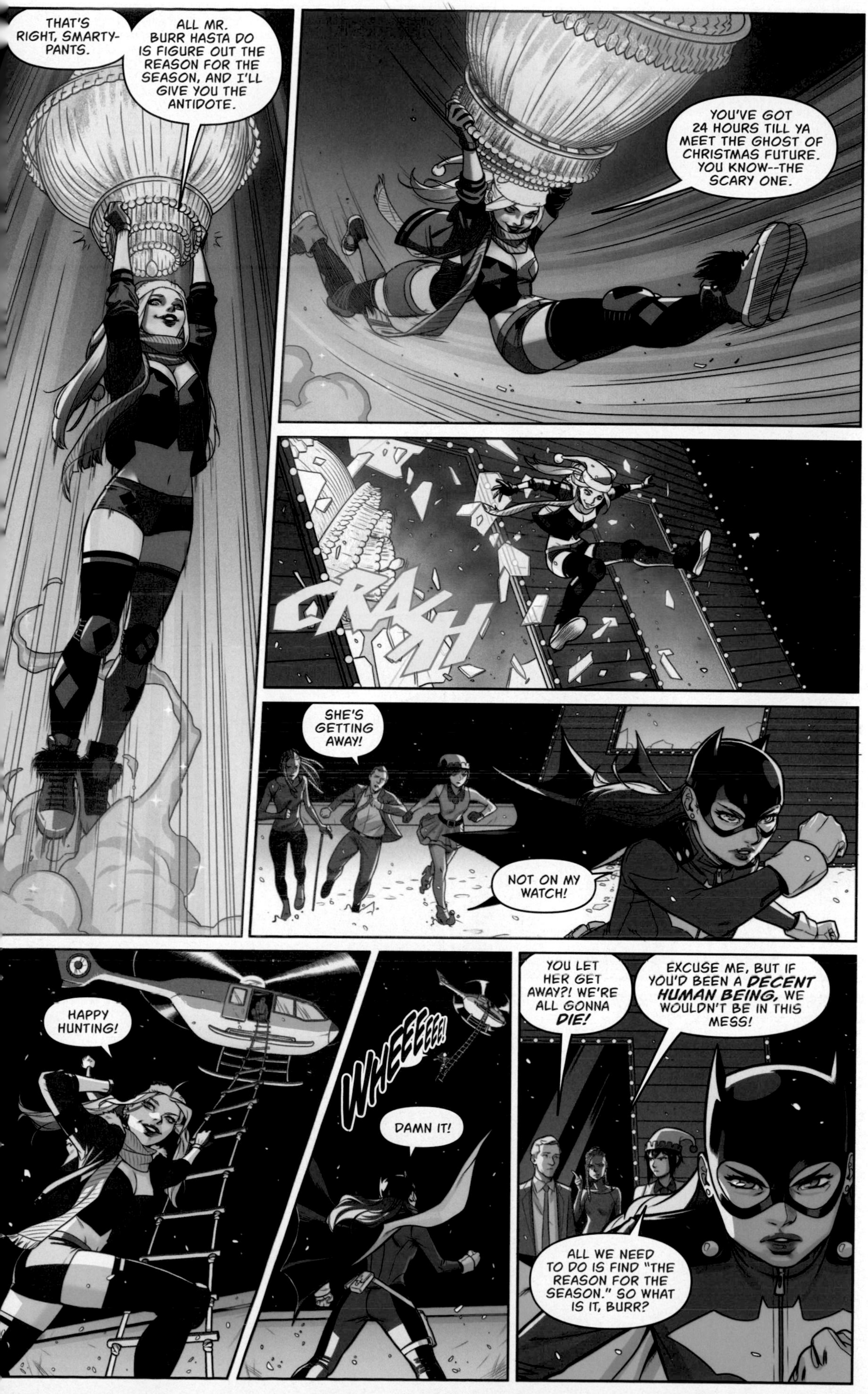
THAT'S RIGHT, SMARTY-PANTS.
ALL MR. BURR HASTA DO IS FIGURE OUT THE REASON FOR THE SEASON, AND I'LL GIVE YOU THE ANTIDOTE.
YOU'VE GOT 24 HOURS TILL YA MEET THE GHOST OF CHRISTMAS FUTURE. YOU KNOW--THE SCARY ONE.
CRASH
SHE'S GETTING AWAY!
NOT ON MY WATCH!
HAPPY HUNTING!
WHEEEEEEE!
DAMN IT!
YOU LET HER GET AWAY?! WE'RE ALL GONNA *DIE!*
EXCUSE ME, BUT IF YOU'D BEEN A ***DECENT HUMAN BEING,*** WE WOULDN'T BE IN THIS MESS!
ALL WE NEED TO DO IS FIND "THE REASON FOR THE SEASON." SO WHAT IS IT, BURR?

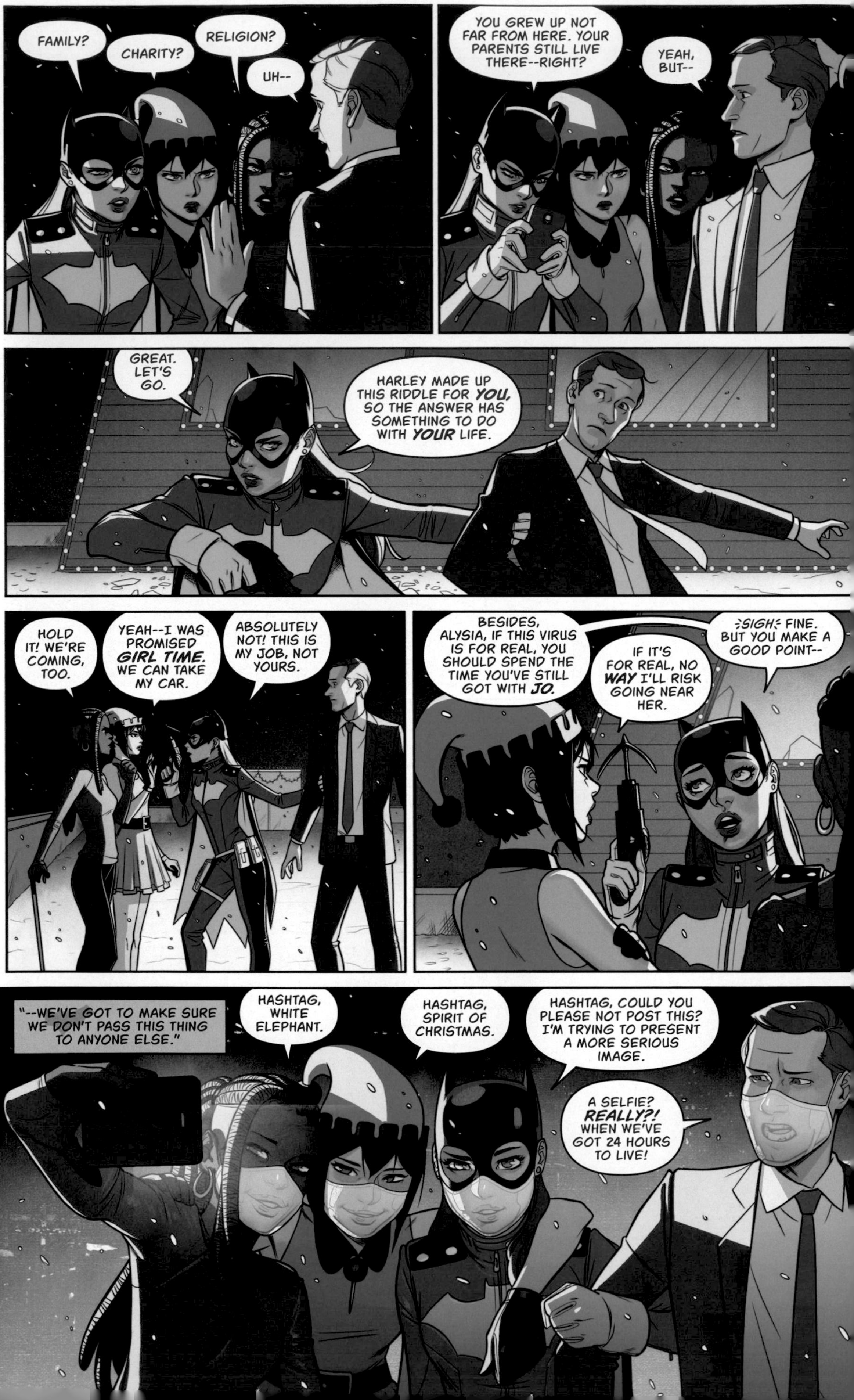
FAMILY?
CHARITY?
RELIGION?
UH--
YOU GREW UP NOT FAR FROM HERE. YOUR PARENTS STILL LIVE THERE--RIGHT?
YEAH, BUT--
GREAT. LET'S GO.
HARLEY MADE UP THIS RIDDLE FOR YOU, SO THE ANSWER HAS SOMETHING TO DO WITH YOUR LIFE.
HOLD IT! WE'RE COMING, TOO.
YEAH--I WAS PROMISED GIRL TIME. WE CAN TAKE MY CAR.
ABSOLUTELY NOT! THIS IS MY JOB, NOT YOURS.
BESIDES, ALYSIA, IF THIS VIRUS IS FOR REAL, YOU SHOULD SPEND THE TIME YOU'VE STILL GOT WITH JO.
IF IT'S FOR REAL, NO WAY I'LL RISK GOING NEAR HER.
SIGH FINE. BUT YOU MAKE A GOOD POINT--
"--WE'VE GOT TO MAKE SURE WE DON'T PASS THIS THING TO ANYONE ELSE."
HASHTAG, WHITE ELEPHANT.
HASHTAG, SPIRIT OF CHRISTMAS.
HASHTAG, COULD YOU PLEASE NOT POST THIS? I'M TRYING TO PRESENT A MORE SERIOUS IMAGE.
A SELFIE? REALLY?! WHEN WE'VE GOT 24 HOURS TO LIVE!

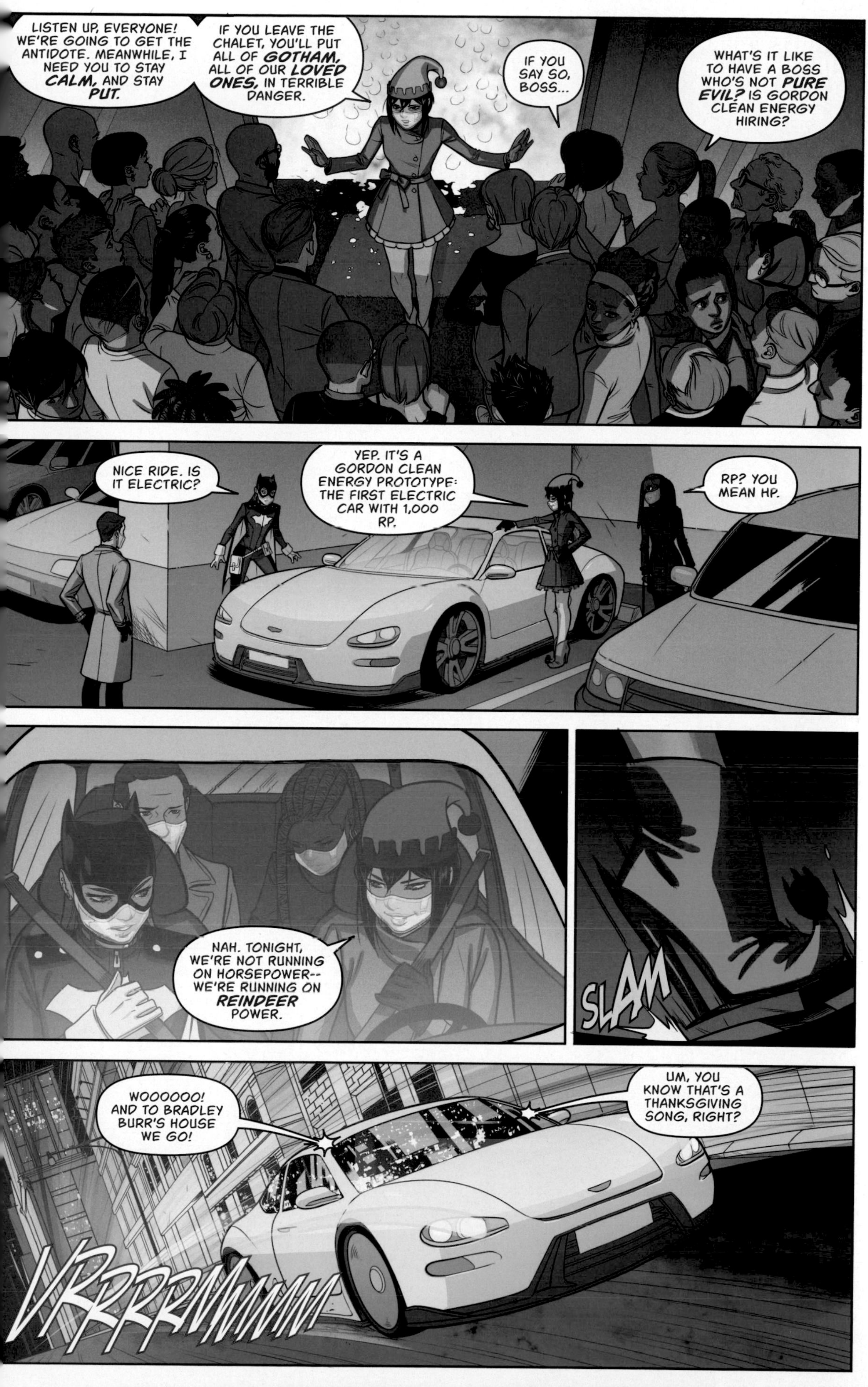
LISTEN UP, EVERYONE! WE'RE GOING TO GET THE ANTIDOTE. MEANWHILE, I NEED YOU TO STAY CALM, AND STAY PUT.
IF YOU LEAVE THE CHALET, YOU'LL PUT ALL OF GOTHAM, ALL OF OUR LOVED ONES, IN TERRIBLE DANGER.
IF YOU SAY SO, BOSS...
WHAT'S IT LIKE TO HAVE A BOSS WHO'S NOT PURE EVIL? IS GORDON CLEAN ENERGY HIRING?
NICE RIDE. IS IT ELECTRIC?
YEP. IT'S A GORDON CLEAN ENERGY PROTOTYPE: THE FIRST ELECTRIC CAR WITH 1,000 RP.
RP? YOU MEAN HP.
NAH. TONIGHT, WE'RE NOT RUNNING ON HORSEPOWER-- WE'RE RUNNING ON REINDEER POWER.
SLAM
WOOOOOO! AND TO BRADLEY BURR'S HOUSE WE GO!
UM, YOU KNOW THAT'S A THANKSGIVING SONG, RIGHT?
VRRRRMMMMM

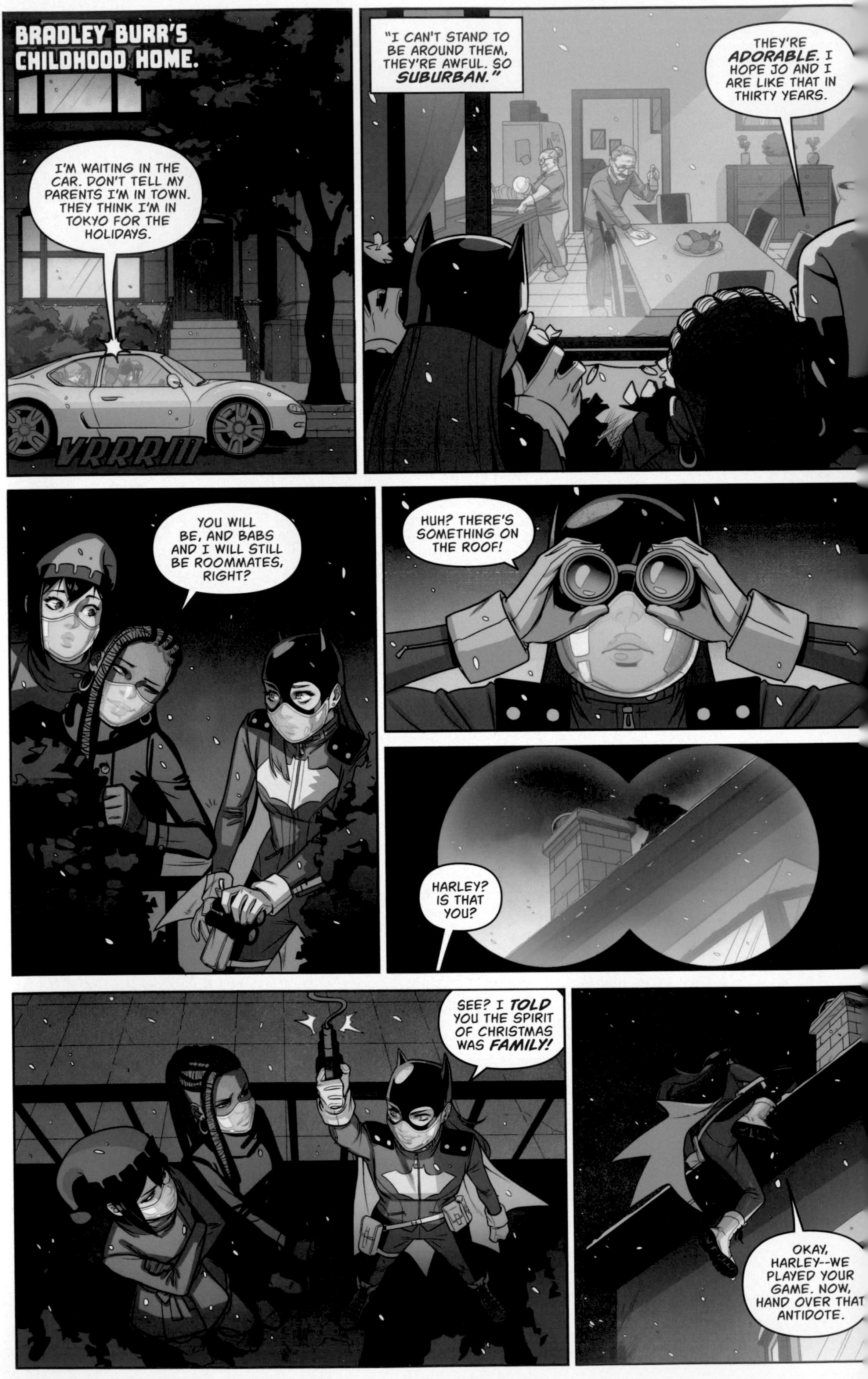
BRADLEY BURR'S CHILDHOOD HOME.
I'M WAITING IN THE CAR. DON'T TELL MY PARENTS I'M IN TOWN. THEY THINK I'M IN TOKYO FOR THE HOLIDAYS.
VRRRM
"I CAN'T STAND TO BE AROUND THEM, THEY'RE AWFUL. SO SUBURBAN."
THEY'RE ADORABLE. I HOPE JO AND I ARE LIKE THAT IN THIRTY YEARS.
YOU WILL BE, AND BABS AND I WILL STILL BE ROOMMATES, RIGHT?
HUH? THERE'S SOMETHING ON THE ROOF!
HARLEY? IS THAT YOU?
SEE? I TOLD YOU THE SPIRIT OF CHRISTMAS WAS FAMILY!
OKAY, HARLEY--WE PLAYED YOUR GAME. NOW, HAND OVER THAT ANTIDOTE.

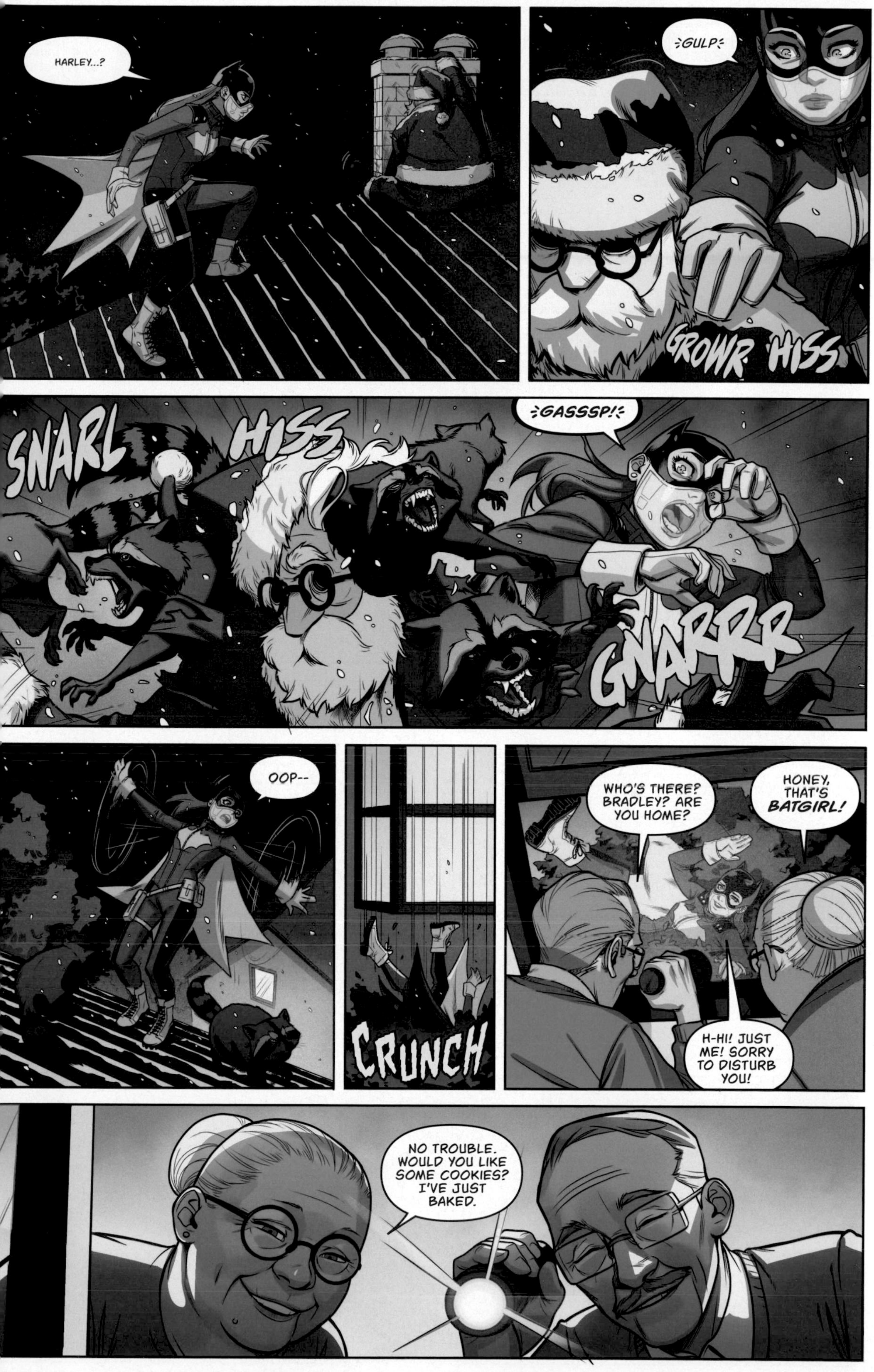
HARLEY...?
:GULP:
GROWR HISS
SNARL
HISS
:GASSSP!:
GNARRR
OOP--
CRUNCH
WHO'S THERE? BRADLEY? ARE YOU HOME?
HONEY, THAT'S BATGIRL!
H-HI! JUST ME! SORRY TO DISTURB YOU!
NO TROUBLE. WOULD YOU LIKE SOME COOKIES? I'VE JUST BAKED.

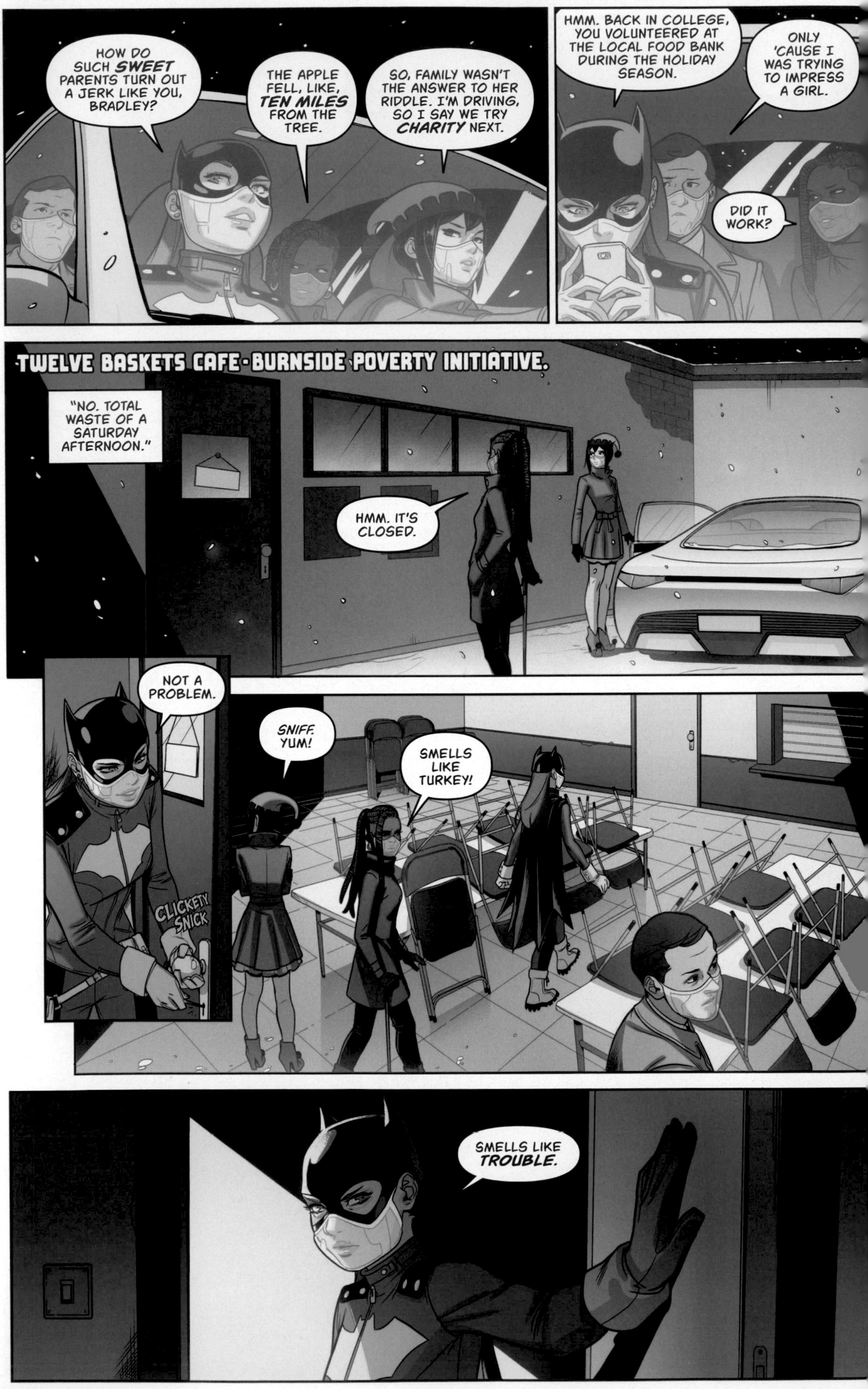
HOW DO SUCH SWEET PARENTS TURN OUT A JERK LIKE YOU, BRADLEY?
THE APPLE FELL, LIKE, TEN MILES FROM THE TREE.
SO, FAMILY WASN'T THE ANSWER TO HER RIDDLE. I'M DRIVING, SO I SAY WE TRY CHARITY NEXT.
HMM. BACK IN COLLEGE, YOU VOLUNTEERED AT THE LOCAL FOOD BANK DURING THE HOLIDAY SEASON.
ONLY 'CAUSE I WAS TRYING TO IMPRESS A GIRL.
DID IT WORK?
TWELVE BASKETS CAFE - BURNSIDE POVERTY INITIATIVE.
"NO. TOTAL WASTE OF A SATURDAY AFTERNOON."
HMM. IT'S CLOSED.
NOT A PROBLEM.
CLICKETY SNICK
SNIFF. YUM!
SMELLS LIKE TURKEY!
SMELLS LIKE TROUBLE.

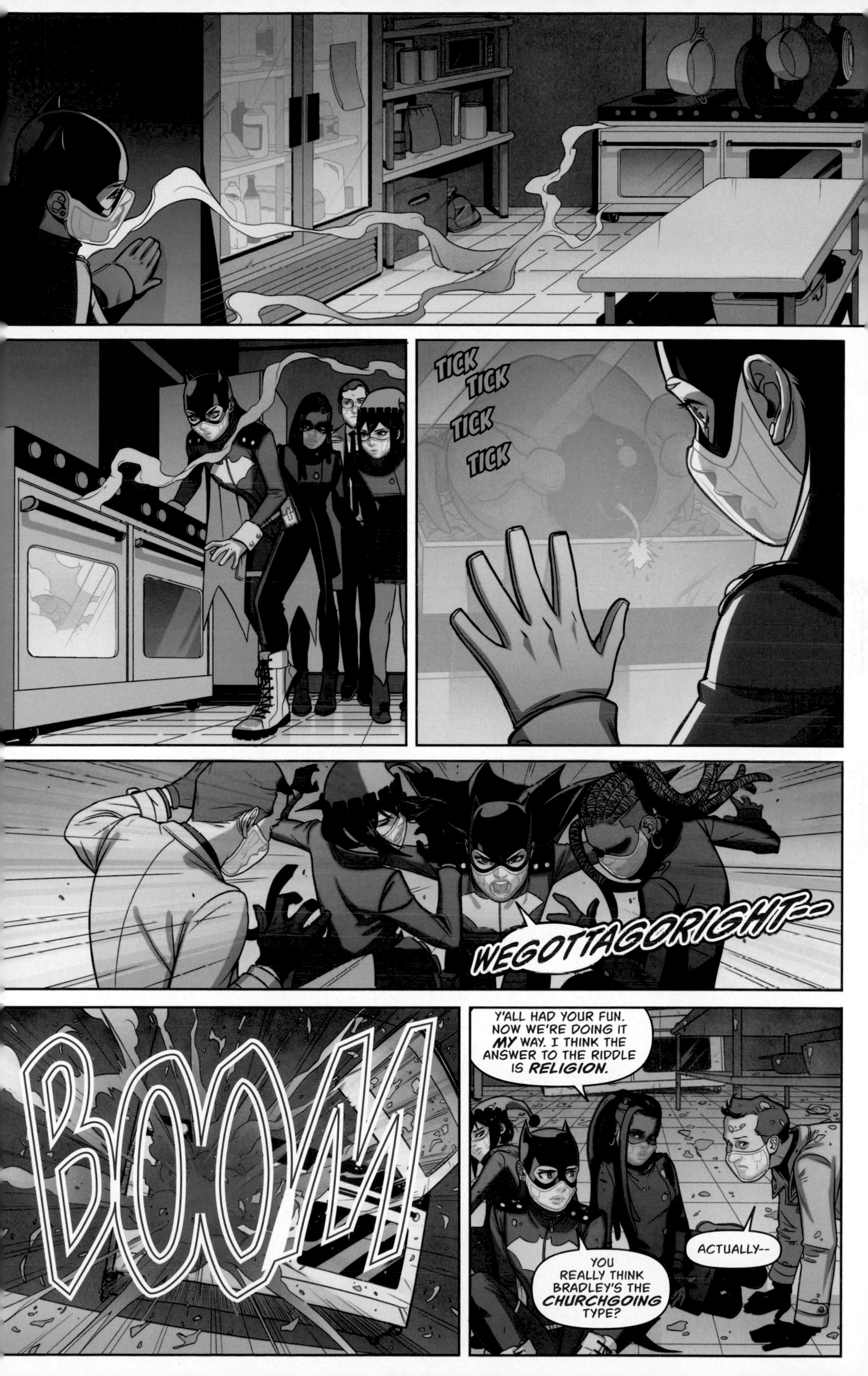
TICK
TICK
TICK
TICK
WEGOTTAGORIGHT--
BOOM
Y'ALL HAD YOUR FUN. NOW WE'RE DOING IT MY WAY. I THINK THE ANSWER TO THE RIDDLE IS RELIGION.
YOU REALLY THINK BRADLEY'S THE CHURCHGOING TYPE?
ACTUALLY--

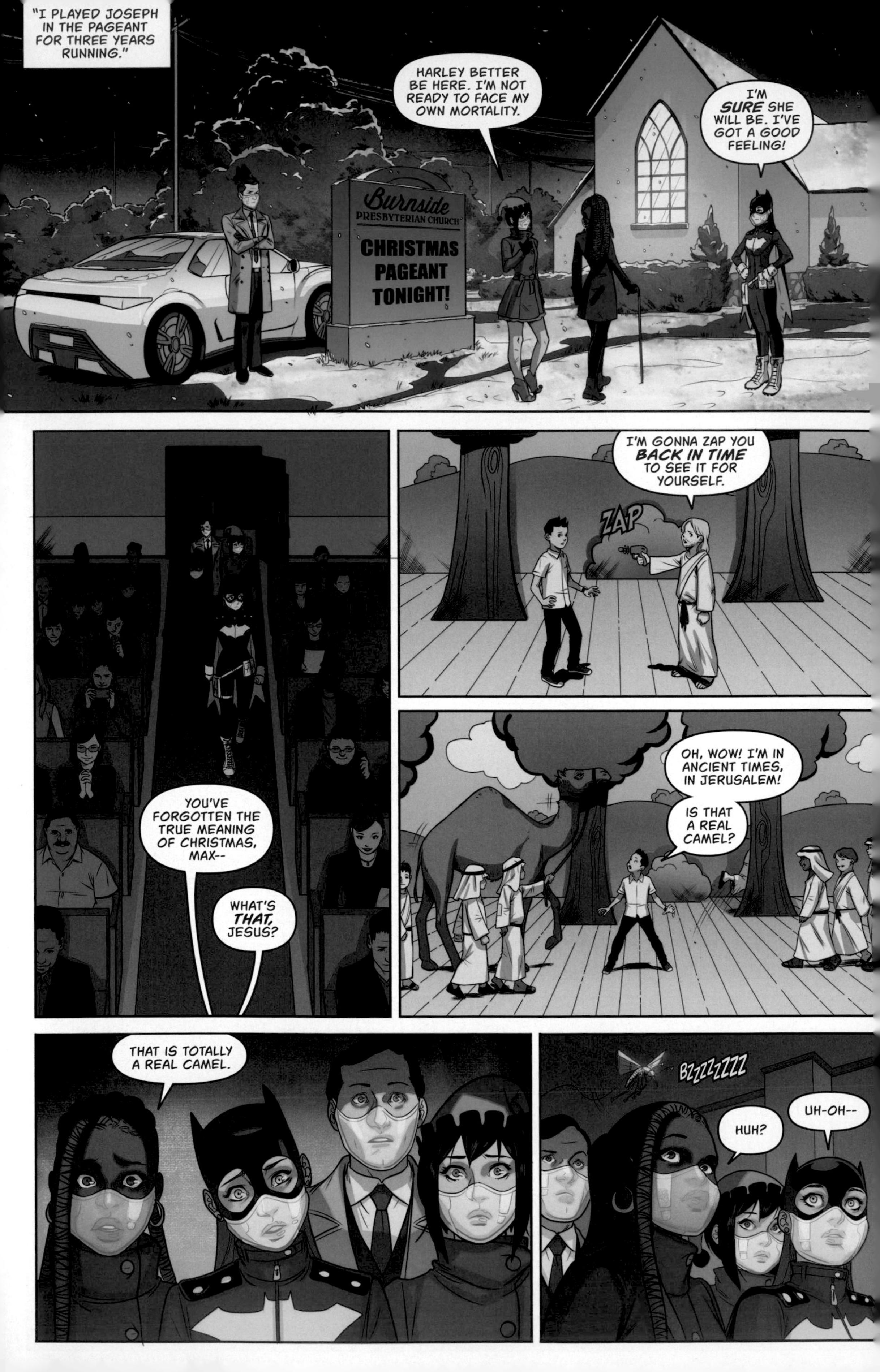
"I PLAYED JOSEPH IN THE PAGEANT FOR THREE YEARS RUNNING."
HARLEY BETTER BE HERE. I'M NOT READY TO FACE MY OWN MORTALITY.
I'M SURE SHE WILL BE. I'VE GOT A GOOD FEELING!
Burnside PRESBYTERIAN CHURCH
CHRISTMAS PAGEANT TONIGHT!
I'M GONNA ZAP YOU BACK IN TIME TO SEE IT FOR YOURSELF.
ZAP
YOU'VE FORGOTTEN THE TRUE MEANING OF CHRISTMAS, MAX--
WHAT'S THAT, JESUS?
OH, WOW! I'M IN ANCIENT TIMES, IN JERUSALEM!
IS THAT A REAL CAMEL?
THAT IS TOTALLY A REAL CAMEL.
BZZZZZZZ
HUH?
UH-OH--

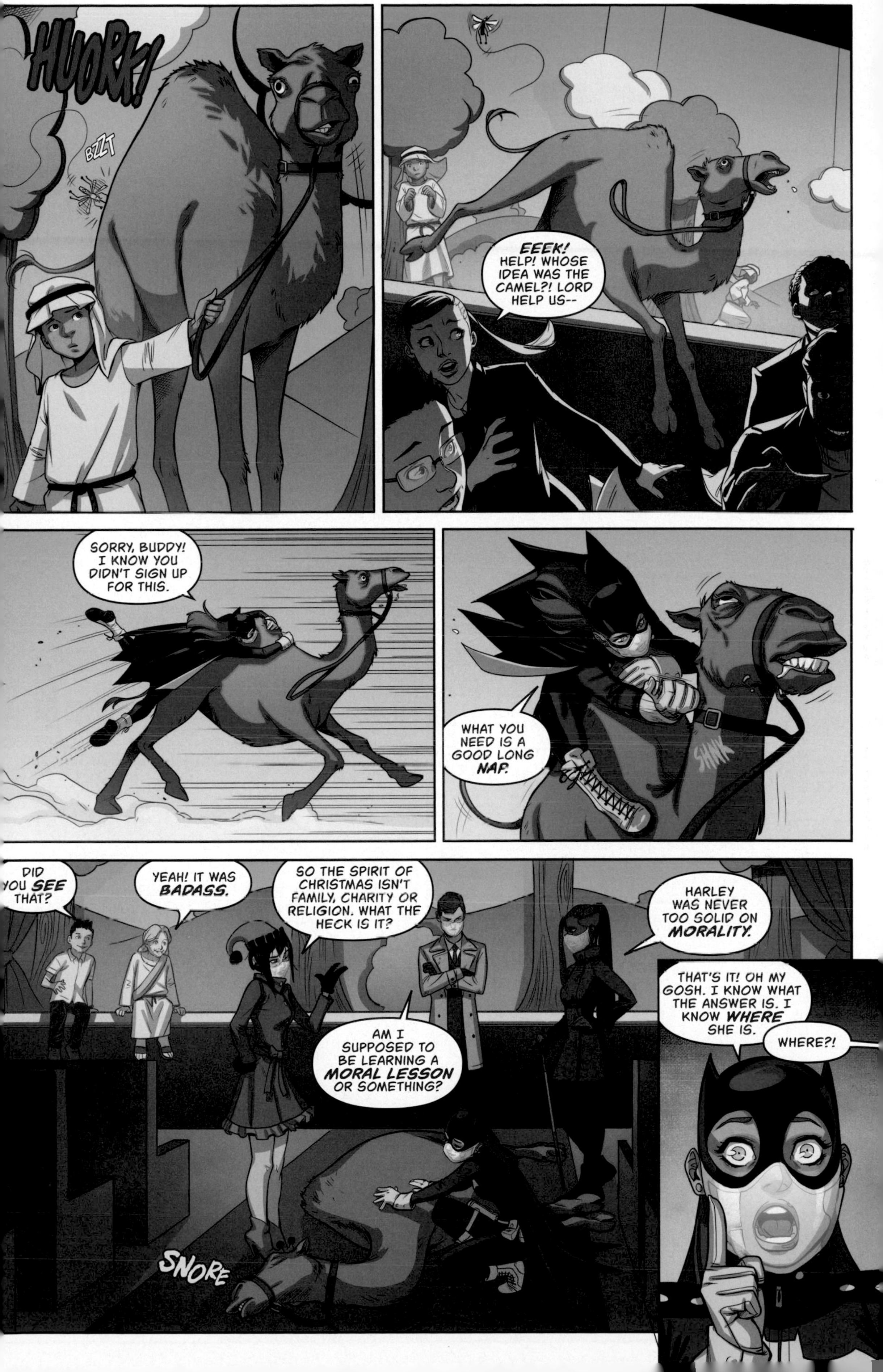
HUORK!
BZZT
EEEK! HELP! WHOSE IDEA WAS THE CAMEL?! LORD HELP US--
SORRY, BUDDY! I KNOW YOU DIDN'T SIGN UP FOR THIS.
WHAT YOU NEED IS A GOOD LONG NAP.
SHNK
DID YOU SEE THAT?
YEAH! IT WAS BADASS.
SO THE SPIRIT OF CHRISTMAS ISN'T FAMILY, CHARITY OR RELIGION. WHAT THE HECK IS IT?
HARLEY WAS NEVER TOO SOLID ON MORALITY.
AM I SUPPOSED TO BE LEARNING A MORAL LESSON OR SOMETHING?
SNORE
THAT'S IT! OH MY GOSH. I KNOW WHAT THE ANSWER IS. I KNOW WHERE SHE IS.
WHERE?!

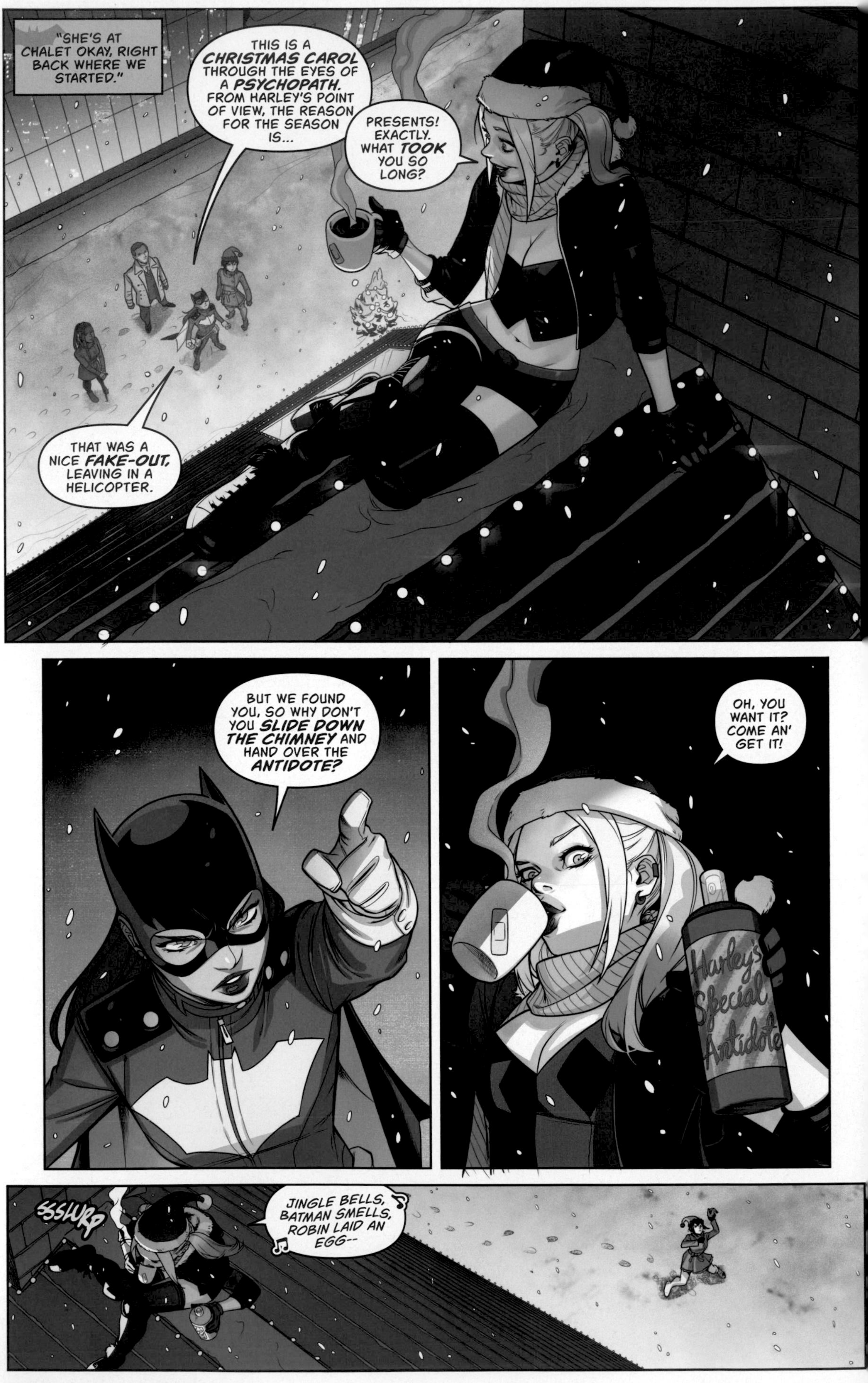
"SHE'S AT CHALET OKAY, RIGHT BACK WHERE WE STARTED."
THIS IS A CHRISTMAS CAROL THROUGH THE EYES OF A PSYCHOPATH. FROM HARLEY'S POINT OF VIEW, THE REASON FOR THE SEASON IS...
PRESENTS! EXACTLY. WHAT TOOK YOU SO LONG?
THAT WAS A NICE FAKE-OUT, LEAVING IN A HELICOPTER.
BUT WE FOUND YOU, SO WHY DON'T YOU SLIDE DOWN THE CHIMNEY AND HAND OVER THE ANTIDOTE?
OH, YOU WANT IT? COME AN' GET IT!
Harley's Special Antidote
SSSLURP
JINGLE BELLS, BATMAN SMELLS, ROBIN LAID AN EGG--

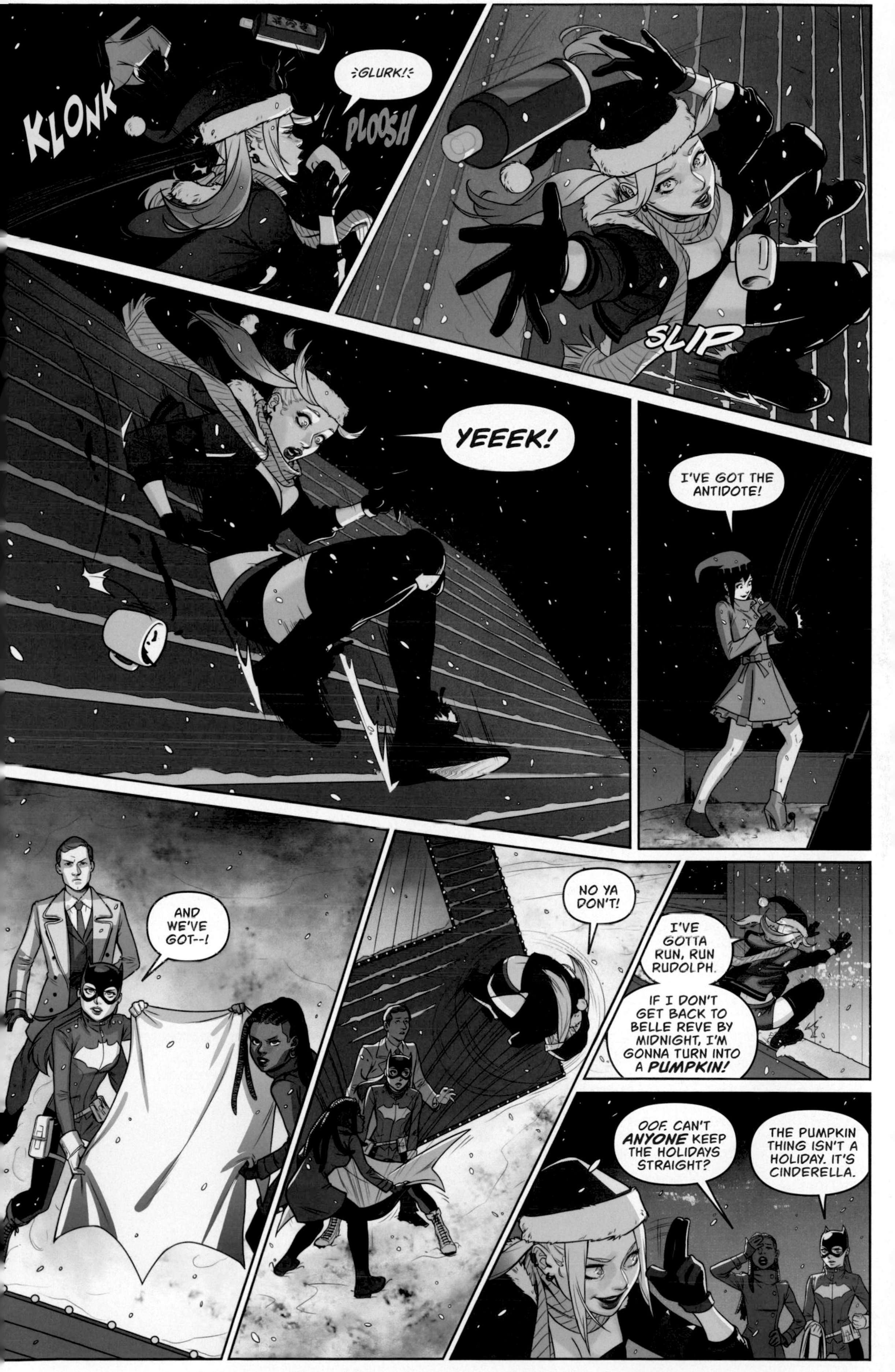
KLONK
GLURK!
PLOOSH
SLIP
YEEEK!
I'VE GOT THE ANTIDOTE!
AND WE'VE GOT--!
NO YA DON'T!
I'VE GOTTA RUN, RUN RUDOLPH.
IF I DON'T GET BACK TO BELLE REVE BY MIDNIGHT, I'M GONNA TURN INTO A PUMPKIN!
OOF. CAN'T ANYONE KEEP THE HOLIDAYS STRAIGHT?
THE PUMPKIN THING ISN'T A HOLIDAY. IT'S CINDERELLA.

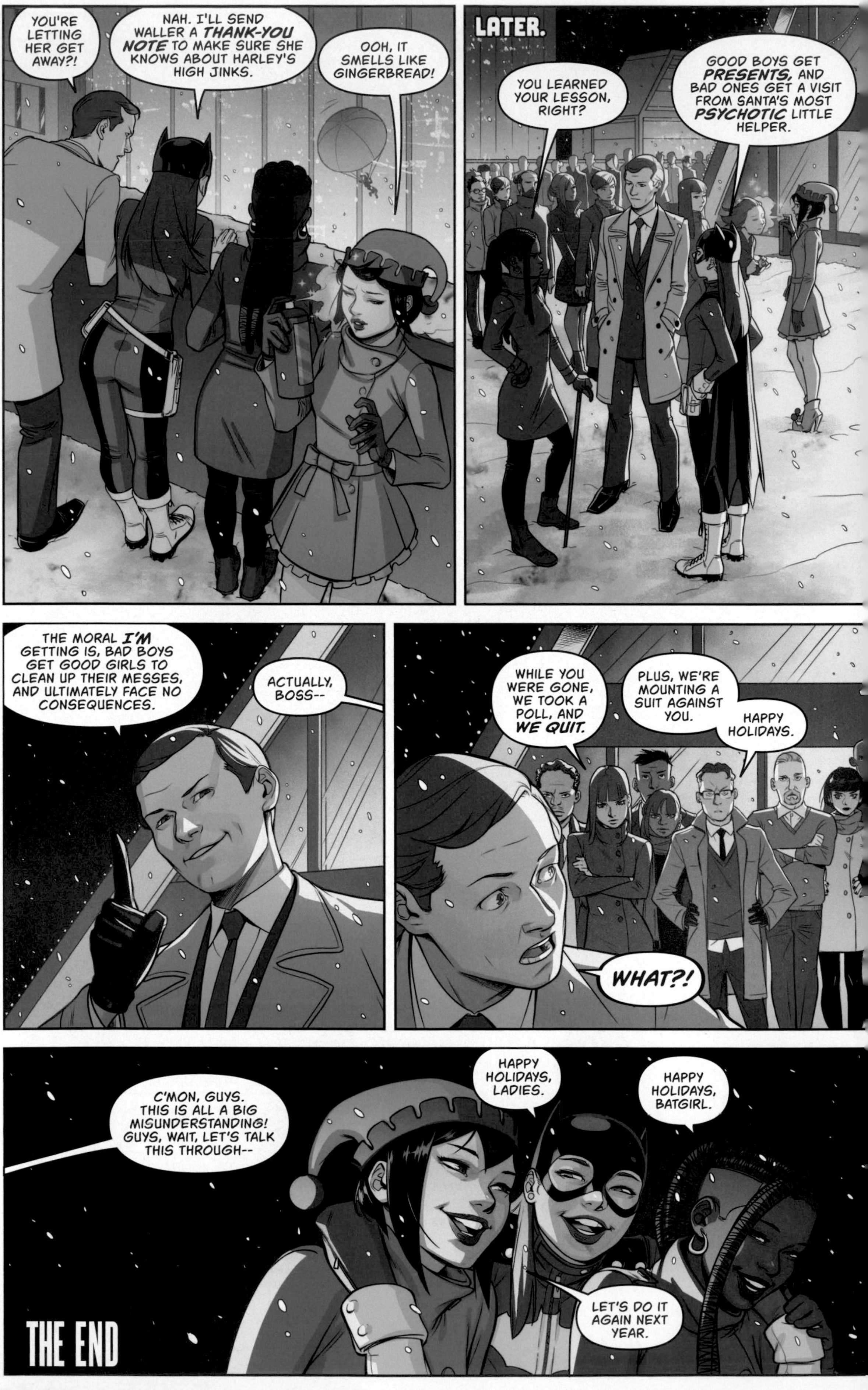
YOU'RE LETTING HER GET AWAY?!
NAH. I'LL SEND WALLER A THANK-YOU NOTE TO MAKE SURE SHE KNOWS ABOUT HARLEY'S HIGH JINKS.
OOH, IT SMELLS LIKE GINGERBREAD!
LATER.
YOU LEARNED YOUR LESSON, RIGHT?
GOOD BOYS GET PRESENTS, AND BAD ONES GET A VISIT FROM SANTA'S MOST PSYCHOTIC LITTLE HELPER.
THE MORAL I'M GETTING IS, BAD BOYS GET GOOD GIRLS TO CLEAN UP THEIR MESSES, AND ULTIMATELY FACE NO CONSEQUENCES.
ACTUALLY, BOSS--
WHILE YOU WERE GONE, WE TOOK A POLL, AND WE QUIT.
PLUS, WE'RE MOUNTING A SUIT AGAINST YOU.
HAPPY HOLIDAYS.
WHAT?!
C'MON, GUYS. THIS IS ALL A BIG MISUNDERSTANDING! GUYS, WAIT, LET'S TALK THIS THROUGH--
HAPPY HOLIDAYS, LADIES.
HAPPY HOLIDAYS, BATGIRL.
LET'S DO IT AGAIN NEXT YEAR.
THE END

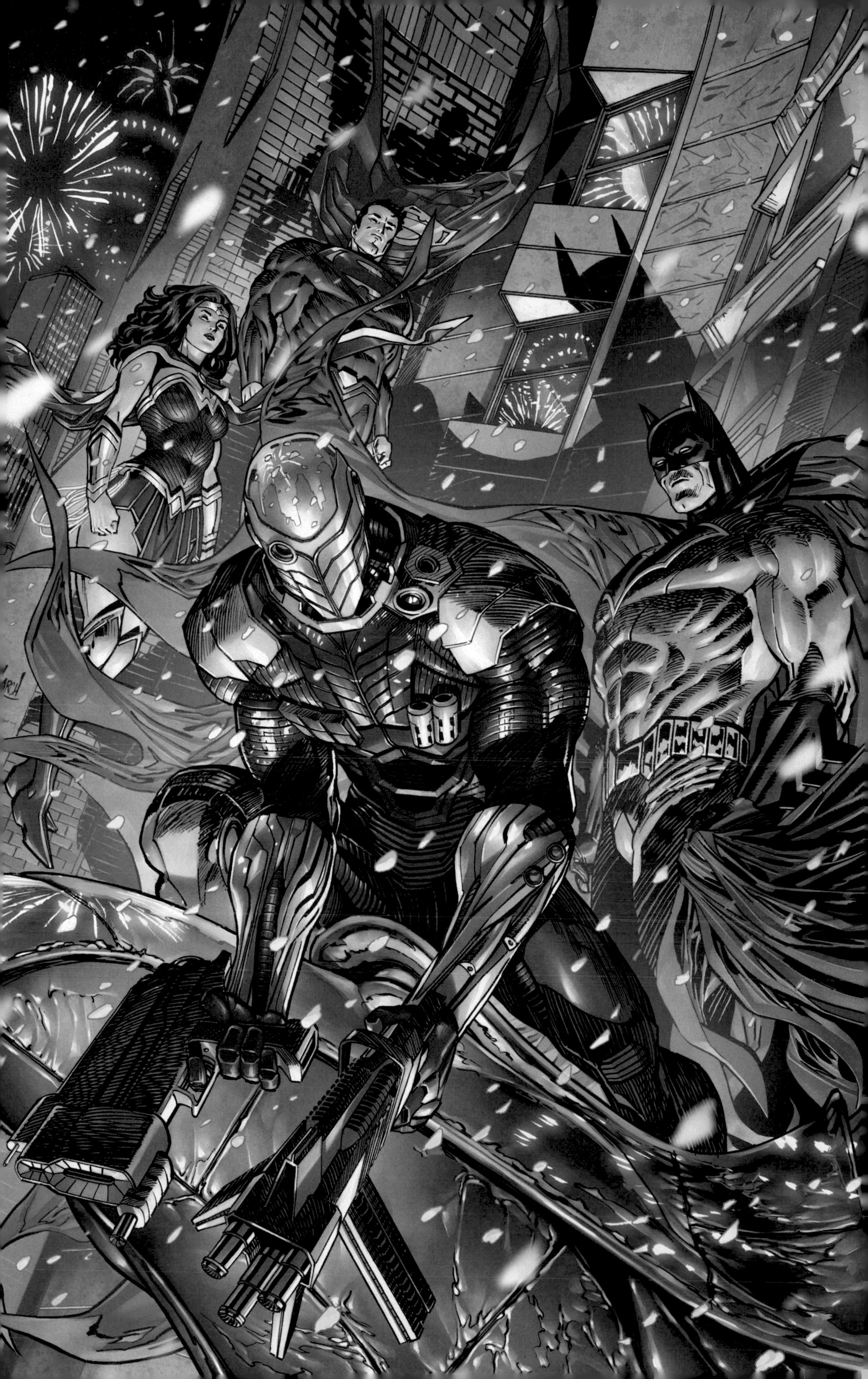

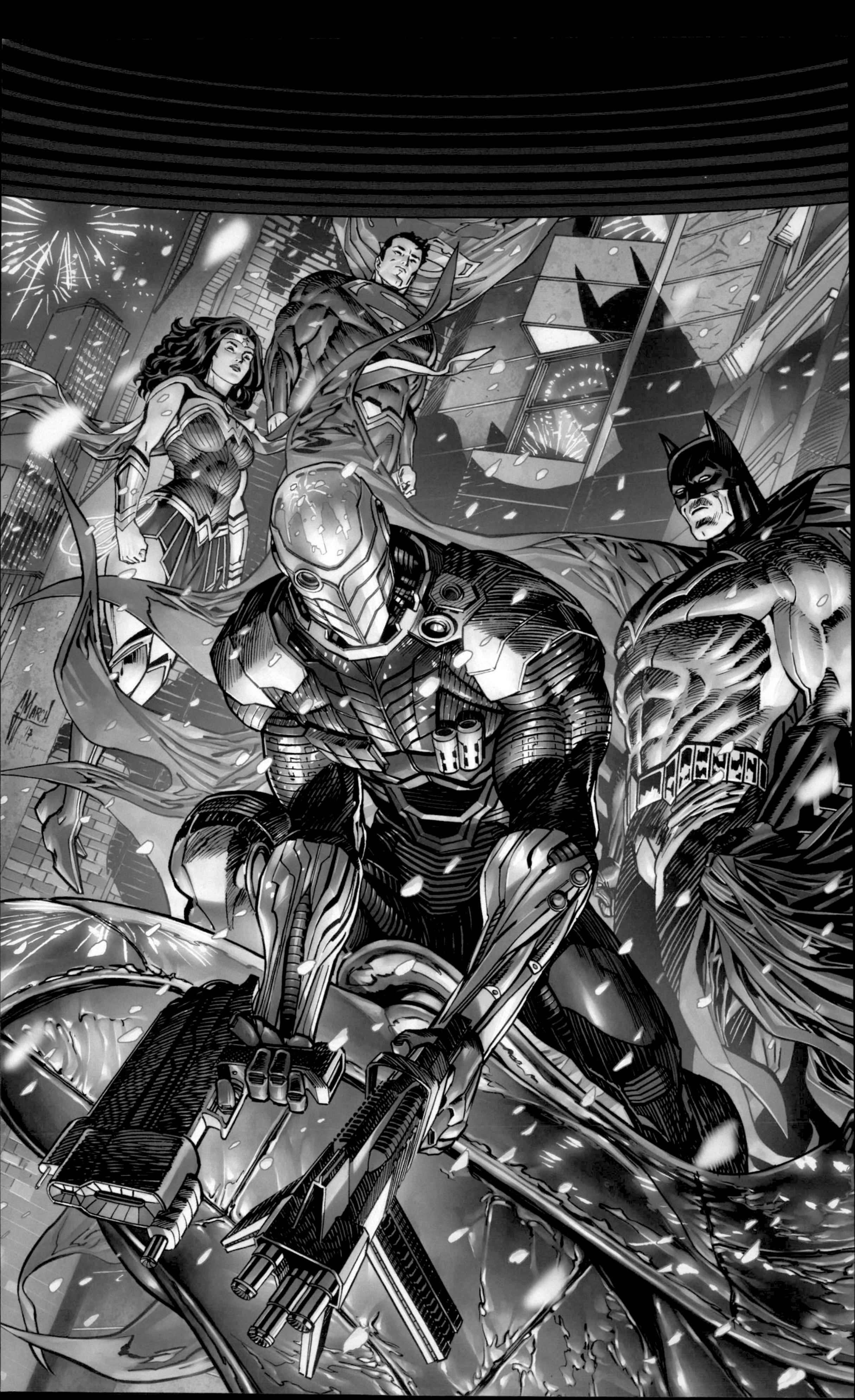

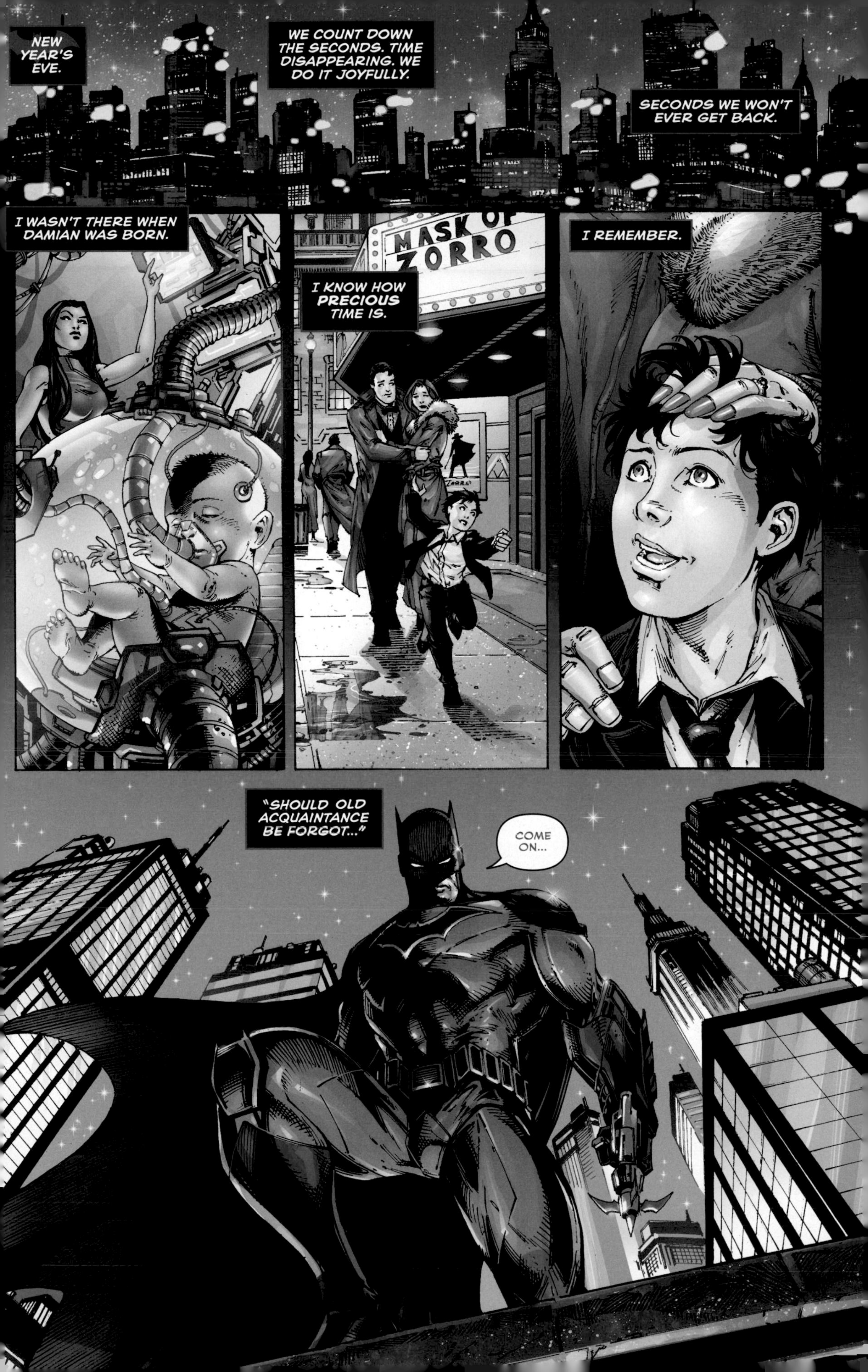
NEW YEAR'S EVE.
WE COUNT DOWN THE SECONDS. TIME DISAPPEARING. WE DO IT JOYFULLY.
SECONDS WE WON'T EVER GET BACK.
I WASN'T THERE WHEN DAMIAN WAS BORN.
MASK OF ZORRO
I KNOW HOW PRECIOUS TIME IS.
I REMEMBER.
"SHOULD OLD ACQUAINTANCE BE FORGOT..."
COME ON...

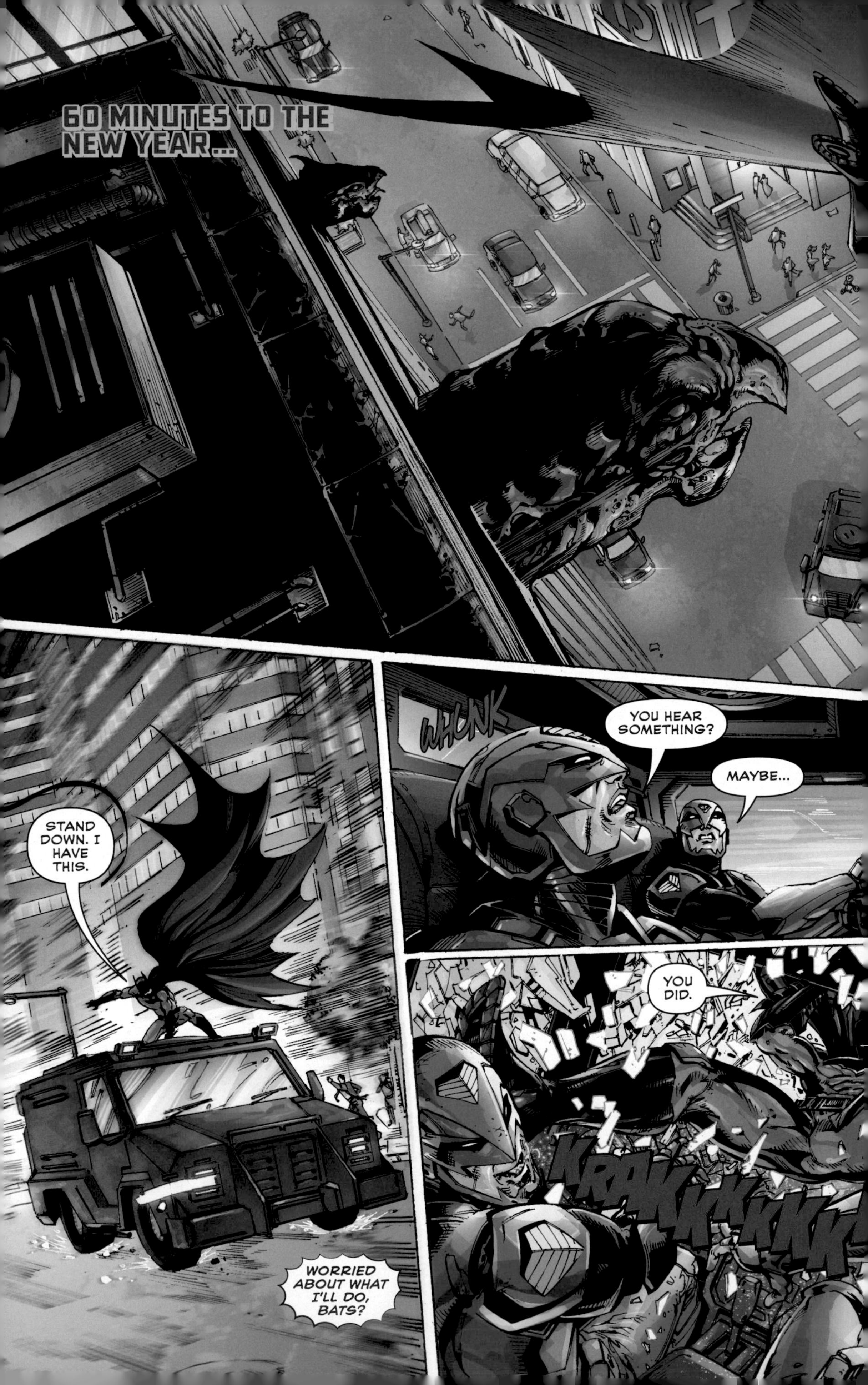
60 MINUTES TO THE NEW YEAR...
STAND DOWN. I HAVE THIS.
WORRIED ABOUT WHAT I'LL DO, BATS?
WHCNK
YOU HEAR SOMETHING?
MAYBE...
YOU DID.
KRAKKKKKK

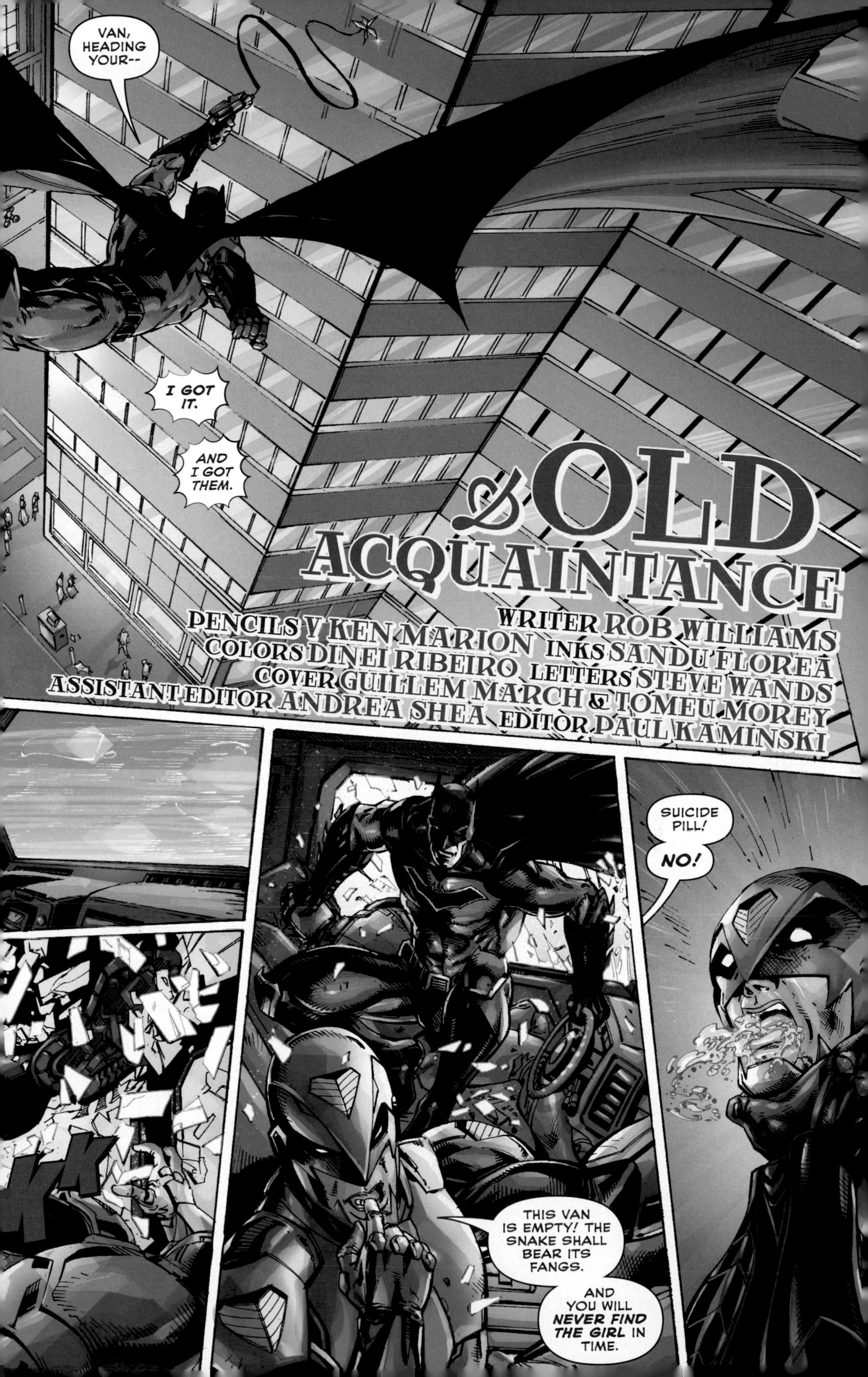
VAN, HEADING YOUR--
I GOT IT.
AND I GOT THEM.
OLD ACQUAINTANCE
WRITER ROB WILLIAMS
PENCILS KEN MARION INKS SANDU FLOREA
COLORS DINEI RIBEIRO LETTERS STEVE WANDS
COVER GUILLEM MARCH & TOMEU MOREY
ASSISTANT EDITOR ANDREA SHEA EDITOR PAUL KAMINSKI
SUICIDE PILL!
NO!
THIS VAN IS EMPTY! THE SNAKE SHALL BEAR ITS FANGS.
AND YOU WILL NEVER FIND THE GIRL IN TIME.

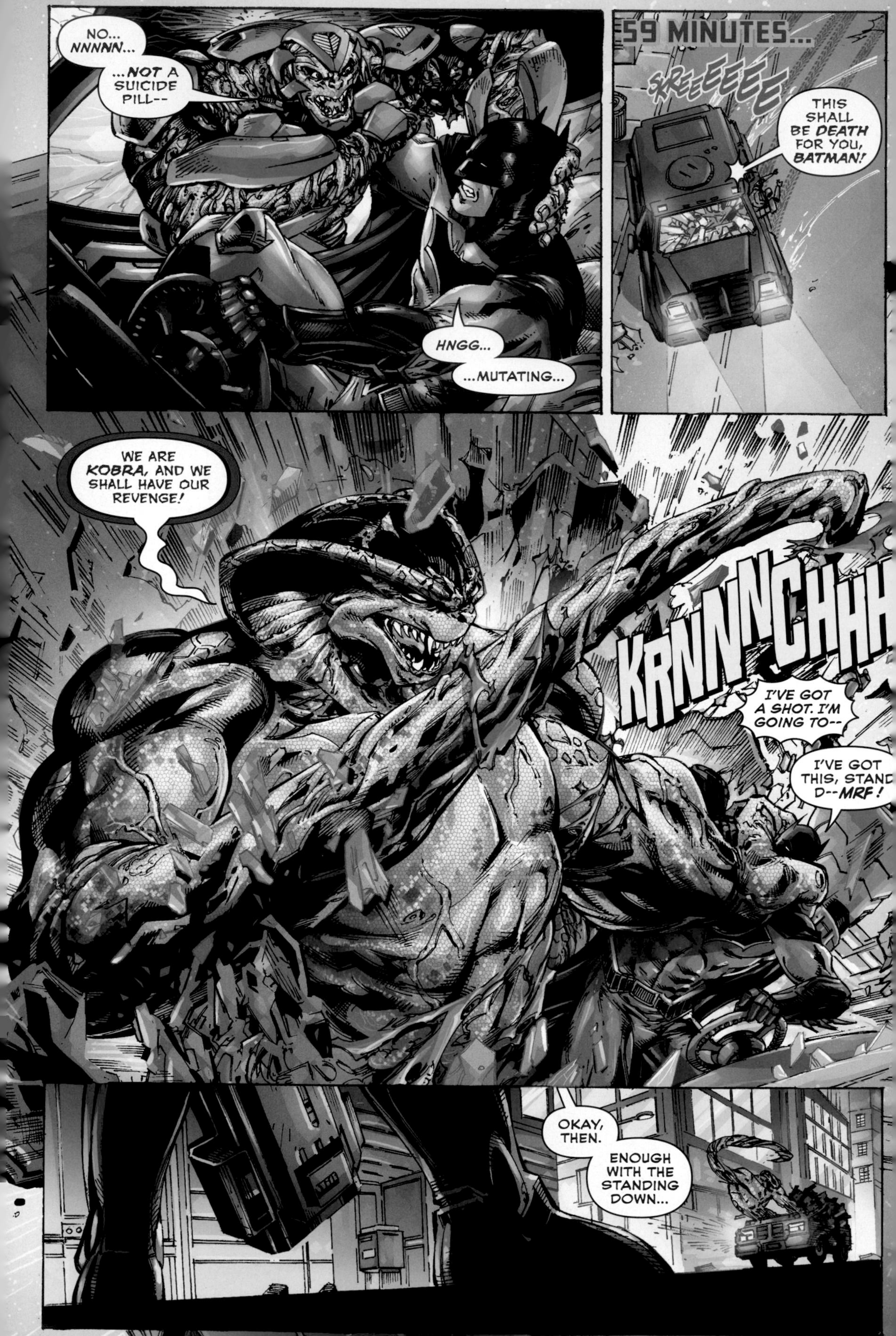
NO... NNNNN...
...NOT A SUICIDE PILL--
HNGG...
...MUTATING...
59 MINUTES...
SKREEEEEE
THIS SHALL BE DEATH FOR YOU, BATMAN!
WE ARE KOBRA, AND WE SHALL HAVE OUR REVENGE!
KRNNNCHHH
I'VE GOT A SHOT. I'M GOING TO--
I'VE GOT THIS, STAND D--MRF!
OKAY, THEN.
ENOUGH WITH THE STANDING DOWN...

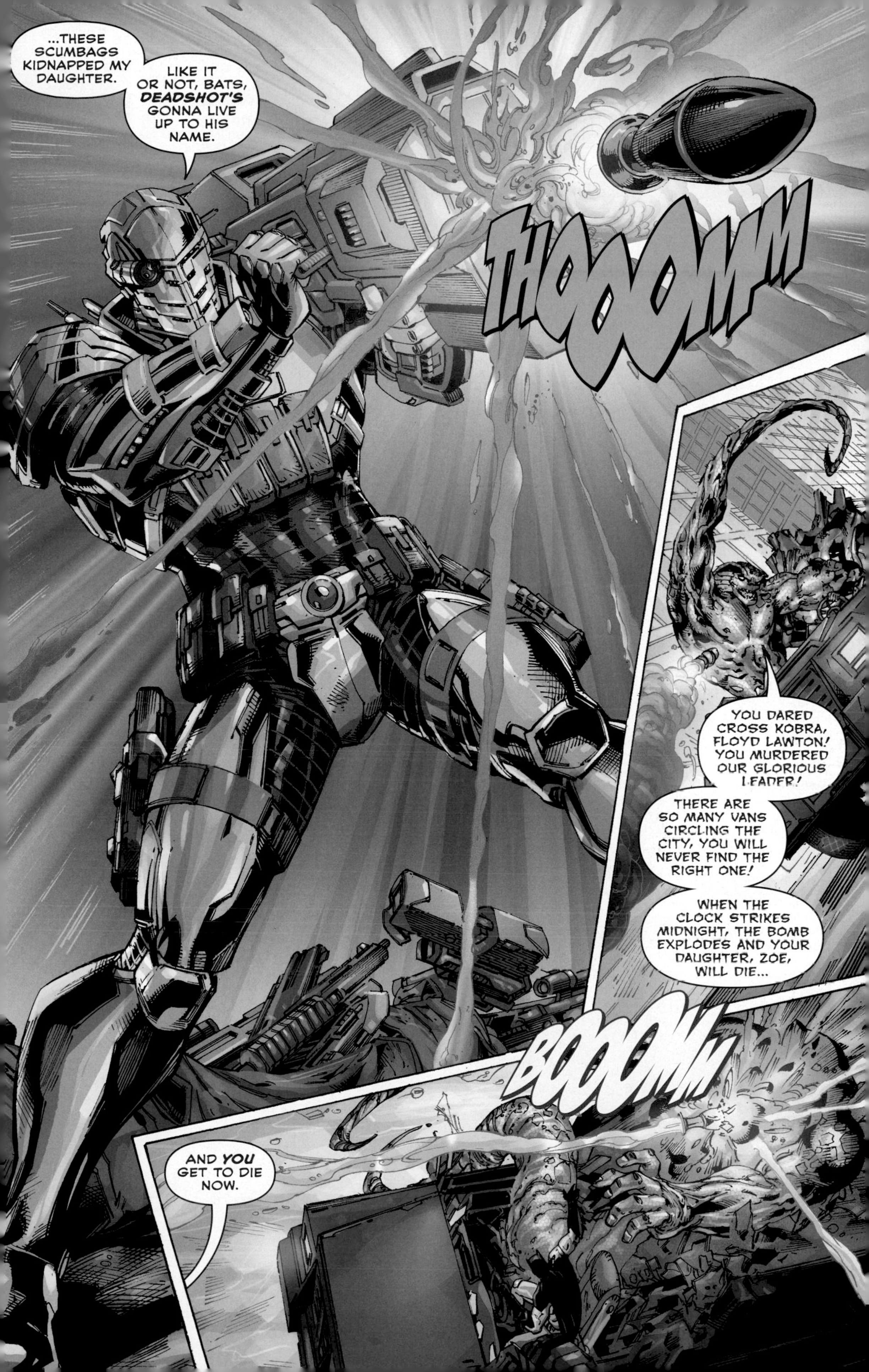
...THESE SCUMBAGS KIDNAPPED MY DAUGHTER.
LIKE IT OR NOT, BATS, DEADSHOT'S GONNA LIVE UP TO HIS NAME.
THOOOMM
YOU DARED CROSS KOBRA, FLOYD LAWTON! YOU MURDERED OUR GLORIOUS LEADER!
THERE ARE SO MANY VANS CIRCLING THE CITY, YOU WILL NEVER FIND THE RIGHT ONE!
WHEN THE CLOCK STRIKES MIDNIGHT, THE BOMB EXPLODES AND YOUR DAUGHTER, ZOE, WILL DIE...
BOOOMM
AND YOU GET TO DIE NOW.

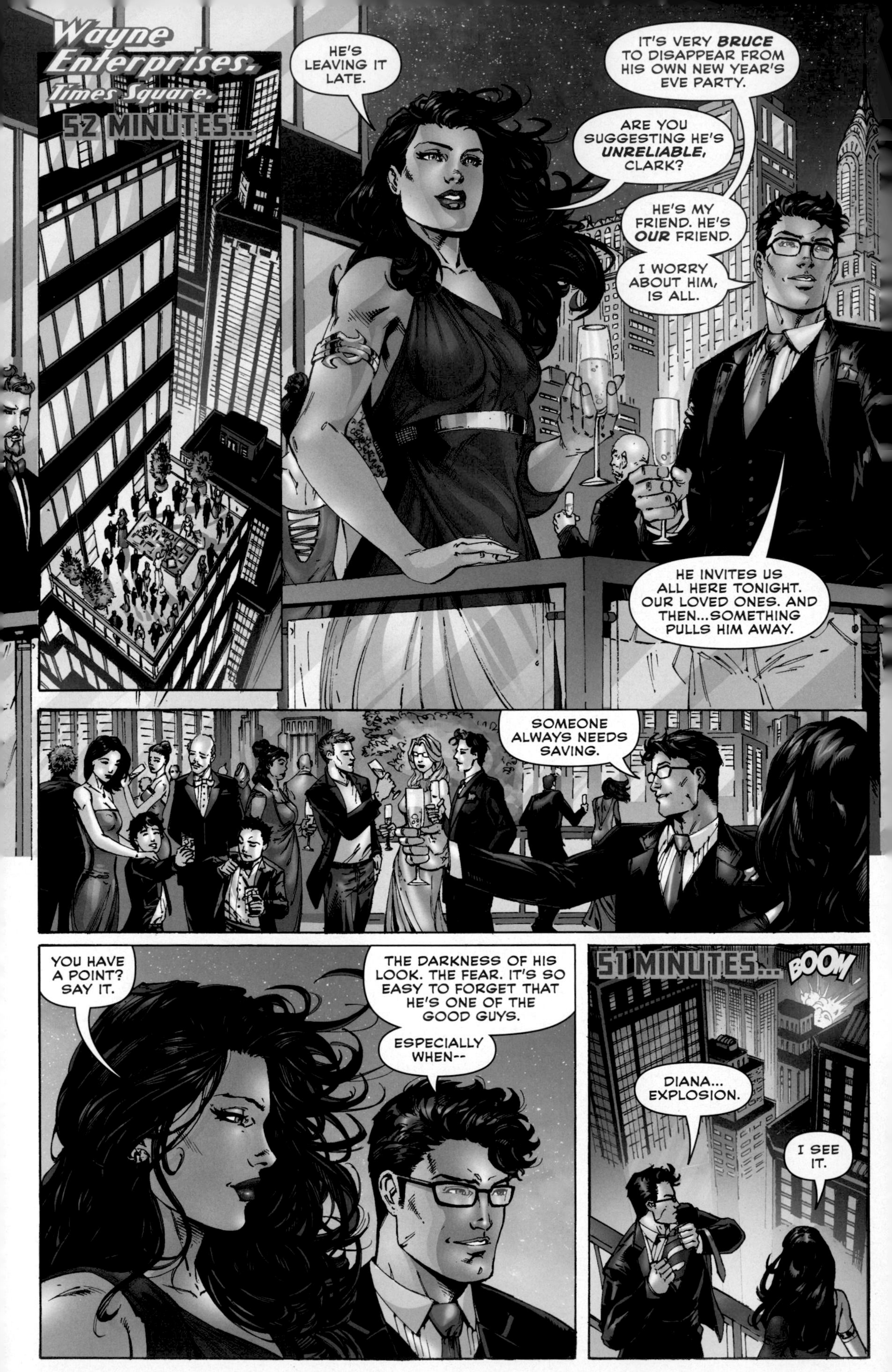

Wayne Enterprises. Times Square.
52 MINUTES...
HE'S LEAVING IT LATE.
IT'S VERY BRUCE TO DISAPPEAR FROM HIS OWN NEW YEAR'S EVE PARTY.
ARE YOU SUGGESTING HE'S UNRELIABLE, CLARK?
HE'S MY FRIEND. HE'S OUR FRIEND.
I WORRY ABOUT HIM, IS ALL.
HE INVITES US ALL HERE TONIGHT. OUR LOVED ONES. AND THEN...SOMETHING PULLS HIM AWAY.
SOMEONE ALWAYS NEEDS SAVING.
YOU HAVE A POINT? SAY IT.
THE DARKNESS OF HIS LOOK. THE FEAR. IT'S SO EASY TO FORGET THAT HE'S ONE OF THE GOOD GUYS.
ESPECIALLY WHEN--
51 MINUTES...
BOOM
DIANA... EXPLOSION.
I SEE IT.

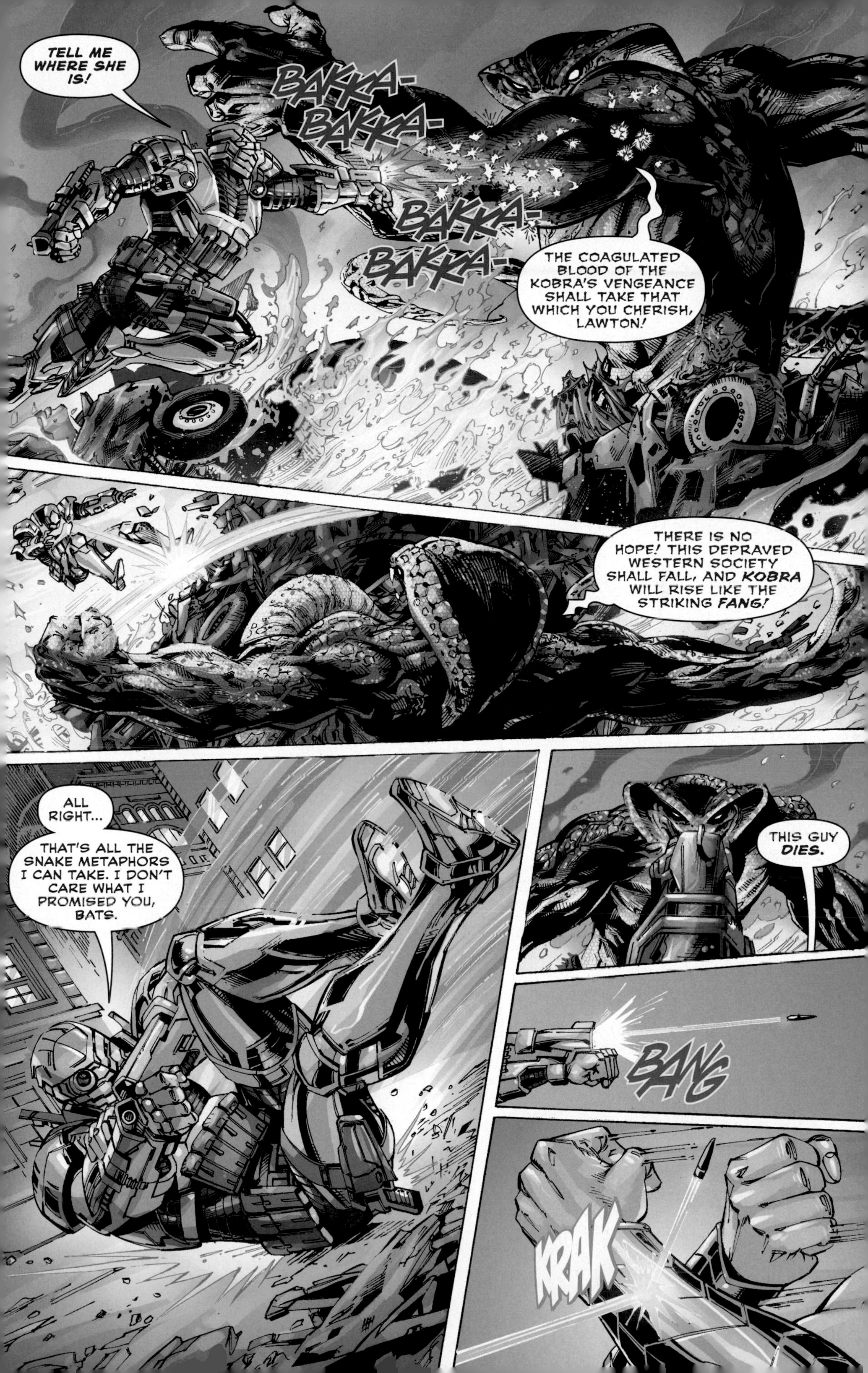

TELL ME WHERE SHE IS!
BAKKA-BAKKA-
BAKKA-BAKKA-
THE COAGULATED BLOOD OF THE KOBRA'S VENGEANCE SHALL TAKE THAT WHICH YOU CHERISH, LAWTON!
THERE IS NO HOPE! THIS DEPRAVED WESTERN SOCIETY SHALL FALL, AND *KOBRA* WILL RISE LIKE THE STRIKING *FANG!*
ALL RIGHT...
THAT'S ALL THE SNAKE METAPHORS I CAN TAKE. I DON'T CARE WHAT I PROMISED YOU, BATS.
THIS GUY *DIES.*
BANG
KRAK

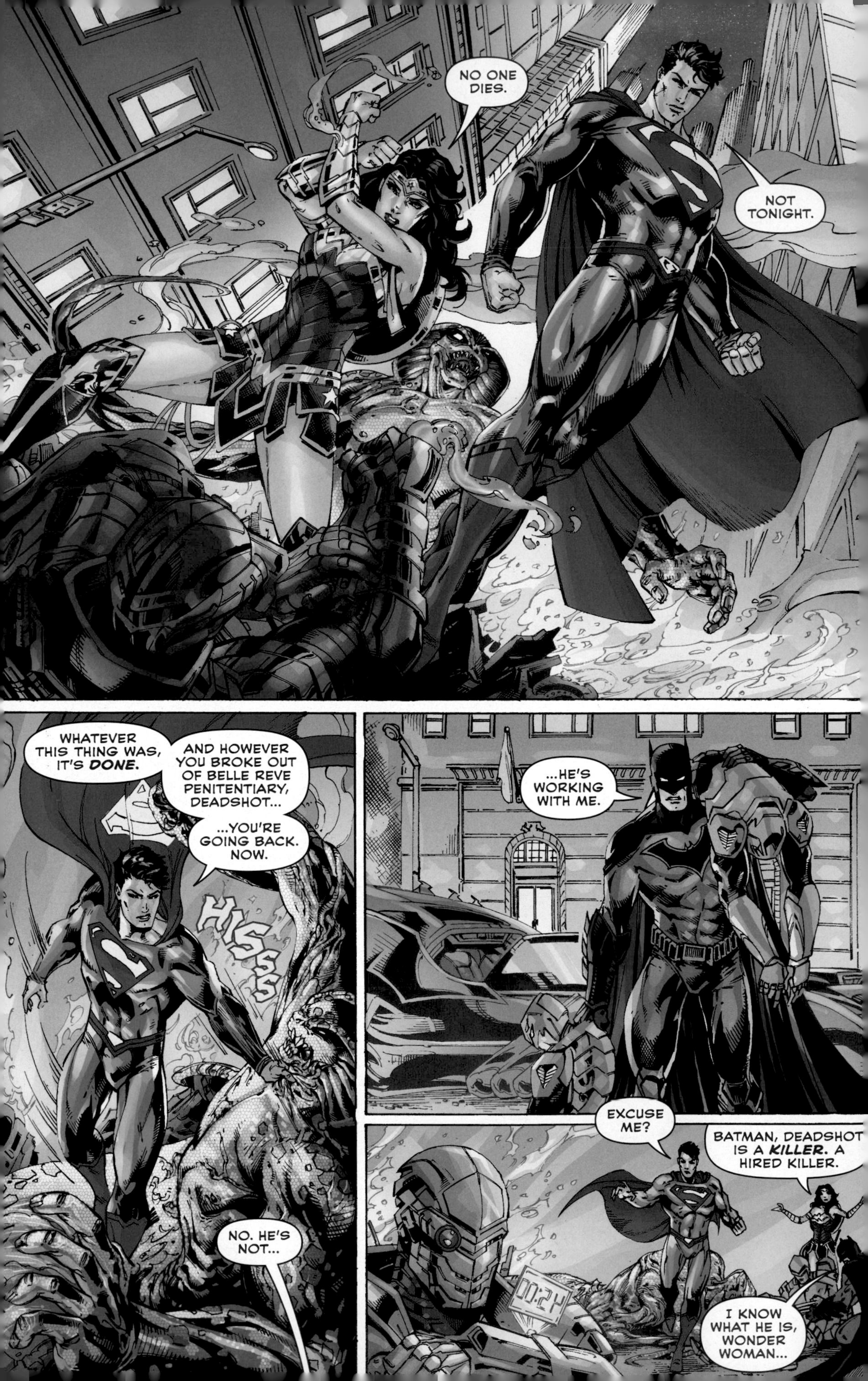
NO ONE DIES.
NOT TONIGHT.
WHATEVER THIS THING WAS, IT'S **DONE.**
AND HOWEVER YOU BROKE OUT OF BELLE REVE PENITENTIARY, DEADSHOT...
...YOU'RE GOING BACK. NOW.
HISSS
NO. HE'S NOT...
...HE'S WORKING WITH ME.
EXCUSE ME?
BATMAN, DEADSHOT IS A ***KILLER.*** A HIRED KILLER.
00:24
I KNOW WHAT HE IS, WONDER WOMAN...

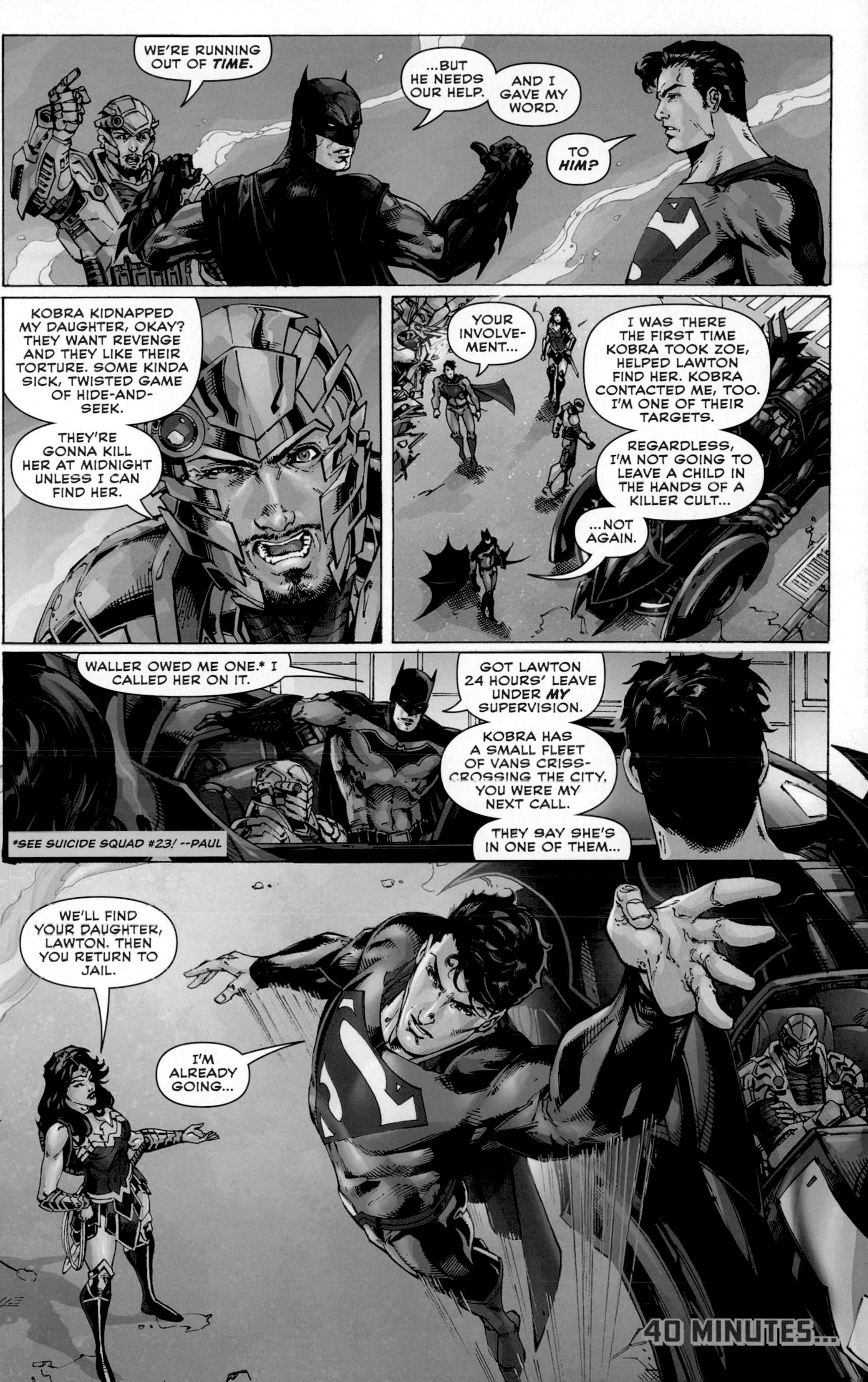
WE'RE RUNNING OUT OF TIME.
...BUT HE NEEDS OUR HELP.
AND I GAVE MY WORD.
TO HIM?
KOBRA KIDNAPPED MY DAUGHTER, OKAY? THEY WANT REVENGE AND THEY LIKE THEIR TORTURE. SOME KINDA SICK, TWISTED GAME OF HIDE-AND-SEEK.
THEY'RE GONNA KILL HER AT MIDNIGHT UNLESS I CAN FIND HER.
YOUR INVOLVEMENT...
I WAS THERE THE FIRST TIME KOBRA TOOK ZOE, HELPED LAWTON FIND HER. KOBRA CONTACTED ME, TOO. I'M ONE OF THEIR TARGETS.
REGARDLESS, I'M NOT GOING TO LEAVE A CHILD IN THE HANDS OF A KILLER CULT...
...NOT AGAIN.
WALLER OWED ME ONE.* I CALLED HER ON IT.
GOT LAWTON 24 HOURS' LEAVE UNDER MY SUPERVISION.
KOBRA HAS A SMALL FLEET OF VANS CRISS-CROSSING THE CITY. YOU WERE MY NEXT CALL.
THEY SAY SHE'S IN ONE OF THEM...
*SEE SUICIDE SQUAD #23! --PAUL
WE'LL FIND YOUR DAUGHTER, LAWTON. THEN YOU RETURN TO JAIL.
I'M ALREADY GOING...
40 MINUTES...

NOT A DAY GOES BY I DON'T THANK THE UNIVERSE THAT JON'S IN MY LIFE.

HE GETS OLDER. EVERY DAY. EVERY MINUTE.

MORE CONFIDENT. MORE HIS OWN PERSON. MAKING THE DECISIONS THAT WILL FORM HIM.

AND I'M **SO** PROUD OF HIM FOR THAT.

BUT IT MAKES ME SAD SOMETIMES.

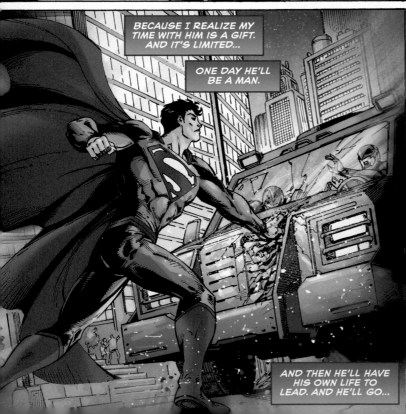

BECAUSE I REALIZE MY TIME WITH HIM IS A GIFT. AND IT'S LIMITED...

ONE DAY HE'LL BE A MAN.

AND THEN HE'LL HAVE HIS OWN LIFE TO LEAD. AND HE'LL GO...

...LIKE A ROCKET SHIP HEADING TO THE STARS.

NO.

30 MINUTES...

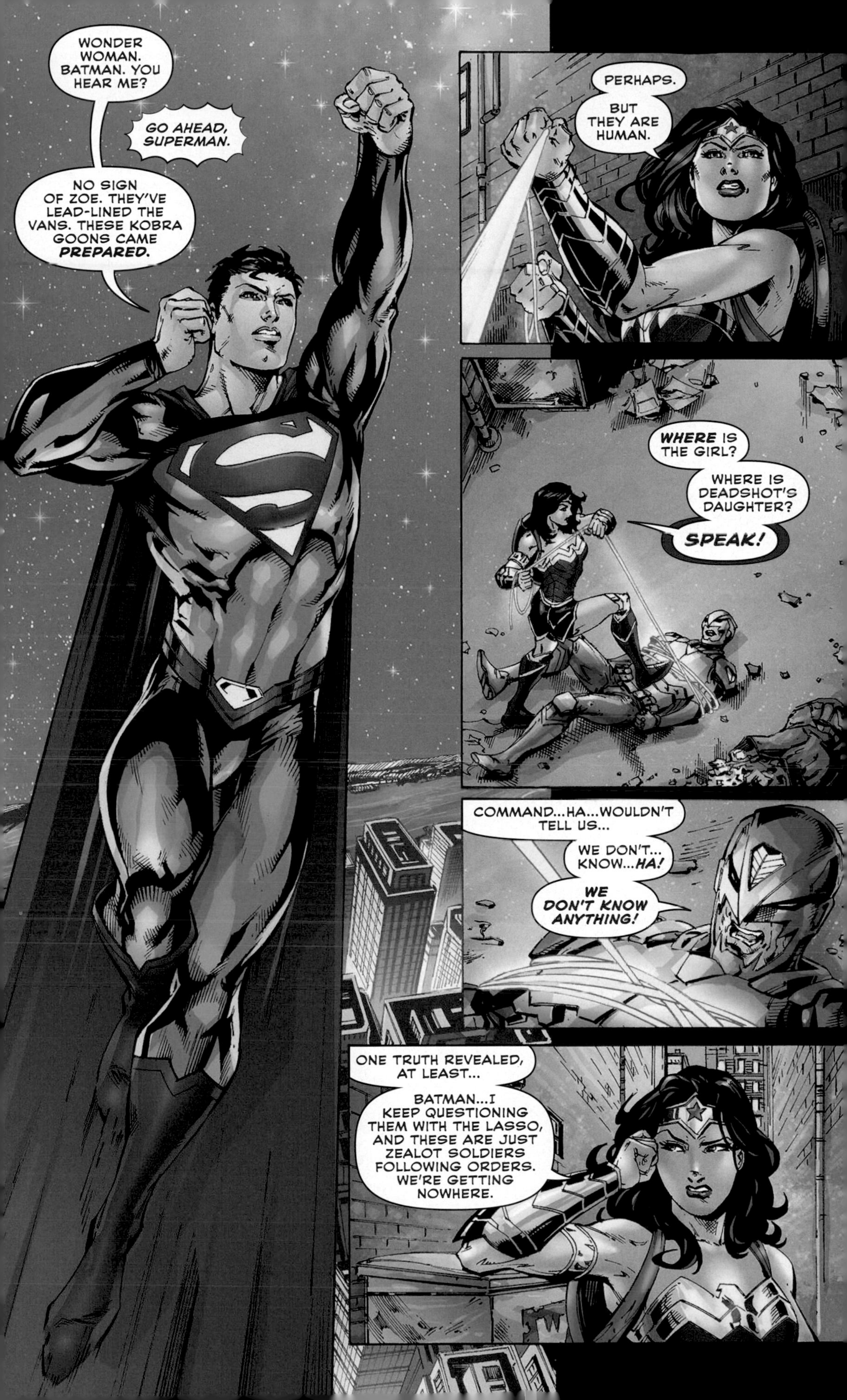

WONDER WOMAN. BATMAN. YOU HEAR ME?
GO AHEAD, SUPERMAN.
NO SIGN OF ZOE. THEY'VE LEAD-LINED THE VANS. THESE KOBRA GOONS CAME PREPARED.
PERHAPS.
BUT THEY ARE HUMAN.
WHERE IS THE GIRL?
WHERE IS DEADSHOT'S DAUGHTER?
SPEAK!
COMMAND...HA...WOULDN'T TELL US...
WE DON'T... KNOW...HA!
WE DON'T KNOW ANYTHING!
ONE TRUTH REVEALED, AT LEAST...
BATMAN...I KEEP QUESTIONING THEM WITH THE LASSO, AND THESE ARE JUST ZEALOT SOLDIERS FOLLOWING ORDERS. WE'RE GETTING NOWHERE.

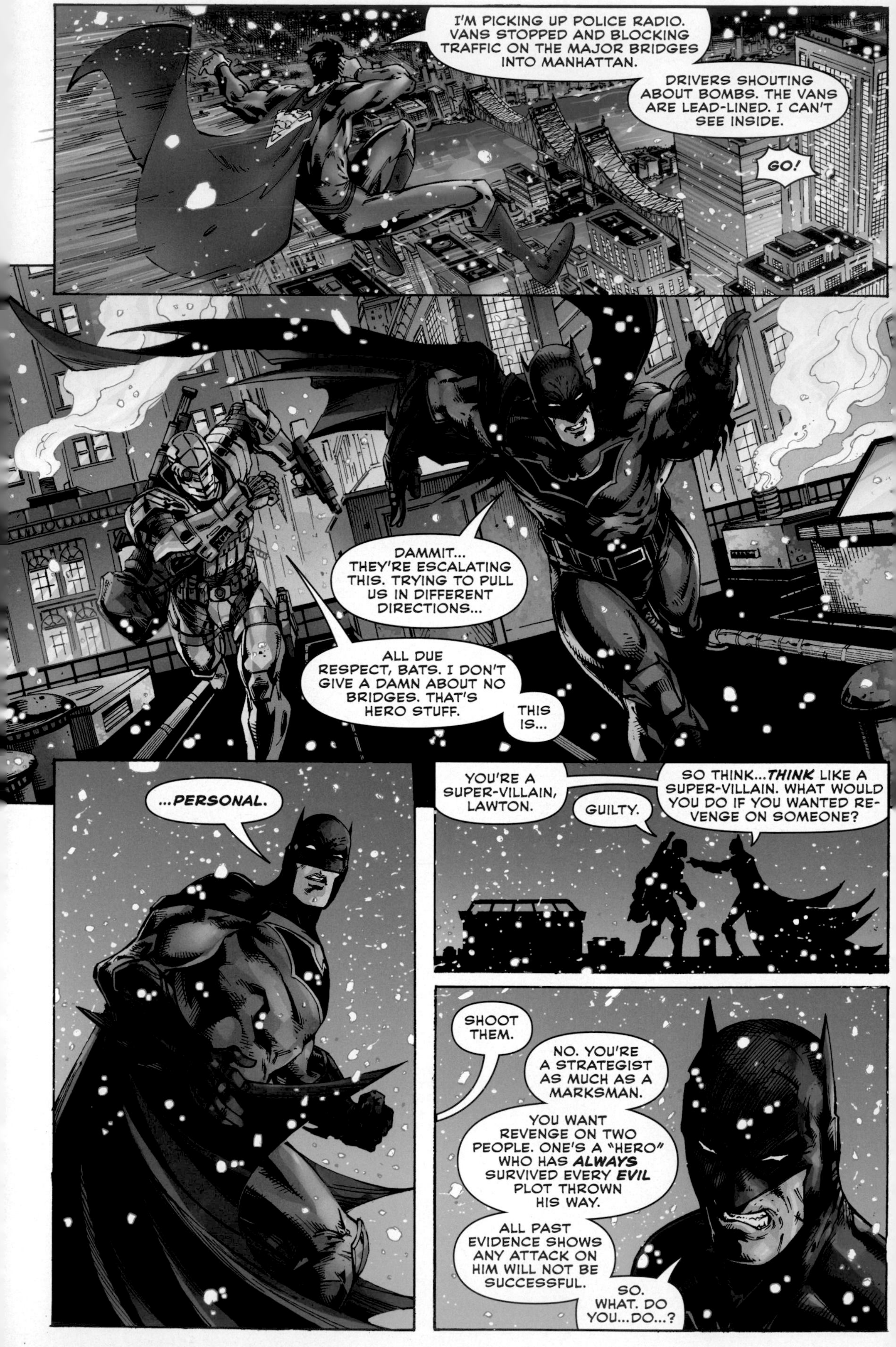
I'M PICKING UP POLICE RADIO. VANS STOPPED AND BLOCKING TRAFFIC ON THE MAJOR BRIDGES INTO MANHATTAN.
DRIVERS SHOUTING ABOUT BOMBS. THE VANS ARE LEAD-LINED. I CAN'T SEE INSIDE.
GO!
DAMMIT... THEY'RE ESCALATING THIS. TRYING TO PULL US IN DIFFERENT DIRECTIONS...
ALL DUE RESPECT, BATS. I DON'T GIVE A DAMN ABOUT NO BRIDGES. THAT'S HERO STUFF.
THIS IS...
...PERSONAL.
YOU'RE A SUPER-VILLAIN, LAWTON.
GUILTY.
SO THINK...THINK LIKE A SUPER-VILLAIN. WHAT WOULD YOU DO IF YOU WANTED RE-VENGE ON SOMEONE?
SHOOT THEM.
NO. YOU'RE A STRATEGIST AS MUCH AS A MARKSMAN.
YOU WANT REVENGE ON TWO PEOPLE. ONE'S A "HERO" WHO HAS ALWAYS SURVIVED EVERY EVIL PLOT THROWN HIS WAY.
ALL PAST EVIDENCE SHOWS ANY ATTACK ON HIM WILL NOT BE SUCCESSFUL.
SO. WHAT. DO YOU...DO...?

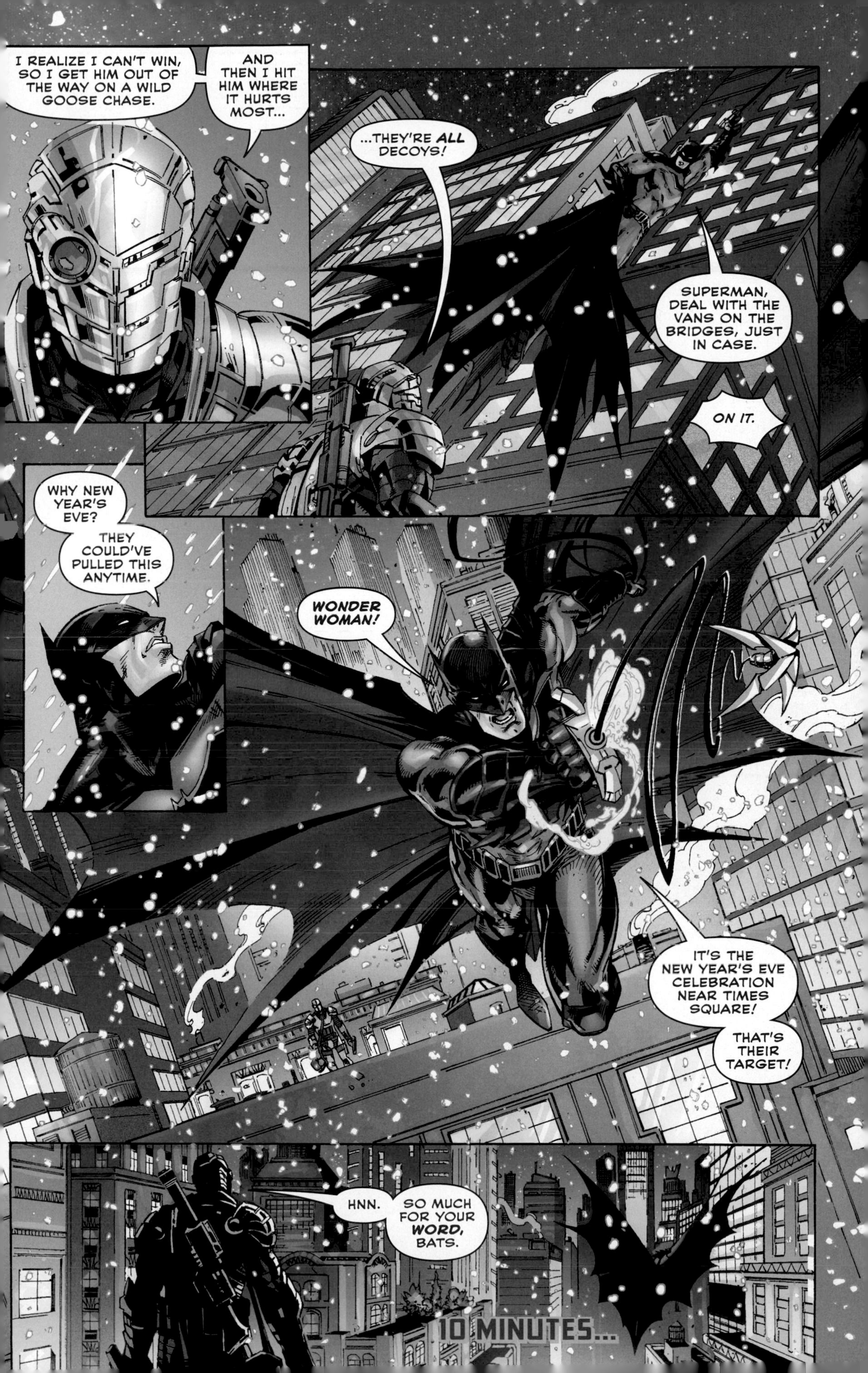
I REALIZE I CAN'T WIN, SO I GET HIM OUT OF THE WAY ON A WILD GOOSE CHASE.
AND THEN I HIT HIM WHERE IT HURTS MOST...
...THEY'RE ALL DECOYS!
SUPERMAN, DEAL WITH THE VANS ON THE BRIDGES, JUST IN CASE.
ON IT.
WHY NEW YEAR'S EVE?
THEY COULD'VE PULLED THIS ANYTIME.
WONDER WOMAN!
IT'S THE NEW YEAR'S EVE CELEBRATION NEAR TIMES SQUARE!
THAT'S THEIR TARGET!
HNN.
SO MUCH FOR YOUR WORD, BATS.
10 MINUTES...

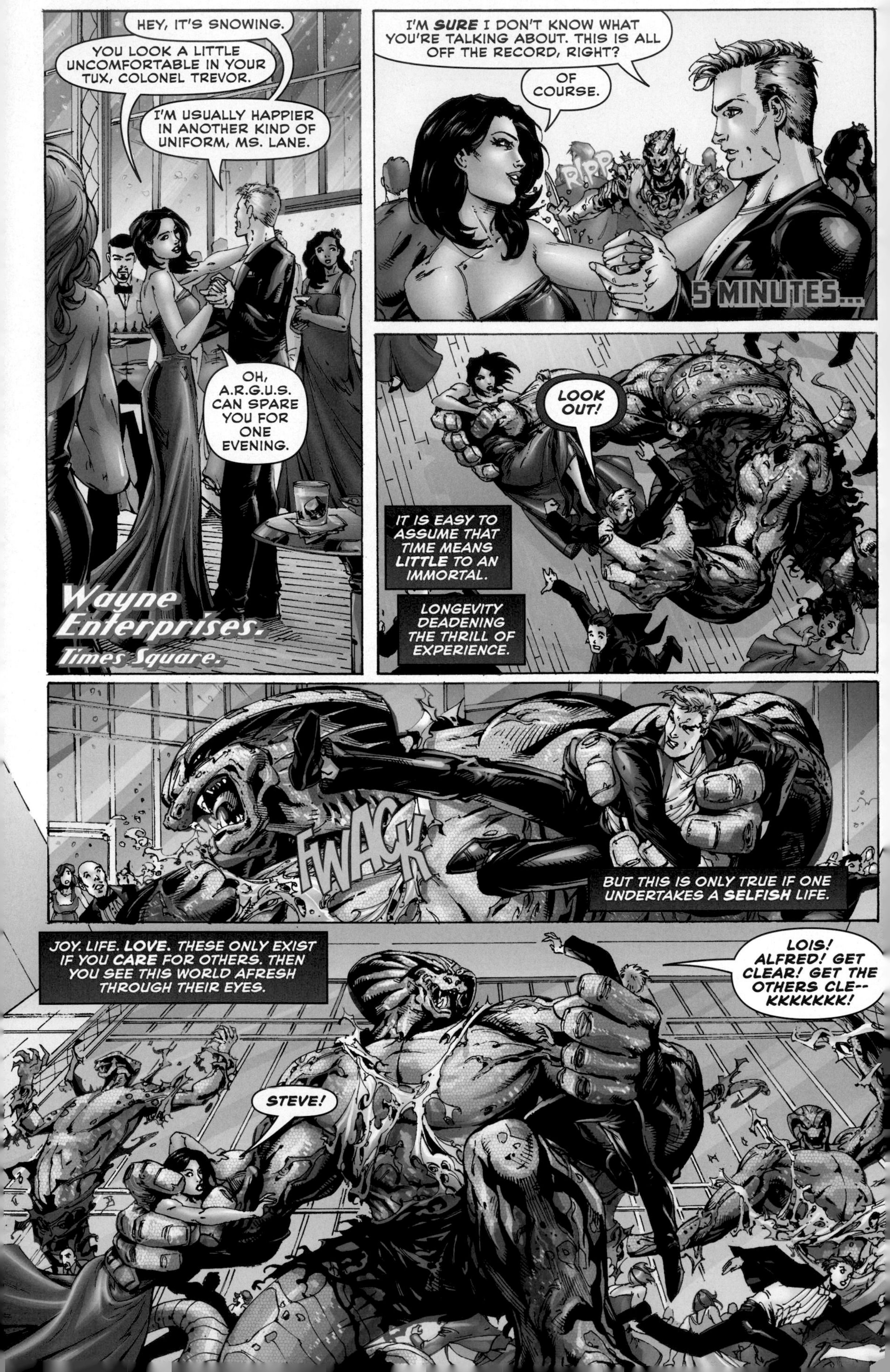
HEY, IT'S SNOWING.
YOU LOOK A LITTLE UNCOMFORTABLE IN YOUR TUX, COLONEL TREVOR.
I'M USUALLY HAPPIER IN ANOTHER KIND OF UNIFORM, MS. LANE.
OH, A.R.G.U.S. CAN SPARE YOU FOR ONE EVENING.
Wayne Enterprises. Times Square.
I'M SURE I DON'T KNOW WHAT YOU'RE TALKING ABOUT. THIS IS ALL OFF THE RECORD, RIGHT?
OF COURSE.
RIPP
5 MINUTES...
LOOK OUT!
IT IS EASY TO ASSUME THAT TIME MEANS LITTLE TO AN IMMORTAL.
LONGEVITY DEADENING THE THRILL OF EXPERIENCE.
FWACK
BUT THIS IS ONLY TRUE IF ONE UNDERTAKES A SELFISH LIFE.
JOY. LIFE. LOVE. THESE ONLY EXIST IF YOU CARE FOR OTHERS. THEN YOU SEE THIS WORLD AFRESH THROUGH THEIR EYES.
LOIS! ALFRED! GET CLEAR! GET THE OTHERS CLE-- KKKKKKK!
STEVE!

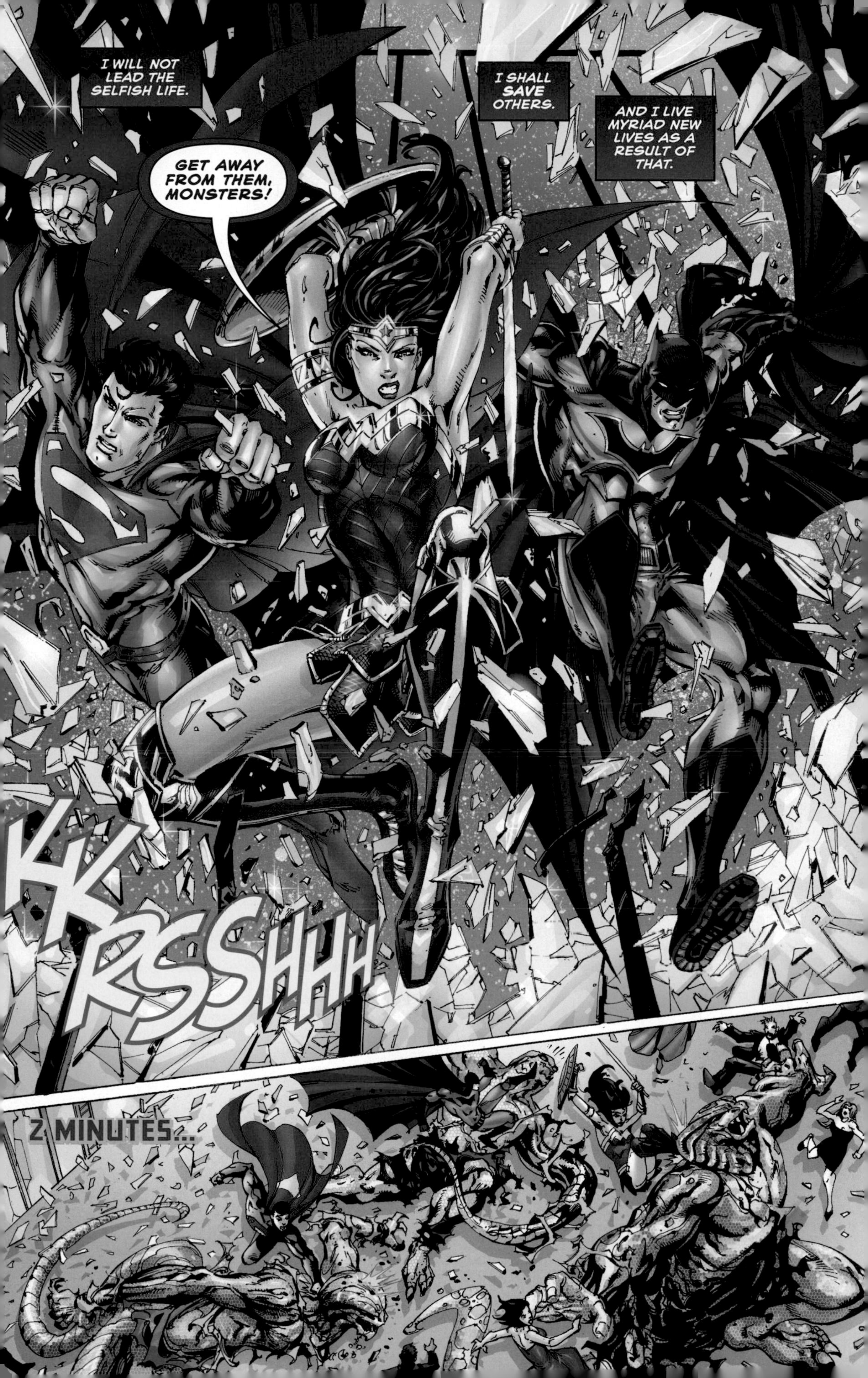
I WILL NOT LEAD THE SELFISH LIFE.
GET AWAY FROM THEM, MONSTERS!
I SHALL SAVE OTHERS.
AND I LIVE MYRIAD NEW LIVES AS A RESULT OF THAT.
KKRSSHHH
2 MINUTES...

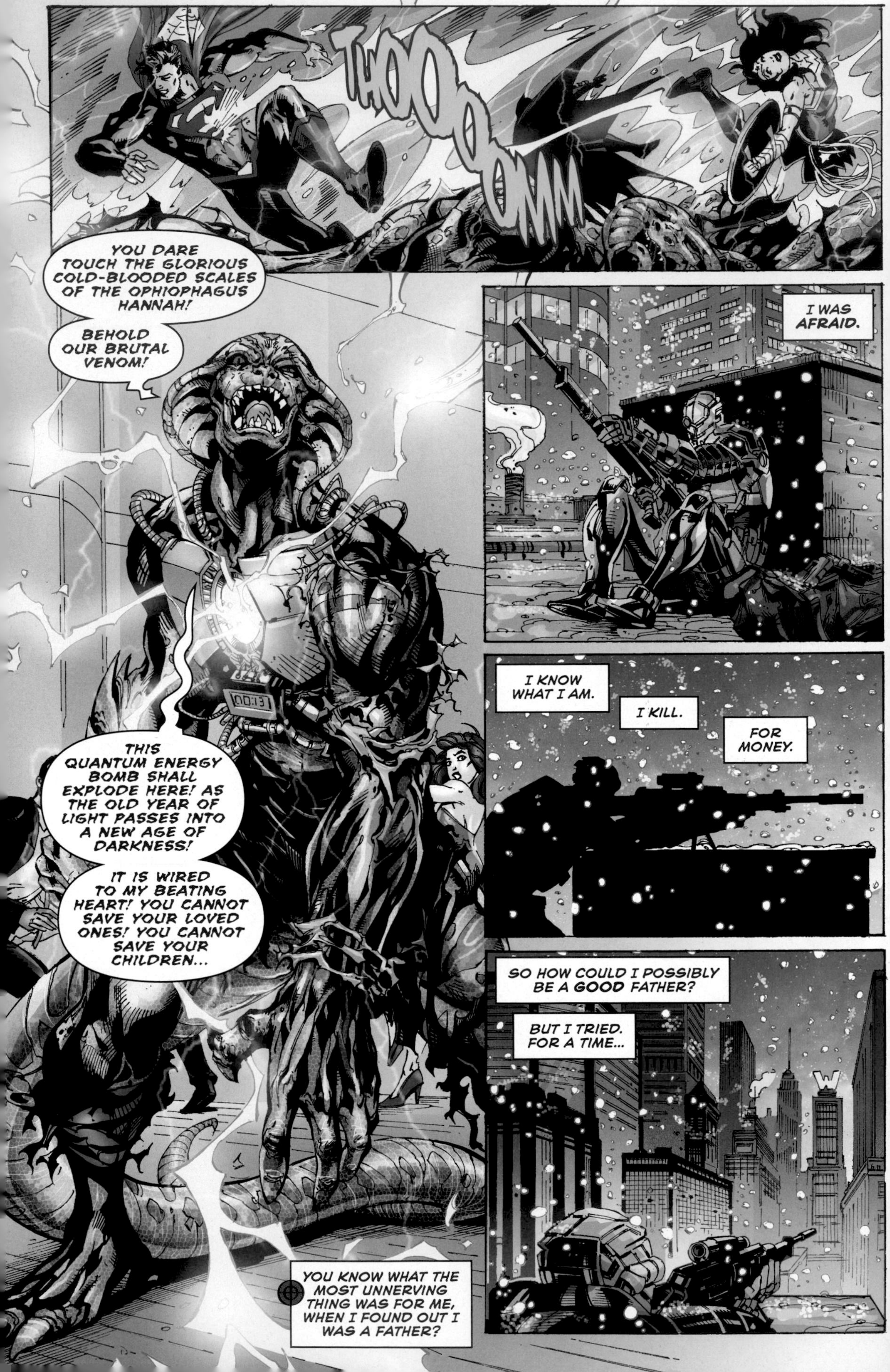
THOOOOOMM
YOU DARE TOUCH THE GLORIOUS COLD-BLOODED SCALES OF THE OPHIOPHAGUS HANNAH!
BEHOLD OUR BRUTAL VENOM!
I WAS AFRAID.
THIS QUANTUM ENERGY BOMB SHALL EXPLODE HERE! AS THE OLD YEAR OF LIGHT PASSES INTO A NEW AGE OF DARKNESS!
IT IS WIRED TO MY BEATING HEART! YOU CANNOT SAVE YOUR LOVED ONES! YOU CANNOT SAVE YOUR CHILDREN...
I KNOW WHAT I AM.
I KILL.
FOR MONEY.
SO HOW COULD I POSSIBLY BE A GOOD FATHER?
BUT I TRIED. FOR A TIME...
YOU KNOW WHAT THE MOST UNNERVING THING WAS FOR ME, WHEN I FOUND OUT I WAS A FATHER?

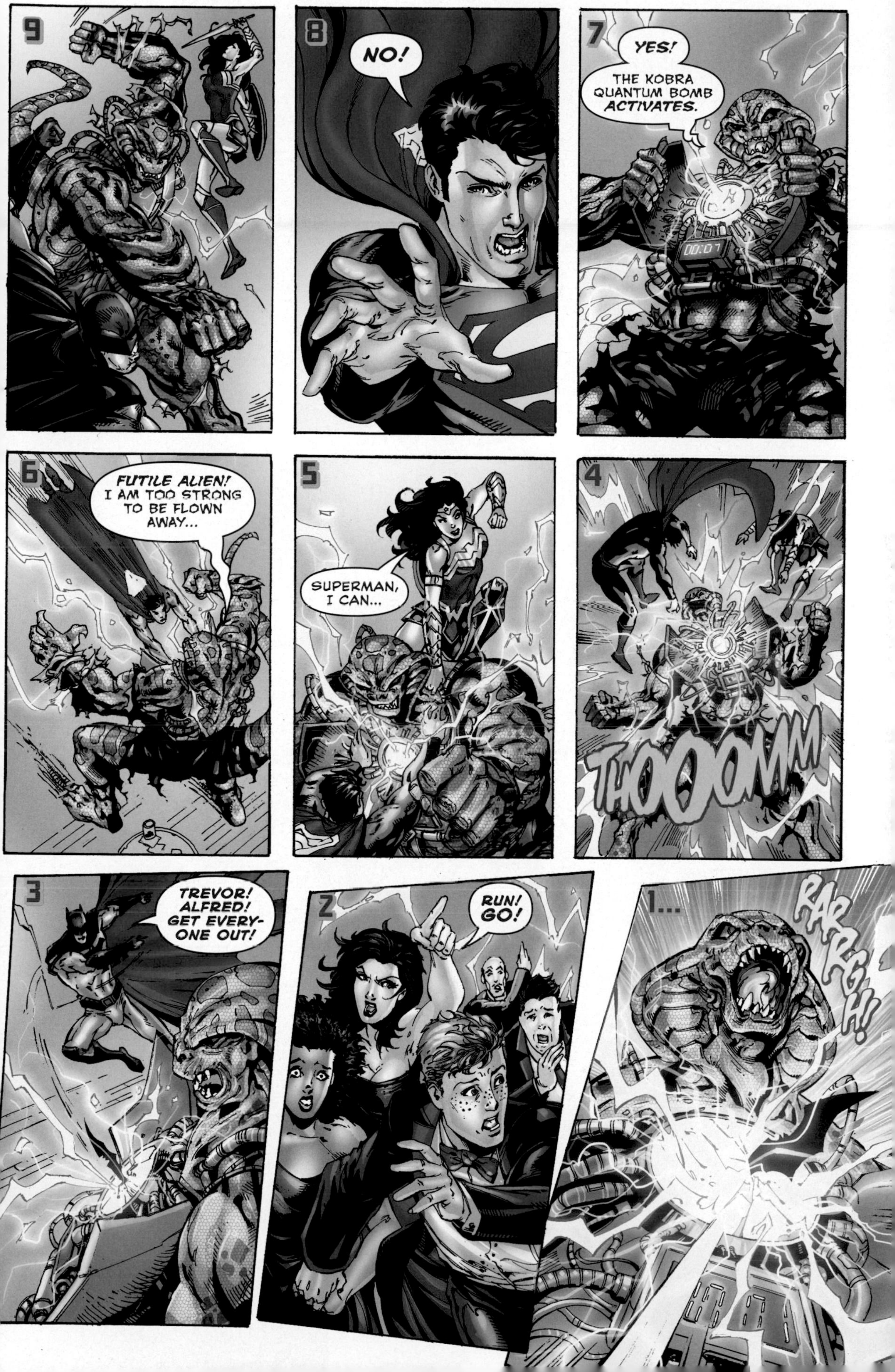
9
8
NO!
7
YES!
THE KOBRA QUANTUM BOMB ACTIVATES.
00:07
6
FUTILE ALIEN! I AM TOO STRONG TO BE FLOWN AWAY...
5
SUPERMAN, I CAN...
4
THOOOMM
3
TREVOR! ALFRED! GET EVERY-ONE OUT!
2
RUN! GO!
1...
RARRGH!

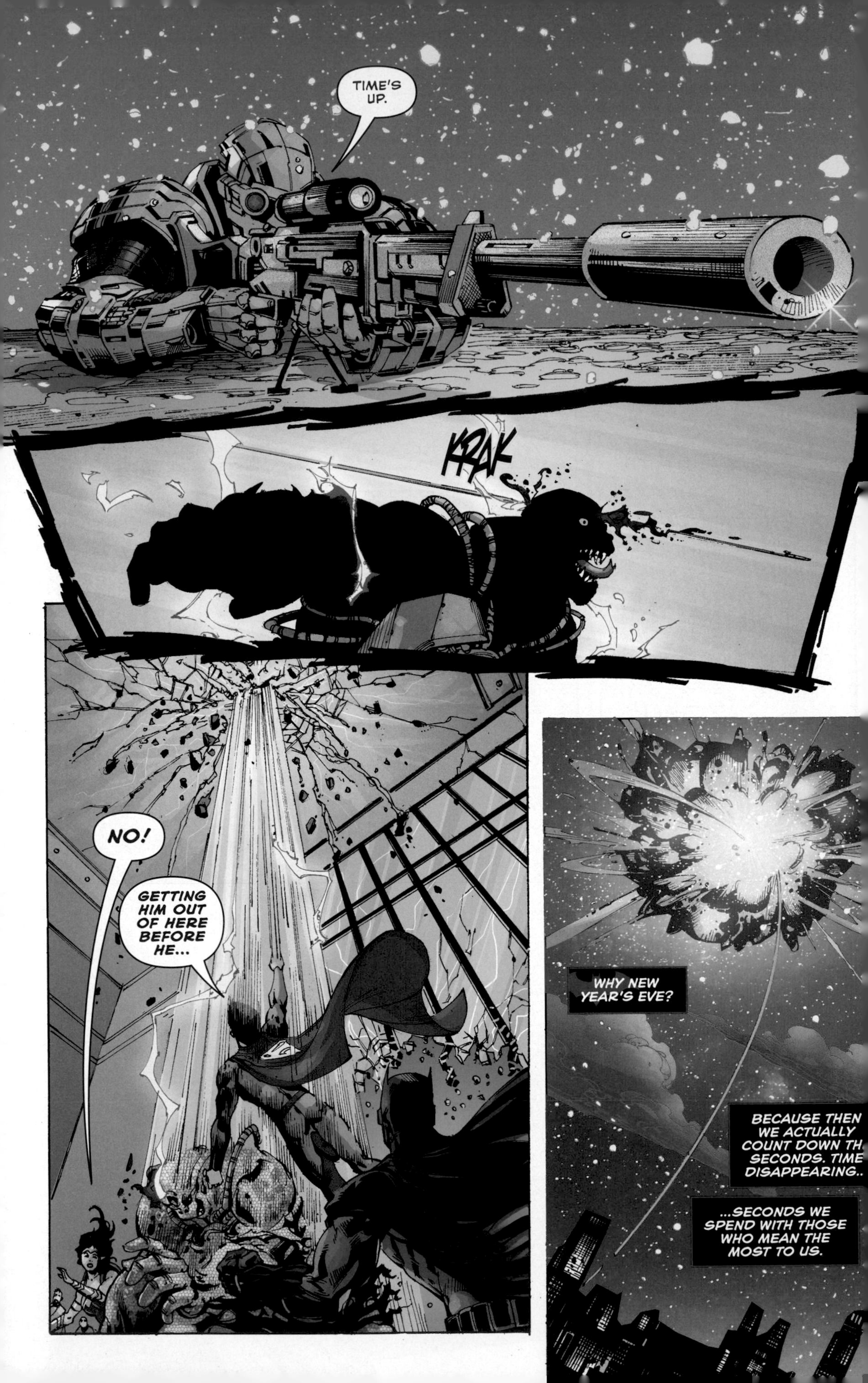
TIME'S UP.
KRAK
NO!
GETTING HIM OUT OF HERE BEFORE HE...
WHY NEW YEAR'S EVE?
BECAUSE THEN WE ACTUALLY COUNT DOWN TH SECONDS. TIME DISAPPEARING..
...SECONDS WE SPEND WITH THOSE WHO MEAN THE MOST TO US.

TIME THAT WE WON'T GET BACK...

DEADSHOT SAVED US.

Soon.

YOU FIRED THAT SHOT. YOU KILLED HIM.

YEAH.

YOU'RE A WARRIOR PRINCESS, RIGHT? THIS LOOKED LIKE A WAR TO ME. AND PEOPLE DIE IN WARS.

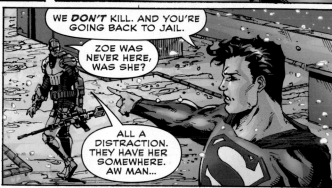

WE **DON'T** KILL. AND YOU'RE GOING BACK TO JAIL.

ZOE WAS NEVER HERE, WAS SHE?

ALL A DISTRACTION. THEY HAVE HER SOMEWHERE. AW MAN...

...I'M GONNA KILL EVERY LAST ONE OF THEM.

LAWTON. WE CAN'T LET YOU...I'LL **FIND** HER. I SWEAR.

STOP!

I CAN'T. YOU KNOW THAT.

STOP.

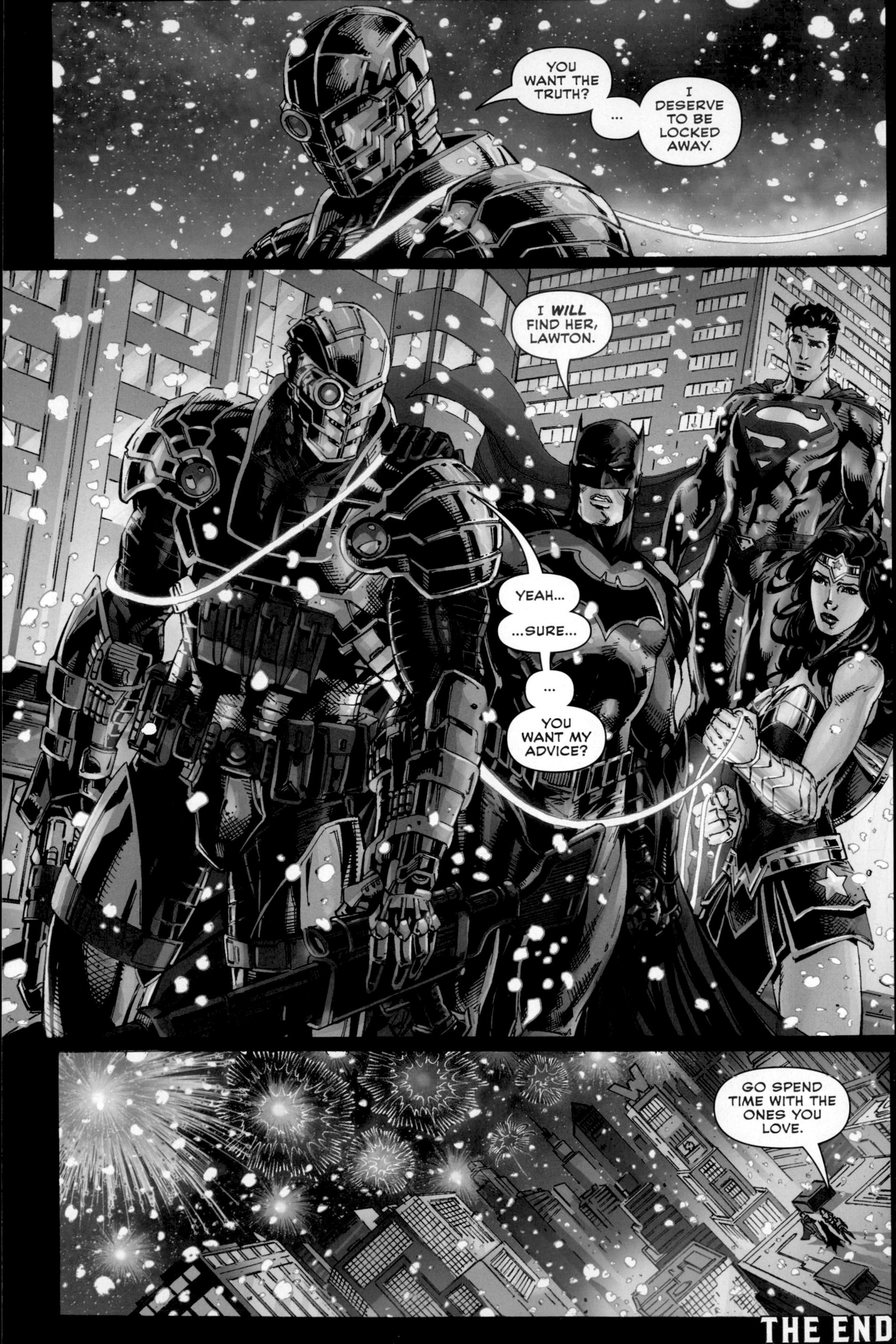
YOU WANT THE TRUTH?
...
I DESERVE TO BE LOCKED AWAY.
I *WILL* FIND HER, LAWTON.
YEAH...
...SURE...
...
YOU WANT MY ADVICE?
GO SPEND TIME WITH THE ONES YOU LOVE.
THE END

BATGIRL #18 variant cover
by JOSHUA MIDDLETON

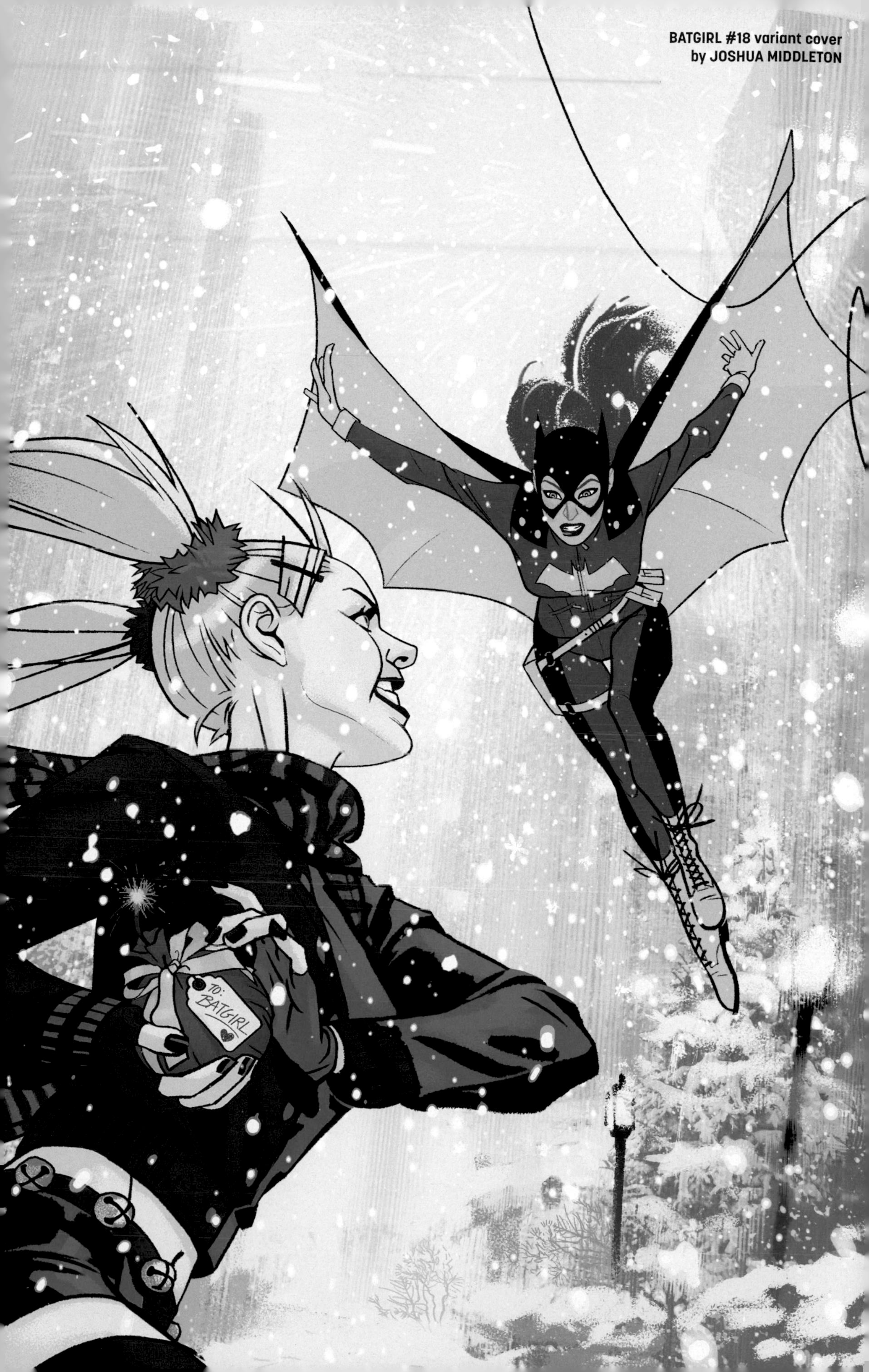
TO: BATGIRL

TRINITY #16 variant cov
by JASON FABOK and BRAD ANDERSO

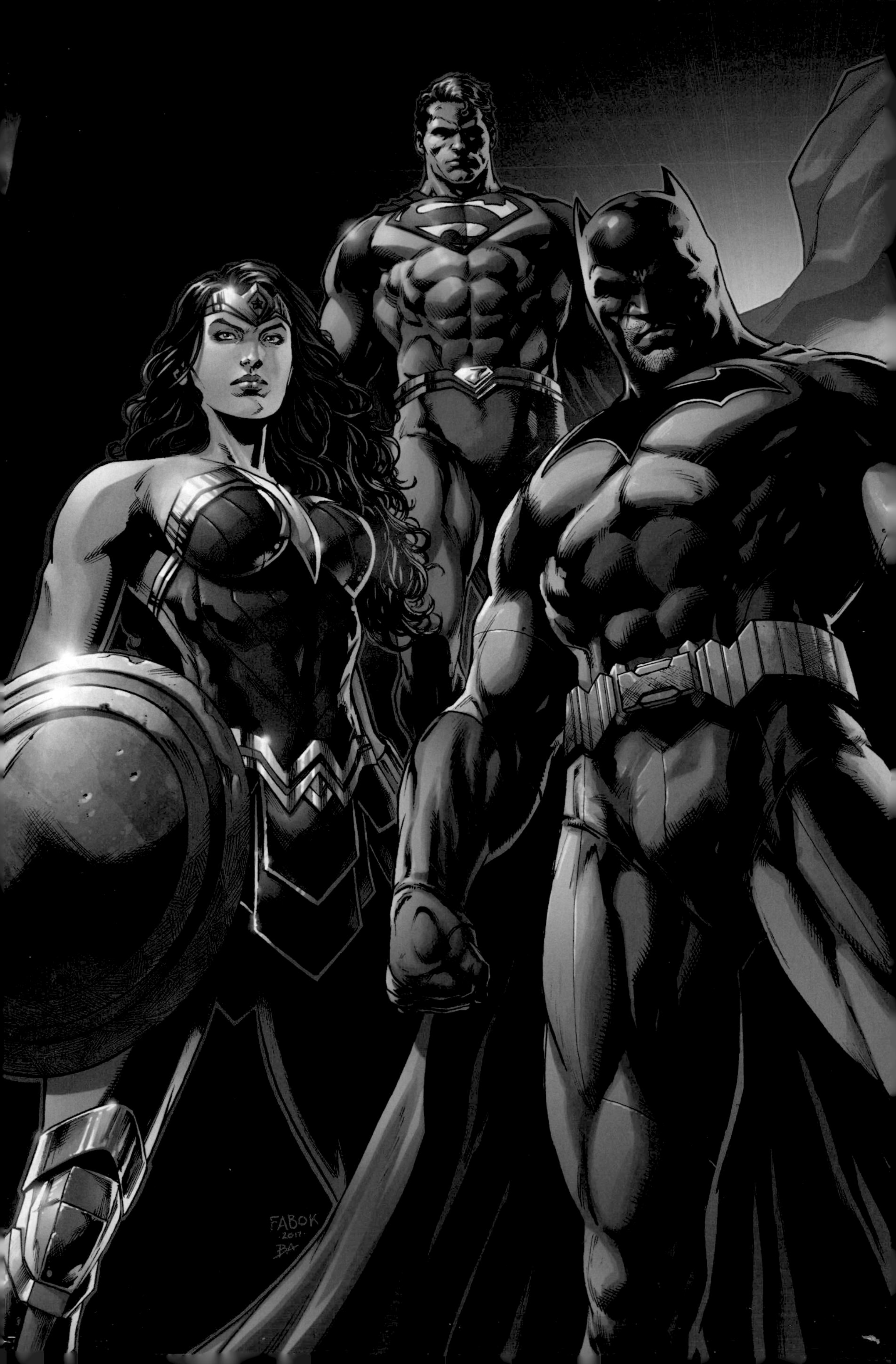
FABOK
.2017.
BA